ADVENTURES IN HOLLYWOOD

A Memoir
by **BOB KOSTER**

"Adventures In Hollywood" A Memoir by Bob Koster
©2012 Robert J. Koster. All rights reserved.

No part of this book may be reproduced in any form or by any means, electronic, mechanical, digital, photocopying or recording, except for the inclusion in a review, without permission in writing from the publisher.

Published in USA:
BearManor Media
P.O. Box 1129
Duncan, OK 73534-1129
www.BearManorMedia.com

ISBN—978-1-59393-266-4

Printed in the United States of America.
Book and cover design by Jacquelin Brough

DEDICATION

The greatest thing my mother and father did for me was to free me from the restrictions of self. They taught me from the beginning that I could be anything I wanted to be, and if I worked hard I could be the best at it, whether it was president, doctor, gardener, or fisherman. Find something you love to do, they said, and work hard at it, and it will support you and give you great pleasure. Thanks, Mom and Dad.

TABLE OF

CONTENTS

Dedication	III
Contents	IV
Acknowledgments	IX
Chapter 1: ORIGINS	1
Chapter 2: TODDLER	7
Chapter 3: EUROPE	13
Chapter 4: OJAI	20
Chapter 5: WEBB	24
Chapter 6: POMONA	31
Chapter 7: LACC and UCLA	37
Chapter 8: DGA	46
Chapter 9: UNITED CALIFORNIA BANK	48
Chapter 10: LAW OF BURNING SANDS	52
Chapter 11: TOP HAT	55
Chapter 12: MR. HOBBS TAKES A VACATION	57
Chapter 13: NEW YORK	66
Chapter 14: WPIX	75
Chapter 15: HARRY COLEMAN PRODUCTIONS	80
Chapter 16: EYE ON NEW YORK	83
Chapter 17: J. WALTER THOMPSON	88
Chapter 18: NEW YORK DGA	93
Chapter 19: UP THE DOWN STAIRCASE	98
Chapter 20: BLACKOUT	101

Chapter 21: VALLEY OF THE DOLLS 107
Chapter 22: GALFAS 113
Chapter 23: RACHEL, RACHEL 115
Chapter 24: FOR LOVE OF IVY 117
Chapter 25: PENDULUM 122
Chapter 26: COMMERCIALS 125
Chapter 27: HELLO, DOLLY! 128
Chapter 28: PEPSI COMMERCIAL 133
Chapter 29: COLGATE-PALMOLIVE DISHWASHING FLUID 135
Chapter 30: CARS 136
Chapter 31: GENERATION 139
Chapter 32: LARCHMONT 142
Chapter 33: BANANAS 143
Chapter 34: A SAFE PLACE 145
Chapter 35: JUMP 148
Chapter 36: ALLEN FUNT 151
Chapter 37: GREASER'S PALACE 156
Chapter 38: L.A. TRIP 1971 168
Chapter 39: AMERICAN TOURISTER 171
Chapter 40: RED CROSS 172
Chapter 41: VIRGIN ISLANDS VACATION 173
Chapter 42: RALPH L. SAVARESE PRODUCTIONS 174
Chapter 43: STICKS AND BONES 178
Chapter 44: CONCORD ELECTRONICS 180
Chapter 45: THE SUPERCOPS 182
Chapter 46: MOVING TO LOS ANGELES 189
Chapter 47: OUTRAGE 194
Chapter 48: CAN ELLEN BE SAVED? 198
Chapter 49: JUDGE DEE AND THE MONASTERY MURDERS 200
Chapter 50: KADOKAWA BUNKO 204

Chapter 51: DARKTOWN STRUTTERS 207
Chapter 52: THE MAN IN THE GLASS BOOTH 209
Chapter 53: THE BARONY 214
Chapter 54: TRILOGY OF TERROR 219
Chapter 55: INCREDIBLE MELTING MAN 221
Chapter 56: FOOD OF THE GODS 223
Chapter 57: FUTUREWORLD 228
Chapter 58: POLICE STORY 235
Chapter 59: SPACE FORCE 240
Chapter 60: BUTCH AND SUNDANCE 242
Chapter 61: FLESH AND BLOOD 250
Chapter 62: MORE THAN FRIENDS 253
Chapter 63: UNIVERSAL INTERLUDE 254
Chapter 64: GIDEON'S TRUMPET 258
Chapter 65: HUSTLER OF MUSCLE BEACH 262
Chapter 66: THE RETURN OF FRANK CANNON 265
Chapter 67: FANTASY ISLAND 269
Chapter 68: DARK NIGHT OF THE SCARECROW 271
Chapter 69: MCCLAIN'S LAW 274
Chapter 70: GAVILAN 278
Chapter 71: RIPLEY'S BELIEVE IT OR NOT 284
Chapter 72: TRAUMA CENTER 286
Chapter 73: PASSIONS 287
Chapter 74: THAT WAS THEN, THIS IS NOW 289
Chapter 75: BETWEEN THE DARKNESS AND THE DAWN 295
Chapter 76: THE SKY'S NO LIMIT 296
Chapter 77: CODENAME FOXFIRE 298
Chapter 78: THE GLADIATOR 303
Chapter 79: THE MAN WHO BROKE 1000 CHAINS 304
Chapter 80: HARDESTY HOUSE 306

Chapter 81: WAR AND REMEMBRANCE 308
Chapter 82: COMPUTER 317
Chapter 83: SUPERCARRIER 319
Chapter 84: PHANTOM OF THE MALL 323
Chapter 85: TRACEY THURMAN STORY 329
Chapter 86: THE BOOK 331
Chapter 87: FAMILY FILMS 334
Chapter 88: TEACHING I 336
Chapter 89: EARTHQUAKE 338
Chapter 90: TRAVELING AND LECTURING 340
Chapter 91: ARCHIVES I 341
Chapter 92: SHERIFF'S RESERVE NEWS 342
Chapter 93: AERO SQUADRON 343
Chapter 94: PEGGY 345
Chapter 95: LEISURE VILLAGE 346
Chapter 96: ANDRÉ 350
Chapter 97: ARCHIVES II 352
Chapter 98: TEACHING II 359
Chapter 99: SAN FRANCISCO 360
Chapter 100: EUROPE 2007 361
Chapter 101: VIENNA 363
Chapter 102: BUDAPEST 364
Chapter 103: A NEW LIFE 367
Chapter 104: TEACHING IN GERMANY 369
Chapter 105: HOME TO CAMARILLO 371
Index 372

ACKNOWLEDGMENTS

Many people helped or encouraged the writing of this book.

First of all, I was writing a book about the life of my father. Still am. While I was collecting material my then wife, Antje Prangenberg-Koster, asked me why I was doing that when my own life was interesting. I should write an autobiography, says she. So I did. N.B. We are still best friends, by the way.

Then I was enjoying an afternoon at the home of Marvin and Kathy Kohner Zuckerman. Kathy is the original "Gidget." Marvin has been a highly respected literary agent for many years. I mentioned my book. He agreed to read a few pages. Next thing I knew I had a publisher, the esteemed Ben Ohmart, head of Bear Manor Media publishing. This was becoming serious.

Ben assigned a marvelous editor/production manager, Sandy Grabman, who guided me through the hazards of syntax among other things. Then the book went to a marvelous typesetter and proofreader, Jacquelin Brough, who worked me through all my typos and then formatted the book the way you see it now. She even designed the cover. Just lovely.

In the midst of editing and formatting, Sandy Grabman retired and was replaced by Michelle Morgan, who did some further corrections and suggestions, all very valid. The great thing about all these people is that they did not tamper with the tone of the book, only helped to make it better.

The marvelous cover photo was made by my friend Tony Verebes. Nobody does it better.

The two lovely paintings of me on the next page were done by my father after his retirement in 1965. He settled down to paint. He had studied art in school in Germany and I think he secretly wanted to be an artist all his life. He was, of course, in so many ways.

I am sure others are involved who are equally instrumental in bringing this book out. If I have not mentioned you please know that I am grateful for your help.

Finally I have to belatedly thank my mother and father for insisting that I have such a splendid education, and for introducing me to this fascinating world. Also my sons, Chris and Kevin, who were encouraging and supportive throughout our lives together, but especially during the writing. Thanks, guys.

And thank you, the reader, for permitting me to entertain you for a while.

CHAPTER 1

ORIGINS

Sitting in my beautiful back yard, listening to the wind chimes and the birds. Moved to write my life story. My family's story and mine are bound so tightly that it will be impossible to write without reference to them, so we may as well begin, as they say, at the beginning.

In those days my father's legal name was Herman Kosterlitz. He would change his name, and ours, legally, in 1943 when he finally was accepted as a U.S. citizen. Then our name changed from Kosterlitz to Koster. I was born Robert Joseph Kosterlitz.

Dad escaped the Nazis by fleeing Berlin on his lunch hour in early 1933, one week after Hitler stole the presidential election. Jews were no longer permitted to work in the film industry so he had to leave the country.

Dad went to his bank to withdraw his savings in order to buy a ticket out of the country. The teller, now in a Nazi uniform, told him that all the Jews' money had been confiscated. Dad showed him the passbook, which the teller tore up and threw on the floor without looking at it. Dad said he wanted to speak to the bank manager. The teller said that Herr Schmidt was out of the office. Dad said he would wait for him. After a few minutes the teller saw that Dad wasn't about to leave. He picked up the phone and said, "Hello, Herr Schmidt? I have a Jew here named Kosterlitz who wants to withdraw his money. (Pause) OK, I'll tell him." Turning to Dad, he said, "Mr. Schmidt is not here."

Dad said "But you were just speaking to him!" The teller then made a big mistake. He said, "You filthy Jew bastard, are you calling me a liar?" Dad picked up the phone and hit the teller on the head with it, knocking him out. Mr. Schmidt appeared at that moment and pulled Dad off the teller, whom Dad was pummeling on the floor. Schmidt handed Dad some money from his own pocket, told him to go directly to the railroad station and take the next train out of Germany. Don't go home and pack, don't go back to work, just leave the country. Dad did that.

As the train approached the border of France the German border police went through the cabins asking for passports and visas. Dad happened to have both with him. He passed through the border with no problem. As the train crossed into France, Dad leaned out the window from the French side, and called to a German border guard, "Hitler can kiss my behind!!" He didn't return to Germany until 1949 or so.

Dad went to Paris first where he made a new name for himself as a writer. Directors and producers traveled from Germany to Paris just to have him write their scripts. He earned a good living at it, too. But he was lonely, having left his girlfriend, Georgia, in Berlin when he fled. She was an up-and-coming young actress, not prompted to leave Berlin for the same reasons as Dad, and she chose not to join him in France where her future was uncertain.

Presently, Dad re-established contact with Universal's representative in Europe, Joe Pasternak. Pasternak had also left Germany and was currently shuttling between Budapest and Vienna where he was producing films for Universal, using blocked European funds. He had noticed and befriended Dad when they worked on adjoining sound stages in Berlin. Joe recognized Dad's talent and promised him that in the future they would make films together.

This was their chance. Joe cabled Dad in Paris from Budapest and offered him the chance to direct once again, and Dad gave it less than one second's thought. He had been directing in Berlin when he left, and that was his first love.

Dad cleaned up his life in Paris for a few days and then took the train to Budapest where Joe had offered him the chance to direct the famous German star, Franceska Gaal, in a comedy. Gaal was very popular in Europe at the time. This was the break Dad had been hoping for.

After a few days in Budapest rewriting the script and prepping the film, the two men were having dinner when Joe asked why Dad never introduced Joe to his girlfriend. Dad replied that he didn't have one, but what he really wanted to do was to get married so he wouldn't have to worry about the dating game any more. He was too busy directing to enter the social whirl of pre-war Austria-Hungary. Joe understood that. He did, however, ask Dad if "love" had anything to do with it, and the answer was that Dad was looking for someone pleasant he could be with who would be his wife. His requirements were that she enjoy good music, have a good sense of humor, and have good teeth.

Mom had been born in Budapest in 1914, the daughter of the two most famous Hungarian performers of their day. Erno Kiraly (translated: Ernie King) was a matinee idol along the lines of Maurice Chevalier, and Hermine Solti was the leading songstress-comedienne of her day. They were to remain popular until the 1930s, but their marriage, ill conceived to begin with, faltered after two or three years and they were soon divorced. Their daughter, Katalin Kiraly, known as "Kato" to her friends and relatives, was a lonely child, not appreciated by either parent, brought up by nannies and private schools including a convent. On her own, but trading on the family name, she played roles on stage and in two or three films by the time she was twenty. Very pretty, not a bad actress; she would have achieved the rank of lead in "B" pictures in Hollywood.

Hermine Solti, my grandmother.   Erno Kiraly, my grandfather.

As was the custom, and still is, between shooting phases in show business there were the parties. Everyone who was anyone met and mingled at Joe Pasternak's parties because he represented Universal, therefore Hollywood, and with the political situation uncertain in Europe all the artists were looking toward England and the U.S. as possible refuge. Not so Solti and Kiraly. They were, they thought, too big to be bothered by the likes of the Nazis, or anyone else.

But Kato, their daughter, without much guidance in her past and with an uncertain future, was looking for someone to whom she could attach herself in a love-match. When Pasternak arranged for them to meet it was a revelation for both. Mom found the love of her life and Dad found a girl with good teeth. They married three weeks later.

Dad neither spoke nor understood Hungarian so Mom had to nudge him gently with her foot during the ceremony when he was supposed to say the previously memorized and much rehearsed phrase, "I do" since he did not understand a word the judge was saying. They repeated their vows in front of an official in the German embassy, both quaking with fear, since Dad was a wanted fugitive in Berlin. The Nazi machine had not yet become efficient enough that his fame as a wanted man had spread to the outlying states. They were married without further ado. And yes, Mom spoke fluent German so Dad did not have to nudge her.

Mom, Kato Kiraly.   Dad, Henry Koster.

The year was 1934. Big changes were happening in Germany and indeed on the European continent. Two people with German passports but unable to return to Germany were essentially stateless.

Luckily, Joe Pasternak kept Dad working. He directed four films for Universal during this period, *Katharina die Letzte*, *Kleine Mutti*, *Peter*, and *Maria Baschkirtzeff*, finishing at the end of 1935. He also wrote *Ball im Savoy*. All were financially and critically successful. Dad's and Pasternak's income was assured. Carl Laemmle, founder of Universal Pictures in Hollywood, loved their work and would have kept them making European pictures and spending the blocked money.

But the mood in Europe had turned ugly. Nazi parties were springing up in the countries surrounding Germany. More and more German and European artists, writers, scientists, musicians, and intellectuals of all beliefs and creeds were fleeing the continent to England and eventually to the United States.

Carl Laemmle, still in charge of Universal's destiny, was busily bringing members of his family from Europe and legitimizing them by giving them jobs at Universal Pictures, sometimes as directors or producers, sometimes as screenwriters or editors. The studio began to deteriorate from within. Many of the new Laemmle people were untalented. And yet the flood of the talented and talentless continued from Europe to the wilds of Hollywood. The studio, which in prior years had produced such classics as *Dracula*, *Hunchback of Notre Dame* with Lon Chaney,

ORIGINS

and *All Quiet on the Western Front*, was churning out low-grade programmers and was losing money.

Laemmle had cabled Pasternak to tell him to return to Hollywood before the Nazis took over Europe. Pasternak cabled back that he would not return "without my director, Henry Koster." God bless him for that. The studio balked, said they already had enough German directors. Pasternak insisted and the studio caved, but promised only one movie "and then Koster will have to return to Europe." Dad knew that his career, possibly his life, depended on making one very big hit.

By train across Europe, skirting the borders of Germany where he was still a hunted man, then to New York on the *Ile de France*, one of the great ocean liners in an age of great ocean liners. The crossing was rough. Many of the passengers stayed in their staterooms, not emerging to partake of the fine French cuisine. Dad was never a victim of seasickness so he ate regularly. And what cuisine it was. The chef told the waiters that they had a surfeit of caviar, and please to find a passenger who was still able to consume the rest before they arrived in New York and had to throw it away. Dad was elected. Why didn't I ever have a job like that? Life is so unfair sometimes.

The boat docked in New York on 21 February 1936. After a night in a hotel the small group, now including Dad, Mom, Joe Pasternak, and Joe's wife, boarded the train for Hollywood. The future looked bright as long as that first movie was a smash hit.

Their arrival was somewhat less than they expected. Laemmle had finally surrendered control of the studio to a financial group led by A.P. Giannini, founder and head of the Bank of America. Good financial brain, not much of a filmmaker. He put in charge of the studio Charles Rogers, a banker. Rogers was charged with ridding the studio of all the recent hires that Laemmle had brought in, good or bad. That included Koster and Pasternak.

Luck was on their side. After one of their meetings with Rogers, as they left the office they ran into an attorney whom Pasternak knew from his stay in Hollywood in the late 1920s. This man took on their case and helped Rogers see that it was in the studio's interest to at least give them the one promised film.

After some difficulties including a national talent search an actress was found, Deanna Durbin, and the film was completed in record time. It broke all records. Deanna Durbin became the darling of Hollywood. She had the voice of an angel and an innocent face. Suddenly Koster and Pasternak were the hot producer-director team.

On their arrival in Hollywood Dad and Mom first stayed in an apartment hotel in East Hollywood on Wilton Place near Franklin Avenue, and then they bought a home on Bronson Canyon Drive.

The Koster-Pasternak team was by now famous at Universal and in Hollywood as a whole. Whenever a new Durbin film, or anything else by Koster and Pasternak was released, the newspapers trumpeted, "Koster and Pasternak Did It Again!" And it was always a big hit, critically and financially. When I was born, a big sign appeared on the gate in front of Universal City. It said, "Congratulations, Papa Koster. Koster and Pasternak Did It Again!"

Deanna Durbin, Mom, and I, a few months old

CHAPTER 2

TODDLER

My parents' marriage was falling apart without the pressure of the Nazi threat to hold them together. My birth kept the marriage together for another year or so before Dad finally moved out. He had commissioned a house to be built in Westwood before the divorce. Mom got that house and custody of yours truly, along with the usual alimony and child support. The divorce was final in 1941. The house still stands at 262 South Bentley Drive. I remember little about those years. Guess I was too young. I do remember the dinners. Mom kept herself busy by joining the Hollywood Canteen and the USO. She also appeared in a traveling theatre group that flew or bussed to several local Army, Navy, and Air Force bases around Southern California. Mom would appear in a play or review and then invite a dozen or so servicemen to the house for a "home-cooked" meal. I remember the dining room filled with various uniforms, the men drinking good wine and eating good food while on leave in Hollywood. I was given to nurses and nannies to be brought up. Mom was busy with her stage career. I did see her when she was home.

I also saw Dad on weekends. I remember him picking me up for Sunday visits in his convertible. He called it "Bonzo." I was put on the back seat, remember, no seat belts in those days, and told to stay put. The top was usually down and there was a row of screws holding the convertible cover on. Dad would tell me to push the third screw from the end with my finger and the car would magically start. I didn't know at the time that his car started with a button on the floor. He pushed it with his foot at the same time I pushed the screw. I loved doing this. Then we would go to his house and I could play with him and his new wife, Peggy. Or we went to a friend's house, maybe Ernst Verebes, or Charles Laughton. Sometimes we went to Franz Waxman's house and I played with his son, Johnny.

My stepmother, Peggy Moran, had been a film star in the 1930s and 40s. At Universal she was known as "Queen of the B Pictures." She was always full of fun and a great hostess for Dad's weekend gatherings. Dad and Peggy had two sons, Nick and Peter. Nick went on to act in six of Dad's films. Peter graduated from Yale and went into public welfare work in the San Francisco area.

One event stands out in my memory. When my mother and I were together we did have fun. She and I would imitate what the other was saying until we both collapsed in laughter. This was particularly funny because she had a very thick Hungarian accent. What Hungarian does not? And I was three years old or so, and I didn't speak too well myself.

Mom was appearing at that time at the Hollywood Canteen. Such leading lights as Donald O'Connor and Fred Clark were appearing there regularly. I remember them coming to the house for dinner as well. In fact many of Hollywood's best actors and actresses performed their wartime duty by appearing at the Canteen to entertain the troops after a day of filming. It was part of the war effort.

On this day Mom decided it was time for me to see her performing on stage, so she obtained two tickets, front row center, to the matinee performance of her play. The audience was jammed with all manner and all rank of service personnel and a few civilians thrown in. My nanny, "Libby," and I arrived on time and the usher (remember ushers?) showed us to our seats. I watched the first act with fascination. All those people on stage saying those funny things. Why, it was just like when they visited us at home. Same people, too.

Mom didn't appear until the second act, but when she did it was just like at home. I imitated, in a high, loud baby voice, everything she said. I did it consistently. The audience, at first startled, burst into laughter. They stopped laughing enough to hear Mom's next line, then burst into laughter again when I repeated it. This went on throughout the scene. Fred Clark, an old hand at acting, was by now speaking with his face turned away from the audience because he was laughing so hard.

At the end of the act there was an intermission, and Libby took me backstage to see Mommy. We sat in the dressing room. Soon a very large policeman with motorcycle boots entered. He said that Libby should take me home. Presumably the show went on without my commentary.

When I was older, I usually spent Sundays during the year with Dad and his family. I saw very little of him when I was at his home. I did play as best I could with my half-brothers, Nick and Peter, under the ever vigilant eye of Libby, and we were all properly nice to each other. We usually got dressed up and went to a good restaurant for dinner. Dad was with us then, although I usually sat several chairs away from him and had little chance to talk to him. He was a kind of untouchable eminence who drifted into and out of my life without actually making any real contact. Most of the time when we were playing at his house he was closeted in his study with a writer or a producer, doing rewrites or shot plots on his current projects. Since he was a very reliable director, always on schedule and on time, and not at all temperamental, the studios kept him working. Fox even loaned him out to other studios for special tasks. He was loaned to Universal, for instance, for *Harvey* with Jimmy Stewart, the beginning of a long and fruitful relationship.

While Dad was working in the office, one of his friends would come and stay with us. Usually it was Ernst Verebes. Verebes had been a very famous comedian in Austria, Hungary, and Germany before the war, but when he came to the U.S. his accent prevented him from having the same kind of success. His wife, Hedy Schoop, was a very accomplished and famous artist and ceramic sculptor, and she was able to keep the family going. They all came over on Sundays to be with Dad. Tony, son of Ernst, is a friend still.

Sometimes we were accompanied by a European actor, like John Banner, or by Robert Cummings, also Dad's friend. And there were others. The beautiful actress Jeanne Crain lived next door and her children came over to play. Across the street was a famous psychologist, Dr. Druckman, whose son, Joelie, is still a friend.

Sometimes we went over to someone else's house to play. We went to Franz Waxman's home more than once, and I remember going to Ernst Lubitsch's house and spending an afternoon with Nicola Lubitsch, his daughter. We also spent some time at Joe Pasternak's house, where we played with his three sons, Peter, Jeff, and Mike, now famous as The Emperor Rosko.

Felix Jackson had been Dad's writing partner in Europe and in the early days in Hollywood, but Mom did not keep up that friendship. We visited Jackson's ex-wife, Jill, and two daughters, Janet and Harley, with Mom, but not with Dad. Mom and Jill had become close friends, even after Felix divorced Jill. She later remarried a great musician and popular composer, Sy Miller, and together they wrote the famous hymn, "Let There Be Peace on Earth, and Let It Begin with Me." Their daughters remain my friends.

Various members of the Hollywood Canteen would stop by from time to time to visit with Mom. Fred Clark was a visitor. Sidney Blackmer came by from time to time.

And Mom had dinners for various friends and parties as well. I remember Al Jarvis, originator of radio's *Make Believe Ballroom* on the music station KMPC. He came over several times. A very nice man, a little short, good sense of humor. And once Blossom Seeley and Benny Fields came over and performed in the living room. More than once Mom invited her former accompanist over, and he played while she sang for the guests. This was a ritual that occurred in many showbiz homes in those pre-TV days.

For instance, Dad would invite some guests, especially one or two singers, and after dinner ask them to perform for the other guests. He asked me once to sit down and play the piano, but I knew how good I was so I refused. He was dismayed at this but no matter how he tried to coax me I would not play for his guests. My brother Nick wasn't so lucky, but he was far more talented than I ever could be. He played gladly for the guests.

In fact, when Dad's family went to London for *No Highway in the Sky*, they were invited for an evening at the home of Richard Addinsell, composer of the *Warsaw Concerto*. That piece had been composed by Addinsell for the British wartime film *Dangerous Moonlight*, starring Anton Walbrook. Originally the producers had requested a Rachmaninoff-like pastiche to be composed, but Rachmaninoff turned them down. Addinsell succeeded. The film was very successful, and the musical piece has drifted into the classical repertoire.

Dad, Peggy, and Nick were invited to Addinsell's home for dinner. After dinner Dad asked Addinsell to play the piece on the piano. He did try, but he had forgotten how to play it. So Nick, then eight years old, sat down at the piano and played it, to the amusement of all. Dad always bragged about the incident later.

Since the parties at Dad's house were held on Sunday evenings I was usually invited, especially later, when I was a teenager. Nick's piano teacher, Mr. Teaford, was always invited for these dinners, and he came gladly, enjoyed the food, and always played the piano for the guests. If any of the guests was a singer, Dad invariably asked them to perform.

When Dad directed *Flower Drum Song*, we made friends with Miyoshi Umeki and her husband, Win Opie. Miyoshi had been a famous singer and musical performer in Japan. Whenever she came over Dad always asked her to sing for the group. She did so gladly and effortlessly. She also spoke perfect English, so it was easy for her to sing her own parody of the American song "Up a Razy Liver."

Dad sold the house in the Hollywood Hills and bought one in Beverly Hills on Whittier Drive. Some reconstruction was done on the home before Dad and the family moved in. A swimming pool was installed in the backyard. It was placed lengthwise facing away from the patio, so the shallow end was where the patio was and the deep end at the other end of the pool, toward the alley in back of the house. Dad designed the pool to be a foot or two narrower at the deep end so the pool would appear much longer because of forced perspective.

Dad also had to have the very latest in music playing equipment. First it was the record cutter. Then Dad got hold of a wire recorder. This was the precursor to the tape recorder, and it recorded the electrical impulses on a steel wire that wound from spool to spool across a recording head. It worked quite well as a recording device but the wire would break and become hopelessly tangled. This was around 1945 or '46. Next came the tape recorder. But before that, Dad bought a Grundig record player for the Whittier house that played both sides of the record. It did not turn the record over. Rather, the record dropped onto three revolving rubber wheels that rested on the record on the turntable. Then a needle protruded upward and played the underside of the record. A pressure arm held the record down on the rubber wheels because the records were too light to make a good connection. It worked well for a few weeks, then the wheels started not rolling properly. Long story short, the pressure arm started breaking the records over the spindle. End of Grundig. Dad got another Grundig but with a more standard playing mode.

The new house was fine for Dad's expanding family. He now had a maid and butler/chef. From time to time there were au pair girls. One was a young Dutch lady, Anita Magnus. Her father had been Dad's acquaintance in Europe. Dad agreed to house her for a year or so in return for her watching over the rapidly growing Nick and Peter. During the day Anita attended Beverly Hills High School. She was not very happy. She was rather overweight and the other kids made fun of her accent. In the evening she was the kids' nanny. She did not join the other kids' activities and was never invited over to the other kids' houses.

One day she broke her leg and it was set in a cast for healing. This made her even less happy because now she could not enjoy recess at school either. And the cast, as they were in those days, was entirely white, and made her stand out in the class which she wished devoutly not to do.

A few days later, Dad invited Deanna Durbin and Marlon Brando for dinner. Brando had expressed the desire to meet Deanna Durbin, who happened to be in town. Durbin had retired a few years prior and was living in Paris, but she was visiting Los Angeles at the time. The two arrived for dinner. During the meal Dad asked Deanna if she would like to meet the exchange student and Deanna said of course she would. Dad mentioned that Anita had her leg in a cast, and Deanna offered to sign it. Anita was delighted. She had known about Deanna for years since her father had told her of Dad's and Deanna's fame. Oddly she had not heard of Marlon Brando.

Marlon asked if he could tag along. He was enjoying Deanna's company. At this point, remember, he had just appeared in *On the Waterfront* and *The Wild One* and was at the height of his fame and popularity. Girls across the country felt their hearts race at the mention of his name. He followed Deanna upstairs to where Anita was sitting, watching television and doing her homework, and Deanna and Marlon entered the room. They had a brief conversation, which delighted Anita, and then Deanna signed her cast. Marlon asked if he could sign also, and did so. Those were the only two signatures on Anita's cast.

The next day when Anita went to school she was the most popular girl in her class, and from then on the house was filled with schoolgirls running in and out to visit their new best friend.

I knew Marlon Brando briefly from a weekend visit to Dad's house to use the swimming pool. Marlon's friend Sam Gilman was with him. I was just learning chess at the time and I had set up a chess set in the back yard near the pool. Sam and I were playing a game. Sam gave me a few pointers on strategy. Marlon wandered over to watch, and he also gave me a few strategy suggestions, which I have never forgotten. His ability to understand the entire board was quite amazing. I also found him to be a very nice, very literate, interesting man whose interests ranged across a wide spectrum, from politics to art. He could discuss any of these with confidence because he was a voracious reader.

He came over to Dad's house on weekends because he wanted to escape the media zoo that collected around his own house in the Hollywood Hills. Paparazzi are not a modern phenomena. Dad's house was quiet, usually with some soothing classical music playing. Marlon usually came over with Sam. A few times he came over with Anna Kashfi, to whom he was betrothed. They were like a couple of school kids in love. I don't remember ever seeing him swim in the pool, as so many others did, but he did enjoy just sitting in the sun and being left alone with his own thoughts.

One of Mom's more constant companions was Joe Valentine. He had been Dad's cameraman during the Universal years, 1936 through 1941. An excellent photographer, he finally won a much-deserved Oscar for his work on *Joan of Arc*, 1948, with Ingrid Bergman. He had been nominated four times prior, for *Wings over Honolulu* (1937), *Mad About Music* (1939), *First Love* (1939), and *Spring Parade* (1940), the last two working with Dad.

He was a great friend. I loved being with him. He was full of fun, doing little magic tricks and telling jokes. Mom must have loved him as well because we spent more and more time with him and his family. It was a large Catholic Italian family and they took us into their hearts. I fondly remember weekend afternoons spent at the Valentine house in Van Nuys in the backyard under the trees. Eventually Mom and Joe became engaged. They were constant companions in 1948 and 1949 until he died in May of 1949. I do not know what caused his death.

I do know that one of his last films was Alfred Hitchcock's *Rope*, a film shot in ten-minute segments. Hitchcock had attempted to omit editing by shooting everything with a fluid camera in one shot, no intercuts. He almost succeeded, too. The cameras, grips, and actors all had to rehearse together because the camera was to appear to flow fluidly from room to room. The grips had to practice moving walls and furniture out of the way for the camera to dolly around, and all had to be done silently. The actors had to memorize their lines in ten-minute segments. This was easy for stage-trained actors, but film actors only memorize maybe ten or twenty seconds of dialogue at a time, shoot it, and then memorize the next shot. Some go so far as to memorize their whole day's scenes, but these are not common. And a day's shoot usually encompassed maybe three or four minutes of film time. Hitchcock was demanding ten minutes.

After the wrap, Joe would come to our house and pour himself a glass of scotch or two. I guess he felt that our home was a "safe" place where he could let his hair down and relax, rather than go back to his own empty, cold house. Anyway, Mom was his fiancée, so why shouldn't he come over?

Unfortunately, Joe died in May of that year. Mom had planned a trip to Europe with me for that summer. It would have been the last time we would have alone together before she sent me away to school and married Joe. We went anyway, after the funeral. Mom had promised many of Joe's relatives, all staunch Catholics, that we would bring their rosaries to have the Pope bless them in person, and this we did.

CHAPTER 3

EUROPE

In late June of 1949, we boarded a Lockheed Constellation flown by Air America, an unscheduled airline, possible in those days. I remember the flight vividly. We had to stop in Kansas City and Chicago to top off the gas tanks because the planes were as yet unable to fly coast-to-coast without refueling. We flew from Burbank Airport, now Bob Hope Airport, and we landed at Idlewild in Queens, New York. We were met at the airport by Uncle Miklos, Mom's uncle. It would be 1963 before Idlewild changed its name to John F. Kennedy International Airport in honor of the assassinated president. We had a bit of wrangling to do because Mom had two big steamer trunks full of clothes for every possible kind of weather and every possible event. I had a drawer or two for my clothes also, and I had my good suit along for those formal dinner events. These trunks weighed a ton. This was before suitcases normally had casters to roll about. Skycaps and Redcaps were absolutely essential then. The tips one paid them were well worth the expense.

We stayed in New York only for a day or two before we boarded the *Queen Mary*, for Le Havre, France, the first stop on our tour. I remember that the *Queen* was too large to dock at Le Havre, so we were shuttled to the harbor by ferry boat. We and our steamer trunks. We had met the other tour members on the *Queen*. We would travel to seven countries in six weeks: France, Italy, Switzerland, Belgium, Luxembourg, the Netherlands, and England, then return on the *Queen Elizabeth*. It was the trip of a lifetime.

From Le Havre we traveled by train to Paris, where we met an old friend of Mom, George Banyai. He was a Hungarian manager, impresario, producer. He originally specialized in stage shows and vaudeville, but later became involved more and more with legitimate theatre in Los Angeles and New York. He and Mom were friends in Los Angeles before the trip. George had married and settled down in Nice, France, with his wife. He joined us in Paris. We stayed very briefly in Paris at the Hotel du Louvre. And of course we saw the Louvre museum, which was across the street. At night I stayed alone in the room while George and Mom went out on the town. That was a pattern we would follow for the rest of the trip with a few exceptions. I didn't mind much. I was used to staying alone at home as long as I had a book to read. Mom had bought me some French comic books and I used them to teach myself the rudiments of the French language, at least as it was spoken by Donald Duck and his family. I was surprised to learn that Huey, Dewey, and Louie had different names in France. I also had a "Supermann" comic book in German. I remember a girl was drowning in a lake, and was yelling "Hilfe! Hilfe!" when Supermann flew in and saved her. Not a bad way to learn a language, through comic books.

One of the two mornings we were in Paris, the Tour de France bicycle race started right in front of the hotel. The riders were on bikes unfamiliar to me. At home I had a J.C. Higgins, the Sears and Roebuck house brand. It cost me $10 new, and had a spiffy little luggage carrier over the rear tire shaped like a jet plane's tail. I rode it around the neighborhood but was afraid to take it to school because the kids were known to steal other people's bikes. But the bikes ridden in the Tour de France were very different. On these the riders bent down over the handlebars, which had a reverse curve to them, much like racing bikes of today. This meant that from our point of view in the hotel window, with the riders peddling away from us, all we saw were multi-colored derrieres bobbing up and down as the bikes disappeared down the street.

We went to the Louvre museum. Saw the *Mona Lisa*—beautiful, but small. The *Venus de Milo* was also impressive.

George drove us to his Nice estate in his Renault Dauphine. I was fascinated by the fact that the directional signal was a tiny lighted arm that swung out from the "B" pillar. We drove at night so we didn't see much. We stayed with George and his wife for about four days then rejoined the tour group and headed down the coast to Genova. Stayed overnight, then bused down to Florence, pausing at Pisa to see the famous Leaning Tower. Mom took photos of the leaning tower, the cathedral, and the Hall of Whispers. I was more impressed by the Hall of Whispers, where one can stand at one end in front of a concave wall, and whisper, and the sound can be heard clearly at the other end of the room in front of another concave wall. Mom and I then went to a gelato place and had some of the lovely Italian ice cream. Back on the bus and on to Florence.

Somewhere on the road to Florence, Mom realized that she had left her cameras at the gelato store. We would have driven four hours from Pisa to Florence. We arrived at the hotel, had the steamer trunks taken to the room, and Mom got on the phone to Pisa. Not easy for a Hungarian who spoke no Italian, but she managed. Mom was good at managing.

Long story short, five hours later, a man appeared at the hotel room door with Mom's cameras in hand. Mom was understandably grateful. She offered the man money, which he refused. She offered to buy him dinner and gasoline for his trip. He refused that too. Finally she persuaded him to take a carton of American cigarettes. He accepted that and left with his booty under his arm. Two valuable cameras in exchange for a carton of cigarettes. Might have cost her $2.00.

In Florence we visited museums like the Uffizi. In the evening, back to the hotel room after dinner while Mom sampled what night life there was in Florence with the rest of the tour. I was the only child on the tour. At that age, of course, I wouldn't have known what a nightclub was if I fell over one, but I was not happy being left alone in the room. I was nervous about being left alone in a foreign country where I did not speak the language. If I needed something whom do I call and how? Mom had locked the door to the hotel room so I couldn't get out, and nobody could get in. I'm sure the manager had a master key, but I didn't know that at the time. After I read some, I went to bed. There were two cords hanging, one on each side of the bed. Pull one and the light goes on. Pull the other and it summons the concierge. I woke up an hour or two later and needed to use the rest room, so I pulled the cord that I remembered as the light cord. I was wrong. Presently there was a knock at the door, and a lady outside started speaking to me very fast in Italian. I answered, of course, in English. I have no idea what she said and I am sure she was equally confused. Luckily she gave up after a minute or two and went away. I never heard from her again, and I went back to sleep.

I should mention that I was just uncomfortable being alone in a foreign country. I was not uncomfortable being alone. I spent many evenings and afternoons by myself as a child, reading and listening to the radio. Mom was working or otherwise occupied and Lucy was cleaning or cooking. The world of Superman and Straight Arrow was just fine for me.

After about 1948 we had a very early TV set in the playroom over the garage, and I could watch TV for hours, even if I never learned how to adjust the picture properly. I always had the contrast too high, and the pictures were always black-and-white with little gray scale. Eventually Joe Valentine showed me how to adjust the brightness and contrast so that the picture was much more pleasant.

After a few days in Florence we bused down to Rome. The highlight of that trip was the visit to the Vatican. I don't remember much about Rome except for that, but that was enough. Mom had a bag full of rosaries that Joe Valentine's family had asked her to have blessed. She still wanted to do that. So we went with the tour to the Vatican to have a mass audience with Pope Pius XII. Eugenio Pacelli was still in the prime of life. Dad recalled having lunch with him in Paris when he was Eugenio Pacelli, Papal Nuncio to Pope Pius XI. Dad described him as a very learned man, well read, and very aware of the world around him.

We were ushered into the big audience chamber. There must have been a thousand people there, divided by a silken rope, with an aisle down the center, down which the Pope was to be carried to his throne. The Swiss Guard were there to carry the pallet bearing the Pope and to act as guard for His Holiness. They all carried large pikes and were dressed in colorful costumes. We were standing at the rear of the crowd, nowhere near where the Pope was to enter. Mom took the rosaries from the bag and handed them to me so they were draped over my hand. She told me to work my way forward through the crowd until I was standing next to the rope where I could see the Pope clearly. When the Pope appeared I was to raise the rosaries in the hope that His Holiness would notice and bless me.

Needless to say, when the Pope saw me holding the rosaries he reached down, touched my hand, and smiled at me. It was a very kind smile. Then he sat back up, made the sign of the cross over me, and continued on down to the throne. His sign of the cross probably included everyone in my section of the audience, but to me it seemed it was for me alone. I worked my way back to Mom, who of course was delighted. Not bad for a couple of Jews, eh? But we did get the rosaries properly blessed for the Valentine family, and that was her main reason for this visit. We continued on the tour. Saw the Sistine Chapel with the magnificent Michelangelo ceiling painting, saw a lot of religious artifacts. We also took a tour of the Vatican and saw many great paintings and statues.

We stayed in Rome for a couple more days, then took the train to Naples. From there we took a small boat out to the Isle of Capri where we visited the blue grotto. This is a cave that opens to the sea just outside of Anacapri. The sunlight bounces off the crystal sides of the grotto and makes the water an unearthly blue. To enter the cave we had to lie down in the bottom of the little boat and pull ourselves in by a rope because the cave entrance was so small. Mom went swimming inside the grotto and her skin appeared silver. Very beautiful. On the way back to Naples the pilot allowed me to take the wheel for a few minutes. On open water, with no other ships close by. Thrill of a lifetime.

From Naples we took the train to Milan on our way to Switzerland. We stayed in Milan for a couple of days going to museums. We went just outside of Milan to the little church where DaVinci had painted the *Last Supper* on the wall. The war had not been kind to the painting. The roof of the church was gone, exposing the painting to the weather. Worse, the painting had been protected by sandbags against the bombing. The bags had rotted and the painting had been attacked by mildew. I recognized it from the fact that there is a stained-glass copy in Los Angeles at one of the several Forest Lawn cemeteries. Much was made by the tour guide in L.A. about the fact that the glass figure of Judas had broken thirteen times in the kiln. The curator who showed us the original DaVinci painting told us that it would have to be restored. The restoration was finally completed fifty years later.

In Milan we stayed at a hotel managed by a former Italian Fascist. He would harangue us at meals about the damage that American bombing had done to his city during the war, and how we had killed women and children and bombed a hospital. He was quite loud, too. This was in 1949 and the city had not been rebuilt yet. There were large neighborhoods of ruined houses that we drove through on our way.

From Milan we went to Interlaken, Switzerland, where we took a ski lift up the Jungfrau. Well, up some Swiss Alp. It was raining and foggy, but we were given heavy insulated raincoats. I remember looking across the valley toward the Eigerwand and the Mönch. Or maybe we were going up the Eigerwand and looking… Anyway it was high and cold. And on the way up the bus driver explained to me that Swiss cows were specially bred so that they could stand easily on hillsides – their left legs were shorter than their right ones. He also told me that the dark brown cows gave chocolate milk. Ah, the Swiss…

We took a bus from Interlaken to Lucerne. On the way we stopped at the Rhône Glacier, the start of the River Rhône. The Glacier had a tunnel carved into it for several dozen yards and one could walk right into it. Inside the glacier, because of light refraction, the tunnel walls, which in fact were clear ice, appeared very light blue. After the walk into the glacier the tour went into a coffee shop next to the tunnel opening, where Mom had some Glühwein and I had some hot chocolate, gotten from those brown cows no doubt.

Later we passed through Altdorf, home of William Tell. The monument there tells the story of Tell, his son, the apple, and his expertise with the bow and arrow. It does not tell the story of the masked man who only shoots silver bullets and has a faithful Indian companion.

In Lucerne I remember seeing the dying lion memorial. It memorialized the Swiss Guard who died trying to save Louis XVI. A granite statue, very soulful. Too bad Louis didn't survive. From Basel we traveled to Luxembourg of which I remember nothing. Then to Brussels.

In Brussels I remember going to the house of a rather morbid painter, Antoine Joseph Wiertz. His subjects were people dying, a cholera victim trying to claw his way out of a coffin, a person's life flashing before his eyes just before he is guillotined. Just the thing for a ten-year-old's imagination.

The other Brussels landmark we saw was *Mannekin-Pis*, a statue of a youth about two or three years old urinating into the street. That must be one of those "Brussels Spouts" we have all heard about.

From there we traveled to Amsterdam. There we stayed with Gabriel Levy and his wonderful wife, Elsbeth. Gabriel had been a very successful film producer in Germany before Hitler, then was forced to flee in the early 1930s. Went to Amsterdam where he produced more films, including *De Kribbebijter*, starring Frits van Dongen and directed by Henry Koster. Van Dongen would later come to Hollywood and have a very active career as Philip Dorn, including as co-star of *I Remember Mama*. He visited Dad's house many times.

But now we were visiting the Levys in Holland. We stayed there for several days, cutting time off the tour's travel to London so we could spend more time with the Levys. Gabriel took me on a bicycle tour of Amsterdam, to the museums, the sights. We stopped on a street corner and bought from a street vendor two herring, which we ate whole. I have never stopped loving that, and whenever I am in Europe I search out street vendors selling fresh herring, which I eat whole.

We also took a train to Marken and Volendam, two medieval Dutch towns near

Amsterdam. The people there still wore wooden shoes and traditional clothing and the buildings had been largely untouched by the war. Fascinating. And the bike ride was excellent. We took the train there, biked around, had some more herring, and trained back. Being with this marvelous man was a real treat. And when we arrived home, Elsbeth had prepared a wonderful German-Dutch meal. I have wonderful, warm memories of these marvelous people.

Next stop was London. Only two memories of London. We visited the Tower, saw the old White Tower, built by William the Conqueror in 1078, saw some battlements. Saw where the "Princes in the Tower" presumably met their fate. Also saw the interrogation chambers. Nice things for a ten-year-old. But then we saw the crown jewels, which are very impressive.

The other thing in London that impressed me was a visit to a travel agent. Not for the travel agent, but because he told us what deprivations were still suffered by the British people due to the recent war. He and his family, wife and two children, were allowed a piece of beef about the size of a fist, for the four of them for an entire week. Coming from America, the land of plenty, I did not relate to that at all and remembered it for the rest of my life. Having been brought up with enough food and clothing, I found it an eye-opener.

We sailed for America from Southampton on the *Queen Elizabeth*. That liner was eleven feet longer than the *Queen Mary*, and the staterooms, especially in tourist class, were correspondingly larger. I must say this about both trips on the *Queens*; the food was excellent no matter in which class one dined. The service was excellent. The accommodations were luxurious even in tourist. Within reason there was enough room in our cabin. I do remember that the ship rolled quite a bit more than modern cruise ships do, probably because modern stabilizers had not been invented yet. I also remember that my daily bath was in warm salt water, and the steward quickly learned what temperature to set it.

I also remember that when we came through customs in New York an embarrassing thing happened. Mom and I both enjoyed real Hungarian salami and she wanted to bring some in. This was not on the customs list of allowed items. Hungarian salami is very aromatic, so Mom wrapped it carefully in wax paper to keep the aroma in. When we visited the Grand Chartreuse monastery in France, Mom bought a bottle of Chartreuse liqueur, also on the import verboten list. This she did not wrap carefully.

The bottle broke in the steamer trunk, soaking the clothing around it and spreading its cloyingly sweet aroma around the customs area. The customs officers were amused, anyway, but in opening the steamer trunk to see what was causing the atmospheric change they also discovered the Hungarian salami. We lost the salami, and since there was nothing left in the Chartreuse bottle, all the customs inspectors kept were the pieces of the bottle. We went to Uncle Miklos' home with aromatic luggage.

If I had my druthers I would give every child an experience like that trip. It left lasting impressions that I have to this day, impressions mostly of people and places of which I had no knowledge before this. Reading all the books in the library cannot give one the experience of experience.

It would also be the last time, and one of the few times in my life, that I spent any valuable time at all with my mother. The next school year I was in the fifth grade in West Hollywood, and the following summer I was sent to Chadwick School, a private boarding school in Palos Verdes. After that I spent very little time at home.

CHAPTER 4

OJAI

Within a week after Chadwick School was out I learned that I would be going away, this time to the Ojai Valley School. Mom sent me away to summer camp there to see if I liked it. Then I was to go to school there for the next two years, eighth and ninth grades.

The Ojai Valley School is nestled in the center of the Ojai Valley, about 80 miles from Hollywood, just inland from Ventura. It was about a three-hour drive. The summer camp was a six-week affair. I lived in a big dormitory with all the other boys. The dorm actually was split into two sections with a very strong door between them, the other section being for the girls. The school had great facilities, including a swimming pool where I took my first swimming classes and a stable with horses to ride. I had my bike there and could ride into town from time to time. I also rode all over the school.

But the school was fun. And for the first time in my life I was becoming aware of girls in a manner more than school-mate. There were possibilities here for sure.

Mom, in the meantime, had gone to a school to learn stenography and speed-typing. Then she got a job as secretary to one of Hollywood's leading literary agents, Laura Wilck. Laura handled such people as Rupert Hughes and Tom and Margaret Coffey. Mom got to know these people and more and more of them came over to the house when Mom had one of her literary dinner evenings. By this time I was away at school and very seldom had the chance to join her for dinner any more. But she seemed to be happier than she had been in a long time.

Also during this time she sold our house on Doheny Drive and bought some income property a few blocks away. This was a four-unit apartment house on the northwest corner of Holloway and La Cienega. It was directly outside the back door of Art Linkletter's La Cienega Bowling Lanes. Handy for me because I loved to bowl. And Mom derived enough income from the other apartments to pay the mortgage.

In the apartment just above us were an actor, Harry Lewis, and his wife, Marilyn. He worked quite often in Hollywood, usually in film noir projects. They had a small son who was just learning to walk, which we were aware of because we lived immediately below them. To supplement his income as an actor they opened a lunch café on Sunset Strip called Hamburger Hamlet. They covered the walls with pictures of famous actors in Shakespearean roles, the majority of them with John Barrymore as Hamlet. Actors of his generation flocked to the place. Heck, even I went there. Eventually they opened more and more branches of the place and sold the business in the mid-1990s for over $30,000,000.

The Ojai Valley School was a quiet, serene spot in the Ojai Valley. It had its share of princes and princesses, some real princes and princesses, although we didn't know it at the time. There was a young man from Italy named Martino de Bourbon, a member of the Bourbon family. Because he spoke with a pronounced accent we made fun of him. He usually was referred to as "Martini Bourbon." But he was a nice lad and joined in the fun cheerfully. Another was a young lady from Japan whom we later discovered was a member of the Japanese royal family.

There was the usual smattering of children of Hollywood celebrities. Since we were given a home weekend every four weeks, we had to learn to get along. I shared a room with Ed Bailey. Ed and I had known each other as children, in fact we went to Boy's Camp together. His mother was a Hungarian actress named Eury Erzi. Ed's father, James P. Bailey, was seldom at home. As chief geologist for Standard Oil of California he traveled the world looking for oil deposits. He had a fascinating wall of photos at home of himself in every conceivable location from Bali to Arabia to South Africa, even to Nazi Germany before the war. Because his mother and mine were Hungarian we had played together as young children.

The setup at OVS was that one of two roommates stayed in the room while the other lived in the common dorm area on the sun porch. At the end of four weeks we switched. So part of the time I slept in the room alone, and part of the time I was on the sun porch. I usually slept on the upper part of a double-bunk, which meant that I was usually about five feet above the ground. This led to an amusing incident. Well, it wasn't amusing at the time.

I went to summer camp at OVS in 1951, 1952 and 1953. I was staying at OVS during the summer of 1952. I was sleeping on that upper bunk on the night of July 21, when around 5:00 AM the White Wolf fault, an offshoot of the San Andreas fault system, slipped two feet horizontally and one-and-a-half feet vertically. It was a magnitude 7.5. Caused widespread damage. We felt it in Ojai, and it was also felt as far south as San Diego, in Las Vegas, and of course in Los Angeles. I was asleep on the upper bunk when it began to sway, quite alarmingly at first. It was rocking back and forth on its legs, swinging side-to-side alarmingly. I grabbed onto the upper corners of the closest uprights and hung on for dear life. The big fear was that the bunk beds would collapse like a row of dominoes.

They didn't. I survived, and even was able to reassure a younger boy who wandered out onto the sunroom porch, crying, "It's an eruption from Mars! It's an eruption from Mars!" For the rest of the morning, before time to get up, there were aftershocks. One or two were so severe that I hung on to the uprights again, but usually they were not very strong. Mrs. Launder, the dorm mother, came out in nightgown and bathrobe to reassure us that the worst was over. Ojai was closer to the epicenter than most places. I don't know if any buildings were damaged in Ojai. I suspect not. But I sure got a good shaking and a healthy respect for good architecture.

Many good memories and a few bad ones about OVS. We used to go camping in the Los Padres National Forest on the Sespe River at Piedras Blancas, the White Rocks. Hiking, horseback riding, fishing. We once caught a rattlesnake. The cook, Mr. Paul Pittman, skinned him and we each had a little chunk of rattler for dinner. Pittman was a real character himself. He also managed the stables, and he kept all the equestrian princes and princesses in line, always very tactfully but very authoritatively. Mostly we were on our own, although the counselors were always present when we needed them. If anyone caught a trout, we always had it for dinner. And in those days the Sespe had plenty of trout.

The school neither encouraged nor discouraged contact between the sexes. We were never alone enough to get into real trouble, but we did form attachments. There were two girls, both in the grade just behind mine, that I fantasized about. One of them was very seductive for a thirteen-year old. We sat opposite each other at the lunch and dinner tables and made seductive faces at each other.

The other girl, Sarah-Jane Futch, was a bit more mature. Her father was a famous surgeon who had made a very fine career for himself in Beverly Hills as an otorhinolaryngologist. Unfortunately he became addicted to the medicines he took to stay awake and to sleep. He shot himself to death in their home. Sarah was there at the time. According to Sarah, her mother ran up the stairs, then came back down and told her that her father had died from a heart attack.

Sarah was a frail youth who overcompensated in many ways to make up for her shortcomings. She had fallen off a horse and suffered from seizures. Her mother was overprotective, at least when she was younger. She also suffered from being the younger sister to Margaret-Ann, who was an aggressive, beautiful, talented lady. Still is, at this writing. Sarah was seven years her junior.

We didn't do much together. Went to a few dances, rode horses. Sarah was an excellent horsewoman both in traditional English style and in Western. After I moved on from OVS to the Webb School she and I corresponded, stayed in touch for a few years.

One thing I do remember about the OVS days was a radio evangelist named "Brother Jessup." The good brother broadcast often and loud, probably from Ventura. In those days Ventura was a kind of country town, not very sophisticated, and the radio fare was usually limited to country music and preaching. Brother Jessup was a real dilly. He advertised two things of note: his book of Soul Saver Sermons and his bottles of Soul Saver Serum. Open your hearts and open your wallets, friends, salvation is about to be yours. For merely five dollars you could buy a book of

Brother Jessup's best sermons, the reading of which would practically guarantee your place inside those pearly gates. But much quicker access was promised by buying a bottle of Soul Saver Serum. Drink this and your soul will be saved, no question about it. A quick lesson in the power of radio (How many suckers actually bought the stuff?) and in broadcast persuasion.

CHAPTER 5

WEBB

Come 1953 I graduated from OVS and it was time to move on. Mom gave me the choice of three schools to attend: Cate, Thacher, and Webb. We went to each of them and toured the campus. Thacher was nice but in order to succeed there one needed a horse. Horsemanship was an integral part of the curriculum. Each student either brought his own horse, or was given one by the school, and the student was graded on caring for the horse as much as for any academic subject. I have always liked horses but the horsy life was not for me.

Cate school in Carpinteria seemed much more than adequate. Had good surroundings, nice teachers, good living accommodations. A few of my classmates from OVS went there so I already knew some of the other students.

We also visited Webb, in Claremont, California. Here too were a few OVS graduates. The spacious campus is located in the foothills of the San Bernardino Mountains, close to Mount Baldy. It had an advantage in that I would have my own private bedroom, with no roommate. The curriculum seemed straightforward enough. It really didn't matter between Cate and Webb. I flipped a mental coin and chose Webb. I considered myself lucky that I had a choice of schools anyway. Most kids my age had to go to public schools, and then they were limited to going near where they lived. I would go to private school, maybe have as much fun as at OVS.

If there was a down side it was that Webb is a boys' school. Once every two months or so they had exchange dances with private girls' schools such as Marlborough and Westlake. I had a problem in that I was already shy. Not afraid of girls, just had no experience in how to approach them or make friends with them. I had taken dancing lessons at OVS but it was square dancing, nothing more. Anyway I was awkward and gangling as a child, a little clumsy, prone to drop or break things at unfortunate moments. Webb's strict protocol did not help much.

Mom at this time was absorbed in dating the author, Ronn Marvin, whom she married in 1954. He would be my stepfather and they would remain married until their deaths in the late 1990s.

After I had moved into my new bedroom I settled down to work into the routine there. There was study hall, there were assemblies every morning. Twice a week we had to put on coats and ties, the traditional Webb color tie, and go to chapel meetings. There were lectures in chapel about all sorts of moral subjects, the usual singing of hymns, some kind of benediction by Thompson Webb, the school's founder. During my tenth and eleventh grades, Webb was involved with building a chapel that Thompson named after his wife. After that, in our twelfth grade, we trekked up the hill to the Vivian Webb chapel.

Girls were something else again. Webb had these dances, but they had a strictly enforced "six-centimeter" rule. The teachers actually went around the dance floor with little measuring sticks, and if you were unlucky to be caught snuggling up to your dancing partner you were given demerits. One demerit meant an extra hour in study hall. I think if one had three demerits one had to give up an afternoon of going into Claremont.

We were allowed to ride our bikes or walk into Claremont on Wednesdays and Saturday afternoons. We could go to the store and buy food to bring back to our rooms. Or we could go to the record store and buy records. Whatever our meager allowances would allow. Some of us had allowances somewhat less meager than others. I quickly learned to buy foods that did not spoil quickly as I did not have a refrigerator in the room. I did have a record player, not a very good one, and a small collection of records. I also had a small radio that did not pick up very many stations, but at least it could play some music. In those days transistor radios were unheard of. They came into general use in another year or so. I finally got one in my senior year. Some of the other boys had a new super-duper radio, a Telefunken, from Germany. It had white ivory keys that you used to tune it, and the sound from its speakers was wonderful. Others had Webcor tape recorders. There were no pre-recorded tapes in those days but one could use the tape recorder to help in memorizing the many poems we were taught in English Lit.

A note on the curriculum. I spent hours learning Latin, by choice. I studied it for three years. Others studied French, and most studied Spanish because Spanish is handy for Californians. But Latin, ah, there's a classic subject that has uses far beyond its founders' dreams. My knowledge of Latin has helped in so many ways, and still does. I can sometimes figure out all kinds of foreign languages because of my knowledge of Latin. Also it opened a whole new world of word analysis for me. If I don't know what a word in English means, many times I can work out the meaning by checking the parts against the Latin dictionary. The luckier boys at Webb studied Greek, which with Latin gave them an even greater advantage.

While I went to Webb, during the summer I was sent to a really great camp—Catalina Island Boys Camp. Many of the Webb students were there. And in fact the camp was managed by Les Perry, who was the athletics coach at Webb. The kitchen staff was the same also. Counselors were drawn from college students around the Los Angeles area. By this time I was one of the "older boys," so I no longer worried about bullies. I had reached my adult height, 6'2." I wasn't particularly muscular, but I could hold my own. That was such a treat. Swimming every day, hiking the back roads of Catalina. Spear fishing and regular reel fishing. Horses, too, although I didn't pay much attention to them. The camp owned several little sailboats and I learned to sail. I took a snorkel and swim fins and snorkeled in the kelp around the camp, looking at the fish. The camp was right on the water at Howland's Landing, around four or five miles from the Isthmus.

One event stands out in my mind. I went to regular six-week camp, and then stayed two weeks for the "post-camp" session. During that time we caught a pig, there are wild pigs on the island, and we had a luau.

If there was a down side to this it was that there were no girls there. There was a girls' camp not far away but we had almost no contact with them. I remember we had one campfire where we sat around with the girls, toasted marshmallows, and sang songs, and then the girls headed back to their own camp and we didn't see them again. I was just as awkward as ever.

During the few weeks I spent at home there was not enough time for me to make any headway with any girls. I saw some but since I didn't have a car there wasn't much I could do about it. I fantasized a lot, usually about Sarah. She was a very fine looking lady, had shown me a great deal of heart. Maybe there would be something there after all.

During the year Webb had dances with girls' schools. One of these was Westlake School for Girls in Holmby Hills. Sarah attended that school. Since I was shy I only went to one dance during the three years I went to Webb, and that was at Westlake. We were bused there. There was a band. And there was Sarah. We were allowed two dances with the same girl, that was all, but I managed to exchange dances with another Webb student so I had three with Sarah. She had by now become a fantasy girl, a wonderful golden angel. In reality she was a lovely girl, just shy of a golden angel, but quite extraordinary nonetheless. And she didn't care if I couldn't dance well.

I had been taking dancing lessons provided by Webb with a few girls shipped in from Claremont High School for the purpose. These only pointed up my inability to dance, and I wasn't getting any better. I stuck with it for the entire course but to no avail.

When I returned home for a weekend, my mother let me borrow her Buick to go on a date. I was now of an age when driving was legal. I took driving lessons and earned my driver's license. I had no car, but because I lived at school the Buick would do. At this time Sarah was living in Bel-Air with her mother, who was very protective of her. I could take her out during the day but not at night. I could live with that. But we were only able to go out maybe two or three times because of my schedule, going back to Webb.

I could not have had a better education than I had at Webb. The whole school was focused on preparing the student for college and for later life as well. We were punished not only for rule infractions but also for infractions of the honor code. After each test we had to write out and sign the following statement: "I pledge my word of honor as a gentleman that I have neither given nor received aid during this examination." The school was very strict about that aspect. If it were later discovered that cheating had occurred, you could be asked to leave the school. Furthermore, if we saw someone cheat on an exam we were expected to go to the offender and tell him to admit to the teacher that he had cheated. If he did, he would have to take the test over, usually. If we did see someone cheating, told him, and he did not admit his offense to the teacher, we were to do it. And if we did not do it, and later it was discovered that he had cheated and we saw it but did nothing, we would both be asked to leave the school. It was strict indeed, but it was a good lesson well learned. Very few students suffered dismissal while I was there. A member of my graduating class was dismissed a week before graduation, but nobody else in my class was dismissed. Another classmate was barred from the graduation ceremony because he had the temerity to swear at a teacher. A younger fellow was dismissed because he kept a car in the canyon next to the school, snuck out his dorm window after "lights out" time, and drove into town to see a girl. Another student was dismissed for stealing. You either hewed to the straight and narrow or you were not welcome at Webb.

We were also taught personal hygiene. No facial hair. Clothes always neat. Rooms always straightened. There was room inspection every day. Strangely enough, when I went there in the mid-50s, smoking was allowed in the twelfth grade. We could smoke in our rooms or around the dorm, but nowhere else. Sam Davidge, a classmate, had something of an emporium in his dorm room, selling cigarettes, candy, and other necessities.

There was not much effort to involve the parents in the school process. We went home once a month for a weekend. Mom wasn't happy about the one-and-a-half-hour drive so she and two or three other parents shared driving responsibilities on alternate home weekends.

A private boarding school is usually a placid place. Big excitement can be caused by improperly conjugating a verb. Our lives were orderly and pre-ordained. The motto for Webb School is "Principes, non Homines"—Leaders, not Men. We were being groomed to be captains of industry, upper-echelon government employees, creative forces in the community. The road to this was made easier by the fact that all the teachers lived on campus, some in the dorms with us. Most had families that lived with them. So at dinner when we sat down to table, each table was headed by a teacher, we called them "masters," and Dr. Webb, or "Pappy" as we called him, was the headmaster. We couldn't take a bite until he picked up his fork at his table. But we usually ate with the table's master and his wife and whatever children he had.

Our daily routine seldom varied. We knew when to be in the common dining hall for breakfast, when to straighten up our rooms, when to go to class, when to go to study hall. Our days were laid out with precision. Wednesdays and Saturdays we were given extra time in the afternoons for free time, and then we could go into Claremont, or just sit around on the lawns, or study, whatever we wanted to do. Other weekdays we did have an hour or two in the afternoon to ourselves. There were specific times for practicing sports also. The "Gauls," the home team, had a regular schedule for football practice and for games with other schools. In any case, nothing was anticipated to disrupt our studies and the routine.

One of the boys with whom I drove home, whose mother alternated as chauffeur with mine, was Bob Roos. He was a diminutive eighth grader. He had buck teeth. He dressed funny. He was shorter than most Webbites. He became the butt of school jokes, a position he seemed to enjoy. He never complained about it. Sometimes some of the older boys would rough him up, not seriously, just uncomfortably. He didn't invite this, but he didn't shy away either. He came from a good family. His father owned a string of clothing stores in Los Angeles. I rather liked him, and I was not happy when the older kids picked on him. Once or twice I suggested that they take their aggression out elsewhere, but they paid me no heed. I probably was mean to him too from time to time.

Roos was one of those few who was extremely intelligent and perceptive. He could turn anything into a joke. He usually interjected himself into any handy conversation whether he knew the people or not. And he was loud. He was also impulsive.

One morning we woke up to the sounds of sirens. Sometime during the night Bob Roos had hanged himself in his room. He used his belt looped over the pipe in the ceiling, and he stepped off a chair. The dorm master found him the next morning when he didn't show up for breakfast. I wasn't particularly touched by this. He hadn't been a close friend. It was, however, disjointing because our orderly lives were disrupted for a day or two while the shock wore off. One of us had actually done it. The ambulance and the police cruiser left the campus, and we were called into an assembly. Pappy gave a eulogy of sorts, said how much he loved the boy, how hurt he was that this had happened. None of the rest of us knew how to react, I believe. We sure didn't make any more Roos jokes and Mom had to find a new mother to share driving chores.

Mom's time became more constricted in 1954. That was the year she married Ronn Marvin, an author whom she had represented as a literary agent. They were very close to each other and their wedding was almost inevitable. The wedding was held at the temple on the corner of Crescent Heights and Fountain. I wore my suit. Mom's father was there but not her mother. Ronn's parents, Isaac and Marie, and his sister, Ebria, were there. I had asked for and been given a leave of absence from Webb for that weekend to attend the event. After the ceremony we went back to the apartment on Holloway Drive. Mom and Ronn were to leave right after the service for a honeymoon in Europe, so I would take the bus back to Webb. I had checked the bus schedules, figured I would be back at the bus station in Claremont by 2:30.

Giving myself an hour to get a cab and get back to school, I checked myself out until 3:30 Sunday afternoon.

The bus broke down. I returned to the school around 5:00 pm. The master in charge of discipline at the school was Mr. Sumner, and he was merciless. I never took a class from him, but those who did said he was a good teacher. I'm sure they are right. He gave me two demerits for being late. I explained that the bus broke down and they had to send a replacement bus. He explained that I should have thought of that. The demerits stayed, two extra hours in study hall. I seldom got demerits for anything else after that.

Webb had a store where we could buy our schoolbooks and supplies. In the same building was a soda fountain. I volunteered to be the soda jerk. There were two of us, and we were kept busy from about 12:30 to about 1:30 making various concoctions for the students. The school paid for the supplies. I think they also charged for the various sodas and sundaes we made. Not much, 10 or 20 cents. But we had to learn to handle money. I taught myself to fashion special combinations, unlikely combinations, for the sundaes. The kids loved it. I usually made myself something as well, and I dutifully put a quarter or whatever it cost into the cash register.

I should mention that the annual tuition for the school was on the order of $5,000 or so in those days. Now it's over $45,000 for the school year. But of course that includes the schoolbooks and food.

There were some memorable masters at the school. Ramsay L. Harris was Burmese. He had been raised by a missionary and took his name. He taught History, English, and Latin. He taught us more about Shakespeare than we could ever have learned from anyone else. A brilliant man. John Pettley, formerly an officer in His Majesty's Navy, taught English, Latin, and Plane Geometry. All the masters there taught in several disciplines. D. Murray Alexander, pride of His Majesty's Royal Air Force, a highly decorated bomber pilot during WWII, taught Physics.

And then there was Raymond M. Alf, teacher of biology and paleontology. He had been a competitive runner in college. The *Claremont Courier* said that he held the record for having run the 10-yard dash in 9.5 seconds, and they should know. Ray Alf had a museum. He took students out on fossil-hunting expeditions into the desert around Barstow and Victorville. One of his students had snagged his pants on something while skidding down a sand hill. Going back to find the culprit, he dug up a skull of the missing link in the pig family, *Dyseohysus fricki*. That was in the museum. Another student discovered an unusual snail, named it *Helminthoglypta Alfi* in honor of Ray Alf. His museum stands on the campus as the only museum of paleontology on a high school campus in the world. The students still go out every year in search of fossils. Sometimes they allow alumni to go along.

My senior year at Webb was spent in the dormitory known as The Alamo. Built on a hillside with the rooms in a line up the hill. Almost all the classmates were returnees from the junior class. We were allowed to smoke in our rooms, which we did incessantly. Philip Morris could have used us as poster boys. I did break the mold from time to time by trying to smoke a pipe. I thought it looked sophisticated. Later, when I was in college, I found pipe smoking to be too involved. Too much junk to carry around. I stuck with cigarettes from then on until my first son was born ten years later. Then I quit. For a while.

I graduated from Webb in 1956. Mom came to my graduation but Dad did not. I was told that they had discussed it and decided that they both should not go, but that Mom would represent both of them. The diploma was encased in a leather-bound Bible, which I still have on my shelf. We had to wear our Webb coats and Webb neckties to the ceremony, the last time I was to ever wear either. We had to wear them during the year to Sunday chapel, every week. They became a kind of joke to us. We didn't like them or dislike them, since it wasn't strictly speaking a uniform, but it was a mark of the school discipline. I know one classmate for sure who tied the coat and tie to the rear bumper of his car and dragged them home.

CHAPTER 6

POMONA

Things had changed at home. Mom and Ronn had sold the apartment house and moved to a different apartment in a duplex in West Hollywood. They had the upstairs apartment. The ground floor was occupied by the owner, Virginia Payne. Virginia Payne was for thirty years the voice of radio's beloved "Ma Perkins." She owned the building, and she lived in the ground floor apartment with her somewhat crotchety mother, whose unlikely name was Queen Victoria Levitt. Mom and Ronn lived upstairs. I lived upstairs too, when I was there, on the couch in Ronn's office. The old fold-a-bed had migrated. I had to fold the bed up every day so that Ronn could write his books.

My first priority after graduation was to get a car. Like most teenagers I wanted that freedom. Dad agreed to buy me a car if I would repay him out of summer earnings. We looked in the newspaper ads for a good prospect, and eventually settled on a 1951 Chevy. It had low mileage, only owned by a movie starlet and driven to the studio and back. And it had a radio. It did not have a heater. In those days one paid extra for radio or heater. Automatic transmission was an unheard-of luxury, air conditioning was an impossible dream, there was no cruise control. If you wanted external rear-view mirrors they were also extra. And you actually had to roll up the windows by hand. But it did go, quite well, and gasoline only cost 25 cents a gallon. Sometimes there were price wars and the gasoline prices went down to 15 cents. The car cost $600. I was in heaven.

In order to repay Dad I went to work as a box boy at the local Ralph's Supermarket, $1.05 an hour, something like that. Two days after I started working a very large, well-dressed person approached me to offer me membership in Local 770 of the food handler's union. He was so persuasive that I accepted right away, and after work that day I went down to the union office to sign up. My first union.

Ralphs was really drudgery. Supermarkets were not anything then like they are now. We often wrapped the food in boxes instead of bags for customers to take home. The store policy was to not accept tips. If we helped a customer out to the car with a big load of groceries and were offered a tip we were to say, politely, "It is a courtesy of the company" and turn it down, which I did. Few of the other box boys did. I still had that old honor code from Webb drilled into me and I was uncomfortable doing anything else. This theme would follow me through my life.

I lived at the new apartment in a somewhat uncomfortable proximity to Ronn and Mom. Mom seemed to be happy with me at "home," but Ronn was not. He was seldom outright in his coldness, and we even had some good times together, although never without Mom being present. I was mostly on my own. I saw Sarah a couple of times. I saw the girl next-door a couple of times. Sarah was still my fantasy woman, a role that well suited her.

It was almost a relief when I went to college. Pomona College is also in Claremont. The Webb School and Pomona College were close in tone. In fact the senior classes at Webb were almost identical to the freshman classes at Pomona. And since I had my own car I could drive to school, move myself in, and attend classes without my parents having to lift a finger. Pomona gave their students a two-room suite for two, bedroom and studying room, and bathroom. And there were girls there, but in dorms all the way across the campus.

I was happy at the school. My roommate, Gerald deSantillana, was a great guy, bright, interesting, and very concentrated on his work. I hadn't really chosen a major yet, so I was studying "English," both Lit and Writing. I quickly learned that writing wasn't my long suit. And Lit was interesting but not something I wanted to do for the rest of my life. I was much more interested in the social life, hanging out with the guys and driving my car around. My grades reflected that attitude. The social atmosphere at the school was much more relaxed than it had been at either OVS or Webb. There was no study hall. We were expected to have enough self-discipline to study on our own. I did plenty of that, but some of the classes I chose were entirely beyond me. German wasn't. I took that because I already spoke a smattering of the language. It was a mistake. I assumed that with my prior knowledge I could ace the course. I flunked it.

I also took Religion, which dealt with some of the more arcane meanings in the Bible. I had never had any sort of religious upbringing. There was no question that I was Jewish by heritage, but I knew nothing about the religion itself. My dad had decided that if the Nazis won the war I would not suffer because I never had any Jewish upbringing. I never had a briss. My dad had had a bar mitzvah and hated it, so I never had one of those either. I had been in temple only twice that I could remember, the first time the day after Franklin Roosevelt died, and Mom took me there. The second time was when she married Ronn. I felt no need for religion, never having been given any guidance in that direction by anyone. I mistrusted any kind of organized anything, much less religion. Having been well schooled in history both at Webb and at Pomona, one of the few classes that I enjoyed enough to pass with good grades, I felt that most wars were religious in nature and that the subject itself was to be avoided. So it was a mystery both to me and to the professor why I took the class. I think it had something to do with a choice between that and philosophy, and with the student's natural inclination to take the line of least resistance. I took the class that I felt was the easier of the two. Silly me.

After hours we had the whole evening to ourselves. The drinking age in California at the time was twenty-one. I had never bought liquor before although I was raised to have a glass of wine with dinner from age four, a habit I have never broken. The European style was to allow children a little alcohol with the main meal of the day, just a small glass, and I was used to wine with dinner. As I went through high school I had beer and once in a while a decent scotch, but wine was still the potable of choice. I wasn't a drinker, never have been. Not until my marriage started to go sour, anyway, and then only briefly. Near Pomona College was the Claremont liquor store. "The Colonel" ran it, a friendly elderly man. I wanted to try buying a bottle of wine. I went to the store, the Colonel asked me for my drivers license. I gave it to him. He glanced at it and asked me what I wanted. Red wine? Right over there. I bought a gallon of Manischewitz Concord Grape and took it back to the dorm. Kept it on a shelf in the closet where the housekeeping staff wouldn't find it, I hoped. Later I heard that the Colonel was unable to see farther than the tip of his nose, that it had been a tradition for all Pomona students to buy their spirits there for many years, and both the liquor store and the students were happy with the arrangement.

One evening I actually set out to get plastered. At Pomona there was an undeveloped area called "The Wash" where one could take a girl with reasonable expectation of being left alone, or one could also take a bottle, with reasonable expectation of being left to drink alone. Usually we drank in groups, however, and seldom to excess, with a few exceptions. Well, maybe with many exceptions. Especially on the weekends.

Never having had this kind of freedom before, I paid much more attention to the freedom part than I did to the studying part. The results of this did not become evident until my sophomore year. I moved into a different dormitory, had a new roommate. Mike Godfrey was a different sort. His father was an oil driller. Mike had been at Webb with me. I never knew him very well at Webb, but then I never knew anyone very well at Webb except for one fellow, Saul Kahan. Saul and I would study together, and his father once in a while drove me home because he also lived in West Hollywood.

Anyway, Mike Godfrey was a more roughneck sort than I was. And he had a really neat car. He was given a 1956 Chevy Bel-Air on graduating from high school. It rumbled a bit more than a stock car should. I got interested in car racing through him. He didn't race his own car, but we did go to the Pomona Drag Strip, at the L.A. County Fair Grounds. Mike's friend Jerry Garrett had a good car which had a few little things done to it to make it go faster in the quarter-mile, and we all went out to watch the drag races every couple of weeks. From time to time we went to a small race track on Arrow Highway where quarter-midget races were held. These consisted of little children, maybe ten-year-old boys, racing around the track in full racing regalia, driving miniature quarter-size race cars powered, I suppose, by washing machine and lawn mower engines. Nobody was ever hurt at these things because the cars weren't going fast enough to cause any damage. The kids all wore helmets anyway.

Between my freshman and sophomore years I got a job in the summer at The Troc Drugs, selling behind the counter, and delivering when necessary. It was necessary quite often. We sold medicine, liquor, and sundries to many Hollywood folk and I was usually the delivery boy. I delivered to Elizabeth Taylor and her husband du jour, Nicky Hilton, in their really big house on Doheny Drive. Never saw them, of course, the butler always answered the door and dealt with such as myself. I remember trying to see around him into the living room. I could hear voices there. He was too large, however. Spike Jones was a different story. He and Helen had a big home in Beverly Hills. When I delivered to him he came to the door in his shorts, tipped me well. Steven McNally also tipped well, but was always well dressed.

The Troc Drugs was owned and operated by old "Doc" Jacobsen. He seemed to feel that if he paid me he could ask me to do personal favors for him. After all, he was paying me, right? One day he told me to go to his house and polish the floor in the dining room. I wasn't happy about that but I didn't expect what happened next. His wife had moved all their furniture out of the room but left some shelves on the wall. One shelf contained some little statues. The really *kitsch* kind that can be bought at the Grand Canyon rim store. I had bent down to adjust something on the floor polishing machine, and without looking I stood up under the shelf, scattering all the little statues, or rather their parts, across the floor. Mrs. Jacobsen wasn't happy at all. But they didn't fire me, just told me to go back and work at the store. They never asked me to do anything like that again. I must have been an adequate salesman/stock-clerk/driver. I never offered to pay for the damage and they never asked, probably best all the way around.

One delivery stands out in my memory. There was a starlet named Darby Donnelly who lived just off Sunset Strip on Larrabee. I only delivered to her once. She had ordered some makeup supplies and some wine. I rang the doorbell of her apartment. I heard two feminine voices inside. She opened the door, and I could see that they were two girls. She was dressed in an absolutely sheer teddy, and her girlfriend, sitting on the couch in full view, wore a bra and panties. A very small bra and panties. I gave them the bag with the order, and then the bill. She went back into the living room and searched her purse for the exact amount of the bill, no tip. I thought, oh well. The view made it worth it. As she turned back into the living room, her girlfriend said, "Well? Aren't you going to tip the boy?" She turned back to me, pressed her whole body against mine, and gave me my very first French kiss. It lasted about two weeks. Then she stepped back, smiled, and closed the door. I could hear giggles coming from inside. I went back to my car and drove back to the drugstore. On the way, for the one time in my life, I lit a filter cigarette on the wrong end. They sure do taste terrible that way. Like I said, I was shy, and very naïve.

I went back to Pomona just before the new semester started so I could get my room set up and decide what classes to take. I was majoring in English, a language I spoke fluently by then. I wasn't really all that excited about English but I needed a focus. I didn't want to follow in the family tradition of show business because I suspected that it was expected of me, and Dad certainly didn't want me to go into the movie industry.

In fact once when I was visiting him at his big house in Pacific Palisades, he told me outright that the movie industry is the meanest, cruelest business in the world, and that I would be much better off as a journalist. He told me to go home and write a short story, that he would critique it. I did, and he didn't. But he kept insisting on a journalism career for me. As an added incentive, he suggested that writing for a newspaper or journal would be very good practice for writing for the screen, and the best route to directing was through writing. After all, that's how he got into the movie business, as a writer. I never brought it up again. He never did either.

One of the students who had graduated from Webb and attended Pomona was E. Pierce Marshall. Pierce was a car nut. His father, J. Howard Marshall, was a multimillionaire. He had a huge house at Lake Arrowhead where we would drive during the winter, through the snow, and the cook would make us dinner. Pierce's father owned a Jaguar XK-120, one of the originals from 1952 or '53. Pierce would drive the car whenever possible. When he kept it at the Arrowhead house, he took the tires off and put it up on blocks so his father couldn't drive it. Pierce loved that car. On graduating from Webb, he received the car as a graduation present. He then kept it at Pomona. Unfortunately, another Pomona student had been given a 1954 Corvette, one of the original 6-cylinder cars. Baseline Road was near Pomona, and at the time it was in an undeveloped part of Claremont. Desert fields around. The boys would go up there and drag race in the evening because the road was almost always deserted. Mike Godfrey and Jerry were frequent flyers up there. Well, Pierce decided to race his Jaguar against the Corvette. We all went up to Baseline Road to watch. The flag dropped, both cars took off… and the Corvette left the Jaguar in the dust.

Pierce, never one to let a little race depress him, went to the Chevy dealer next day and bought a brand new Corvette.

Pierce was a hands-on car nut, however. My old 1951 Chevy came without a heater. In Pomona it gets cold on winter nights. I went to Pep Boys and bought a new aftermarket heater. Pierce installed it, and it worked perfectly.

Just for the record, Pierce was the same E. Pierce Marshall who got into a legal battle with Anna Nicole Smith over his father's fortune. As I would have expected, Pierce eventually won a court of appeals ruling that Smith was entitled to none of the millions. Pierce, who had died the year before, would have been proud. There wasn't any evidence that Old Harold willed the money to her. But it sure was amusing for a while. Thinking that her baby daughter was about to inherit millions, everyone from Frederick von Anhalt to Santa Claus claimed fatherhood of the baby.

I took several courses in English and one in biology. None of them were of interest and I treated them accordingly. The result was that toward the end of the school year Dean Beatty called me into his office. He showed me my grades thus far that year. Then he suggested that my talents might be better served at another institution. He didn't outright tell me that I didn't make the cut. In fact I asked him if I could stay and try to bring my grades up. He answered that I could, but he didn't think it would be much use. I couldn't get my head around this kind of work. He was right. I had no interest in what I was studying. I accepted the inevitable, finished the semester, and returned home to Mom's apartment.

Neither she nor Dad were very happy about my leaving school. I decided that I should start being serious. I was not independently wealthy and would have to fend for myself soon. I had no direction. I needed to figure out, all by myself, how my life would plan out. I had no guidance with this. Mom sent me to a testing service that was supposed to help you figure out what your professional direction would be. The best they could do was to tell me that I should consider teaching. OK, teaching. I can do that. I have always been shy in front of strangers, but a room full of students? I don't know but I'll try it.

CHAPTER 7

LACC AND UCLA

I first went to UCLA and applied but my grades were not good enough. So I went to Los Angeles City College, a two-year school that at the time dealt with students from the poorer sections of town. If I could make the cut, I would enter UCLA next year. I took courses in Shakespeare, microbiology, and teaching. This place was a breeze. I took French, got an "A." Still can't speak the language. The education classes were as interesting as watching eggs fry but I soldiered on through. In fact I aced all the courses I took. The Microbiology teacher was an elderly, cynical man. His joy was to show one of the old Army films about venereal disease. Emptied the classroom of girls within five minutes.

I remembered that when I went to Webb we all took an attitude test, comparing our likes and dislikes with those of members of various professions. This was an attempt to match us with a group of people with similar interests, not an aptitude test. They asked questions such as whether we liked people with big noses or small noses, classical or popular music, riding a bicycle or a motorcycle. I had always loved all kinds of music, and I didn't care whether someone had a big or small nose, so the test was lost on me. It was no surprise that the professional group I matched closest was mortician.

But this was the here and now and I had no idea what direction to take. Teaching? Maybe. English? How can I make a living at English? McDonald's was still a hamburger joint in Pasadena. I had gotten a job with Clara Blore's Catering Service, washing dishes and delivering food to movie stars. Clara's main feature was if you were in from New York just for a week or so, working at a studio, she would make a meal for you and deliver it to your hotel room. Her specialty was Lobster Thermidor. Mrs. Blore was the wife of Eric Blore, the British actor who played the butler in the Fred Astaire-Ginger Rogers films. He had retired long since and was no longer very mobile, so she had her own business to supplement his pension. I delivered to Melville Cooper, Reginald Denny, all the Hollywood Raj folk in fact. I also delivered once or twice to Burl Ives, who was staying at the Chateau Marmont. I introduced myself to him as the son of Henry Koster. Dad had directed him in a film a few years prior, *The Power and the Prize*. He greeted me warmly and we talked for a while, but I had other deliveries to make before the food grew too cold, so I had to move on.

Once in a while Mrs. Blore, to give me a real treat, would make Lobster Thermidor for my dinner also. Not long after, she made it for another client and I watched her make it. She sat at the kitchen table peeling the caps off a big bowl of mushrooms. It was a work of art. She sipped a glass of scotch. She also had a cigarette hanging out of her mouth. From time to time the ashes fell into the mushrooms. She saw me staring, and she smiled and said gaily, "Well, Bob, what they don't know won't hurt 'em, eh?" I never told 'em, but I never ate her food again.

I did get into UCLA. That summer I took a few courses there, including one on the introduction to motion pictures. It was taught by Hugh Gray, who had written several films, including *Helen of Troy* and *Quo Vadis*. I had not seriously considered going into the movie industry before. Maybe Dad was right. Hugh Gray was a small Englishman who suffered from the beginnings of Parkinson's disease. As he spoke his head shook back and forth. But what he had to say and the way he said it was special. He took us through the history of some of the finest films ever made, explaining what made each of them exciting. I had never looked on cinema as an art before, just a way to make a living. Now I was looking at films in a whole new light. Now this was much more interesting than English or teaching or anything else. I was hooked. I went to the admissions office and officially changed my major to Theatre Arts, with Motion Pictures as a specialty.

Considering that my father's grandfather was in the opera, his mother played the piano in one of the first movie theatres in Berlin, my mother's parents were famous performers, she was an actress both onstage and off, Dad was a director, in hindsight I can't see how I could have done anything else. What was I thinking? English? Teaching? I have always loved this language. I also love teaching.

I paid the $75 for my tuition. The next two years were a great bargain for me. I studied film. I took courses in camera, editing, acting, directing, writing. In those days there were no courses in the business of film, only courses in the making of. It was assumed that we would be artists, not administrators. In fact many of us were. Such leading lights as Francis Ford Coppola, Laszlo Kovacs, Noel Black, Steve Burum, Carroll Ballard, and Paul Bartel were all there in one class or another. It didn't matter; we all studied together. Karl Freund, Charles Clark, Arthur Ripley were instructors. Dorothy Arzner taught directing. Dorothy Adams Foulger taught acting. It was a stellar class with stellar professors. I never had so much fun before. Saul Kahan was there also, for a while. And there was a comedian named Ken Greenwald. Kenny and I hung out together quite a bit, since I loved going to the coffee houses in those days—the Troubadour, Ice House, Ash Grove—and Kenny enjoyed performing there with the likes of Bud & Travis, Miriam Makeba, and Leon Bibb. I also made friends in a poker party setup with Al Rossman and Ron Waller.

The work was not easy, but I was interested enough in learning the crafts that I kept at it. There was not much homework. I had already done the grunt work on that in the previous three years. I did have to read some classic plays and poetry, but these were a pleasure, not a travail. I again tried my hand at creative writing and again it was no use. I can put two words in front of another as well as the next person but it is impossible for me to create stories of any value. I can tell them but I can't invent them. Never could.

I really enjoyed the camera classes and editing. Sound recording also. And I found that I was most comfortable in the student productions when I was working in the "production department" as an assistant director (AD) or production manager (PM). I enjoyed taking other people's work and arranging it properly. In any case, the mechanical part of UCLA Theatre Arts was out-of-date camera equipment, and our editing facilities were at least ten years behind the times. We made movies in the old style. There was a Houston Fearless dolly that must have been manufactured in the 1920s. It weighed tons, or appeared to, and was controlled by turning huge iron wheels to pan or boom. Very cumbersome, almost impossible for us to use, but we had to make it work so we did.

I was assigned to be the property master on one student production. Ken Greenwald was the assistant cameraman and his use of the slate would send us into gales of laughter. There were student actors and student crew persons. There was a faculty advisor, but like many faculty members there he had never made a good living in the business and had decided to teach. So we basically ran our own productions for better or for worse. This usually took far more time than we would have had professionally, but we were students and we were learning. And even if we had outdated equipment we learned that we had to load a camera and reseal it to make it light-tight before filming. We learned that if we used the wrong makeup an actor would not look very good. Actors did not like not looking very good. I had an advantage because I had also studied makeup.

I had the pleasure of working one summer at 20th Century-Fox as a day laborer. I learned several things very quickly. I learned that I would have to join the Studio Utility Employees Union, IATSE Local 724, in order to work. I learned that I would have to buy a good solid hammer, and I would bend a wire clothes hanger to fit over my belt and hold a hammer for easy use at my waist. That would be my principal tool. I learned to make my own lunch and to bring it in a steel lunchbox. I learned to carry an extra wire coat hanger and bend it straight with a hook at each end, so I could hang the lunch box from a tree limb and not worry that ants would get to it. They couldn't crawl down the wire.

When I was there, a new film was being made with an unknown actor who was known better as a singer, Elvis Presley. I saw him working on the back lot one day and walked over just to say hello. I saw some fairly amazing things as well. The trees and shrubbery around the "Southern Mansion" exterior had all been dead for many years, but were used over and over again in films. Crews went out just before filming, sprayed them off, spray-painted the leaves green, added other bushes as necessary, and the front of the house was ready for filming.

One day a fire broke out on the back lot at the "Mill," the huge building in which set walls were constructed. There were fire trucks and the usual gaggle of reporters to cover the event. Predictably, a Corvette drove up and Pat Boone stepped out. He quickly removed his shirt so he was bare from the waist up. He grabbed a hose from a fireman, started spraying the fire with the water jet. The reporters took his picture. He quickly returned the hose to the fireman, put his shirt back on, and drove off. The whole episode took maybe two minutes.

I quickly earned my stripes as a "high man." I wasn't afraid to climb trees or stalagmites, chop off the tops, and work my way down. Heights didn't particularly scare me as they did some others on the crew.

I also relished making $1.37/hour. It wasn't a great deal but it helped to pay for the Chevy. And there was a little left over for other pleasures. In those days a respectable dinner for two at a good restaurant might cost $5.00-7.50.

My mother at this point was still a literary agent. Laura Wilck had retired and left her the business. One of the books she arranged to publish was the *Westmore Book of Beauty*, written mainly by Perc Westmore. That's pronounced "Perse" by the way, not "Perk" as most people erroneously said it. In the mid to late fifties and into the sixties the beauty salon of choice was the House of Westmore on Sunset Boulevard across from the Crossroads of the World. There came movie stars and starlets, the cream of L.A. society, usually on a Saturday or Sunday before some fancy do, to have the master, Perc, minister to them.

The Westmore family was legendary in Hollywood. The father, George, was an English wig maker who had come to the U.S. in the early twentieth century. He had numerous children, all of whom went into the makeup field, but Perc, the oldest, was the head of the family after George died. It was he who opened the House of Westmore Beauty Salon, and it was he who wrote the book. To give it more legitimacy, however, he ascribed each chapter as having been written by one of his brothers. Each of his brothers, by the way, was the head of makeup at a major studio. Their children and grandchildren are still excellent makeup artists. I have worked with most of them.

Upstairs from the salon was a makeup school, probably the first in Hollywood and certainly the best. As a gesture of thanks for my mother representing the book Perc, who had become a family friend, offered to put me through the makeup school at no cost. I spent that summer learning how to do straight daytime and evening makeup, as well as prostheses, blood bags, scars, fangs, the whole nine yards. I was good at it, too. Not an artist like the Westmores, but capable of doing a very respectable job with straight makeup, age, and the simpler effects.

LACC AND UCLA

"I made up my friend Ron Waller as Vincent Van Gogh. Notice the ear..."

It was one of the most satisfying jobs I ever had, when I was doing it on productions. When I had finished a good makeup I could see it. It was right there in front of me. I didn't need someone, a director or producer, who usually didn't know good makeup when it happened, to tell me that it was a good job. It had to be good. After all, if an actor's face is going to be blown up and shown on a seventy-foot screen in a large theatre, every blemish and discoloration will be seventy times as big as life on the screen, so good makeup is essential.

I learned makeup quite well. In fact in the makeup class at UCLA the teacher did not know as much as I did. Being a teacher who had not actually performed any makeup in his life but only taught about it, he was a little intimidated by me because I had studied it at the House of Westmore and had actually performed makeup on stage plays and movies. From then on we taught the class together, and he deferred to me if his film experience varied from mine. I deferred to him in matters of stage makeup because he had actually done some. It was a good relationship.

I did not know quite as much about camera and editing. I eagerly learned how to load and operate cameras, and how to work by Braille in the black bag when the film had to be reloaded. Youngsters today have no such problem since the recording media are not light sensitive. Nowadays we seldom use film, usually tape or hard or flash memory drives to record scenes. In 1960 the most current editing device was the "hot splicer." It was miles ahead of the old cold splicer. The bond made by the cement was nearly instantaneous under heat, whereas with the cold splicer we had to stand there and blow on the juncture to dry the cement. Today all editing is electronic and most editors would not recognize a Moviola, our principal viewing tool, if it were in bed with them. Gone are the days when a young Richard Lester had to edit film by viewing against the white surface of a trap drum.

The fact remains that when I actually got out into the business world I had to re-learn most of what I had learned at UCLA because the school's equipment was so obsolete. I did not have to re-learn the aesthetics of it or the basics, but when one learns how to load Auricon or Maurer cameras and then one actually works with Mitchells or Arriflexes, one is at a bit of a disadvantage vis-à-vis someone who has used the professional cameras before. The basics were always the same; every film camera has a magazine, a lens system, an intermittent movement, a viewing system, and a light-tight box. But the operation is different from one manufacturer to another. Bolex, for instance, can auto-load the film, whereas Arriflex must be threaded. In the Éclair the feed and takeup reels are side-by-side, whereas in most other cameras they are separate, looking like Mickey Mouse ears.

Another common thing with cameras is that they should always be cleaned between reels of film. Dirt is our enemy. Minute specks of dust can scratch film. If film breaks in the camera, a very rare thing outside of film school, the camera assistant must unload the magazines and carefully clean out the interior of the box to prevent later problems. The dreaded "hair in the gate."

All this is the same no matter what the camera, so we did have a certain basic understanding of the photographic process. We also learned what f-stops are, how to vary the shutter speed, basic elements of exposure. A little about composition, although everyone always tried to break the rules regarding that.

Regarding editing—it is like camera work. You can always learn the mechanics of it but you need to have some sort of intrinsic artistic sense in order to do it properly. Now, with Final Cut and other electronic editing systems, an editor can sit alone at home on his own computer, if it is properly equipped, and edit to his heart's content in much the same way that an artist can paint or a poet can "poe." He may need an assistant to help to log in new footage, but that's all. The drudgery we knew is no longer necessary. The glue, the razor blades to scrape away the excess emulsion, it's all gone now. A lost art.

One of the people I made up at the House of Westmore was Sarah, and we renewed our friendship. She was still the prettiest girl I had ever dated, and the nicest. She had been to boarding school, as had I, but she hated the rigid stultifying life of a debutante that her mother was trying to force upon her. Her sister, Margaret, had been a debutante, but Sarah resisted the parties and the formal occasions, the coming-out party, all the folderol that goes with high society, much to her mother's annoyance. We went to movies together and I took her to dinner, but we never had the chance for intimacy. It was enough for me. I was still shy around girls, still unsure of myself, and Sarah was the perfect companion. Not demanding, always willing to try new things or go to a new place. She probably felt safe with me. Although from time to time I saw another girl or two, Sarah and I were each other's main squeeze.

Two years prior the old Chevy had given up the ghost, and I bought an Austin-Healey sports car. A Sprite it was. It was very troublesome, but very cute. It did not go very fast. Its little engine did the best it could, and it certainly saved me tons of money on gasoline, as cheap as it was then. And it was much fun to drive. Especially with the top down. Sarah had moved with her mother to a condo in Palm Springs. I phoned and she agreed to have dinner with me if I drove down. On a bright Saturday I got into the car at around 10:00 am. In those days there was no Interstate 10 running almost all the way to the Springs, so a lot of the road was on what was then Route 66. It was a long drive, maybe three hours or so. I thought to get there early. I had my swimming trunks in the car trunk, and planned to lie around the condo pool with Sarah until dinner time, then have dinner, then drive home. Ah, youth.

It was a warm summer day in July. As I drove farther and farther east, the sun got hotter and hotter. Austin Healey Sprite could never have an air conditioner, so the only way for relief was to take the convertible top off and stow it in the trunk. I drove through Beaumont and Banning with the top down, and arrived at Route 111 to Palm Springs. The air was clear, the temperature hot and getting hotter. Perfect sports car weather. I had left my driving cap at home. The music was playing on my aftermarket radio. Life was good. I arrived in Palm Springs around 1 or 1:30.

The Austin-Healey and I

Adventures In Hollywood: A Memoir By Bob Koster

I was quite thirsty, so I pulled into the first gas station I saw and took a long drink from their ice-water fountain. I don't remember anything after that except I woke up in a shower with warm water spraying on me. I don't know for how long I was out. I do know that it was 115 degrees that day. I had been taken across the street to a motel by the gas station attendants and put in the shower with the hot water on. Slowly over the next period of time they made the water cooler and cooler to bring my body temperature down. That worked. When I was coherent again I got Sarah's phone number and phoned her, told her the reason I would be late. I finally got to their condo at around 5. I was reasonably back to normal. I did take her to dinner that evening, at the Doll's House, and I did drive the three or three-and-a-half hours back home. What I wouldn't do for love.

I had been living at my mother's apartment on the couch for a while. I stayed there through the school year just for the convenience of it. Mom and I, and Ronn, rarely did things together. They had their own life; he owned the largest wholesale hat company in Los Angeles, Anchor Hat and Cap Co. "If it adorns the head, we have it!" As the school year drew to a close, I learned that my father had placed in a savings account some money for me to get my career started, and I put this into a savings account. Shortly thereafter, Mom came to me and explained that since I was living there I should be helping to pay the rent. This did not seem unreasonable, and I agreed to give her $135.00 every month as my part of the rent. It was a roof over my head, after all. Not too many months passed when I happened to be in Mom's office and I saw the rent bill. It was for $135.00 per month. I had been paying their rent.

I immediately went out and found my own apartment on South Robertson Blvd., across the street from Hamilton High School. It cost $50 a month, and was my own bungalow. Large-ish living room, bedroom, huge walk-in closet, full kitchen. What more did I want in life.

I went home and started to pack my things to move. Mom became quite angry with me for moving, said I didn't know how to live on my own, couldn't I just wait another few months. I moved. We still saw each other sporadically but not often, a pattern that would recur for the rest of my life.

I graduated from UCLA, they tell me, with honors. I have the diploma here. I never went to the graduation. Ritual is boring. Mom and Ronn never even asked about it, and Dad did, several months later. I told him I had graduated from UCLA and was now working as a freelance makeup man. He suggested that since I was hell-bent on joining the film industry I should go to the Directors Guild of America and apply for membership. At least I could make a proper living as an assistant director.

I had one item to dispose of before I could begin anything. I had to register for the draft. In those days the military service was required. World War II was too recent, and we had the Red Menace just outside the door. I went to a local recruiter and asked where I should sign up. He arranged for me to have my physical and be put on the list. I wanted to attend the Army Pictorial Center on Long Island. Four or five of my UCLA buddies were there. I could work in film, making training films, get paid a little money, and have three hots and a cot.

I reported as requested and went through the physical exam. I flunked in two places. One, I could never go to the pictorial center because I am colorblind. Those stupid eye charts that have a bunch of dots and if you see number 4, for instance, you are OK, but if you see 9 you are blue-green colorblind. I am red-green colorblind. I still sometimes wear one black sock and one dark blue sock. And forget seeing aquamarine. I have no idea what that is.

The other item was more serious. I still have a heart murmur. The doctor heard it and declared me 4-F, or medically unfit for duty. I was disappointed that I couldn't make films for the Army but on the other hand I was free to pursue my career without any military interruptions.

CHAPTER 8

DGA

The Directors Guild is the premier union in the entertainment industry. Any director must be a member in order to work in the United States for a major producer. Also, the assistant directors, production managers, stage managers, and associate directors are all members. So on any production the bulk of the people who manage the show are in this union. People who hire other people, and fire them, and make schedules and budgets, and stick to them, are in the DGA. In 1960 there were very few nonunion films. The studio system was fading fast but still had some power and the studios were all signatories to the DGA agreement.

In those days there were set, decades-old ways of entering the DGA. Each of the major studios could denote two people they wanted to hire as production people, and these would be accepted. On top of that, the DGA admitted two sons of members each year. There did not seem to be anything wrong with that at the time. Almost any industry has some nepotism involved. People do what is familiar to them, whether it be shoemaker or iron worker or factory owner, or artist or musician. You grow up admiring what your parents do for a living and you gravitate toward that. It's familiar and comfortable.

The problem with Hollywood is that there are huge numbers of people who have come to Hollywood for fame and fortune, drawn by the entertainment section of their local newspapers. Usually the life in Hollywood is painted as carefree, sunlit days on the beach, evenings at nightclubs dancing the hours away, hobnobbing with the stars. Not many people I know here hobnob. And when I worked it was bloody hard. I often worked sixteen- to eighteen-hour days, six days a week. Sunday was for sleeping late, the last day possible before the grind began again. Some feature films were a little more relaxed, not much. But for episodic television, the grind was immediate and intense. I likened it to trying to paddle a canoe upriver against the rapids. For the first hour or so, it can be exhilarating, exciting, energizing. Then as your arms get more tired it becomes a little difficult. Eventually you wish you could get off the darn thing, but you can't stop paddling or else you will crash against the rocks. You must keep paddling no matter what the pain.

The life of a well-known actor or actress is even worse. Not only is there the daily grind, which usually begins well before the crew arrives because makeup and wardrobe need time to do their magic. But after a level of fame is reached you can barely go out into public. Everywhere you go you are stopped and asked for autographs and photos, and could you please just sign this for my sister in Detroit. Dinner at a restaurant is impossible. I once watched a local weather reader trying to have dinner at a restaurant. He was beset by well-meaning people who wanted to be photographed with him, and it did not stop throughout the entire meal. He took it with great grace but he could never finish the meal. After one fan left his table another appeared, preventing him from eating anything. And the waiters all wanted to wait on him also, so nobody else that evening received any kind of good service either. Going shopping is like that as well. I can't imagine why anyone would want that life but some do, probably without understanding the real ramifications of it.

Well, here I was, twenty-one years old, looking for a way to work in the movie industry. I had an advantage and I took it. I went to the DGA and filled out an application. On the application, by the way, I had to sign a loyalty oath. This was 1961 and those awful commies were still the big bugaboo. "I swear that I am not now and have never been a member of any organization whose purpose is the overthrow of the United States government." I would have to wait for a few weeks to see if the Board had approved my application.

It was around this time that Mom came to me and asked to borrow some money. She said that things were hard in the hat business these days and they just needed a little money to tide them over so they could order some stock. She would pay me back in a month or two. Heck, it was my mother, wasn't it? How could I refuse, she who had brought me into this world.

In my UCLA work there was one thing missing. In order to work properly in a production department I needed a passing knowledge of accounting practice. I already had a passing knowledge of most of what happened on set, but behind the scenes someone must do a budget and make sure the books balance. There is always an accountant on the production team, but it helps if the UPM knows enough about accounting that he or she can catch any mistake before it becomes dangerous.

UCLA had no accounting classes for movies. They were far more involved with focus, f-stop, jump cuts, and change of direction. There were accounting classes at school but they were not part of the Theatre Arts Department, and not conveniently scheduled so I couldn't take them and still work on student films. Think, Bob. Where do you go to learn accounting?

CHAPTER 9

UNITED CALIFORNIA BANK

I went downtown and applied for a job as a management trainee at United California Bank. My record was good and the application was accepted. During the interview I was asked why I wanted to work at a bank. My answer was that I had had my fill of the movie industry, with all its dishonesty and immorality. That satisfied them and I began working at a UCB branch in Hollywood. Later I would be transferred to a downtown branch in a rather depressed area of town, and finally I would be working in West Hollywood near Wolper Productions and the Beverly Center shopping center. But right now I wanted to learn accounting. I was first given a couple of days' orientation. And I needed a suit. One always wore a suit when one worked at a bank in those days.

I soon found myself working in the tellers' area, handling day-to-day banking transactions for clients big and small. It was actually quite interesting. One big problem was that the bank was VERY LOUD. Electronic Data Process had not been adopted by all banks yet, and much of the bookkeeping was done by hand, using huge LOUD machines to log in each check individually. UCB was in the process of changing over to EDP but it would be months before it was complete. In the meantime it was the old way or nothing. And those checking machines were LOUD!! For a serene, conservative institution it certainly was not serene. But it was a way for me to gain accounting experience, so I just spoke a little louder.

After I had some experience in the Hollywood office I was transferred downtown to a branch on San Pedro Street and Pico Blvd. This was even more interesting because in those days this was a terribly undesirable area of Los Angeles. The bank branch there had as clients some of the local businesses and a few local residents, just enough to pay for itself. The drive to work down Pico Blvd. every morning alone was fascinating. And every day was a new adventure just because of the people who came in. One local gentleman, for instance, having partaken more than adequately of the fruit of the grape, desired some more. He tried to cash a parking ticket. More than one client came in to cash a check and were flummoxed to find out that their bank accounts did not have the necessary balance. "What do you mean I can't cash a check? I still have checks in the checkbook, don't I?"

Presently I was transferred to the branch on the corner of Santa Monica and

UNITED CALIFORNIA BANK

Highland Blvd. It would be my last assignment for the bank. I knew just about everything I needed to know about accounting, from a bank's point of view anyway. Movie accounting couldn't be that far different, could it?

I stayed at that branch for about two months. The monotony was broken by three incidents. The first happened just before I arrived at the branch but it was fresh in everyone's mind. A man had been released from the local mental institution, probably Camarillo. He had nowhere to go, no family, nobody who would take him in. He was not capable of taking care of himself and had no idea what to do. He decided that if he robbed a bank at least he would be put in jail where he would have a bed and food. He stole a table knife from a diner nearby and somehow got a paper bag. Then he entered the UCB branch in Hollywood, went to a teller's cage, and demanded that she put all the money from her desk into the paper bag, all the while brandishing the knife.

The teller had just begun working there the day before and had not yet been briefed on how to handle bank robbery. Not knowing what else to do, she complied with his demands and filled the bag with money. Not knowing what else to do, he left the bank, holding a table knife in one hand and about $2,000 in a paper bag in the other.

The teller in the next cage saw the robbed teller standing with a shocked look on her face. Snapped her fingers in the girl's ear a couple of times. The girl said "I've been robbed." The neighbor teller immediately kicked the emergency button that locked the bank and called the police. They arrived about a half-minute later. Upon interviewing the robbed teller they put out an APB on the culprit. He was discovered two blocks away, walking slowly down the street, with a table knife in one hand and $2,000 in a paper bag in the other, and a very confused look on his face. Taken into custody, he achieved his goal of being put in jail where he had, as we say, "three hots and a cot."

The second incident was more personal. I discovered at the bottom of a drawer in my dresser an old U.S. war bond. It had been bought in 1943 or so for $18. And was to have matured in 1953 at $25. It was made out to "Robert Joseph Kosterlitz, a minor under legal guardianship." By now, in 1961, the bond was worth maybe $32.00. I wanted it.

First I took it to my bank to cash it. They asked me, naturally, for my driver's license, which named me as "Robert Joseph Koster," not "-litz." I explained that I was born "–litz" but our names were changed legally in 1943 when Dad and Mom got their citizenship papers. "Prove it!"

OK. Remember, there was no Internet in those days. Where do I get proof? The tallest building in Los Angeles then was City Hall, a thirteen-story skyscraper of a building. Inside was the Hall of Records. Birth certificates, death certificates, marriage certificates, anything official that happened in Los Angeles was kept there. I drove downtown and asked them to search out the court order that changed our names, which they did. I then paid a small amount for them to photocopy it. There were no Xerox copiers in those days either. I was told I could come back in three weeks for the copy. No, they would not mail it. For $32? Oh well, in for a penny, in for a pound.

Three weeks later I drove back downtown having phoned ahead of time to be sure it was ready for pickup. I retrieved the court order copy and drove back to the bank. Went to the same teller who had requested it three weeks earlier. OK? This document do? Yes, it shows that you changed your name, but how do we know that you are the real Kosterlitz? Better bring in your birth certificate. Are you kidding? Back to the Hall of Records and another three weeks for photocopy? Sure, no problem.

Drove back to the Hall of Records, saw the same clerk. With a small smile she said, "They want the birth certificate, right?" "Right."

Three weeks later drove back down to the Hall of Records to retrieve birth certificate. Back to the bank. Same teller. Paperwork OK now. Oh, wait a minute. It says here, "A minor under legal guardianship." "But I am twenty-two years old. Here's my driver's license." "You'll have to prove it." "Isn't the license enough? And the birth certificate? Do I need to bring in my mother to verify it?" "Say, that's a good idea!"

"Hello, Mom? Are you home for a while?" "Sure. What do you need?" "I need you to come to the bank with me to prove I am not a minor under legal guardianship." "Didn't they see your birth certficate?" "Yes, but they want to see you in person." "Oh, OK. Come pick me up."

Drove home, got Mom, drove back to the bank.

"Good afternoon, Mrs. Koster." "My name isn't Koster, it's Marvin. Mrs. Ronn Marvin."

Merely three more weeks to get copies of Mom's divorce papers and her marriage license, and I had my $32. Now it was $32.50, so I guess it was worth it after all.

The third incident also had to do with Mom. It had been several months since I loaned her some money to pay the bills. I was ungrateful enough to she who brought me into his world to ask her when she would pay me back. I had forgotten that she was a) Hungarian and b) an actress. Two days later I was behind the teller cage helping clients when in my teller line suddenly my mother appeared. She had her purse and an opaque bag about as large as an oversized sandwich bag.

When Mom got to my teller's window she switched to a stage whisper, designed to sound as if she was speaking confidentially to me when in fact everyone within thirty feet or so could hear everything she said very clearly. "So. You wanted me to pay you back? My own son? I didn't have money, so here are my jewels. You can sell them and keep the money." With that she opened the bag and dumped a handful of necklaces, earrings, bracelets, brooches, and rings on the counter between us.

They rolled all over the place. I quickly gathered up the items and stuffed them back inside the bag. Handed the bag back to Mom and told her quietly to go home and we would discuss it later. She took the bag and left. I never discussed it with her and I cannot honestly remember if she ever repaid me or not. It doesn't matter. Perhaps she was right and I never should have mentioned it.

I left the bank soon after to go to work in the film industry. If I couldn't immediately be D.W. Griffith, at least I could be a pretty good cameraman or editor, or AD. I had learned what I felt I needed to know about accounting.

CHAPTER 10

LAW OF BURNING SANDS

With nothing better to do I accepted a job working as a makeup man on a film. Frank Luter, a Hollywood drugstore cowboy with a vague resemblance to The Duke, an impressive 6'4" physique, and a deep, manly voice, had raised some money to fund a western film he had written. He made several crucial mistakes. One was that he had hired the guy next-door as cameraman based on his brilliant use of an autoexposure 8mm camera to make his baby-on-the-lawn films. Remember, these were the very earliest days of autoexposure. Autofocus was years in the future. Another was that Frank had written his own script which all his friends had told him was sheer genius. It had deathless lines in it such as "Blade (the hero) faces Sam Wade (the villain) down the street. Blade reaches for his buns."

The title was *Law of Burning Sands*, and it was set in the small western town of Burning Sands until we were at the location, the Hertz Ranch in the San Fernando Valley foothills. Thought Hertz only rented cars, did you? When we arrived on location we saw that the pre-rigged western town had the Silver Springs Saloon, the Silver Springs Bank, the Silver Springs General Store, and the Silver Springs Stables. As if by magic, the film title changed. I set up my makeup room in one of the storefronts on the main street of Silver Springs.

For the first day or two I was a very conscientious makeup man. On the first day the cameraman was lining up a shot in the saloon. The five bad guys were at a table, sipping whiskey and plotting the bank robbery. The actors were what one would expect for the price. We had to take the shot over and over until at least all the lines were spoken without stumbling. After the fifth or sixth take the camera suddenly began making loud protesting noises, grinding and moaning. The cameraman shut it off. We all waited expectantly. Being a curious sort, he turned the camera back on for a moment and the noises only grew louder. He shut it off again, flexed his fingers, and opened the camera door. About 200 feet of film came flying out of the box at us, unspooling on the ground. Some of it was shredded inside the camera box. Cameraman sheepishly admitted that he had forgotten to thread the take-up reel.

The camera having been cleaned and reloaded, we tried again. This time it worked.
At the end of the second day we all gathered around in the saloon to see yesterday's

dailies. Surprisingly, there was no image. There were vague shapes floating around on a muddy gray screen, but no crisp, sharp picture. All the first day's filming would have to be re-shot. That didn't bother Frank Luter, by God, it was his buddy from next-door and he was going to keep him on as cameraman.

The second and third day's dailies were equally invisible. It was obvious that our film needed a cameraman who knew an f-stop from his elbow. Frank Luter did the only possible thing. He fired the director and hired a new one.

The new director was faster than the old one. He also had some knowledge of camera work. But not much.

By this time I was relaxing in the makeup room most of the time. I kept a horse tethered just outside the makeup room in case I was called to the set on short notice. One of the actresses was in character, playing a bargirl. At night after filming she worked at the Kit-Kat Club in Los Angeles, so the part required little acting ability. I didn't inquire as to how she had been cast in that role. She insisted in being made up from the waist up. I naturally obliged. Those were in the days, so many years ago, when girls at the Strip-Tease joints wore pasties, so this was a special treat. She didn't seem to mind even when the soundman came into the makeup room to discuss the scene.

One of the villains had been named "Bad Eye." From my years of experience I knew that he would not like one of his eyeballs worked on, so a scar near the eye would have to do. I gave him a very proper scar just below his right eye, reaching diagonally down his cheek. I sketched a chart of that so we could reproduce it. We kept reproducing the scar for three days. After the second day's dailies it became perfectly obvious to everyone except Frank Luter that this film would never see the light of day. There was no film. After three days filming there were perhaps two minutes of usable footage.

With that in mind, on the fourth day I put the scar on the opposite cheek. Nobody noticed except the actor. There was no script girl on the set so continuity was not a problem. Luter hadn't thought that one was necessary. In any case so much of the film was laughable that there was no chance it would ever be released.

One of the five villains had never ridden a horse before and was frightened to death of horses. When the bad guys mounted up after the bank heist to ride out of town, he and his horse just stood there at the hitching post while the other four rode hell for leather down the street. The director asked and he admitted he had never ridden before. The remedy was to tie his horse's reins to another horse's saddlehorn. This was worse, because now the poor actor was flopping around on the saddle like a flag in a stiff breeze, hanging on to his saddlehorn for dear life, and leaning this way and that to try to keep his balance. His horse, meanwhile, was tethered to the other horse and was straining to break away and go in his own direction. The second remedy was simpler. Five robbers enter the bank and rob it. Four exit the bank and ride away. Later, at the side of the river where they gather to split the loot, there are mysteriously five robbers again. But by this time Bad Eye was wearing his scar on his forehead.

A week later we wrapped the film and had the traditional wrap party, still at Hertz ranch. We saw more dailies. By now there were less than ten minutes of barely usable footage. But, you know, a wrap party was a wrap party, and a good time was had by all.

CHAPTER 11

TOP HAT

The next job was a stage makeup job on a new musical, *Top Hat*. This was being produced in a small theatre near Hollywood and La Brea. (La Brea in Spanish means "The Tar." Ergo, the La Brea Tar Pits really means "the the tar tar pits.") Hollywood Boulevard had not yet become the tourist Mecca it is today. There were no Chaplins or Spidermen prowling the sidewalk stalking the unwary photographer. The theatre was on the second floor of a building near the southeast corner. This made it very handy for having dinner in the neighborhood. And there was always CC Brown's just across the street. Scientology had not yet taken over so many buildings on the boulevard and the concomitant proselytizers were not yet on the sidewalks.

Top Hat was a musical, of all things, about the assassination of Abraham Lincoln. The good thing for a makeup artist was that I was able to practice my hair work. Here were lots of beards and moustaches, and the ladies' hairstyles were exceptional. Ladies seemed to have a lot more hair in those days. We solved that problem with wigs. I had to design and fashion the beards and moustaches on applicable cloth pieces for the men, including the long sideburns for almost everyone and of course Lincoln's trademark beard. There were around two weeks of prep time for this because it would take that amount of time to get everything ready.

I never saw the play. For all the rehearsals I was upstairs in the makeup room getting actors ready for the next scene. Once in a while when the door opened I heard pieces of music drift in, but usually the door was closed and every noise from outside the room was muffled. The actors were a combination of energized and cynical. Oh, another play, ho hum. The dress rehearsal went off very well as planned. Everyone seemed to be satisfied that there was a hit aborning.

Opening night was different. There were very few in the audience and those were probably relatives of the actors and staff. Few outsiders came. No critics showed up. Of course, not much advertising had been taken in the newspapers. After the performance we had a wrap party and the producer told us that there would be no second performance. I wasn't very surprised and I suspect neither was anyone else. The concept of a musical about one of the most traumatic events in U.S. history is not ideal. Almost laughable, in fact. At least it wasn't a musical comedy with John Wilkes Booth dancing and singing his way offstage with a broken leg. There were jokes to that effect amongst the actors.

Free again. This wasn't bad, this freelance stuff. I would always be my own boss to some extent, and after I finished one job I could move to another company or another production. I did not have a family that instilled in me the desire for security that plagues so many others. I didn't have the example of a father figure who had a regular job, went to work every morning with a lunch box and came home at the same time every night.

CHAPTER 12

MR. HOBBS TAKES A VACATION

Soon after the play was over Dad called. He had accepted the idea that I would be going into his business. He was about to begin a new movie, *Mr. Hobbs Takes a Vacation*, and for a pittance I could be his assistant. It would be my real introduction to professional filmmaking. I wasn't a DGA member yet so I couldn't be officially on the production team but I could befriend those who were, and I could learn from them. And in the meantime I worked half as Dad's secretary and half as a production assistant.

The first assistant director is the sergeant major of the set. He (in those days there was only "he") was the leader of the crew, the prime communicator who made sure that everyone knew what they had to do and when. He usually made the schedule using a device known as a strip board. This was translated into a proper schedule by the secretarial staff and then typed up for all the department heads to know what the order of battle was. This is necessary because a film is almost never shot in sequence, in the order in which the scenes appear in the script. You usually try to combine locations to make the filming more efficient. Shoot all the office scenes at once, all the scenes in the home at the same time, no matter where they appear in the script. It eliminates the biggest time-waster of all, moving the crew. The first assistant on *Mr. Hobbs* was Joe Rickards, an old veteran of many years at Fox and a few other major studios. He knew the drill so well it was second nature to him. He was also very fair. I never saw him yell at the crew. He always spoke in a very calm voice and was very polite to everyone. I learned that most of the time much more can be accomplished with that approach than with yelling, which some assistants tend to do.

In those days the production manager of the studio was the virtual studio production chief; he usually hired the production team for each movie, or in a major studio, each "unit." The individual production chief for a single movie is therefore called the "unit production manager," or now, the UPM. The head of production at 20th Century-Fox was Lewis B. "Doc" Merman, a man whose name struck fear into the hearts of production people who met him. Since I had nothing to lose, I was not afraid of him at all. The first day he saw me, he smiled and said, "Hi, Koster." I smiled back and said "Hi, Merman." He smiled wider and said "How's it going, Koster?" I replied with "Just fine, Merman, and with you?" After forty years of experience I probably wouldn't dare to be so snotty, but then it was a hoot. It worked, much to my surprise. He greeted me every day the same way with the same result, and he appeared to take me under his wing. Joe and Nat were very helpful too in showing me how to make out the various forms, how to manage extras, all the tools in the AD's tool kit.

In those days the production chief usually was the lord of the studio no matter at what studio. It depended on their style. Some worked through fear. One of the most famous was Jack Fier, who ruled at Columbia for many years. And at Columbia TV, the same could be said for Seymour Friedman, a man with whom I worked for several years. But Doc ruled the roost at Fox. He was ably assisted by UPMs Gaston Glass and Bill Hough. Hough later married Jean Peters after she divorced Howard Hughes. I worked with both Glass and Hough. Both were gentlemen, understanding, willing to listen to new and sometimes outrageous ideas, and adaptable. Doc managed to mask his softness, if there was any, with a very raspy voice and a heavy New York accent. That accent he used as a weapon. The UPM on our movie was Art Leuker, also a veteran of many years at Fox. In the days of the studio system you worked for a studio and if you were adept at the job the studio would not put you under contract, but they kept you working and during down time they gave you schedules and budgets to do, just to keep you at the studio. Art, Joe, and Nat Merman, the 2nd AD, were such.

I went to the production meeting. The meeting usually lasted several hours and was held in the main production office. During the meeting the director and the department heads, everyone from camera to property master to makeup, and even the editor and script supervisor, read through the script together to decide what elements had to be prepared ahead of time for each scene. Done properly—and this was—it saved a lot of trouble later in the production. The crew has the opportunity to clear up any ambiguities in the script and the director can clarify his or her vision about the various scenes.

The producer was present also. In this case it was Jerry Wald, a legend in Hollywood history. He came with two of his assistants. I knew one of them from his recent graduation from UCLA. These two gentlemen stood behind Jerry Wald at the conference table, not entirely at attention but almost. Don Feld was the wardrobe designer, before he changed his name to Donfeld. He had fashioned several sketches of key wardrobe pieces for the film, mostly for Maureen O'Hara. Jimmy Stewart was known for wanting to wear his own clothing, and since it almost always fit the character this was allowed. Don Feld would pass the wardrobe sketches over to Dad, who would comment. He then passed them to Jerry Wald. Jerry would give them a cursory glance, then pass them over his shoulder to the assistants. These would have a brief conference, or share a glance, hand the sketches back to Jerry while whispering in his ear. Jerry would then give his opinion of the wardrobe.

MR. HOBBS TAKES A VACATION

There might be a brief discussion with Dad, and then the wardrobe was approved, or an inch was added or snipped off here or there. This method endured throughout the meeting.

One other item of note which taught me a lesson about the practicalities of film production. In one of the opening scenes, Jimmy Stewart is driving an absurdly small car, like a Renault Dauphine or a Morris Minor. He is stuck in traffic between two large trucks, the exhaust from which is making him cough and choke. This would have added to the impetus for him to take his family on a vacation, and added a note of humor when he bent himself into and out of the small car.

The subject of the car came up in the production meeting. Doc Merman reminded the group that Fox had an arrangement with the Chrysler Corp. to provide their picture cars without charge. The car was changed to a Plymouth Valiant and the humor of the scene, except for the truck exhaust, was lost.

Nat Merman was the second assistant. It was his job to make out the call sheets and production reports, and to hire and direct the extras. He was Doc's brother, and Doc kept him working at Fox. For good reason. He was extremely competent and a good diplomat as well, keeping everyone happy in many ways. This was not easy. Movie stars under the star system had their own fiefdoms which should not be invaded by the outsider. We had several, each of whom had his or her own entourage, and those entourages did not always work together well. An interesting exercise was assigning limousines to take the various groups to location in the early morning. You didn't want to put Jimmy Stewart's makeup man in the same car with Maureen O'Hara's hair stylist, and so forth. It was Nat Merman's job to handle all this arrangement along with the head of transportation. In those days there was also an iron-clad contract with the Teamsters union. It stated that every crew member must be transported from the studio to location by bus or limo. No exceptions. Even me, and I wasn't even officially on the payroll because Dad was footing the bill. Oh yes, there was one exception. The unit publicist was permitted to travel from his home to the location to the studio, or in the other direction. He was not allowed to go from the studio to location and back without a driver.

There were amusing anomalies that this unsettled truce between the unions and the producers had generated. There is a job called the craft serviceman. When filming is done on a carpeted set, or in someone's home on location, the practice is to roll out thick brown paper over the carpet so the crew cannot track mud or debris in from outside. It's a protective measure. This brown paper comes on great rolls and is known as craft paper. The person who rolls it out is the craft serviceman. He can also sweep the set and do minor housekeeping. With such a job there was a bit of down time. Craft servicemen used the down time to make coffee in large pots for the crew, which they sold for maybe a dime a cup. They also usually stopped on the way to work and bought several boxes of donuts that they also sold at a profit. So a little pocket money could be made by the craft serviceman. He may or may not have shared this profit with the head of the labor department, for the privilege of having the job and earning a few extra dollars. I never could prove it but quite possibly it did exist.

On *Mr. Hobbs* there was a grip. Freddie the grip. He worked the grip wagon, a rolling supply wagon with all kinds of shading devices such as flags, nets, and the stands used to raise them in front of the lamps. The grip cart was essential. Freddie's cart had a minor difference. It had an electric system in it, and Freddy had a pot in which he made soup. He sold the soup for a dime a cup. He did not share his profits, if such was the case, with the head of the labor department, or with anyone else. He did share his soup with us.

Presently the head of the labor department came down to the set to see if everything was all right in his domain. Of course he was concerned that Freddie the grip was taking valuable income away from the craft serviceman by selling soup, and he started complaining that Freddie was not doing his job. He went to Art the UPM and insisted that Freddie cease and desist immediately. Art said he would look into the situation and the labor boss went back to the studio. Driven in a studio limousine, according to the Teamster contract. Well, it turned out that everyone on the set liked the soup, and that they were still buying the coffee and donuts from the craft serviceman who was losing no money at all, but the perception was that Freddie was siphoning off the labor department's income even if untrue. So Freddie, in spite of the warnings from the labor department, kept making soup and we kept drinking it.

Until three days later, when the labor boss returned to the set in his limousine. This time he really got angry. He filed a complaint with the National Labor Relations Board. They dutifully sent a commission to the set to resolve the soup issue. Three people. They arrived from the studio in a Teamster-driven limousine. They interviewed everyone concerned, from Dad and Jimmy Stewart, Maureen O'Hara, all the way down the totem pole to me. And of course Freddie the grip, and the craft serviceman. They took voluminous notes. Then they left in the limousine.

Two weeks later Art Leuker appeared on the set with what looked like a 100-page manuscript. It was the NLRB's report on the soup issue. The bottom line was that it would be perfectly legal for Freddie to make and sell soup on the set as long as a member of the culinary workers' union was present to serve it. Freddie moved the soup pot into the grip truck where it was less visible to visiting dignitaries, and kept making soup for us without the required waiter. Nobody mentioned it after that.

We filmed for about two weeks on the beach at Leo Carrillo State beach. Our caravan left the studio early and traveled up Pacific Coast Highway. We spent the day filming, then caravanned back. Each day Nat Merman made out the transportation list, went over it with Joe Rickards and then with the transportation captain, and then sent it back to the studio for mimeo. Same with the call sheet for tomorrow's work. They were careful to show me how all this was done properly. The Fox format was very clear and logical.

During one of Doc Merman's daily visits to the set he told me that he wanted me to stay at Fox and work after my DGA card became final. This would have been a big boost to my career in Hollywood and I was grateful to him for it.

After we finished our location work at the beach we had a day of filming at a house in nearby Cheviot Hills, a block or two away from the studio. It was a kind of generic house, no particular architecture, could have easily been in the Midwest where Mr. Hobbs lived in the story. The scene called for Hobbs and his family to drive up to the front of the house, and his son-in-law to come out the door to greet them after having been separated from them for two months. His line was something like "Welcome home." The car pulled up, the son-in-law came to the driveway, and he stood there for a moment before he gave the line. Dad called "Cut!" and asked him why he didn't give the line immediately. The actor said, "But what is my motivation?" Dad did nothing more than give the crew a "Jack Benny" look, and the scene flowed smoothly from then.

I was fascinated by sound stage shooting. I had enough time to watch each of the crew people do their magic. I arrived early in the morning to watch the makeup and wardrobe artists at work. Jimmy Stewart's personal makeup man was Frank Westmore, youngest of the Westmore brothers. He was a kind, easy-going man who knew his craft well. He had been head makeup man on *The Ten Commandments* for Cecil DeMille. For that film he had invented a spray-makeup system to be able to make up the hundreds of extras using essentially a spray-paint machine. Saved the company hours of work. When the picture was released his brother Wally, head of Paramount makeup department, got the screen credit, as was customary in those days. DeMille recognized Frank's contribution, however, by giving him 1% of the film, according to Perc. This seemed to be adequate.

In makeup I had the pleasure of getting to know the actors in a relaxed mode, including the teen idol Fabian. Fabian was at the height of his fame in 1961. He had an entourage that followed him around, but seldom into the makeup room. No more than one or two, anyway. A really nice kid from the streets of Philadelphia, he was easy to talk to and we shared some of the more arcane fantasies of youth. Had he not been a creature of his "handlers" we might have been friends. Dad liked him enough to cast him in *Dear Brigitte* a couple of years later.

Another actor whom I enjoyed was Lauri Peters. She had a big success on Broadway as the oldest daughter of the von Trapp family in *Sound of Music*. At the time we were filming she was engaged to marry Jon Voight, whom she had met when they both were in *Sound of Music* on Broadway. But he was in New York and I in Los Angeles, so Lauri and I had a few dinners together. I enjoyed her bright, cheerful demeanor and her obvious love of stage. This was different from my feelings about Sarah, who had no knowledge of stage or film and whose parents looked on show business as a bastard form of making a living, even if they secretly harbored a love of showbiz folk. Not unusual for her segment of society. Lauri had no such reservations and we could talk for hours about stage plays we had seen and films of note. Few subjects on which she could not converse long and intelligently, in fact, as long as they were in the entertainment realm.

I also enjoyed a couple of lunches with Jimmy Stewart. A quiet, almost shy man, he preferred to have a table in a corner of the commissary where he could eat in peace. He had very definite ideas about almost everything and was most persuasive. Show biz wasn't his most important subject. He also was rightfully proud of his work with the Air Force. He had been colonel on active duty, had earned the DFC and the Croix de Guerre. After the war he remained in the Air Force Reserve, achieving the rank of brigadier general. He was quite active, a good pilot, and much of his spare time between films was taken up with military activities. He was justifiably more proud, and more conscious, of his Air Force work than he was as a movie star. Only two show-biz types outranked him. Director John Ford had become a two-star admiral, and of course uncle Ronnie from across the street became commander in chief.

I also became friends with John Saxon. A good actor, a very pleasant man to just sit down and talk with between scenes. He had a great appreciation of beauty. We could sit on a wall at the beach where we were filming, watch the waves and the seagulls, discuss art and music. I had the pleasure of working with him much later after I returned to Los Angeles, and I was delighted to find that he had not changed one whit. It is notable that he has credits in over 310 films and TV shows, from 1954 to this writing. A credit to his professionalism and easy set manner.

Jimmy Stewart and The Infernal Machine

MR. HOBBS TAKES A VACATION

John Saxon and I

All too soon the filming was over. As would happen for the next forty years, I was out on the street again. But now I had a trade. I could be an assistant director. I knew how to make call sheets, production reports, how to design a strip board, what elements go into making a schedule, how to manage background talent, or extras as they are sometimes known, transportation charts, what to do if a makeup person or an actor is late for a makeup call, how to get actors to give me their private home numbers to phone if God forbid they oversleep. I learned to get by with four or five hours sleep for five days at a time. I learned what foods gave me the best energy without being fattening.

Most important, I learned that the single most important thing anyone in production can do is to communicate. An AD has to tell the crew what the next shot is, and the shot after that, and if possible the shot after that. The next shot has to be prepared for, quietly, while the current shot is being made. That is what gives a set its efficiency. What actors must be made up now to be ready in a half hour? What props must be prepped? Set dressing? Will there be a stunt or special effect two or three shots from now? An AD must tell those departments to be ready shortly and for what. This can be done through a bullhorn, loudly and in my opinion disruptively, or it can be done quietly and efficiently without distracting the rest of the crew from their tasks. I found over the years that the second method is far more efficient. There are times when a bullhorn is necessary but they are few. The quiet approach also invites dialogue with the crew to clarify necessary actions for the next few minutes, always a good thing. In that two-month period on *Mr. Hobbs Takes a Vacation* I learned about good production from these professionals. A better education does not exist.

I was free. Spent a couple of days at home doing necessary cleaning and paying bills, all the things I had been neglecting during production. This pattern would repeat during the next forty years.

I also dated Sarah a few times. The more mature she was the more she appealed to me. When *Hobbs* was over I finally took the step and proposed marriage to her. I never saw someone disappear so fast in my life.

That was the end of it. I never saw her again. She did not answer my calls, wouldn't answer the door, nothing. I was at a complete loss as to what had gone wrong. In my romantic world we would be inseparable, and nothing I had done would cause such a disastrous separation. I did date other girls from time to time, became very close to a few, but in the back of my mind Sarah was always the Golden Girl Who Got Away.

Shortly after this I received a phone call from the DGA. My application had been approved and I could come down and collect my Guild membership card. I paid the required $750, had a brief conversation with Joe Youngerman, the National Executive Director. Also chatted with Morrie Abrams, DGA head of the AD/UPM section, regarding my employment possibilities. They were pretty good. These were before the floodgates opened and twenty or so new members were admitted every month. It would not have been advisable to have large numbers of DGA members anyway since TV had not yet become the huge force it would be in just a few short years. The major studios conceived of it as an enemy, an entity that kept people at home and away from the big screen theatres. It would have been inconceivable on those days for a studio to make a "Movie of the Week" or even a TV series. These were produced mostly by advertising agencies that also lined up the sponsors. So we saw Pillsbury Playhouse, Milton Berle's Texaco Star Theatre, and such. There were the networks, of course, CBS, NBC, and ABC, and they produced their own shows and obtained their own sponsors. Most of their studios were in New York, with some satellite studios on the major population centers like Los Angeles, Chicago, Houston, etc.

I called a girl I knew and treated the two of us to a good dinner at the Imperial Garden, a Japanese restaurant on Sunset Boulevard. It was traditional, so there were private booths where diners sat on cushions on the floor with crossed legs, drank sake, ate sashimi and sukiyaki, and generally felt oriental. The craze for sushi had not yet arrived and sukiyaki was the in thing. Each booth was surrounded by shoji screens so there was privacy while we ate. Of course the shoji screens had very thin panes of paper, so anyone in an adjoining booth could hear whatever was said in the next booth. One had to be careful about what one did or said. But it was all very discrete, and the food was delicious. The girl was lovely. I was still getting over the sudden rejection by Sarah, but not enough to prevent me from having fun with girls. It didn't have to be serious. And this girl was lovely. Spoke with a slight middle-European accent, always charming, and we enjoyed each other's company for the entire evening.

MR. HOBBS TAKES A VACATION

In Hollywood, the major studios—Fox, Universal, Paramount, Warners, Disney and RKO—ruled the roost. The major film stars were still usually under contract to one studio or another at a fixed weekly income. It could be quite wonderful, or it could be drudgery for the actors. They were not free to work at another studio if a good role were offered them. There was the "loan-out" system, however. Fox, for instance, could loan a contract star to Warners and charge for his service. The star, let's say Jimmy Stewart, was already making a good salary at Fox of, let's say, $5,000 a week, whether he was on camera or not. If not on camera he was expected to do publicity appearances in Hollywood and other areas as well. If Warner's wanted him they could offer $7,500 a week to Fox for his services. Fox could give Jimmy Stewart his $5,000 and keep the extra $2,500 for themselves. Neat, huh? When Dad was under contract to Fox he was loaned to Universal for *Harvey* in that manner. Then later to Universal again for *Flower Drum Song*.

Well, I had my DGA card and was ready to go to work. I applied at Warner Brothers. Filled out the application, turned it in. The guy in personnel said, "Oh, Henry Koster's kid, eh?" That didn't sit very well because I felt that if I were to have a job it would be on my own.

I went to MGM, Dad's old stomping grounds from the 1940s, and applied there as an AD. The fellow who took my application said, "Oh, Henry Koster's kid, eh?" Hmmm... I admitted that, and asked if there were any openings. "Not right now, kid, but we'll let you know."

I tried Paramount. "Oh, Henry Koster's kid, eh? Nothing now, we'll let you know."

This was quickly becoming boring. Nothing wrong with being Henry Koster's kid, but how about hiring me just because I'm good? Hollywood didn't work that way.

I went back to Fox and spoke with Doc Merman. Yes, he remembered that he had asked me to come back when I had my DGA card. Yes, he would like to hire me. However, the only thing filming at the moment is *Cleopatra* with Elizabeth Taylor, and that is shooting in Rome. If I pay my own way to Rome, pay my own per diem, he would put me on payroll at the same rate as the Italian ADs. Didn't sound like a good idea to me, so I thanked him kindly and left.

Now what to do? I have a DGA card and no job. I've been abandoned by Sarah. I am free of all obligations in Hollywood. Time to do something I always wanted to do, drive cross country to New York and see what the industry is like there. After all, many really good films had been shot there, from the early D.W. Griffith films to the more recent *On the Waterfront*.

CHAPTER 13

NEW YORK

By now the troublesome Austin-Healey had given way to a VW Beetle. I needed a reliable car, not necessarily pretty, but one that would keep on ticking if it took a licking. VW filled the bill admirably. It would take me cross country three times and have well over 100,000 miles on it when I let it go some years later. I even splurged and had a Blaupunkt AM-FM-Shortwave radio put in. And a sunroof for those balmy days. I eventually bought for $10 a kit by which I could convert the VW seats into beds, to lie down flat.

I told Mom and Dad where I was going. Mom asked me to stay for a few more months and keep trying in Hollywood, advice I did not feel like following. Dad entered into the spirit of the thing with me and was all in favor of my trying someplace entirely new, someplace where I would be entirely on my own without parental help, where I could stand or fall on my own hook. I was ready.

It took one day to secure the apartment on Robertson Blvd., pack some traveling clothes, and gas and oil the VW.

The drive to New York was interesting. I had flown across the country in 1949. In 1962, Route 66 was still a dirt road in places, and there were stretches in Arizona and New Mexico where the only available radio station was at Window Rock, AZ, and it was in Navajo. Route 66 in those days went all the way to Chicago. I stayed in cheap motels and for cuisine I discovered the pleasures of Howard Johnson. The motels still included groups of faux Indian teepees and little bungalows, usually unheated. It was an adventure.

It almost became more of an adventure just outside of Needles, California, a tiny town on the border of Arizona. I had been driving all morning and the gas gauge showed that I was at quarter tank. My VW was the first to have a gas gauge anyway, the prior models having no gas gauge but a reserve tank. When the engine began to sputter the drill was to turn a handle on the firewall that released the gasoline in the reserve tank. Then there were around 30-40 miles left, and the driver had to find the next gas station. But my model actually had a gas gauge and it showed that I was down to a few miles. I had never driven across country before except for one trip to Las Vegas, so I had no idea how far Needles was from where I was at the moment. Remember the days before GPS screens?

NEW YORK

I spotted a gas station off the road and pulled in. It was just as dusty as the rest of the desert, and it appeared deserted. Nobody was evident. I pulled next to a gas pump and wondered what to do. In 1962 it was unusual to pump one's own gasoline, unlike today. There was always an attendant. Well, an attendant did come out of the office and approached the car. He was at most ten years old, and he was wearing work overalls. As he approached he walked more and more slowly, stopping a few feet away from the car. Then he said in a very loud voice, "Buy American." "I beg pardon?" "I said, Buy American. We don't sell to fer'n cars here." "Oh? And why not?" "Because we don't believe in sending all our money overseas."

It took me fully ten minutes of explaining that VW employs Americans in their showrooms and their service shops, and a lot of good Americans make a very good living from the coffers of VW, and anything else I could think of. The kid's father had probably gone into town for vittles and left him in charge. He finally agreed to sell me some gasoline, I guess, against his better judgment. A few bad moments there, wondering if I could make it all the way into town on less than quarter tank.

The rest of the trip was also fascinating. One odd event happened just off the Pennsylvania Turnpike. I had a couple of hours to kill and decided to find Wheeling, West Virginia. I drove off into the countryside, saw Wheeling, West Virginia, and tried to get back to the turnpike. It was growing dark and not all the street signs were lit. The map from the AAA showed where I wanted to go but not necessarily the route there. I stopped in to a local gas station to ask for directions and was faced with the fact that the attendant did not speak the kind of English I was used to if it was indeed English. I thanked him and left. Here's where the sunroof comes in handy. I opened up the top and looked for the North Star. Driving so that it was more or less in front of me, I kept going north until I ran into the turnpike again, then turned east and followed it until I found a road with an onramp. Primitive GPS system, but it worked.

I arrived in New York a day later, drove up the New Jersey Turnpike and entered New York through the Lincoln Tunnel. I was like a hick from the sticks. The buildings were so tall and my VW was so short. Luckily I had some idea of how Manhattan was arranged. Down at the bottom of Manhattan the streets begin with 1st street just north of Houston (House-ton, not Hews-ton), then the numbers get higher the farther north you go. Beginning at the East River, there is First Avenue, then Second to its west, then Third, etc. All very logical, until you come to Lexington, Park, Madison, then Fifth, Sixth, etc. on up to Eleventh, close to the Hudson river. All very logical. Except of course for the address numbers. These do not at all match from one block to the equivalent in north-south direction. Fifth Ave. and 40th Street is 458 Fifth Avenue. Sixth Avenue is 1050, and Seventh is 560. So you have to go by the cross streets. You get used to it after a while. I only lived in New York for 11 years so I just didn't have enough time to get used to it.

I found the Park Sheraton Hotel, Seventh Ave. and 56th, and checked in. Needed to get my bearings. The Sheraton was a famous old hotel, made even more famous by the shooting of Albert Anastasia in 1957 in the hotel barber shop. The room was comfortable if small, enough for my brief stay. I had come to see if I could make a living in the Big Apple. I began calling film producers in the local film directory. After numerous interviews with old producers, young producers, all kinds of producers, I was interviewed by Konstanin Kalser of Marathon International Productions, a maker of documentaries. The interview went well. And as an added incentive, Konstantin's mother had been Irma von Cube, a German writer who had worked with Dad. So I was greeted warmly, and told to go home, pack up, and move to New York. That was good enough for me. As an added incentive, Mr. Kalser asked me to send my UCLA student project to him so he could see what I could do. He wanted to hire me as a producer of documentaries, and my student project had been a documentary about sports cars.

I still had relatives in New York, Miklos and Ilona Kiraly, and we spent a couple of lovely evenings together. He was a doctor and she a psychologist. The conversation sparkled. He looked enough like my late grandfather that the whole situation was familiar to me. He also had grandpa's whimsical sense of humor. We got along just fine.

There was also a girl in New York whom I had known in Los Angeles, not well, but at least it was someone whom I could take to dinner a couple of times. Luckily she lived in the East End Hotel for women, on East River Drive and 78th Street. Whenever I visited her she always introduced me to her roommates and a couple of other girls so I knew that I would not be wanting for feminine companionship.

Now that I was certain of a job in New York I could relax a little and enjoy the city. My friend from UCLA, Ken Greenwald, arrived in New York about this time, and we started going to nightclubs in Greenwich Village where he would perform comedy and pick up a few dollars. The plan was to stay for a few days, then drive back to Los Angeles. I would close up my apartment and hire a mover to move all my furniture to NY, put as much as I could into the VW, and drive back to NY myself. I could stay in a hotel for a few days until I found an apartment. Then after I had moved in I would go back to Marathon International Pictures, start work, and then go to the DGA and check in.

The drive back across the country with Ken was fun. We did "shtick" from New York to Los Angeles. We even stopped in Chicago where Ken performed at the legendary "Gate of Horn" coffee shop. In Denver, Ken performed at the "Exodus" coffee shop. I had phoned ahead, said I was Ken's agent, and he was going to be in town for only one night, and wouldn't they like to have him do a guest shot. Sure they would. He was a big hit there, in fact, doing the routines he had perfected at the Ash Grove and the Troubadour in Los Angeles, and which had gotten him spots on the Steve Allen and Merv Griffin shows. The Exodus was in the midst of one of those silly lawsuits that happens when attorneys get together for lunch. The Exodus

Coffee Shop was suing Leon Uris, author of *Exodus*, for copyright infringement for using their name, since their coffee shop was older than his book. The lawsuit brought out that the second book of the Bible, Exodus, was probably earlier than both. But everyone had fun, the lawyers made a little money, everyone including the Bible got some publicity out of it, and nobody was hurt.

Highway 6 from Denver west is one of the most spectacular drives one can make. It travels through the Rocky Mountains, next to rivers, along cliffs, among tall pine trees, through the Arapahoe National Forest. It goes for miles and miles with very little civilization to break the beauty. Takes your breath away. Also can make you very thirsty. Kenny and I were very thirsty when we stopped at a small general store by the side of the road. There were just a few houses visible on the hill amongst the trees behind the store, and a sign on the road had proudly proclaimed the name of the town, and "Population 325" or thereabouts. So we stopped the VW, went in, and asked the elderly gentleman, there was only the one person there, if we could buy a soft drink. Of course we could. He showed us to the refrigerator where we helped ourselves to drinks. The place was so charming and lovely that I thought I'd send a postcard from there to Dad. There was the usual postcard rack, and I picked a good one. Borrowed a pen, wrote a couple of lines and addressed it. Ooops—no stamps. Asked the gentleman if we could buy stamps. Of course we could. He moved to another counter in the store, changed hats, and voila! He was also the postmaster! Kenny and I looked at each other. Ken asked him if he knew where we could find the local constable. He moved to another counter and changed hats again, and voila! Seems everyone except him in that town worked in the next town over, and left him in charge of everything, a fact of which he was justifiably proud. And he had a good collection of hats to boot.

A few days later we had returned to Los Angeles and I set about packing my few belongings and contacting a moving company. I packed into the VW what I felt I might need for a few weeks' stay until I could find and populate an apartment in New York, gave up my little apartment on Robertson and Venice, and looked for a place to stay for a week or so while my furniture was being transported to NY.

I set out again for Manhattan. The trip was relatively uneventful. The VW was so reliable, so opposite from the Sprite, it was a pleasure. It was not as much fun to drive as the sports car but it made it up in practicality. And the radio was a wonder. In the area of the Southwest where only the Navajo station was audible I could listen to the BBC, Hilversum, Deutsche Welle, even Radio Moscow. The latter seemed to have a somewhat skewed version of events that were reported properly on American radio. This set a pattern I would follow to this day, listening to news from around the world. It was also interesting to listen to the speech patterns of local announcers and news readers. In those days the accents were not yet homogenized and they changed from state to state.

I arrived back in New York on a fall day. It was still hot, much less comfortable than I was used to in Los Angeles. I would become accustomed to it later but I never liked it much. I checked into the Sheraton again. My furniture would not be in New York for more than a week, which gave me time to look for a flat. I discovered the pleasures of *The New York Times* Classifieds. I also discovered that the in crowd got their copies of the *Sunday Times* on Friday night, minus the latest front page news, business section, and sports. News vendors ordered a few extra of these "stripped" papers for those who were searching for bargains in flats, cars, and other time-sensitive items. The best of these had been bought or rented by the time Sunday morning came around because the Friday evening readers had gotten the jump on them.

I found a flat on 60th Street between Second and Third Avenues, a half-block away from the entrance to the 59th Street Bridge. This was fine with me because I went to Queens often to visit friends there. Each time I returned over the bridge I could see the United Nations building and the magnificent New York skyline. I was in the center of the world. The financial center, the artistic center, the center, period. It was a heady feeling.

I also had the pleasure of listening to the two greatest radio comedians of all time, Bob and Ray. They were broadcasting on WHN in the morning for four hours a day. Their lampoons of radio shows were famous, and their cast of odd characters, including Webley Webster, Natalie Attired, and the ubiquitous newscaster, Wally Ballou, kept me in stitches. I learned not to drive while they were on the radio because I would become so enrapt by their show I could easily forget where I was going and just drive aimlessly. I still have that problem. In those days I tried to listen to them on the way to work in the morning but I usually had to change the station and listen to the news broadcasts, just to keep my mind on my driving.

My 60h Street apartment was on the fifth floor of a walk-up building. Two doors away down the street was a marvelous store called Serendipity which carried wondrous things. And just up the street on Third Avenue were the Coronet and Baronet theatres that showed art films and foreign films of all kinds. Across the street from the theatres is Bloomingdale's department store, one of the wonders of New York. It was a short walk, and an exciting one, to Fifth Avenue, where I could visit all sorts of places I had only read about in books: Museum of Modern Art, Museum of Natural History, Metropolitan Museum of Art, Central Park, Madison Square Garden, Lincoln Center. 711 Fifth Avenue was the corporate headquarters for Columbia Pictures. 55th Street and Sixth Ave. was HQ of MGM. The largest film studio in the city was owned by 20th Century-Fox, corner of 10th Ave. and 56th Street. I would know it very well in the next years.

Having moved in and gotten my bearings, and having found a place to park the VW a block away, I set about to establish myself in New York. I already had an introduction to New York dating scene because of my contact at the East End Hotel for Women. It was their quaint custom not to allow male visitors outside of the first floor lounge. This worked most of the time. There were the usual wags dressed in women's clothing who tried to sneak up to their girlfriends' rooms but they were usually caught. I dated a few girls at the hotel, off and on. One of them even moved into my apartment briefly but we were not as compatible as we both would have wished.

Now that I was settled I made an appointment with Konstanin Kalser to be shown around Marathon International Pictures and to begin work. Mr. Kalser very politely but firmly told me that there were no openings for a producer at that time. He had seen my student film. He strongly suggested that I never show it to anyone else. He wished me luck and showed me the door. I was so stunned by having my job disappear that I said nothing and left. Walking home, I thought of all the things I should have said, that I had just uprooted myself from L.A. and moved to New York based on his promise of a job, that I knew nobody in the city and needed work, that I would settle for any job no matter how small, just so I could begin working somewhere, anywhere, in New York. I needed a start.

My next stop was at the DGA office in New York. That was a rude awakening. To begin with, the DGA in New York had no jurisdiction over film production; it only had contracts at the time with the TV networks and not all of those. Film directors in New York were represented by the Screen Directors International Guild, or SDIG. ADs and UPMs were represented by Local 161 of the IATSE, the International Alliance of Theatrical Stage Employees, which also represented script supervisors. I was in the wrong union. Even if I were in the proper union I would have to apply to the East Coast Council for membership and they would have to vote on me. I'd have to start all over again. Thanks, Joe Youngerman and Morrie Abrams, for telling me about this when I told them I was moving to New York. I was still getting bills for quarterly dues from the DGA in Hollywood so I knew I was a member somewhere at least.

This was also a big lesson for me in how little effect Hollywood has on anyone else. Here I thought that just because I was a DGA member there I could work anywhere. Not at all true. Further it was becoming clear that the two coasts had a less than friendly rivalry. New York had far less theatrical film production, preferring to concentrate on commercials and industrials for the corporate headquarters which were almost all in Manhattan or nearby. Films were made in New York by a few renegades like Elia Kazan, Sidney Lumet, and Woody Allen. There were maybe three or four major feature films produced on the East Coast each year, while hundreds were produced in Los Angeles. But New York considered the films made there to be the best in the world, and they generally frowned on the typical Hollywood output. Truth be told, there was a serious difference between Hollywood and New York films, and for seriousness of purpose and artistic intent, if not always execution, New York seemed to have the edge. It also became obvious that there was a well-established hierarchy of production people in New York, and those at the top of the pile got the plum jobs in theatrical films. I was crazy to have moved there. But in for a penny, in for a pound. I would stick around for a year or two and see what develops. I would eventually start up my own production house and then start producing feature films myself. How hard could it be? The producers I had known in Hollywood had nowhere near the sterling education I had, and they were successful, weren't they? I had the edge.

I found that Times Square was the theatrical center of the universe. One could find anything there concerning theater or film. *The Hollywood Reporter* and *Daily Variety*, as well as *Weekly Variety, Backstage*, and all other theatrical publications were sold on the street there. Magazine stands and bookstores were filled with theatrical publications. I walked down to Times Square and bought a copy of the New York Theatrical Directory. In my flat I went over it thoroughly and decided just to start phoning all the producers in the book and ask for an interview. I had no resume to speak of, a movie on which I had done makeup, a film where I was the director's assistant. No experience at all in New York. A degree from UCLA and membership in the DGA. I had a car so I could run errands, although in New York the subway was always faster and cheaper. A token in the subway cost 5 cents.

I started by phoning the major studios, none of whom would even interview me. Then I started phoning producers whose names I knew from the screen. Got a few interviews but no job. Then I started phoning producers at random. This was getting silly. Someone somewhere must need an assistant who knows how cameras work, who can do makeup, who knows how to edit. Can act if necessary. I finally found a producer named Bern Robertson. His company, Industrials Illustrated, was looking for an assistant everything who knew a wide variety of film tasks. Hey, that's me. I was hired at $65 per week.

Bern was a very kind, very energetic man. He had just finished a TV special about the famous PR man, James Moran. Moran had been famous for his publicity stunts. He a) found a needle in a haystack, b) sold a refrigerator to an Eskimo c) led a bull through a New York china shop, and d) opened a bogus embassy in New York for *The Mouse That Roared*. One of his most famous gags was his publicity for his friend David Merrick, who had produced a play, *Subways Are for Sleeping*. Moran found seven New Yorkers with names identical to those of the most famous seven theatrical critics. He invited the namesakes to the play, then had an ad printed that quoted them all saying how great the play was. The TV show that Bern had produced and directed was accompanied by a song written by Jim Moran entitled "George Washington Bridge." The song consisted of the words "George Washington Bridge" sung over and over again to the tune of "It's the Loveliest Night of the Year." Very inspiring. Bern had finished filming it and was just adding the sound track in post production when I came aboard. The process was fascinating and Bern was a good teacher. About two weeks after he had finished the show and delivered the elements he told me that he no longer needed an assistant. He was sorry but I needed to find another job elsewhere.

Around this time I learned that Otto Preminger was looking for an AD for his next film, *The Cardinal*. I phoned his office in the Columbia Pictures Building at 711 Fifth Avenue and made an appointment for an interview. I dressed in my best suit and showed up on time. Mr. Preminger's secretary ushered me into the presence of the director, who was seated behind a slab of marble whose sole occupant was an intercom. No papers, no pencils, no blotter, just an intercom on a bare piece of marble. We chatted for a few minutes, and Mr. Preminger concluded the interview by flicking a switch on the intercom, saying to his assistant, "Mr. Price, I have a young man here from Hollywood who would like to work with us. You will see what you can do for him!" He clicked off without waiting for an answer.

I left the office and was greeted in the hall by Mr. Price, who showed me to his office, a tiny cubicle down the hall. This cubicle was decorated with posters from Preminger's pictures all around the wall: *Anatomy of a Murder*, *Laura*, *Advise and Consent*, *Exodus*, and others. Mr. Price asked me what I wanted to do. I said I wanted to be Mr. Preminger's assistant director. "No, no, what do you want to do for a career?" "I'd like eventually to produce films." Price gestured around the office at the posters and said, "You can get an eight-millimeter camera and go out in the street and make a movie right now that's ten times better than this shit." I left.

Back on the street, I decided to try my luck at Local 161 where the ADs and UPMs called home. If my DGA card wasn't any good in New York, maybe I could get a card that was. I had an interview with Milt Felsen, then business manager for the union. He was cordial but firm. The local already had enough ADs and UPMs and didn't need any more. Furthermore, in the production world of New York there was no point in being the son of a director. It counted for nothing.

Milt Felsen was a real character himself. A former member of the pre-war Abraham Lincoln Brigade that fought in Spain during the civil war on the side of the Republicans against Franco's Nationalists, really Fascists, after the Spanish War he returned to the States and joined the OSS, precursor to the CIA. He worked undercover in Europe against the Nazis. Milt was parachuted into Eastern Europe and worked with partisans against the German forces there. He was captured and interned. He escaped and walked across Europe to rejoin the OSS forces in England, where he was sent back to the continent to fight again. After the war he joined the International Longshoreman's Association as a union organizer. Kept that job until the late 1950s.

At that time, Local 161 was in trouble. The ADs, UPMs and script supervisors had hired a bad egg for their business manager. He managed to embezzle all the money in their operating fund, then disappeared. The union local needed help very badly. They pooled their money and placed an ad in *The New York Times*, an ad that Milt Felsen answered. A very intelligent, energetic, aggressive man, he immediately took the reins of the union local, put their finances back on a sound footing, put systems in place to ensure no recurrence of the problem. He had a job for life after that. My meeting with him was not adversarial at all, just matter of fact. This would serve both of us well in the future. I asked to be placed on a waiting list for membership, or if their availability list were exhausted I should be given the opportunity to "shape up" at the local for jobs. He allowed that, but neither ever happened.

I decided if I had to work in TV, I might as well start now, so I went to all the major network headquarters and filled out job applications. I was told politely by all that there were no openings right now, but if something came up…

CHAPTER 14

WPIX

I chanced to walk on 42nd Street and 3rd Ave. Gleaming in the sky a block away was the tower building owned by the *New York Daily News*. It was the really awful newspaper of New York—sensational, yellow journalism, bad reporting, the lot. But it did own WPIX-TV, Channel 11 in New York City. The station of the Yankees. It had little else to recommend it. In 1962 it was still showing *Highway Patrol* and *Superman* series. It also had Sheriff John, Engineer Bill, and a slew of children's programs, including *The Bozo Show*. Its news programming was an embarrassment. It still broadcast in black and white when the other stations were beginning to broadcast in color. It was the perfect place in which to learn. I went in, applied, and was hired on the spot to type up the daily log. There were no computers, no spell checkers, nothing so sophisticated in those days. I had to use a relatively new IBM Electric typewriter with a letter-ball system. Bob McEvily was the head of the operations department, a very nice, slightly harried man, but very calm and a good supervisor. We all wore suits to work. McEvily explained what to do, and I picked it up right away. I had been hired for an eight-hour day and typing logs took maybe four to five hours, so I had time to walk around the station and watch the operation. I always carried a clipboard with me to take notes. It gave the impression that I was doing something "important" anyway.

Bob McEvily's immediate superior was Alice Cook, VP Operations, a lady in her fifties who sat in her glass-enclosed office just off the log typing room. She had four TV sets on the wall in front of her desk so she could watch the major networks and WPIX at the same time. She had arranged for several noted personalities to broadcast on WPIX, among them a televangelist named Jack Wyrtzen. Wyrtzen would appear in a different auditorium every week around the Eastern seaboard. After his sermons he would have an open house where the faithful could meet him in person and have him minister to their problems. At that point in the broadcast a card would appear on the screen that said, "Meet Jack Wyrtzen in Person," and the next card would have the venue. The log said, "Go to card: Meet Jack Wyrtzen in Person." After typing this a few times in successive weeks, I guess my finger slipped on the typewriter. I don't know what came over me. But I typed "Meet Jack Wyrtzen in Pyrtzen." Mrs. Cook was not happy. She emerged from her office, snorting and huffing, came to my desk and slammed the offending log down on the desk in from of me. Saying "Who is the filthy pig who did this?" Sensing that I was about to be fired for the infraction, I explained that I had been very tired when I typed it, and I was oh so sorry, it would never happen again, I assure you, etc. It had never occurred to me that she was a fanatical follower of the Gospel according to Jack Wyrtzen.

There were interesting people working at WPIX even if their programming was antique. Salvatore D'Amico was the head of the WPIX editorial department. They had very little to do except to edit the films to fit the WPIX time slots. Sometimes they edited news footage but not often. I liked Sal. He did a great job against terrible odds. Once he had to edit *The Moon Is Down*, a classic World War II film, to fit a ninety-minute time slot. The movie was ninety minutes long already, which meant that Sal had to delete twenty minutes from the film for the commercials. He asked me what I thought he should cut, and I told him in my opinion he should cut nothing. But if he had to cut I would gladly sit with him and help to edit the film down. He thanked me and disappeared into Editorial muttering that they hadn't given him time for that. Ten minutes later he appeared at my desk again with a reel of film in his hand, saying, "Well, it's finished." I asked him how he did it, and he told me he had arbitrarily edited twenty minutes out of the center of the film. No choices, just a slug of twenty minutes. I guess it had to be done that way.

Sal Amico did me another favor. He introduced me to Helen Oursler Balaber. Helen's father was Fulton Oursler, author of *The Greatest Story Ever Told*, a book about the life of Christ. Made him quite rich and was an iconic book in Christian history. Helen was the widow of Barney Balaber, a film salesman. At least that's what he fancied himself. He wandered around Times Square with a suitcase full of film reels of original footage. Rented it to some of the art houses and revival theatres. "Hey buddy, wanna rent a Chaplin? No? Howzabout an Arbuckle?"

Anyway the gentleman had passed away the previous year and his wife had some films she wanted to dispose of. Asked Sal Amico if he could help her put a value to them. He didn't have the time so he gave the job to me. She lived in a high-rise apartment in Queens. It was the dead of winter when I appeared at her door, dressed in my suit and a Chesterfield coat. Helen appeared at her door wearing sequined pedal-pushers, a tight blouse, and smoking a cigarette in an absurdly long cigarette holder. A rather well put-together lady for her age, and very nice to boot.

I entered and gave her my coat, getting ready to catalogue her films for her. She took my coat to the hall closet, opened the door, and realized it wasn't useful. Piled floor to ceiling with film cans. Same with the bedroom closet. She put my coat on the couch. I have no idea where she kept her own clothes. I asked her where I could begin, and she said I could start anywhere. She had no idea what was here or where to begin. I took a stack of film cans from the closet and started to open them. This one was labeled *Blood and Sand*. It was a pristine print of the classic 1922 film with

Rudolph Valentino. It was on nitrate film.

Nitrate film is very, very volatile and dangerous. A nitrate fire in a Paris theater in the 1890s killed a number of French nobility. Nitrate film has been banned since 1951 when acetate-based film replaced it. Tri-nitrocellulose, nitrate film's base, is chemically equivalent to TNT. Once lit it cannot be extinguished with normal means, continuing to burn even if held under water. Very dangerous stuff. Also known as "guncotton."

I suggested that Helen snuff her cigarette and never, never smoke in the apartment again. She followed my suggestion. I decided I had better determine the value of these films immediately so she could get them out of her apartment. The copy of *Blood and Sand* alone was worth hundreds of dollars. There was much more. Newsreels from 1905-1906, original prints of Laurel and Hardy from the 1920s, Chaplin, Francis X. Bushman, Mary Pickford. What seemed like hundreds of reels of film, a treasure trove for the collector. All nitrate.

I started to make a list. Helen was helpful. I must have stayed three or four hours, told her I would return the next day after work. We spent three or four consecutive days listing the films and were only about a quarter of the way through. Mentally I had gone through several hundred thousand feet of film, easily worth half million dollars in those days. When I returned on the fifth day Helen again had a cigarette in its holder and was puffing away. I told her to put it out, but she pointed to the empty closet and told me the film was gone.

There wasn't a foot of film left. Helen was delighted. She had made a killing, selling it to a collector. A man named Raymond Rohauer had heard of the film and had come late the day before, and carted it away. How much? $1,500. I didn't have the heart to tell her that she had been flimflammed royally. She just wanted to get rid of the stuff, didn't know what it was worth, and was relieved that it wasn't there any more so she could smoke. I left and never saw her again.

A few weeks later the brand new Huntington Hartford Gallery of Modern Art opened on Columbus Circle in New York City. The announcement included the fact that the gallery would have a prize collection of rare films from the early cinema, including *Blood and Sand* and some Mary Pickford footage, recently discovered by the curator, Raymond Rohauer...

One of the better people I met at the station was a performer, Chuck McCann. He was a madcap comedian, great entertainer. He had an hour-long children's show every afternoon and we always looked forward to his arrival because he brightened up the studio with his presence. He played to the adults in the audience as well as the children. He later became friends with Stan Laurel, and Chuck and Dick van Dyke had a "Laurel and Hardy" act that they performed for years.

One day the programming head came into the log room and asked us to come to the videotape room to see an audition videotape of a new comedian whose agent had submitted him for WPIX viewing. We all crowded into the tiny video room to see the tape. It was a comedian named Soupy Sales. I started laughing at him right away, as did one or two others in the room. I also mentioned to the programming head that Sales had been known in Los Angeles for some time and was very popular there. The programming head thanked us, said he probably wouldn't go over well in New York, and took the tape away. Sales eventually appeared in New York on another station and made many advertisers very happy.

WPIX was the local outlet for the *Bozo Show*. Larry Harmon had a school somewhere in which he trained Bozos. He had the franchise for training every Bozo in the country, and there were many. There was also a surplus of Princess Ticklefeathers, Bozo's sidekick. When I worked at WPIX the *Bozo Show* had been on for several years and generally the children of New York paid it little attention. It was a live show and there were guest children every day who sat in bleachers and watched Bozo be Bozo. By 1963 there were only three or four children each day, so to fill the seats in the studio, WPIX decreed that the parents would be sitting with the children in the bleachers. It was a stopgap measure at best. Soon there were maybe four mothers and six children sitting in the bleachers. They cheered and laughed and made as much childish noise as possible but it wasn't the same as in the good old days when there were thirty or forty children present.

Another event that caused a big stir in the station was when the son of one of the vice presidents of *Daily News* appeared with a 16mm stag reel. These were not commonly available in those days. Usually one needed to be invited to a stag party or a bachelor party to be able to see one, and the owner, usually a large burly fellow, accompanied it to make sure it wasn't somehow defaced. But this young man had one, and he wanted to have it transferred to videotape. Why? Nobody knew. Videotape for the home had not yet been invented. Not even Betamax. The procedure was to put the film on in a "film chain" in telecine, send the video through Master Control, where it was routed into the video room where it was recorded. For this to happen, however, Master Control had to bring up the picture on its monitors to make the proper connections. Unfortunately the perpetrator had not informed Master Control what the subject of the film was, and they chose to make the transfer just before the *Bozo Show*. Master Control's monitors were all entirely visible to the hallway leading to the studio, with big picture windows from the hall into the control room so visitors could watch the operation without disturbing the staff. That's the hallway that the parents and children followed to get to Bozo's studio. The control staff shut the videos off almost in time. A couple of them were fired as well as the film chain operator, and the young man was barred from the station from then on. The WPIX staff retained the film in question just in case any further legal action was necessary.

Another time, about four months after I stated work at WPIX, I was typing the daily log for the Yankee game. There was no definite time mentioned in the log, only the length of the commercials to be inserted during inning changes. After the commercials I would type, "Go to field," indicating to Master Control to return the feed from the telecine in the studio to Yankee Stadium. This happened, of course, at least nine or ten times per game. There were two or three games each week, and each week I would have to type "Go to field" over and over and over. I became pretty good at it. Also hated it. I asked Bob McEvily if there weren't another phrase I could use. No, there weren't. The inevitable thing happened. One day I typed, "Go to field. Go directly to field. Do not pass Go. Do not collect $200."

CHAPTER 15

HARRY COLEMAN PRODUCTIONS

Back on the street, I wondered what to do next. I still had the *New York Production Guide* and the list of producers, so I went back to it. After a couple of days of fruitless phone calls I got an interview with Harry Coleman, president of Coleman productions. His office was on 45th Street between Sixth and Seventh Avenues. By now Sixth Avenue was renamed Avenue of the Americas, in honor of The Americas. Everyone in New York still called it Sixth Avenue anyway. 45th Street was just off 7th Avenue, then Broadway. Right in the heart of the theatre district.

Harry Coleman had a small industrial movie outfit. His main client was Pan American World Airways for whom he had produced a series of "Wings to…" films. Wings to Argentina, Wings to France, Wings to Japan, etc. These entailed a lot of traveling, of course. And some expertise with film. Harry had the former, not the latter. But he knew how to hire people who did, the mark of a good producer. Bill Moeller, an expert cameraman in New York, filmed the "Wings to" series. The Pan-Am producer who at least had a sense of that art form supervised the editing. This actually formed the bulk of Coleman's income. I worked with him on two small projects. I was his staff technician, expected to manage camera, sound, editing, props, everything in fact. On one shoot I found myself looking through the camera viewfinder with my right eye, working the camera panning and tilting wheels with my right hand, and with my left eye and hand I was recording the sound on a Nagra tape recorder on the ground next to me. I told Harry that we really needed two people to handle both tasks but Harry didn't want to spend the money.

In 1963 we produced a film for the Ford Motor Company that required us to fly to Detroit and film at the factory. We were in the office of the head of Public Relations, high up in the Ford building, discussing what was to be filmed. I glanced out the window and saw several small four-seat sports cars, some convertibles and some coupes, driving very quickly around a test track. I had never seen cars like these before and I asked the PR man what they were. He swore me to secrecy, said they would probably be called "Mustangs" in keeping with Ford's habit of naming its cars after horses. Pretty little things they were, too, and very agile.

We were assigned the company camera car. A camera car needs pairs of steel beams running fore and aft, and side to side. These beams are arranged so that camera platforms can be attached just outside the doors, hood, or trunk of the car. The suspension needs to be strengthened so the car does not lean due to the extra weight of the camera and crew. In keeping with the company philosophy, their camera car was a Lincoln convertible. It worked beautifully, and it looked beautiful.

I did most of the filming. We took the undeveloped film back to New York with us where Harry insisted that we have it processed at Berkey Film Labs, an independent film lab in New York with a reputation for being inexpensive. Perfect for Harry Coleman. I took the sealed film cans downtown to the lab and checked them in. The drone at the desk was new to the job, and he asked me what kind of film we had used. I told him Kodak and gave him the stock number. He said he had to check. In spite of my repeated warning I watched him open one can and look at the film, which of course was now ruined. I protested and suggested that he not open any others. He didn't. His supervisor came straightaway because by now I was protesting at high volume. I never saw that clerk again. Thank God. The lab, of course, replaced the film.

Labs guarantee that if they ruin film they will insure the loss only for the cost of the film stock, nothing more. Every film company carries what is called negative insurance. This pays the producer to re-shoot any film that has been lost in the lab, or if there is a camera glitch. If the producer can prove that it was an accident and not the result of the producer's negligence, the insurance company will pay for the cost of reshooting the footage that was lost, nothing more. That could also entail flight and hotel costs if necessary, however.

It never occurred to me that Harry would not have negative insurance. Everyone did. True to form, Harry blamed me for the film loss. It was only one of four film rolls, so we still had footage to edit, and the people at Ford were none the wiser.

During this time I asked Harry when we would be filming another "Wings to…" show. He answered that Pan-Am no longer made those films and we would be filming for other companies. I later did some work for Pan-Am and asked them. I was told that Harry's contact at Pan-Am had been fired, for, you guessed it, taking bribes from Harry Coleman.

We made one other film; Harry was hired by a company that had built an archery range on Long Island and wanted a record of the grand opening. Celebrities had been invited. The hope was that the establishment would become ubiquitous as a bowling alley and other branches would open in cities across the country. I was acting as the producer on this shoot. We had hired a cameraman, a Frenchman named Leon Perer. There was also another assistant, John Wlosek, a very efficient technician with a very wry sense of humor, most welcome under the terrible stress of filming at an archery range.

The celebrities were Joey Heatherton, an actress and nightclub performer, and the famous boxer, Rocky Marciano. They were on camera a very small part of the time. The focus of the film was on the locals who came to use the archery range. Some were quite good, and others, well, not so good. But the owners had hired a couple of experts to coach the tyros. There were free food and drinks for all. It was quite the festive occasion. We shot the heck out of it and immediately took the film to the lab. Movielab this time. Later Harry picked up the film and edited it himself. I never saw the finished product, and if history taught us anything, neither did anyone else.

I knew that my career at Coleman Productions would not be long. I had been looking for another gig during my free time, and one of the places where I had applied suddenly called to say they had an opening and was I interested? Was I interested?

CHAPTER 16

❖

EYE ON NEW YORK

WCBS is the flagship station of the CBS-TV Network. Its main offices are in the Black Tower, the national headquarters of the CBS network on the corner of Fifth Avenue and 59th Street. In 1963 CBS decided that New York needed a CBS documentary unit. It would produce a half-hour show entitled *Eye on New York*, referring to the famous CBS eye logo. There was a need for four producers, each with a researcher/writer, secretarial staff, some production supervisors and some production assistants to handle the technical end, and an editorial staff. Clem Stigdon would oversee the unit. Offices would be in the DuArt building on 55th Street between Broadway and 8th Ave. The production unit would be on the eleventh floor and editorial would be on the twelfth floor.

They already had a full complement of producers and researchers. They had even hired all the production supervisors they needed. What they needed were production assistants. I was more than willing. I filled out another application and two days later they phoned to ask me to report for work on Monday morning. Of course I did.

By now I was beginning to have a résumé. I also found out that my references were being checked. WPIX, oddly, had given me a good recommendation. Harry Coleman had complained so long and loudly about me that CBS considered him a nut and disregarded his rants. I had the job.

There were four production supervisors I would be working with. Tony Alatis had come from programming at NBC Network. Bill Turque had worked with John and Helen Secondari at the Secondari Unit, which made documentaries. Sheldon Lubow had been in production for several years in New York, and John Gramaglia had also been a production supervisor before. All very good workers and all very easy to get along with. Good teachers, too. I stress that last part because no matter how experienced I became in my years of work I always found that I could learn something from the people around me.

It was our job to make documentaries about life in New York City. The producers came up with the subject ideas, it was passed through legal, then up to WCBS hierarchy, and eventually to the desk of the station manager, Norm Walt. His decision was final. We made some very interesting shows, and a few very dull shows. When a show was green-lighted the producer and researcher started doing background work on it, and in a short period of time a scenario was written which was passed to the WCBS hierarchy again, and if approved, we filmed. The four producers were very gifted and the subjects were almost always approved.

As a P.A. I did a great deal of everything. We had contracts with the local IATSE union so we were bound to hire union camera, sound, and editors. Since there was no studio work, only location, we needed no art directors, but we did hire property masters from time to time.

We had a crew that we kept working for the months we were in business. Hal Seiden was usually the cameraman. A big, cheerful, easygoing man with an innate sense of composition and a good eye for lighting, he was a pleasure to work with. Tommy Gavin, Jr. was usually our gaffer. A gaffer is the head electrician. He had many of his own lights, which were also his father's. Tommy Gavin, Sr. was in his late seventies but he still worked with us when he could. He had worked with Billy Bitzer, D.W. Griffith's cameraman, back in the old days, and he could care for lights like nobody I ever met before or since. At other times we worked with other crews but these people seemed to be there most often.

We produced a show about the rich and their apartments in New York. Photographed inside such buildings as the revered "Dakota" apartments, where John Lennon lived. Another was called "Behind the Looking Glass," about New York's modeling industry. Our main actress was the first supermodel, Susie Parker. We broke new ground with a show called "Crosstown," which dealt with gays in New York. This in 1964. We were sent to Vermont in the winter for "Bunnies, Bachelors, and Broken Bones," about the ski industry. We examined "Angels on Broadway" and followed the funding of a stage play through to opening night. The show was about *A Funny Thing Happened on the Way to the Forum*, starring Zero Mostel. Mostel had just emerged from the blacklist and was a top performer again. His interview was completely unrehearsed, spontaneous, and hilarious. He broke from the interview a couple of times to chase chorus girls around the stage.

We did a show entitled "Brains and Brawn." One half was about Mensa, the high-IQ club. The other half was about Vic Tanny gyms. I only worked on the "Brains" part. We spent an evening documenting a Mensa meeting. Those Mensa people were certainly smart. They were discussing subjects far over my head and I trust the rest of the crew felt the same way. It was also possible that they did that for a goof, just for the cameras, and that during normal meetings they discussed the virtues of good cheese and vintage wine. I never found out. They did invite me to join, as they did everyone else on the crew, and I don't believe any of us took advantage of it. In any case the show was never aired because, unbeknownst to us, Norm Walt was a member of Vic Tanny Gyms and he felt our coverage of that segment was demeaning.

We also did a show about slumlords. In one case the man who owned the apartment house next door to a really badly rundown building we were photographing sued CBS for defamation of character. We had managed to catch two or three of the bricks of his building in our master shot of our subject slum building. It was one of those annoyance suits that people file against a "deep pockets" defendant in hopes of getting a few thousand dollars out of it, and it worked. Another lesson learned.

We produced one show about breweries in the New York area. During research we discovered that Augie Busch, owner of Anheuser Busch, maker of Budweiser, really disliked beer and at heart wanted to be a vintner. But his beer became so famous that he had to promote it, even though in private he referred to it as "Dat Schlop."

We did one show about the opening of the New York World's Fair of 1964. Interviewed the man himself, Robert Moses, the master builder of New York. He had been responsible for the construction of many of the most famous structures in and around the city, including the thruway system, various bridges and tunnels, stadiums, anything large and impressive. And he oversaw the construction of the fair. He gave great interview, as our audience found out. And truth be told his vision was magnificent regarding the structures for which he was responsible.

One day in the office we on the eleventh floor heard a great commotion down in the street. We looked out the window and saw people not acting normally, running around crying. I was sent to find out what was the matter. There was a newsboy selling copies of the *Daily News* with the headline, "Kennedy Shot in Dallas." There was no article, just the headline. We worked for CBS, one of the world's finest news organizations, but had no idea what was happening. It also became apparent that even though we worked for one of the great news gathering agencies, our office had no TV set or radio. We phoned CBS headquarters and they kept us apprised by telephone when he had died. They soon sent over a TV set so we could get our own news.

The production room was in deep shock and depression for a brief period of time after the news broke. Then we got back down to the business at hand. One of the great things about the USA is that it is resilient enough to keep going smoothly even after such a shock. That's what happened. Johnson was sworn in. The nation went through mourning. And we got back to work.

We produced a show, an entire half-hour and that was not long enough, about the noted cartoonist Al Hirschfeld. This marvelous man caricatured the famous and near famous on Broadway, in Hollywood, in politics, worldwide. His wife was Dolly Haas. Dolly had starred in the last film Dad directed in Berlin, in the middle of which he had to leave the country. She remembered him fondly, especially since he had been one of the people who sponsored her move to the USA through the Film Fund. I introduced myself to her. From that moment on during that show I was no longer a production assistant, but a noted Hollywood personality. Al and Dolly showed me around their town house in Manhattan, and Al took me into his studio to show me his latest works, superb as always. The next day, of course, I became a P.A. once again.

We photographed all over New York City and environs. From Tony Alatis and the others I learned to be "street smart"—how to adapt to rapidly changing conditions during production, to keep the cameras rolling no matter what, and how to use a little clever repartee to disarm potential opponents. This did not always work but it worked enough to make the attempt worthwhile. I learned much more than I had known before about cameras, lenses, sound equipment, how to order it, where to obtain it, how to maintain it. I made acquaintances at various movie equipment houses where I would be renting equipment in the future, and this was all in aid of helping me to add more tools to my professional briefcase. Many of the people with whom I worked would work with me again in the future on commercials and in feature films. It was a great school.

Hal Seiden had become a friend. He invited me for dinner at his home on Long Island. His wife was an excellent cook. At that time I was steadily dating a secretary at CBS, Lucy Fried. She was bright and pretty, had a very good sense of humor. We shared many of the same likes and dislikes. Her family accepted me as a kind of interesting and amusing outsider, partly because I told stories about show biz, of which they had no knowledge. Lucy and I alone were a good match. I started seeing her exclusively. She accompanied me to Hal's house that evening for dinner.

Another guest at that dinner was Jeanne Harrison, an executive at J. Walter Thompson Advertising. JWT at that point was the world's largest agency. Its clients included Ford, Liggett & Meyers Tobacco, Unilever, and a host of others. Bill Dwinnell, an old friend from the Webb School, worked at JWT also. The evening was most pleasant, and I found Jeanne to be a charming guest. Hal was his usual boisterous self, irrepressible and funny. Hal's son, a college student, was an excellent singer and guitarist and he entertained us with a few folk songs. It was a very comfortable, easy evening with friends.

CHAPTER 17

J. WALTER THOMPSON

The following Monday I returned to CBS to find a message from Jeanne Harrison. Asked me to phone JWT. I did so, and she told me to make an appointment with Bill Tenneson, head of the film commercial producers' department. They wanted to discuss with me the idea of producing TV commercials for them. It paid a great deal more than CBS was paying. It was a grand opportunity.

Bill Tenneson greeted me warmly. Jeanne Harrison had apparently told him about me and recommended me highly. I was flattered and elated at this chance. I had the job. I just had to go through their personnel department's system to be hired officially. I told Bill that I had to give CBS two weeks' notice and he agreed. In the meantime I would make the time to go to personnel and fill out the papers. Bill, and all the people at J. Walter, were more than understanding. They bent over backwards to make me feel welcome and to help me get my feet on the ground in the new job.

I phoned Jeanne and thanked her. I also phoned Hal Seiden and thanked him for setting up the dinner. I phoned Lucy and told her I was leaving CBS, and why. We had worked in the same office, which made it easier for us to date. Now I'd be spending more time on the road.

Much as I enjoyed the Manhattan life, I needed to move to a less expensive apartment. I found one in Jackson Heights, Queens, a one-room/kitchen/bathroom place a block away from the "El." Sometimes Lucy came out to my place and we spent quiet evenings watching TV, punctuated by the friendly roar of the elevated train and the sirens at the emergency entrance to the hospital across the street. It was romantic, sort of.

I went to CBS the next day. They knew where I had been and they expected me to resign so I could take the new job. They were all very supportive, wished me well. The next two weeks I was in the office off and on. I never met the person who took my place, and I didn't have much to do because there were no productions in process at that time. Lunches at Brannigan's or the Brittany were still in order, however. Once even the Stage Deli, but that not so much because the waiters are so rude and I was still at heart from Los Angeles.

My elation about the new job lasted a few days. I went to the personnel department and signed all the papers. I had an orientation meeting. I was still smoking cigarettes at the time and had become enchanted by the taste, and the snob appeal, of Nat Sherman Cigarettes. When I sat down in the comfortable personnel office, I noticed on the table a tray of L & M Cigarettes. There was a little glass jar with a carefully arranged spray of L & M Cigarettes. There was an L & M logo cigarette lighter on the table. I absentmindedly pulled out my Shermans and started to light one. The personnel man said "Wait a minute—why don't you… Oh never mind. You'll learn soon enough."

Later I was in Bill Dwinnell's office, and I pulled out a Sherman. He reminded me that L & M was a JWT client and the company expected its employees to be supportive of their clients. He told me that most employees who smoked used L & M packages but kept their own cigarette brands in them, so at least clients thought they were smoking L & M even if they weren't. I started wondering how I could disguise a VW as a Ford.

The next indication that something was wrong was the fact that nobody there seemed to want to make eye contact. I could walk down the corridor and everyone who approached was looking at the floor, not at my face. Maybe they were checking to make sure I wore Rockport shoes or whatever the JWT-sanctioned brand was. I was not accustomed to this. Everywhere else I worked people greeted you, even if they had just seen you ten minutes before. A quick "Hey there" or "How's it going?" was enough. But at JWT there was mostly silence.

I was given a cubicle in the middle of a large office. There were a number of cubicles around me. My cubicle contained a desk (empty), a desk lamp (lit), a telephone with two extensions, a trash basket, and an ashtray. That's it. I searched every corner of the cubicle but could find nothing to sit on. That's funny; all the other cubicle occupants had chairs. Apparently the former occupant took his chair with him. Oh well. I looked around and saw an empty office close by with a very nice, well-upholstered desk chair on casters, springs so one could lean back a little. The full shot. I wheeled it into my cubicle, sat down, and started to take my office supplies from my attaché case and arrange the desk. I would still need a blotter and a small table for my typewriter. Oh good, here comes the office supplies person. She bid me a very welcome good morning and asked if I needed anything. I mentioned the blotter and—ooops—"Where did you get that chair?"

I explained that there was no chair when I was shown the cubicle so I took it from that unoccupied office right over there. She explained that that is not permitted. A cubicle may have a padded chair, or an armchair, but not a padded armchair. With that she wheeled the chair back into the office. I asked her what I was expected to sit on and she said that she would arrange for a chair to be brought later today. And until then? We'll have a chair for you shortly. Be patient.

I wandered around the office, hung out with my senior producer, Hank Selverstone, a very intelligent gentleman who knew the ropes far better than I.

J. WALTER THOMPSON

Since I didn't have a chair yet by lunch I went out to one of those little pizza joints on Lexington Ave. that has far better pizza than anything I had eaten in L.A., then I went to a local furniture store and bought a folding director's chair. Took it back to my cubicle and opened it up, sat down and started reading old commercial scripts so I could see what I was supposed to be doing. Presently I could hear whispers in the passageway outside my cubicle. I looked out and saw a small gaggle of secretaries and producers staring at my director's chair. The head of office supplies reappeared. She asked me where I got the chair. I told her that it was my chair, I bought it, and showed her the sales slip. She seemed a little unnerved be this. She explained that this was not standard cubicle furniture. I told her that the alternative would be an apple box if she did not approve of this. I kept my director's chair for three or four days until the office supplies powers managed to find me an armchair without padding. Then I folded the director's chair and put it in the corner of the cubicle, handy in case my regulation armchair disappeared again.

I was treated to an afternoon of watching commercials in the screening room so I could see what kind of visuals were used. I had been assigned to the Unilever group, which covered a lot of territory. There were foods and cleaning supplies galore. I would shortly go on my first commercial shoot, a day trip to Connecticut. The Lever Bros. copy group had written the commercial, and all the prep had been done. The production company was close by, MPO productions. This was considered the MGM of commercial production. Offices were in a building on 45th Street where they had four or five floors. Nine sound stages, not very large, and one big one with a cyclorama that was usually white, but could be repainted sky blue if necessary. Offices for producers, and an entire floor for the editorial department. There was a well-appointed commissary to entertain clients, conference rooms, and a really good staff. The director assigned to our commercial was Joe Kohn, and the cameraman was Zoltan Vidor, a Hungarian whom I had known from days of yore with my mother and grandmother. He had actually worked in Europe on Dad's films in Budapest and we had stills of Dad and him together on the set. He and I would grow to be good friends. The AD, George Marvin, a member of Local 161, was a former stand-up comedian from the Catskills. Joe Kohn had directed numerous films for Columbia back in the 1940s. This was a highly experienced group.

Hank Selverstone, the copywriter, the cast and myself were put up overnight before the shoot in a motel in Connecticut close to the location. The crew would follow up early the next day and set up at the location. The cast had been carefully chosen to represent the typical all-American family: Mommy, Daddy, and a boy and girl. The scene was a campsite next to a lake, and Daddy is cooking pancakes in a skillet. Mommy is getting the kids ready for breakfast. The commercial is for Mrs. Butterworth's Syrup.

It was a perfect setting. It was sunny with a slight mist on the lake surface. While we were setting up the first shot, the copywriter asked to see the shot through the camera. The cameraman told her to go ahead. With that she went to the camera and tried to peer through the tripod handle. The assistant cameraman, bless him, gently showed her the viewfinder.

My first commercial went off without a hitch. After a few days in the office it was a pleasure to be outdoors in the woods next to a lake, far away from the stifling atmosphere of Lexington Avenue. In fact, I learned quickly that JWT producers found excuses to look for locations and go on scouting trips to Los Angeles and other exotic places just to get away from Madison Avenue for a few days. It would be a few years before I was able to return to Los Angeles, however. Now that I was working productively, had my own place, had a steady girlfriend, Lucy, there was no draw for me to return.

Lucy and I grew closer. She lived in Great Neck on Long Island, just across the border into Nassau County. Her father was a school principal and her mother taught History of Economics in high school. Lucy had attended Cornell University and had a lively sense of humor, if a little dark. Extremely intelligent, probably much more than I am. Enjoyed dancing, even though I am quite awkward and my dancing skills are nil. But the dancing of those days did not require much personal contact, just some kind of frenetic movement. I could do that. Lucy's parents and family seemed to be attentive and friendly. Over the years they became more so.

My career was going well at JWT in spite of itself. I was not very happy there. There were too many rules. Too much regimentation. Some took comfort in that; I chafed. One day I noticed that the girl at the front desk was checking our names off a list as we entered. She explained that she was giving everyone who arrived between 8:45 and 9:00 am an "A," 9:00 and 9:05 a "B," 9:05 and 9:10 a "C," etc. to after 9:20, an "F." I usually was a few minutes early. The office was quiet early and I could get some work done at my desk before everyone else arrived and the phone began ringing. I usually arrived around 8:50 or so. At the end of the week I received in interoffice mail a report card that gave me an "A." Showed what time I arrived every morning. Hey, not bad. Next week was the same. The week following I needed to do some quiet work before my usual arrival time, so for the entire week I arrived at 8:30. On Monday of the following week I received my report card. I had gotten "F" for each day because I had arrived long before the girl was at the desk. She assumed that since I didn't pass her desk at the requisite times I had not arrived at all. It never occurred to her when she saw me passing through the lobby later that she might ask when I had entered in the morning.

Soon the head of my department came to my cubicle to discuss my absence with me. I explained that I arrived early. He asked me not to do that any more because it threw their record keeping ability off. I told him that I was able to do better work at 8:30 because the office was empty, but it appeared to be more important to him for me to get a good grade than to do good work. Hmmm. At that point I knew my days at JWT were numbered also. The production department suggested that I might be able to make more money and operate more independently if I were to join the copy group. There I could write commercials, think up new ideas, exercise my own creative energy, and not feel quite so stifled as I did in the production department. Credit to them for that.

The personnel department called me and suggested that I write a commercial so they could see if my talent lay in that direction. Use any product with which I was familiar.

One way or another I was ready to leave JWT so I didn't take the suggestion seriously. I still had friends there, Hank Selverstone, Bob Kronenberg, and a few others, Bill Dwinnell. These were people with whom Lucy and I had dinner and spent leisure time. I sat down at my typewriter and wrote a commercial for Stripe Toothpaste, a Lever product. The red stripes on the white paste purported to be a breath cleanser. Most toothpaste commercials were set in a sunlit, bright bathroom with the mommy helping the kiddies put a curl of toothpaste on the brush and watching lovingly while her kids(s) brush their teeth in an up and down motion like no kid on earth does. It usually ended with the kids showing off their pearly whites as Mommy does the same.

My commercial started at a dark pool in the middle of a foreboding forest at midnight. A green mist rises from the pool and the wind howls menacingly through the trees. Out of the pool rises a monster like the one in *Swamp Thing*, a horribly ugly evil creature. He is carrying a gorgeous girl in his arms. Her torn dress barely covers her assets. He puts her on the grass at the edge of the pool (I guess I was influenced by the Mrs. Butterworth Syrup commercial location) and tries to kiss her but she is having none of it, screaming and pounding on his chest. He stops trying and asks her what is wrong. She says it is his repulsive breath. Cut to his underwater bathroom where he is brushing his teeth with Stripe toothpaste. The foam from his mouth flows out into he water around him. He mentions how the toothpaste is cleaning the algae out from between his teeth. Dissolve back to the grass patch at the dark pool. He is making passionate love with the girl. He is wearing a Stripe Toothpaste sweatshirt.

I thought that was outrageous enough that it could never be produced. I had left my name off the script because I really didn't want the copy group to know who wrote this travesty. Needless to say, two weeks later I saw my script on the desk of a copywriter. I asked him about it and he answered that someone had turned it in to personnel, the client's representative saw and loved it, and it became his job to make the monster "cute."

Two events precipitated my departure from JWT.

About the time I wrote the commercial I went back to the Directors Guild to see if there was anything else I could do. Heck, I would have worked in the legitimate theatre at that point if I could. I found out that at this time the DGA had merged with the SDIG and Local 161, leaving 161 to represent only the script supervisors. Now the DGA represented all directors, ADs and UPMs in New York for commercials, feature films, TV shows, network, everything except legitimate stage. That had happened a few months before. I also found out that during the previous month the DGA AD/UPM council had taken up the subject of a member who had moved to the East Coast from Hollywood, and had voted to allow him to work in New York in category. That meant I could find work as an AD again; especially in New York where nobody knew who my dad was. I would be making my own way. I didn't bother to ask why nobody had called me to tell me about something that had happened a month ago, I was too elated at being able to work again.

The other thing was that I felt enough in love with Lucy that I proposed to her. She accepted. We set our wedding date for November. I was now twenty-five years old and ready to accept the responsibility of married life. I phoned my mom and dad. They discussed it and decided that Mom would come to the wedding but not Dad. True to form. Lucy and her mom set about planning the wedding.

There had already been small foretastes of the chaos to come. Two or three months earlier Lucy's younger sister, Alice, had married her boyfriend, Michael Baker. Mike was a very pleasant man, trained in accounting and business. He was being groomed to take over his father's real estate construction business and had excellent prospects for the future. Lucy was shattered that her sister should marry before her. She had far too much to drink at the reception and thankfully disappeared into a hotel room at the wedding site to sleep, but not before she had been quite vocal about all sorts of wrongs that had been done her. I'm being polite. She was plastered, and she laid into me and everyone else around her in an unnecessarily vicious diatribe. Being the innocent I was, I overlooked that aspect for years. I've always been a softie, sometimes to the point where it hurts me. And being naïve I thought I could handle anything. I would pay for that.

CHAPTER 18

NEW YORK DGA

I returned to the DGA where Milt Felsen was now the business agent for the ADs and UPMs. He invited me to attend the next AD/UPM council meeting. I went to the DGA offices on the appointed evening and listened to my very first AD council meeting. New York and Los Angeles branches had not yet entirely merged and the two coasts had different pay scales and working conditions. It would be a gradual process, a few years in the making. The West Coast, with the philosophy that the AD and UPM are in fact management positions, was charging a set amount for an entire day. There was no overtime. The daily rate covered a reasonable amount for a day's work, and it was deemed unnecessary for those in charge to quibble about hours of overtime. On the East Coast the AD was paid for an eight-hour day with overtime after the eighth hour. There were other differences as well. In New York there was much less differentiation between UPM and AD since the vast majority of the work was in TV commercials in which both crafts were covered by a single person. In L.A. they were mostly two separate crafts and on a typical production there was a UPM, and 1st AD and a 2nd AD. If needed, to wrangle large numbers of extras for instance, there could be additional ADs. In New York, except for the feature films and TV, there were production assistants. These were ubiquitous in the commercials industry where they were everything from gofers to paper wranglers. There were over a hundred of them in Local 161 who were now in the Guild and they needed to be addressed somehow. These problems would be worked out over the next few years. There were also several contracts with management that had to be standardized over the geographic spread. There was a Chicago branch that had its own production problems that had to be addressed. But for now there were separate contracts for commercials, TV shows, and feature films that had to be merged.

These were all problems that would be addressed in the future by the national board. For now there was joy and relief that we were all one Guild nationwide. I went to the meeting and was welcomed as a bit of an oddball. I was one of the only two or three members who had moved in the "wrong" direction. The usual move was from NY to Hollywood, where NY-trained ADs and UPMs were highly regarded because of their "street smarts." The subject arose of my pension and health situation since the two coasts had contracts with different carriers for those funds. This was moot because I had not really worked on the West Coast so was not vested at all. I gladly signed all the necessary papers for salary deductions and so forth to make my DGA membership complete and official.

I returned to J. Walter Thompson, visited with Hank Selverstone and Bill Dwinnell, and submitted my resignation to Bill Tenneson. I had been there for only four or five months, worked on a number of commercials with several well-known commercial producers in NY, and had built a very small but positive reputation as one who knew his filter from his obie light. I even worked from time to time with other producers at JWT who wanted me at their side during production.

I spent the last two weeks at JWT finishing production paperwork and paying my respects to those who had worked with me during my stay. All had been teachers one way or another and I was grateful.

Lucy was beginning to move into the Queens apartment. We were not close enough yet to our wedding date that we were overly concerned. I wasn't concerned at all, in fact, since this would be a traditional wedding and Lucy's parents were covering the costs. I had to rent my own tuxedo. In fact I bought a tuxedo for the occasion, thinking that I would wear it to awards dinners and such. In fact I only wore it one other time, and I can't remember what that was. I just remember fiddling with the cufflinks and the cummerbund.

The wedding took place at a large hotel in Manhattan on 59th Street near 7th Avenue. We had a view of Central Park from the bridal suite. All of Lucy's relatives were there it seemed, and a few of my friends. Mom, too, and Ronn. Hank Selverstone came, Tony Alatis, and Kenny Greenwald. I had maybe six guests. I think my brother Peter was there also. Charlie Turecamo's band played. Mom disappeared for a while with Lucy for a "heart to heart" talk. I paid it little attention, my time being taken up with the guests and generally having a good time. Lucy returned shortly to tell me that they had just discussed the wedding and how Mom had welcomed her into my family. We danced until about 11:00 pm and then retired to the bridal suite. We used the bridal suite in the manner it was intended until 1:00 am the next morning when the phone rang. I should have ignored it. I knew who it was. It was Mom, asking if everything was all right. Everything had been all right until she called.

The next morning Lucy and I went on our honeymoon, a skiing trip to Vermont. One of the better trips in my life, if only for a few days.

I left JWT and was unemployed for about four days when the phone rang. TV Graphics was making a commercial and needed an AD. I took the job and arrived the next morning bright and early, around 8:00 am. In those days it was the custom for the production company to prep a commercial and only have the AD manage the set during shooting. In this case they gave me a day to prep. I made a few calls to hire their usual crew from a list they had. I knew none of the crew and none of the TV graphics staff, but I did the best I could, keeping everything flowing smoothly during the shoot. I made more money in those two days than I had in a week of producing at JWT.

The director was Frank Papp. I would make many commercials with him in various production houses during the next few years. The cameraman was Teddy Pahle, a talented Austrian who had photographed Dad's last European film, *Katharina die Letzte*, at Rosenhugel Studios in Vienna. I was happy to meet him and we spent a bit of time discussing the old days in Europe.

This was living. Lucy and I could walk to the nearest Food Fair market and buy an entire week's worth of groceries for around $10.00. Gasoline cost 30 or 35 cents a gallon. I usually didn't drive into Manhattan because the subway was so inexpensive and safe in those days. Of course the down side was that I was unemployed after three days' work.

This was OK with me. I knew there was always another job around the corner. It did not sit well with Lucy who was accustomed to having a steady paycheck every week. In my case sometimes I was paid more, sometimes less. If I did not work in a week at all, I got paid nothing. I learned to save money to cover the bare spots.

Lucy and I knew we would need a larger apartment and started looking in Forest Hills. We found a place on Yellowstone Boulevard near the town of Forest Hills. It had two bedrooms and two bathrooms, a living room with a dining alcove. Much more suitable. And it was a doorman building, which offered a modicum of safety. We moved within the week. I also bid goodbye to the old, trusty hide-a-bed which had served me for so many years. Now we would have a real bed.

I was beginning to get more work. The biggest commercial producer in New York, MPO, called me often. I had begun to build a group of directors with whom I enjoyed working. The crews were nice also. New York, it turned out, is a character all its own. If I had consciously sought to move to a foreign country I could not have made a better choice. This was the very best kind of education in production. The crews were extremely knowledgeable, the producers willing to share their expertise, the directors understandable. Even the casts were good, many of them old-timers with much stage experience, who were all professional and on time, knew their lines, willing to help, willing to accommodate sudden changes in production requirements. For a young AD this was heaven.

The best part was that I was entirely on my own. There was no backup most of the time. Hollywood's big studios had large camera, grip, lighting, prop, sound departments. The AD or UPM was not required to know every nuance of lighting or camera lens or filter. The department took care of that. In New York the AD/UPM took care of that. I did the equipment ordering and I better know what I was doing. I arranged for the locations. Hired the crew. Even, in some cases, had the film developed and printed. I never really worked for a commercial production company in Los Angeles, only made one commercial there as I recall, so I don't have a frame of reference as to how commercial production is handled on the West

Coast, but the same problems beset us in feature filmmaking in New York as we had in commercial production. That certainly was not the case in L.A. The major studios had large departments that handled everything from camera to editing to sound, post-production, all smoothly and without the UPM having to attend to too much detail. UPMs in Hollywood had to be good communicators, however, because someone had to liaise with the departments to get things done. But the departments handled the detail work, whereas in New York the UPMs did that.

The city of New York did pose its own unique problems. Filming in Central Park was amusing. In those days there was no official police detail designed to help filmmakers. Usually when a filming company appeared in a particular precinct, someone from that precinct would appear and ask if any help were needed from the police department. So the first time I took a crew to Central Park, suddenly an NYPD sergeant appeared and asked if we needed any assistance. Not having been briefed in the normal routine, I told him no. He stood in front of the camera lens and asked again if we needed assistance. I again told him we did not. He was getting a little frustrated by this time, as was I. He kept saying, "It's procedure," and I kept requesting that he get out of the way of the camera. The gaffer came over and clued me in. I quickly made up an envelope with cash in it for the desk sergeant, the sergeant on the set, the lieutenant, and for several other officers of that precinct. I handed it to the sergeant who promptly disappeared. The police did not bother us again by for the remainder of the day.

I found that filming on public streets went much more smoothly if one carried a large amount of petty cash for such exigencies. It was not only the police. The owners of the shop next-door to where we were filming would approach us to complain that our activity was disrupting their business. If we did not reimburse them for income lost they would sometimes call the police, sometimes actually start legal action against us. More often they would turn their radio so loud that we couldn't film.

One of the big lessons of those days is that the public's perception of the movie industry is that we are all millionaires. It says so, right there in the entertainment section of your newspaper. Last weekend such and such a movie made over 30 million dollars at the box office. Of course we were all millionaires, and as such we were subject to every nut in the city thinking that we were a money tree whose branches would drop money into their pockets at the slightest provocation. The same thinking pervades Hollywood, by the way.

Incidentally, some years later I was filming a commercial on East River Drive. John Lindsey had been elected Mayor of New York and one of his first acts was to make New York more "movie friendly." He did this by eliminating police interference with production. A special unit of the NYPD was formed, the TPF or Tactical Patrol Force. It could work anywhere in the city regardless of the precinct. Among their duties was the aid and abetment of filming. There was to be no charge for this. Whatever filmmakers wanted they were to be given, within reason. Traffic was flowing smoothly on East River Drive at midday, but the commercial called for a traffic jam. I knew that if we would stall a car in one lane of the freeway we would have a traffic jam of major proportions, but that as soon as the car moved the jam would free up and traffic would flow smoothly. We could make a traffic jam for five minutes, enough to make the commercial's master shot, and then we could move the car to a parking lot nearby and shoot the close-ups and the product shots.

I asked the lieutenant assigned to us where I could stall the car. He replied that he could not allow us to do so. Traffic in New York was more important than a TV commercial. For a $20 bill I arranged the most beautiful and temporary traffic jam you ever saw. This after the mayor had decreed that no policeman would take a single penny from a film company.

When I began to work in production in New York it was still the Golden Age. The big exodus to Hollywood had not yet happened and many of the best of the best were still working on Manhattan streets. Roger Rothstein was head of production at Video Productions Inc., VPI. Ted Zachary was there also, as was Bob Schneider. Michael Herzberg had not yet worked with Mel Brooks. Fred Gallo was an AD, Burt Bluestein was a PA. These would move to Los Angeles in the early seventies.

CHAPTER 19

UP THE DOWN STAIRCASE

George Justin was one of New York's premier UPMs. I worked with him on *Up the Down Staircase*, one of my first feature films in NY. Don Kranze was the 1st AD on that film, and Joseph Coffey was the cameraman. Bob Mulligan directed. The brilliant Sandy Dennis starred. She had a fondness for cats and kept an apartment in downtown Manhattan that she had filled with old used furniture, just to keep her cats. I remember filming at our location school on 1st Avenue and 107th Street when she spied a kitten hiding under a car. The next half hour saw a good part of the crew trying to catch the little monster who ducked out of one car and under another, seeming to enjoy being chased, until we finally were able to catch and cage the critter so Sandy could give it a good home.

We had hired many kids off the streets of NY to act as students in the school. We had to film during the summer when school was not in session so we could work with the kids all day. This caused a problem on the days when we had to simulate a winter storm. It was 105 degrees in the shade that day and we had wind machines blowing around fake snow made of tiny bits of Styrofoam. This evil substance would slide down the neckline of the kids' jackets and itch like mad when it touched the skin. The result was a hundred or so kids who were squirming with the uncomfortable stuff that had crept down their backs, wearing heavy winter clothing in the humid heat, and generally doing this without complaining. Not audibly.

I was one of the 2nd ADs on *Staircase* and it was my job to keep the extras believable. They had to act like real students. My job was a cinch because they were real students, and all I had to do was to keep them choreographed so they stayed mostly in front of the camera's view, not wandering off into classrooms where they could not be seen. I worked very closely with Tom Ward, who supplied the extras. He had two assistants, Marty Richards and Tommy Fiorello. Marty would later win an Oscar for producing *Chicago* with Richard Gere. Tommy was hired because he was a street person and knew how to keep the kids coming back and where to find them if they didn't show up for the morning call. He later became a very good extras casting person in his own right.

At home we had our apartment in Forest Hills. I paid the manager a little more money so we could have two parking spaces instead of one. I was still driving the old VW, but we bought a Volvo 144S for Lucy to drive or if we took the family on an outing. It also served us well when we went on one of our infrequent skiing trips. At first it didn't serve us well at all. When we first bought it from the Volvo dealer in Manhattan the mechanic who prepared it forgot to replace the drain plug on the differential when he put the working lubricant in, and all the oil drained out on the ground on the way home. This would not have been so bad, but two or three days later Lucy and I took a trip to Cape Cod. On the way up the differential started to moan softly, a noise that I attributed to the new car sounds. On the way home however, the car started to wail like a banshee, but by golly it did make it all the way home and then the next day back to the dealer, who had to replace the differential at his own expense. An expensive lesson for him.

The other little problem was annoying rather than destructive. Every time the car braked, as for a stoplight, there was a noticeable "clunk" coming from the right rear of the car somewhere. When the car accelerated there was another clunk. These were not loud and they did not change their volume as time wore on, but they were noticeable. Finally after a couple of thousand miles when we took the car in for a regular checkup and oil change I mentioned it to the service rep. When we picked up the car he told us that he had noticed it also, but his men had removed the right rear tire, checked the brakes, opened the trunk, checked the wheel well, pretty much examined everything in the right rear of the car to find the clunkmacher but to no avail. By this time I had changed Volvo dealerships since I felt that the seller's shop was really incompetent, and we went to a dealership in White Plains to have the car serviced. This service department found the problem. One of the factory workmen had put a Coca-Cola bottle inside the right rear door and it was sliding back and forth in the door slot every time the car sped up or slowed down.

After that the car became so reliable that it was boring. We drove it across the country three times and eventually sold it around 1973 or '74.

Lucy gave birth to our first son, Christopher, in May of 1965. He was a happy, energetic child, quick to learn and happy to do so. I was still mostly involved in commercials so had not yet begun the difficult grind of feature film and TV production. I was able to spend more time at home. Lucy and I shared the child-caring duties. I got up in the wee hours to change and feed Chris just as much as she did, and when I was off working she handled those chores.

One of the commercials I did was for Chesterfield cigarettes, one of the last TV commercials for smoking. The date was November 9, 1965. We filmed at a baseball stadium in Philadelphia. Drove down one day, checked out the location, stayed overnight at a local hotel, filmed the next day, and drove back that evening. This day was different. Usually we drove up the New Jersey Turnpike, listened to the traffic report on the radio, and went through the Lincoln Tunnel into Manhattan, then back to the offices to return the film equipment and the station wagon, then picked up my own car and drove home over the 59th Street Bridge. Traffic in Manhattan was normally very heavy in the late afternoon and early evening so getting across town was difficult but local radio stations usually tracked which were the roads less traveled.

CHAPTER 20

BLACKOUT

Today would be no different. We drove up the turnpike toward Manhattan, listening to the news. Suddenly the radio station went off the air. We waited a couple of minutes to see if it would come back on, but it didn't. Bernie Hirschenson, the cameraman, sitting in the passenger seat, began turning the radio dial to find a station we could listen to. There were very few, and only in New Jersey. Slowly we came to the realization that something was terribly wrong in New York but whatever it was had not yet spread to New Jersey. The Jersey radio stations were reporting that some sort of electrical problem had shut down the New York radio stations. Slowly, one by one, New York stations came back on, some reporting that they were broadcasting by candlelight. Nobody seemed to know exactly what the problem might be or how widespread.

It grew dark. We were approaching New York. As we drove closer we looked across the Hudson River to where Manhattan was, and in the dark we saw absolutely pitch-black. Nothing. Manhattan had disappeared. We approached the Lincoln Tunnel, and noticed that the lights were out. By now many of the radio stations had come back on the air with emergency generators. The reports were that at least the entire New York metropolitan area was having an electric blackout. It may have extended to parts of New England as well. Nobody seemed to know much.

The drive through the tunnel, which normally took maybe five minutes, took around 45 minutes until we finally emerged, coughing from the fumes, into absolute chaos on New York's streets. I dreaded the cross-town drive from the tunnel, on 11th Avenue, to 1st Avenue all the way across Manhattan. Traffic in Manhattan had always been a huge problem especially in the movie business when a minute could mean the difference between regular hours and a half hour of overtime for a crew, which could cost several hundred dollars. The street lamps were out and the only light came from headlights. The traffic signals also were out. What to do? I had to return the equipment to the office, on 45th and 2nd Ave., somehow wrangle it up thirty flights of stairs to the equipment room, secure the room, retrieve my car from the locked garage (Was the electric door working?) and drive home.

I appealed to the better instincts of the crew. They would not charge overtime for just this one case. I decided that I could not get the equipment up the stairs if the elevators did not work. I would drop the crew at the office building and drive the company station wagon home to my apartment in Queens. I hoped the electricity would return tomorrow and I could easily return the equipment then. In the meantime I could keep the equipment in my apartment until the electricity returned, and keep the exposed film in the refrigerator until the labs were back in business. Cell phones had not yet been invented so I couldn't phone anyone to tell them, but I figured that phone service was still working so I could call from home.

But for now, how to get across town? We were lucky. Normally a cross-town drive could take up to half hour or more. But the traffic lights were out and each intersection had one or more civilians directing traffic through the intersection, sometimes more than one with conflicting signals. I happened to arrive at each intersection as traffic was being directed in my direction. It took less than ten minutes to arrive at the office. I dropped off the crew who had mostly arrived at work by subway. Since the subways were also not working, I took as many in the station wagon as it would carry and laid a route that allowed me to drop them within a block of their homes, and then I went home myself. This process took three hours or so. Traffic on the 59th Street Bridge was impossible. What was usually a ten-minute drive at worst, this time took an hour.

Arriving home I found that I had an understandably nervous wife and a five-month-old infant who needed to be fed regularly with refrigerated but warmed formula. By opening the fridge door a crack, reaching in and yanking out the formula bottles, then heating on our gas stove, we kept Chris fed. We had stocked up on candles beforehand so we were not entirely dark. We had hot water. The phones worked. I called the necessary relatives, found that Lucy's sister in Connecticut was also without electric power. I called the production manager of Filmex, the producing company, and explained what we had done. He agreed with everything and told me to return the equipment as soon as possible. That would be three or four days later. In the meantime I had my family and my baby to care for. Now that I was home I could concentrate on the basic things. We had plenty of canned food in the pantry. Plenty of formula. Plenty of diapers had just been delivered the day before. These were the days before disposable diapers and the usual drill was to hire a diaper service and keep the soiled diapers in a big bag, exchanging it every few days for a new bag full of freshly washed diapers.

The blackout lasted a few days before I could return the equipment to the producer, but nothing was filming in New York anyway for that period. When the electricity went back on Lucy and I caught up with grocery shopping and restocking our supplies, candles, etc. Then New York seemed to sit up, shake itself off, and get back to work.

By now I had several companies that called me regularly for work. I worked about nine days out of ten, and the tenth I usually went to a production office or to the DGA. I found that business lunches kept me on the good side of the heads of production. Anyway I usually liked these people so this was far from an unpleasant task.

One of these companies was MPO, Madison, Pollack and O'Hare. It was the biggest of them all, with a big building on Third Avenue, nine sound stages, a complete camera, grip, electric department, makeup facilities with staff makeup and wardrobe people, set construction, all within the same building. I made several friends who worked there. Tommy Gavin, Jr., and Frank Shimko, the best electrician and grip anywhere, worked there often. There were also Al Wertheim and Kurt Baker in the office. Al went on to become a well-known AD on *Saturday Night Fever*, among other films,. Kurt was first assistant on *The Supercops* with me.

Also a regular at MPO was Marty Hornstein. He would produce *Silent Running*, then move to Hollywood. It was my pleasure to work with him again on *Futureworld* and *The Ultimate Warrior*. He would later produce four of the last *Star Trek* films. He introduced to me one of the writers on *Silent Running*, a quiet man named Mike Cimino. He would later direct *Deer Hunter* and *Heaven's Gate*.

VPI, Video Pictures Inc., lived in a big building on 44th Street just west of 8th Avenue. Ed Casper founded it. He had previously headed Filmways Studios, with headquarters on 125th Street. His chief salesman had been Martin Ransohoff, a charismatic man with a talent for writing and for finding the right market for the right project. Originally Filmways had been a very large and successful producer of TV commercials. With the advent of their first TV show, *Mr. Ed*, the story goes, Ed Casper and Marty Ransohoff had to decide whether to stay with commercials or to branch out into feature films and TV. The story, which may be apocryphal, is that this was decided on the flip of a coin, which Ransohoff won. He bought out Casper. Then he went on to make *Beverly Hillbillies*, which was a very big hit, among other films and TV shows.

Ed Casper, a successful TV commercial producer, still wanted to produce. Walking down 44th Street after the split-up, he noticed a large warehouse available for rent. On a whim he rented it and formed VPI, which grew into one of the largest, most successful TV commercial producers in the city. His list of directors and cameramen was a virtual who's who of New York production. When I worked there his head of production was Roger Rothstein who would later head production in Hollywood for Paramount Pictures; Bob Schneider, later a very successful UPM in Hollywood (*Officer and a Gentleman*), and Ted Zachary, later to work as head of production for Tri-Star Pictures, also worked there. A carrier of film cans for the editing department at the time was John Nicolella who would rise to produce *Miami Vice* and *Nash Bridges*, among other famous shows, before his too early passing at age 53 in Hollywood.

One of the more amusing directors I worked with at VPI was Jerry Kaufman. Jerry had absolutely no concept of budget and imagined that the entire staff at VPI was hired to service him and him alone. He wore jodhpurs and riding pants and carried a riding crop, just as he had seen Cecil DeMille do. He took out a full-page ad in the local TV commercial newspaper with a photo of himself walking on Fifth Avenue in this outlandish get-up, with just the caption, "The Director," nothing more. Not even his name. Confused more possible clients than attracted. He fancied himself a cameraman as well, but with little concept of how a camera worked. We filmed a commercial on Fifth Avenue and 59th Street once. He took the same shot with the camera five times; at f/5.6, f/8, f/11, f/16, and f/22. His assistant cameraman, an exacting, precise man named Arnold Farquhar Trelawney Kotis, whose hobby was making exquisite watches, watched Jerry reset the f-stop this way. Jerry said, "I want you to know that I have a very good reason for doing this." Arnold replied, "I already know the reason; you don't have to tell me."

Jerry had a way of charming clients, especially lady clients. He would say very silly things and they would die laughing. When touch-tone phones came into general use I watched him convince a client that he could dial the phone by saying "Boop-boop-beep-bop" into the phone, imitating the dial sounds.

When we went out for a location shoot we usually had lunch delivered. It was originally a box lunch, quite good, really, with either a large sandwich or two regular sandwiches, an apple or other fruit, a sweet roll for dessert, some milk and fruit juice containers, and plenty of napkins. It was rather like a picnic. Nobody complained. Rather, everybody complained but nobody took it seriously. During the later 1960s, mobile kitchens sprung up, and the food began to be better. At least warmer. Sometimes the food was prepared at a kitchen in Manhattan and brought to the set in chafing dishes, but as time wore on more and more mobile kitchens came into use. For commercials the producers usually tried to impress the clients with elaborate meals such as prime rib, ham, steak, even lobster and crab. Such meals are normal now for TV series and features as well. The craft service man who started with coffee and donuts now is a catering service all in itself. A set I visited recently proudly showed me the craft service kitchen where the crew was being served sushi, of all things, on demand. I guess that's progress. Are the commercials better? Do the products sell more because the crew eats sushi? I'm sure that would make an interesting study.

The larger TV commercial producers in New York in the 1960s operated much like the major studios in Hollywood. They had departments and department heads who supplied the units with equipment from their own stock rooms, and crews they had on staff for the purpose. Or at least crewmembers that were well known to one or another company and stayed available for that company, knowing that they would have a choice of jobs when they became available. Like all good production managers I had a regular crew, usually staffed two or three deep so if one were not available I could call another. Many of these department heads owned their own equipment, including the cameramen who could supply their own cameras. One cameraman, in fact owned BNC #1, (Blimped Noiseless Camera), a real collectors' item. First sound camera built by the venerable Mitchell Company. Of course the most popular, and the best, underwater cameramen owned not only their own cameras but had usually built their underwater housings, which they maintained themselves. Jordan Klein owned a famous yacht completely rigged out for underwater photography.

The commercials field was just as full of certified characters as was the feature films field. I worked side by side with assistant director Steve Gluck on many commercials, where he was on one sound stage and I on another. He had a violent temper. Knocked out a director who crossed him once. In school he had been expelled for throwing a teacher out a window. First floor window. Excellent AD, if a bit eccentric. For a car commercial to be filmed in Yankee Stadium with Mickey Mantle he had the car washed the day before the filming, then entirely covered in Saran Wrap so it would keep its shine no matter how much junk fell out of the air onto it. New York air is famous for being among the dirtiest in the world. Literally tons of dust and dirt fall from the air into Manhattan every day.

Lucy and I lived in the Forest Hills apartment until 1968 or so and then decided that my income would permit us to move upstate to Westchester County. Instead of buying a house right off, we moved to an apartment in Scarsdale so we could be closer to where we would be looking. Also we could enroll little Chris into a Montessori School which would give him an advantage in his education. We found an apartment on Wiltshire Road, right near a Gristede's supermarket, and moved in. A few of my friends from the movie industry were living in the neighborhood also, which made it convenient. Not convenient was the new commuting schedule I had to keep. Non-shooting days were not bad. Shooting days could be brutal. With traffic, even early morning traffic when the trains did not yet make their regular work-hour runs, it was not unusual to take an hour or an hour and a half in each direction. On snowy days it could be more.

The really good part was that I had a sanctuary far away from the madness of New York. I was accustomed to somewhat more leisurely life rhythm. New York had a rhythm all its own. I have traveled around Europe and North America and have never again seen life as in New York. Now, in Scarsdale, it was quiet and more tranquil than in the city. I did not like Manhattan. It had lost the charm I felt when I first saw all the famous landmarks, the Statue of Liberty, Empire State Building, Triborough Bridge. I had felt I was in the center of the world. Now the center was beginning to have a few rough edges.

Regular passers-by when we were filming took on a whole different aspect. Some would without a second thought stand in front of the camera so we couldn't shoot. We had the TPF with us, but they usually explained that the New Yorker had as much right to be on the street as we did, and nobody could move the obstructers. This happened regularly. Or we would be filming on the street and a shop owner nearby would come out of his store and begin to make a huge fuss, and a lot of noise, until we paid him to leave us alone. This became a lucrative kind of game with New Yorkers, and a costly one for filmmakers.

Another annoyance was and still is parking. In any other city one "posts" the streets, putting up signs saying that a film company needs this block of parking spaces and no parking except for film trucks is permitted between certain hours. New Yorkers normally ignore such signs and park wherever they wish, legally or illegally. There might be a dozen trucks, everything from camera truck to property carriers to wardrobe, makeup wagons, "Honey-wagons" with six or eight dressing rooms in a row in the trailer. The first remedy was to have a line of tow trucks appear at the filming site an hour prior to the film tucks arriving to tow illegally parked cars. This was costly and time consuming. The second remedy was also costly but more efficient. Hire Teamsters and the trucks for an extra day prior to filming. Have the trucks standing by to move into a parking space vacated by a local. This the day before filming. This usually worked best on the first day of filming or on a Monday, but during the week the trucks would move overnight from the previous day's location to the one for the following day. The trucks could not afford to wait all day the previous day because they were in use on the set. So we went to Plan "B." This consisted of having the crew's family arrive with the family car the day before filming and park in the trucks' spaces for the next day, to preserve them for the trucks' arrival the following day.

The corollary to this is that the film company also then has to pay for the families' meals when waiting for the spaces to open. And the parking fees. And gasoline. And any parking tickets incurred. In almost any other city in the country this problem does not exist, since people usually obey "No Parking" signs.

Traffic in Manhattan has always been a problem. The city was built when most people had horses, long before the automobile was invented. When I first moved to New York many of the streets were still paved with cobblestone, which is very hard on car suspensions. Much of this has been changed by now. But fifty years ago it was still medieval. The streets were built narrow enough to be practical, just wide enough to accommodate a horse and carriage, or two horses going in opposite directions, certainly not cars. Almost all the New York streets are now one-way which alleviates the problem somewhat. But there are still odd incidents. I once witnessed a fire truck driving down a narrow street to get to a fire. A passenger car had blocked the street by double-parking, and the driver was standing next to the car. The fire engine had its siren cranked up to its loudest volume, shrieking and wailing. The car driver not only refused to move, but also walked back to the fire truck and complained about the noise. He didn't seem to care that a house was burning down a block away.

CHAPTER 21

VALLEY OF THE DOLLS

After 1968 I worked mostly on feature films in New York. Began with *Valley of the Dolls*. Mark Robson was directing for producer David Weisbart. The Jacqueline Susann novel was partially based on biographies of those involved. Judy Garland had been signed to play the role patterned after her, but Susan Hayward, an actress far easier to manage, eventually replaced her. Mark Robson was a wonderful, intuitive director. I learned much from the AD from L.A., Eli Dunn. The PM was the legendary Francisco "Chico" Day, brother of the actor Gilbert Roland. Twentieth Century-Fox produced the film. I could never be sure but I was fairly certain that Doc Merman had a hand in hiring me. I worked on several films for Fox in New York.

Hollywood of course is more comfortable filming. But sometimes it serves their purpose, for reasons of accuracy or atmosphere, to film on location in New York, to catch the flavor of the city. Every major studio has a "New York Street" on the back lot. Nothing will ever match the real thing, however. Films like *On the Waterfront* and *The Supercops* were filmed entirely in New York for that reason. There is a texture to the city that doesn't exist on any back lot. TV shows like *NYPD Blue* and *Law and Order* also take advantage of the New York atmosphere to great effect.

But most of the films only shot for a week or two in New York, and did most of their filming, and all the studio work, in Hollywood. This entailed quite an expense, because due to the union contract only certain crewmembers were allowed to travel to the other coast and those must be matched by native members from the location. There was therefore an extra cameraman, gaffer, key grip, and so forth. I was the additional AD. Eli Dunn actually ran the set and I acted more as a 2nd AD, doing paperwork, and handling extras. Sometimes when Eli had to leave the set for any reason I took over, but normally he was the boss.

Two people came to tragic ends immediately surrounding the filming of *Valley of the Dolls*. David Weisbart, the producer, suffered a fatal heart attack while playing golf in Los Angeles during the filming. On the set the word was that he hit the ball, said, "It's a wonderful life" and fell to the ground. Weisbart, whom I met a couple of times, was what is known in Hollywood as a "mensch." Sharon Tate was to be viciously murdered by the Manson gang two years later.

Adventures In Hollywood: A Memoir By Bob Koster

She was a fine actress and a lovely person.

I had my first real taste of New York major filming with *Valley of the Dolls*. (The very first film I had worked on in New York was *Up the Down Staircase*, but I only worked that for two weeks to help with the extras. I was assigned to *Valley of the Dolls* as the 1st AD from NY.) We filmed at Rockefeller Center near the ice rink. There were two cameras, lights, cables all over the sidewalk, police keeping the gawkers back, movie stars, and perhaps a thousand tourists and locals watching the filming from behind the police lines. I was carrying my clipboard, so I must have been one of those in the know. Presently a local caught my eye and asked me a question. "Are you shooting a movie?" It wouldn't be the last time I was asked that question.

Paul Burke and I, I found, were brothers under the skin. He slept overnight in his motor home right at the location so he could have his morning coffee and walk right out to the set. Every morning he and I had the same routine. I knocked on his door and identified myself. He asked me in. He was in the back bedroom, always attended, usually with a different lady every day. As the two looked up sleepily from the bed he would say, "Bob, I want you to meet my new secretary, (insert name here)." I paid the lady her due respect, even if she was stark naked, and left the motor home confident that Paul would be on set in a half hour. He always was.

The surprising person was Patty Duke. She had a reputation for being temperamental and eccentric. I found her to be professional in every respect, worked well with the crew, and generally belied all the rumors. Good actress, too.

Bill Daniels, the cameraman, was a Hollywood standard. In his heyday—from the time he started to the time he retired—he was the cameraman of choice for many of Hollywood's more famous actresses because of his magnificent lighting ability. He was also a shameless tyrant to the production department and delighted in making us look foolish. One learns however to indulge the artist if the finished product reflects the effort, and that was the case with Bill.

After *Valley of the Dolls* I worked in the commercial world less and less. I much preferred to have a job lasting four months or longer to one lasting four days. I also discovered that the Hollywood studios considered me one of their own since I had joined the DGA on the West Coast. For this reason I was called on regularly to handle the "New York Unit" for several companies. I was still working on pieces of film, never a real, whole, movie and I was always second banana to the Hollywood production department, who looked on themselves as the real professionals and the New York boys as day players. Obviously the reverse was the case. We New York boys considered the Hollywood crowd a bunch of spoiled children who could not operate outside the studio system, and were not street smart like we were.

The reality is that a good production person can adapt to any contingency and can work equally well on either coast. Chico Day certainly could, and Dave Salven as well. I worked with both, and I worked with crews on both coasts, and

I found that there are real eccentric characters on both coasts, good workers, and a few bad apples. One adapts.

New York seemed to have more than its share of legends, however. Tommy "Mother" Brown was a legendary key grip, had worked with Elia Kazan on his New York films, knew the gripping business better than almost anyone on either coast. I saw him carry twelve-foot flats around, perfectly balanced off one arm. There were also property masters who became legends. Norman Koppleman was one. He became an instant legend when he was asked to return a priceless Ming vase to the museum after shooting was finished. He tripped getting out of the cab, and delivered a bag full of vase pieces to the curator. Later, when the union decided to put him into a less fragile position, he became a sound boom operator. To my knowledge he still holds the record for unwiring the Fisher boom, at about five seconds. He unscrewed the wrong bolt. Another prop man, Jack Porte, dropped a heavy washing machine on the foot of the producer, severely damaging it. The pain was so great that the man went into shock and uttered not a word. Then Jack asked him to pick up his side.

Studios were also legendary in New York. Filmways Studio on 125th Street had yet another legend attached to it after advertising that although it was all the way uptown it was the safest studio in New York. No burglaries had ever happened there. Within a week someone talked their way past the studio gate guards and drove off with a yacht. I myself was working on that lot and just to see if it could be done I walked off the lot with a very large silver bowl filled with fruit. Nobody stopped me or questioned me. I immediately returned and took the bowl to the head of security, who perhaps changed the system to make it more secure.

Then there was Boken Studios. It lived on 55th Street near 8th Avenue. When I filmed there the one bathroom, meaning unisex, was in an alcove behind the cyclorama at the far end of the stage. In what must have been an economic effort, no lock was put on the door, which opened outward. To insure privacy the user sat on the commode holding a rope that held the door shut. I was there the day a diminutive lady producer from the agency used the facility, and one of the heftier grips needed to. He yanked the door open with the expected result.

Fox Studios was on 55th Street and 11th Avenue. It was famous for having one of the largest sound stages in New York. Attached to that, and accessible only through the large sound stage, was a smaller stage for lighter work. This gave rise to another legendary story. A commercial director named Peter Elgar was working in the big sound stage. He was famous for having a terrible temper. This day he became enraged at a grip and ordered his UPM/AD to fire him. "Pay him off and get him out of here!" The AD did. Wrote him a check and told him to go home. The next day the grip landed a job on the smaller stage with another company. Naturally he had to go through the larger stage to get to work. When he did, Peter Elgar saw him. He lost his temper as usual, and yelled at the AD, "I thought I told you to fire that man! Now pay him off and get him out of here!" The AD protested, "But sir..." "No buts! Pay him off and get him out of here!!!" "Mr. Elgar, he doesn't..." "I don't care what he doesn't do!!! Pay him off and get him out of here!!!" The AD wrote out another check and told the man to go around in back of the sets to get to his smaller stage for work.

Working in TV commercials was an excellent school for learning how an AD/UPM is supposed to work. In a compressed period of time it was necessary to produce an entire little film. Sometimes this effort was compressed into a few days, or a week. I arrived at the office, saw the script and storyboard. Then I sat with the director and producer to find out what elements were necessary to make the spot work. Next step was writing a budget. Sometimes this was done in concert with the company's production manager. This was given to the company producer who passed it to the advertising agency. The agency approved it, let's say. Sometimes the budget had been submitted and approved before I ever got there, and I started with the next step. Next I hired a crew, or gathered a crew from those already on staff at the company. Usually this was done in conjunction with the director who had his or her favorites. Most of the time this was done in concert with the cameraman who had his own set crew.

Next step was finding the proper location. Very few commercials were filmed in more than one location, and we usually knew what the producer and director wanted in this regard. Many times we only filmed in a studio. At the same time the advert agency was casting the commercial from the very rich supply of good actors in New York. It was my pleasure to work with such varied and talented people. Kenny Delmar was memorable. He performed as "Senator Claghorn" from the old Fred Allen show between takes for us. Margaret Hamilton, who had played the "Wicked Witch" in *The Wizard of Oz*, made commercials for Maxwell House Coffee, and was one of he nicest, sweetest ladies I ever knew. Many other people came in and out. Ed McMahon did beer commercials. Outside of the fact that he arrived in a limousine he was no different than anyone else. Wilt "The Stilt" Chamberlain made a memorable commercial for Volkswagen in which he managed to fold himself into a Beetle. He arrived early, performed well, and left late. Easy to direct.

If a comedian were cast in a commercial the other employees of the advert agency and the production company found reasons to go to the studio or location, just to check it out. Some of the comedians were compulsive and fed on the laughter they got from the crew. This could hold up filming for a while until everyone settled down again.

It was also not unusual for agencies to insist on location filming so they could get out of NY to milder climates, during the winter. During the summer, Canada was popular.

Next step was the actual filming, which could take a day or two, or in rare cases, more. If we were going to distant location where the cast and crew had to stay overnight, it could take a day to get to the location, a day to film, and a day to return. Many times this was done in an area that necessitated an overnight stay for no other reason than that the agency people wanted to go away on an overnight stay and were willing to pay for it.

The last step in the commercial production process is post-production. The film has to be edited, music applied, sound effects, and prints made to send to TV stations all across the country. That was then, of course. Nowadays the editing, effects and music are all done electronically, and the distribution, I assume is over the Internet by secure channel. No film is ever used, and no physical elements ever change hands. The editing is electronic. The product is an MPEG file. This can be easily transmitted over the Internet quickly. No "chain" such as we used at WPIX exists any longer. The editing process probably takes a couple of days, the approval another day or two, and then the commercial goes out over the air like magic.

All these elements exist but in much larger volume with TV shows and feature films. Your average TV commercial takes a week or two to produce from start to finish. An hour-long show takes seven or eight days to shoot, then another week or two to finish the post-production. Maybe a month or a bit longer, all told. A movie of the week a little longer than that. Say, average 18-20-day shoot, six weeks or so in post production. Feature film can take two months to shoot, or if it's a big blockbuster film it can take a year or more. James Cameron takes much longer than that. Then another two or three years in postproduction what with all the computer generated imagery and special effects. The budgets reflect this difference as well. When I was budgeting films for the major studios in the late 1970s and early 1980s our average cost was $3½ million below-the-line, meaning the direct cost of the film less the cost of the actors, director, producers, and script. At this writing that has risen to well over $50 million. And a good name actor can cost $10-20 million, plus the extras. By extras I mean how the studio has to pad the actor's contract in order to persuade him or her to be in the picture, such as chauffeured limousine, bodyguard, perks for the family, and so on. It can add up.

Back at WCBS in New York, *Eye on New York* spent maybe $15,000-20,000 per half hour show. When I worked on TV series back in the 1970s and 80s an hour show cost around $250,000-$300,000 unless you were in the super class range and your producer had lots of pull with the network. Then a show could cost up to $1,000,000.

I got into TV and feature film production around 1968, having served an apprenticeship for four years or so in commercials. After that I did not work in commercials very much, just sometimes between films. Then I found that my presence in the commercial world was enhanced by my theatrical work. TV ad agency producers wanted to employ me because I had stories to tell about the films I had worked on. It added to their prestige in the office to tell some stories from the feature film set. In any case after four years I was one of the more steadily employed

ADs in the commercials business. I worked ten to eleven months of the year, took time off when I wanted to, and Lucy and I took vacations in the Virgin Islands and the Bahamas when we pleased. Not really, just between shoots, but that was really our call, not anyone else's.

CHAPTER 22

GALFAS

I did work for a brief period for Timothy Galfas as his PM/AD on staff. We did a number of in-house commercials on Galfas' own sound stage. Timothy was a Greek eccentric. Some of his ten children or so worked for the company as well. I came in as the production manager, budgeting all his commercials and eventually working the set as the AD.

I took this photo of the Matterhorn from Zermatt

We did one memorable commercial for Swissair Airlines that took us to Zermatt, Switzerland. One of the most beautiful little towns in the world, directly in the shadow of the Matterhorn.

We filmed on the ski slopes in March when the weather was just perfect. If anything existed to keep us from the point of boredom, it was the agency producer. This gentleman, who later won awards with the commercial and a promotion to VP within the agency, startled me on the flight over to Europe by asking me why he had to set his watch forward five hours during the flight. I explained to him that the Earth rotates on its axis and at any one time part of the Earth is lit by sunlight and the other part is in shadow, and so forth until he understood the day-night relationship. And what causes dawn and dusk. You just never know about people. He seemed well educated when we met.

The last commercial I made for Galfas was for Skippy Peanut Butter. It was one of those "Let's go to Hollywood and film on the beach" jobs. The agency producer was a grossly overweight lady whose back was constantly in pain, a fact she did little to hide from us. The cameraman, Dick Glouner, divided his time between filming and giving her back rubs just to keep her from moaning. Timothy, as was his wont, managed to rent a Mustang Shelby 500 KR for his own personal use while we were in L.A.. This car was halfway to a racer and as such had no power steering. Tim gamely kept tugging at the steering wheel to turn the car during parking, not an easy task. But Tim would rather keep tugging than admit the car was a bear to drive, so he drove alone most of the time. I guess it was no worse than his Aston-Martin DB4 he had in New York. Car nut? You bet.

Like many commercial directors Tim dreamed of hitting the big time in feature films, and was constantly making appointments with publicists and Hollywood producers toward that end.

A week before we left Tim had hired a new VP Production, Dick Lowe, who felt horribly threatened by my presence. He was not a DGA member, knew next to nothing about commercial production, but he had a pleasant voice and manner and could be a good salesman. While we were in L.A. he fiddled with the books to make it appear I had taken more money in petty cash than I was due, which pitted me against Tim Galfas. Rather than fight the issue I paid the difference and left the company. I had plenty of work without them and figured it was their loss if that's what they wanted to do.

CHAPTER 23

RACHEL, RACHEL

I was hired by Kayos Productions to be the second assistant director on Paul Newman's second directing effort, *Rachel, Rachel*. Filming was done entirely in Danbury, CT. Most of the crew was put up at the Danbury Inn, but I lived only a half hour away in Scarsdale at the time, so I could drive easily. Harrison Starr was the production manager and Alan Hopkins was the first assistant.

This film was a real treat. We were away from the hustle and bustle of New York City. Our crew was excellent. Gayne Rescher was on camera and Dede Allen edited. Harrison had designed the shoot to be as efficient and as accommodating for Paul Newman as possible. Paul was an excellent actor's director but did not have a great feel for editing or camera angles, and that's where Gayne and Dede sparkled. Paul's choice of actors to surround his wonderfully creative wife, Joanne Woodward, was also outstanding. Kate Harringon, Estelle Parsons, Donald Moffat, and Jim Olson, not to mention Terry Kiser, who brilliantly played an evangelist preacher who spoke in tongues, all added immeasurably to the project.

(N.B. Sometimes it pays to hire local talent. I usually tried to do so whenever I was on location. We checked with local theatre groups and drama schools for talent. In this case the fellow who played the local pharmacist was the local pharmacist, who happened to also be an amateur actor. He played the role remarkably well.)

One amusing incident: There was an exceptionally handsome crew member whose name was also Bob, and whose voice was similar to mine. One day I was alone in the production office when the phone rang. "Hello." "Hello, Bob?" "Yes." "Look, Bob, I can't meet you tonight. My husband is growing suspicious." "Are you sure you are speaking to the right Bob?" Click.

At the time Paul was driving a VW convertible, the old Beetle. Except it had a Porsche engine. In those days the mounting hardware for both cars was essentially the same. He enjoyed driving it home after work, putting the car in low gear and driving it away, up to 40-50 miles per hour, without ever shifting gears into second. It sounded quite wicked. Paul and Joanne lived in Weston, CT, not far from Danbury, so they were able to drive home every evening.

A few of the minor crew people later rose to prominence. We had three production assistants who later became well known production people. Phil Goldfarb would move to Hollywood and manage the production department for Steven Bochco. He also produced several films, including *Flyboys* and *The Librarian*. George Manasse would later be the production manager of the TV series *The District*, among other projects. Ed Foulger would found the Inuit Broadcasting Company, by and for the Eskimos, and spent years living on Frobisher Bay in Northern Canada.

Cast & crew of Rachel Rachel. I stand at upper right.
Joanne Woodward and Paul Newman second row center

CHAPTER 24

FOR LOVE OF IVY

Around this time I was hired by Palomar Pictures, Edgar Scherick, to work as the 2nd AD on a new film by Danny Mann, entitled *For Love of Ivy*. This starred Sidney Poitier and Abby Lincoln in the leads, with Beau Bridges, Carroll O'Connor, Nan Martin, Leon Bibb, and a host of other good actors in supporting roles. The UPM was Joel Glickman and the 1st AD was Johnny Murphy.

I joined the crew about three weeks prior to filming. Sets were already being built and locations scouted for the show. John Murphy had been on payroll for several weeks and had prepared a schedule. He had been following Danny Mann around scouting locations. I had never worked on an entire film before except for *Mr. Hobbs* six years prior on the West Coast.

Before accepting the job I had spoken to several people who had worked with that crew before. They were unanimous about the abilities of Joel Glickman. "A disaster looking to happen," said one. "The most unqualified UPM in New York" said another. It turned out these were gross understatements. Further, John Murphy had never worked on a film before and had not the slightest idea how to either break down (analyze) a script or to schedule a production. His production board was a joke. Made absolutely no sense. I could not even schedule background talent from it, much less actors. In his efforts to save the company money Joel had hired an entirely inexperienced, and consequently inexpensive, AD.

Joel fired Murphy two days after I joined the crew and promoted me to 1st AD. He told me I had two weeks to prepare the film. I told him that was impossible. I had to make a whole new schedule. I had to see the locations with Danny Mann. There were a hundred and one details that needed attending to for the film to be shot with any expectation of efficiency. I begged him for two extra weeks of prep. I told him that he would have to pay in overtime for the lack of preparedness. It would be costly. He suggested that I come into the office every day, work during the day, then go home at night and do the breakdowns and schedule. No matter what I or anyone else said, Joel refused to budge and Ed Scherick, a novice producer, did not know enough.

In New York it was traditional for the paycheck to be handed out on Thursday to cover the work for the prior week. On Thursday of the second week I opened my paycheck and realized that a mistake had been made. I had been working many hours of overtime to get the schedule done but the check showed none. Something was wrong here. I went upstairs at the studio to the office to ask Joel about it only to find a long line of crew waiting outside his office to talk to him. I mean, a LONG line. Maybe twenty-five or thirty people. Naturally as the 1st AD I went right to the head of the line. I was important and I had important things to do. I couldn't wait for thirty people to talk to Joel. I had to go back to work. Leif Pedersen, one of the best set dressers in New York, was at the head of the line. He said, "Pay check?" I said, "Yes." He said, "End of the line. We all get to punch him first." In an effort to save the company money Joel had erased everyone's overtime from their time cards. The lost work time cost Joel more money than he had saved and he had to pay the overtime eventually anyway after a visit from various union representatives.

For the first two weeks I averaged two hours of sleep per night. My weight began to drop. I became less and less able to concentrate. Somehow I managed to finish the schedule on time, and the set construction resumed. We began shooting on location on Long Island.

Our locations were large. We were filming in a house on the North Shore, several acres of property. This was 1967. Walkie-talkies had not yet come into general use. The ADs had to operate with bullhorns, hand signals, signal mirrors, anything that could help us communicate. I needed a bullhorn just so the crew could hear the command to "Roll it!" Electric bullhorns had just come into use, making the old megaphones obsolete. Joel refused to rent me a bullhorn so I did so with my own money. Eventually Ed Scherick saw what had happened and reimbursed me.

Joel was one of those unfortunates who are unable to see any further into the future than the ends of their noses. He lived for the moment. He did whatever he could to save money right now at the expense of paying twice as much later. This became more evident as time went on. He was also a legend in New York for his lack of understanding and his temper.

One day Joel came downstairs to find the set painter working on the walls of the set. Joel had a list of actors and the director who needed to have their set chair backs personalized with their names. The better known ones had taller chairs with leather seats and backs, with their names worked into the leather and with pockets on the side arms for scripts and other papers. Joel read off the list to the man—"Abby Lincoln, Sidney Poitier, Danny Mann…" Joel paused, and then he said, "Oh, and by the way, make me one, too." The painter, never having seen Joel before, said, "What is your name?" "Joel Glickman." "What?" Then Joel said loudly, "Glickman! Glickman!" and stalked off. You guessed it. He got a chair whose back read "Glickman! Glickman!" From then on in New York he was known as "Glickman! Glickman!"

We did some filming in a nightclub known as the Village Gate. It was a kind of hippy nightclub scene with a few dozen beatniks listening to a poetry reading by a defrocked priest. We called the Screen Actors Guild and asked them to supply the proper amount of kids, but they had no such numbers in their ranks. Joel got permission to cast kids off the street as long as we paid them union minimum for extras, maybe $25 per day. We had an open casting call and Danny Mann chose three or four dozen kids from the streets of Greenwich Village to act in the movie.

The scene took three days to film and all those kids came back each day. Every day the 2nd AD had them make out extras vouchers for their paychecks. Each day they handed the vouchers in. Because of the stumbled prep time, the scene had not been prepared properly and we went quite a bit overtime each day. We did finish within the three days however. On Thursday of the next week all the extras lined up outside the studio to collect their paychecks, only to be told that there were none. Joel had gone so far over budget that week that he took the extras' vouchers and threw them away in the trash.

A few hours later, Phil Foster, the head of the Screen Actors Guild in New York, appeared at the door demanding to know why the extras hadn't been paid. Joel replied that there were no vouchers to pay them from so he assumed they had not worked. Phil then asked the assistant UPM, Pepe Saraga, if he had seen the extras vouchers. Pepe had. In fact he had collected them for Joel, and as a safeguard, had copied them all on the newly invented Xerox machine. Faced with that evidence, Joel paid, and a concomitant fine was imposed by SAG.

Another time a set was built for Sidney Poitier's apartment. The studio was the old TV Graphic Studios where I shot my first commercials. This was on the seventh floor of the building on Columbus Circle at 59th and Broadway and 8th Avenue. All the set materials had to be brought up in a huge freight elevator from street level. The studio was well constructed for its time. Mary Miles Mintner and Marie Dressler had trod the boards there. Now the floor was covered in Bakelite substance to give it a smooth dollying surface.

The floor plans called for the living room to be sumptuous, with the centerpiece a cylindrical aquarium for tropical fish in the center. The aquarium held maybe 100 gallons of water. The most efficient possible shape for an aquarium is cylindrical because the water pressure is equal throughout the glass, whereas when the aquarium is rectangular the water presses against the glass with more pressure in the center of the glass pane than on the edges. The art director knew this when he specified a cylinder standing on its end. Although the weight of 100 gallons of water, over 800 pounds, is considerable, the studio floor was well built and could take it.

The problem happened when Joel decided that a cylindrical water tank was too expensive. A rectangular one would have to do, with the same thin glass. This would work for the movie's budget but not for the laws of nature. During the filming the crew watched in horror as the sides of the aquarium began to bulge outward and eventually burst, spraying 100 gallons of water all over the floor. Fish were flopping around and seaweed was evident. The crew quickly grabbed as many fish as they could and dumped them into the nearest water pot, sink, toilet, anything available. The water went where it wanted to go.

First it severely warped the Bakelite floor, making its replacement necessary. Secondly it seeped through the floor to the ceiling of the floor below, where it dripped onto the contents. Just below the sound stage, I am told, was a mapmaker. Joel had saved the company perhaps $500-600 in glass, and cost the company thousands in floor replacement and map redrawing. By this time I had left the movie so I did not see this happen in person. I had stayed on for four weeks of filming. I had never recovered from the first two weeks and the two hours of sleep per night. I dropped from my normal 165 pounds to 135. Steve Barnett became the 1st AD and I, thankfully, was relieved. Joel stayed on to shepherd the film through to its severely over-budget wrap. He had the last laugh, if that's what it was. I found out months later that he had not paid my social security payments. The DGA, God bless them, interceded on my behalf and forced the payment. By that time I had regained my 165 pounds.

Both Chris and Kevin were born via Caesarian section. Right after Kevin was born Lucy became pregnant three months later. My fault. I couldn't resist Lucy any more than I could resist anyone else. This was not good because her Caesarian scar had not had a chance to heal yet. If she carried the baby to term it was nearly certain that the scar would rupture and she would hemorrhage internally with really bad results.

We told our doctor that we wanted to have an abortion immediately, possibly to save her life. The laws of the U.S. and the State of New York would not allow it, surprisingly. It was imperative that it happen soon, though. Through friends we were connected within a couple of days to a religious group that arranged for abortions —flights and hotel bills included— in London, where abortion was legal. We booked a trip for the following week.

Upon our arrival in London we rented a Vauxhall Viva, cute little compact car. Driver was on the wrong side of the car and the car was on the wrong side of the street, but I had done enough driving on location in the Bahamas that I was used to it. Lucy was not. Never mind. We went straight to the doctor's office, a pleasant place in a medical complex. In those days two doctors had to independently agree that an abortion was necessary for one to be legal in Britain. Our ob-gyn had an arrangement with the doctor in the next office to examine patients and give his opinion for that purpose. So Lucy was examined by the ob-gyn, and then went next door to the other doctor for the second exam. The next-door doctor was an ophthalmologist. Lucy sat on the examining table with her feet in the stirrups and read the eye chart between her legs. The opinions were duly given and the procedure was scheduled for the next day.

That evening we dined at a wonderful restaurant, Inigo Jones. I enjoyed the best London had to offer in gustatory delights. We went to bed early in preparation for the morrow.

While Lucy was occupied in the clinic I called an old friend who had worked many years before at Anchor Hat & Cap Company. Eddie Aspis lived in London, had married, and had a successful garment business. As most proper Brits, he belonged to several private clubs in London where he could eat, drink, wager, and dance to good music. He invited us to join his wife and him that evening. I accepted, not knowing if Lucy would be up to it. She was. We had a splendid meal, and we did dance that evening. It was a proper ending to a day of abortion.

Not knowing how she would feel I had arranged for our flight to be two days later, so we had a day to see London. I of course wanted to see the British Museum, Buckingham Palace, the usual sights. Lucy, who worked for *Mademoiselle* magazine at that time, wanted to go shopping. We went shopping. I still have my Turnbull & Asser shirt and tie.

CHAPTER 25

PENDULUM

In March 1968 John Vietch, production manager for Columbia Pictures, called me to help out with *Pendulum*. This film was produced by Stanley Niss, one of the truly great radio writers, and directed by George Schaefer, legendary director of many *Hallmark Hall of Fame* shows. Filming was at the beginning of April in Washington D.C. George Peppard, Jean Seberg, Richard Kiley, and others were to be in town. We stayed at the Washington D.C. Hilton on 14th and K streets. Dave Salven, the UPM/AD from Los Angeles, did a superb job of organizing this diverse group of artists into a well-orchestrated whole even under very trying circumstances.

We began filming on April 1, 1968, in Washington DC. We filmed at Lafayette Square. George Peppard was accompanied by his father and in between shots the two men sat at the side of the set playing chess. Jean Seberg was accompanied by her then-husband, the famous French writer Romain Gary. He held her coat while she was on camera. On Tuesday April 2 we filmed at the Jefferson Memorial. There was a considerable crowd gathered to watch the filming. Washington was full of tourists at that time of year and most of them came to the Jefferson Memorial and stayed to watch the filming. The 2nd AD, Howard Koch Jr., and I had our hands full keeping them away from the actors and keeping the film crew insulated from the hubbub. Somehow it worked.

The next two days took place at the office of Senator Vance Hartke in the Senate Building. I was approached by one of Hartke's staff who had written a thrilling screenplay about a senator who solves a murder mystery. He thought that since I had a clipboard I must be important and could possibly help him to get his film produced. This was not the first time and would certainly not be the last.

On the 4th of April, while we were filming at the U.S. District Court Building at 3rd and C Streets, Martin Luther King Jr. was assassinated. After that things happened very quickly. We were filming a scene in which Jean Seberg drives up to the courthouse in a taxi, exits the cab, runs up the steps, and enters the revolving doors. In the second take, just as she was running up the steps, suddenly the brass doors protecting the revolving doors swung shut and slammed with a sense of finality. At the same time a large group of angry D.C. citizens started marching down Constitution Avenue in our direction, carrying picket signs and making menacing gestures. Dave Salven quickly called a wrap to the filming. We packed the equipment into the trucks as fast as possible and beat a hasty retreat to the hotel. The crew and extras went into the buses and the trucks took off for the hotel as well.

The hotel was on 14th and K streets, the location on 3rd and C streets. The distance is about 1½ miles and normally takes about ten minutes to drive. This was by no means normal. The streets suddenly were filled with angry rioters, government officials trying to leave downtown to get home, chaos everywhere. In the distance gunshots could be heard. The police were struggling to keep order. It took a full three hours to return to the hotel, and then we were quarantined inside the hotel for two days while the war roared on around us.

The hotel was guarded by Army soldiers in battle uniform, flak jackets, plastic shields, full battle regalia. They hustled us into the hotel and told us to stay there until the all clear was given. This would not happen for two days. Any time we even came near the front door of the hotel we were warned back by the soldiers. There just had not been enough police to manage the city, and there were riots all over the place.

This was outrageous. Here we were, moviemakers in our country's capitol, for goodness sakes, and we couldn't even shoot. Not only that, but we couldn't leave the hotel. There were frantic discussions on how we might sneak out of the hotel just to grab a few shots so the time wouldn't be entirely wasted. There was great disappointment that the airport had been shut down. We couldn't leave town. Didn't these people realize that we were their friends? We were innocent, I tell you. We shouldn't be punished this way. We had a schedule to keep. We were being prevented from just doing our innocent job of entertaining the public. It was an outrage, and it was felt in Hollywood as well as in our hotel rooms and offices. The myopia that attends filming was never more in evidence than during those few days.

Our offices and hotel rooms were well above the 14th floor of the hotel so whatever happened did so on the streets below. It was distant and interesting. We did not feel threatened in the least. Dave Salven had laid in a good supply of potables and munchies in the office and since filming was out of the question we partook liberally. The secretaries were on the phone trying to arrange for the Los Angeles crew to return to Hollywood as soon as possible, a task made more difficult by our not being allowed to leave the hotel. The few crew from New York wanted to drive home. For now we were safely locked in the hotel with our cars parked safely in the underground parking lot. We were hampered by the fact that fires were breaking out throughout the city. Looting was rampant. People could be seen on the streets pushing racks of clothes looted from clothing stores, carrying TV sets, carrying anything they could carry. If they saw a car driving their reaction was to break all the car's windows and steal the car from the hapless owner. Some D.C. natives managed to scrawl "SOUL BROTHER" and other terms on car windows with soap but this usually merely slowed the rioters, did not stop them entirely.

Many people were dragged from their cars and beaten. A few people could be seen on rooftops with rifles shooting at people on the streets at random. We, on the 14th floor, were safe.

Leaving the city was a big problem. National Airport was shut down. Driving the twenty-five miles to Dulles was out of the question. We could look out over the city from our hotel windows and see fires on practically every block. We could hear people shouting, occasional gunshots, the sound of riots. We could see people down on the streets running about, congregating in small and large groups, going into and out of stores with whatever they could carry. It was frightening. For our part the movie people had trouble understanding why their needs for returning to Hollywood were put on such a low priority by the travel people who had an entire government to cope with. Everyone wanted to leave town. Congressmen, clothiers, shop owners, everyone, and finally movie people. It took three or four days to make the proper connections, and the Hollywood cast and crew finally were given clearance to leave the city. The caravan with buses and equipment trucks left the hotel the next morning early. The buses went to the airport and the equipment trucks started the long drive back to Hollywood.

I stayed in town for an extra day with Dave Salven to find areas where we would be filming background plates for rear projection. If we couldn't bring the actors to Washington, we would bring Washington to the actors and work on the sound stage with rear projection to emulate Washington DC. I took extensive notes, then drove back to New York.

From our apartment in Scarsdale I phoned John Vietch at Columbia. We decided that I would take a cameraman and assistant, and an "insert car" to Washington in one week to film the background "plates" for RP. This was done. When we returned to Washington the city was still burning in scattered areas. In the film now, especially during Jean Seberg's taxi ride through the city, through the rear window of the cab can be seen some smoke from fires still burning in the streets.

CHAPTER 26

COMMERCIALS

Back to New York and more commercials for a while. Motion Associates hired me to manage a commercial they were making for Gulf Oil. I have always been something of a car nut so this really appealed to me. It consisted of a Chevy Camaro, heavily modified, driving around the Bridgehampton Racetrack at speed. The owner/driver explained his arrangement with the Chevrolet factory. He worked for Kodak. He was trading Kodak resources with a photography enthusiast at Chevy for racing help and supplies. His car was superbly prepped. Easily topped 175 mph. You can imagine my surprise and delight when he asked me if I would like to take a drive around the track as a passenger.

I draped myself around the roll cage in the cabin. There was no passenger seat and no seat belt. He cut loose and went around at maximum speed, 175–180 mph. I was yelling in glee but nobody could hear me over the sound of the motor. Heck, I couldn't even hear me. This was one of the most thrilling rides I have ever had.

Another commercial was for the Tourist Board of the Bahamas. We were hired by the advertising agency to make commercials designed by psychologists to lure tourists down to the islands. We had at our disposal fourteen of the most beautiful models in New York. The director was Silvio Narizzano who had directed *Georgy Girl*. He had a fine sense of directing personal films.

We flew down to Nassau and checked in to one of the more plush hotels. The agency had insisted on only the best. No second-class hotels for their models. The commercial had these models sitting on the water in various seductive poses. The lead model was to say, "Let's say I'm an island. I have warm, inviting beaches…" At the same time she was to hug herself and caress her shoulders and arms in a loving way. When this was voiced in the production meeting in New York I saw Silvio, one of the finest directors in the world, merely nod and smile. His substantial salary served to support his feature film career and he was more than happy to serve the agency however they wished.

I had seen this before. Sir Laurence Olivier, for instance, admitted openly that he appeared in Hollywood films to support his British stage appearances. Same with Gielgud and most other actors of note.

For myself I found when I got into theatrical films and TV shows that about one in four was a "magic" show in which everyone got along and the final product was more than a mere movie. *Man in the Glass Booth* was one, as were *Greaser's Palace* and *Judge Dee*. These films were such a pleasure to work on that the routine shows in between served to pay for the special ones. Of course, while I was working on them, almost all were special in my mind.

Here we were on the most beautiful islands in the world. We needed some things in order to film. For one we needed a means of making the models appear to be sitting on the water. This would entail building some structure that would float an inch or two below water level. We hired a local contractor to design and build the platform. It would be a wooden platform, about 20 feet on a side, large enough for fourteen models to sit comfortably. Underneath would be a steel structure on which we could place sandbags to weigh it down to where it rested just below the surface. Luckily the beach the agency had chosen had very little wave motion so the water was placid. But it did have a very sharp drop off to deep water, which made it difficult to place the sandbags so as to keep the platform level.

All these problems were made worse by the Bahamian sense of urgency. There wasn't any. If we wanted to begin work at 8:00 am, the Bahamians might show up early, like at 10:00 am. Or at a more normal time, 10:30 or 11:00. What should have been a two-day job was finished in four days.

Then came the second problem. We needed manpower to place the sandbags on the steel structure. There were only about five or six of us capable of doing this, and we needed another dozen or more if we were to proceed in a reasonable time. I phoned my friend Cordell Thompson, our contact at the Bahamas Tourist Board, and explained the need. A dozen strong men? No problem.

Next morning a white bus pulled up at the beach. First out was a very large guard with a rifle. Next were a dozen strong men in striped uniforms, all chained together by their ankles. The chains were duly removed and weighted balls attached to their ankle chains. They were shown the stack of sandbags and the pile of sand. They divided themselves up into the bag fillers and the bag placers. That job was finished in a half day. The gentlemen in the striped pajamas left in the bus. We shot the commercial the same day.

We needed some extra shots around the islands so we stayed for an extra three days to do that. At noon the second day we received the dailies for the first day's shoot. The agency wanted to see them soon. I walked a block down the street from the hotel to the town cinema. Sure, the manager would be happy to let us show our dailies in his theatre. That evening we showed up at the theatre, not knowing exactly what to expect. The manager had roped off the two rear rows of chairs for our use. The movie was playing and we took our seats. After about ten minutes, the movie suddenly went off and our dailies were played for us, and for about 100 Bahamians who had come to see a movie. They did not seem to realize that the dailies were not part of the film. The dailies played for fifteen minutes or so, then they went off and the movie went back on. The audience never knew the difference. It was all part of the same show for them. We went back to the manager's office, retrieved our film, and returned to the hotel.

(NB: We also looked for locations at Cabbage Beach on the windward side of Pig Island. Just beautiful and relatively untouched, but too far away from Nassau for the construction to happen. A couple of years later Howard Hughes would buy the island and rename it Paradise Island. "Cabbage" Beach became "Paradise" Beach. Hughes built a bridge to Pig—er—Paradise Island to make it more accessible.)

CHAPTER 27

HELLO, DOLLY!

Next week I went to work on *Hello Dolly!* 20th Century-Fox was filming just upstate from New York City. We had taken over Garrison, NY, the town directly across the Hudson River from West Point. It had been rebuilt to look like Yonkers around the turn of the century.

If ever there were a star film, this was it. Barbra Streisand and Walter Matthau led an all-star cast that included Tommy Tune and Michael Crawford. The producers included legends such as Ernest Lehman and Roger Edens. Gene Kelly directed, along with his friend Michael Kidd. Kidd did most of the choreography. Harry Stradling was cameraman. I was the 1st AD from New York. Paul Helmick actually ran the set, being the L.A. AD.

During large crowd scenes I got into costume to be able to work with the extras more closely.

Kurt Baker, another assistant director, and I,
in front of Vandergelder's hay and feed store.

There were several 2nd ADs, most with amusing activities on this film. I had to let one go because he was never to be found. I eventually found him hiding underneath a pile of wardrobe with a female extra. He was upset at being fired. After all, he said, he wasn't actually screwing her, just feeling her a little.

We had an extra on the film whom I wanted to release but the Fox people decided not to. He was one of those people who always forced his way to the front of the crowd, waited for the camera to roll, and would mop his brow with a brightly colored handkerchief to attract attention to himself. I explained that Streisand and Matthau were the stars and should be featured, but he was insistent. Finally I decided to render him completely harmless. The next scene had Streisand walking down the street in Yonkers. The camera dollied along with her, showing the shops just behind her, with passers-by. One of those shops was a poultry store. 20th Fox had stocked the store with chickens, ducks, eggs, whatever a poultry store would have had in that period. These were live animals who had to be fed and tended daily. I told this extra to take a chair, sit in it on the boardwalk outside the poultry store, and for heaven's sake just sit there and don't do anything.

He went inside the store and brought out a chair. After the camera rolled, he went back into the store and got a live white chicken. As the camera passed by him he started to pluck the chicken. The chicken shrieked appropriately, then died of a heart attack. On camera. At least that gave me the chance to fire him off the picture.

Walter Matthau's mother would visit the set regularly. She always brought a big tin of her own homemade chocolate chip cookies, which she passed around to the crew. She wanted them to treat her son nicely and this was her way of showing her gratitude for their doing so. We would have done so anyway. Walter was a prince of a man, kind, professional, fun to be with. This was true of most of the people on the film.

Barbra Streisand was not as easy. She had in her contract that she was to be given a private house in Garrison and various other perks. She did not seem to be very comfortable with the crew. She did have a few differences of opinion with Gene Kelly which turned into production problems. Streisand took four hours in makeup and wardrobe, so if she argued with Gene Kelly at noon and cried, and her mascara dripped down her face onto the wardrobe, we would have to quit filming for the day because we would not have her back on the set for four hours. Very difficult. She and Water Matthau did not appreciate each other's abilities and said so with loud volume from time to time. This also tended to hold up production.

A person who did get along with the crew very well was her then-husband, Elliott Gould. He was virtually unknown at the time and a few of the crew called him "Mr. Streisand," which did not please him. He would visit the set with their son, Jason. The crew loved Jason.

Every production has one person who causes unexpected problems. In the case of Streisand the problems were expected. In this case the unexpected problems were caused by a Garrison resident. We had rebuilt Garrison to resemble Yonkers around 1900. The railroad station was rebuilt into a church. The station parking lot was covered with dirt and there were a few bushes where there had been pavement before. We built a very large barn structure to house the commuter cars that normally were parked next to the station. This hid them from the camera. No sense having a 1969 Chevy in Yonkers around 1900. Nearly everyone in Garrison parked there for the commuter train ride down to Manhattan. Everyone except one man. He owned an old rusty Peugeot. He felt that he had as much right to be in that parking lot as we did.

Every morning he would arrive at the station/church and park right next to it in the open. The car was perfectly visible to the camera. The crew waited until his train left, and then covered the car with greenery to make it look like a big bush. We knew the time when he returned from the big city, and just before his arrival we would uncover the car and brush it off so he wouldn't suspect what we had done.

This worked for about three weeks. Then the fellow got ill in the office and returned early. Naturally he did not call us to warn of his arrival. Naturally he discovered that his car was a big bush. Quickly the crew removed the greenery and brushed off the car, but we were busted. The guy knew.

He also knew a little about film continuity, because from then on he parked his car in a different spot near the church every day. It's not obvious because there is so much else happening in the film, but in the film there appears to be a big bush that hops around the parking lot mysteriously.

We were heading into the final scene of the film, where several hundred extras sing and dance their way across Flirtation Walk at West Point campus. Producer Roger Edens had been a friend of Bobby Kennedy, who obtained permission for us to use Flirtation Walk as a location. Unhappily for us, and for the USA, Bobby Kennedy was assassinated the day before. There was a mad scramble amongst the production team to make sure that even though Kennedy was no longer with us, we still had the permission. Roger Edens, in spite of his obvious sadness because of the loss of his friend, was prevailed upon to call the contact at West Point to ensure our permission to film, which he did. Little attention seemed to be paid to the consequences of the assassination outside of its effect on our schedule. Our priorities held true once again.

There were further complications. The weather in New York is neither as predictable nor as unremittingly pleasant as in California. And much of the time, when it rains it does so with great authority. The Hollywood production crew got their weather reports from the National Weather Service based in L.A. In those days the weather predictions were nowhere near as accurate as they are today, if today can be held as any kind of criterion. Getting a weather report for New York from a Los Angeles forecaster bordered on the absurd.

I did what I always did. I phoned the local airport and asked for cloud cover and rain probability for the next 24 hours, a course that has served me well for many years. Airport weather must be the most accurate as lives depend on it. The airport said it was going to rain all day the next day.

This could cost Fox a lot of money if it were not handled properly. Two hundred or so extras had been ordered for the next day for Flirtation Walk. They would each be paid for three days' work, since they had to catch a train known as the "Hello Dolly Special" from Grand Central station at around 5:00 am, and would not return to Manhattan until around 9:00 pm, well after dark. Add to that the cost of the special train, extra makeup and wardrobe people and their overtime, extra meals from the caterer, extra wear and tear on the period costumes, extra props and other necessities of filming, and there would be a substantial cost. Ordering the extras when it was pretty certain that there would be no filming would be a big expense. This might be offset by weather insurance. But it would cause a lot of unnecessary trouble for a lot of people. The extras were ordered.

I cannot forget driving through a driving rainstorm to Garrison the next day to the location production office and walking in, seeing one of the Hollywood production people staring out the window at the rain, and saying, "Well, it looks like it's letting up." It did not let up for two days, and we spent the time sitting in tents and waiting for it to let up. With all the extras, extra makeup and wardrobe people, and the Hello Dolly Special. Even today when the movie plays it is possible to see little spouts of water around the dancers' feet at Flirtation Walk. The rain had stopped but the grass they were dancing on was soaked.

The company moved back to Hollywood where Fox had built a replica of 1900 Manhattan in the streets around their sound stages. The set still stands and is still in use. All in all, considering the monumental job of transporting so many people and so much equipment from one coast to the other and back, and considering the effort that went into filming on location for a month far away from any production center, having to create our own village with eating facilities and all the other support systems necessary for running a film production, this was a magnificent accomplishment in spite of the few glitches here and there. It was Hollywood at its best. Was it worth the effort? Of course it was. Not only did a great film emerge from this work, but also many people worked very hard and earned substantial incomes from the effort, money spent to employ other people and to buy goods and services.

Parenthetically, a study made by the Illinois Film Commission prior to our shooting *Flesh and Blood* in 1978 determined that for every dollar spent by a film production on location, ten dollars of local revenue is generated because of the trickle-down effect. This is why each state and most major cities have their own film commissions whose purpose is to lure filmmakers from Hollywood to work in their area. It provides employment for local craftsmen and income for local purveyors of equipment, catering, food supplies, housing, and so on down the line. When I worked on *Butch and Sundance* for Fox in 1978, New Mexico had allotted over $50,000 for its film commission to provide us with helicopter scouting, meals, location personnel, and other services to help us make up our minds. We eventually spent over $1,000,000 of our own money in that state, which, according to the Illinois study, generated $10,000,000 in revenue for the state and its citizens. Even if it was only half of that, that $50,000 was a bargain.

CHAPTER 28

PEPSI COMMERCIAL

Hello Dolly! being wrapped, it was back to commercials temporarily for me. Need to keep income coming in. My next job was back to Washington D.C. for a commercial for Diet Pepsi. One of the "The Girl Whom Girl Watchers Watch" jobs. The producers hoped to have the Diet Pepsi girl walking around the city, in front of various landmarks such as the Lincoln Memorial, Washington Monument, Capitol building, reflecting pool, etc. The script called for the girl to finish up in front of the White House, with emphasis on one of the upstairs windows, showing the window drape being pulled back a little. Implication was that the President was watching.

In order to film anything in Washington D.C. for commercial purposes permission must be granted by the Department of Parks. They watch over the capitol like hawks. Their job is to ensure that no photograph reveals a hiding place to a potential assassin, or a weakness in the capitol defenses. We were categorically denied permission to photograph the White House under any circumstances, and the only shots we could take of the capitol building would be from the mall. We could not go close to the building itself.

The agency producers were outraged. This was, after all, Pepsi-Cola, a very substantial contributor to the Republican Party. In fact, Nixon himself had used the Pepsi corporate jet extensively during his 1960 presidential campaign. The fact that Democrat Lyndon Johnson was the current president and the entire administration was run by Democrats seemed to escape them. The agency producer knew someone high in Republican hierarchy. We'd get our permission. They can't do this to us. Didn't they realize that we had a commercial to film? This was commerce, as in "What makes America great!"

We occupied ourselves with making all the other shots while waiting for the inevitable permission to photograph the White House. Since we had official permission to photograph all the other monuments, we had a small contingent of Capitol police to help us with traffic and crowd control. The Pepsi Girl was a celebrity, after all, and the producers expected crowds to be surging around her begging for autographs, just like what happens in Bakersfield or Evanston. Nothing like that ever happened, of course, because the crowds in Washington D.C. were there to see their senators or representatives, or maybe even the President. NOT the Pepsi girl. There was some minor interest but nothing that could disrupt our filming.

We ended up on the street in front of the White House, still hoping for permission to make the shot with the curtain. We never got the shot, and I never saw the commercial on the air.

CHAPTER 29

COLGATE-PALMOLIVE DISHWASHING FLUID

I also worked on a series of commercials for Colgate-Palmolive Dishwashing Liquid. They starred the great actress Jan Miner as "Madge" the manicurist. The client is always astounded by having dipped her fingers into a bowl of Palmolive Dishwashing liquid, and always says "Hmm... Pretty green!" We did these for three years. Jan Miner did them for twenty-seven years, easily the longest run for the same actress doing the same commercials in history.

We all got to know each other very well. The director, Don Horan, cameraman, Tom Mangravite, and agency producer, Stan Lacey. We always used the same studio and the same equipment. And Don always found an excuse to tell the same joke: "Love is the answer, but what was the question?" at least once during the filming. At first Filmex, a mid-size production firm, employed us all. Then one day Filmex ran into financial troubles and a marshal appeared at the studio to confiscate the film. We begged and pleaded to finish the commercial and he relented, but he stayed with us and watched us very carefully lest we try to smuggle the film outside the studio without his knowledge, which we did anyway. Between shots he serenaded us with his bagpipes. He was good at it, too. We gave him some cans of unexposed film and he went away happy at the end of the shoot. The next day the doors of Filmex closed for good. Bob Bergman, the president of the company, spent all his hard-earned profit wining and dining potential clients.

CHAPTER 30

CARS

Winters in New York can be very cold and uncomfortable in the snow. Being a native Angelino I was not used to living in the stuff. I had seen it, sure, even walked around in it at Lake Arrowhead when we went for dinner at Pierce Marshall's house. I had never seen it actually falling until I moved to New York. Then for the first couple of years I lived in apartments, and the streets were plowed right after a snowfall. The roads were salted, too, to keep the snow from freezing and making the roadways slippery and dangerous. The salt would spray up under the cars, and this helped to rust the frames. It wasn't a good situation. Very difficult for someone who owned a Fiat like I did.

The Volvo stood up under the worst winter weather imaginable, but what did I expect from a Fiat? I should have known when I bought the car. The Volvo dealer in White Plains also sold Fiat, being from an Italian family. Fiat was, more or less, supported by Fiat-Roosevelt Motors in Teaneck, New Jersey, or thereabouts. Fiat-Roosevelt was the American distributor for the Italian firm, and was owned in part by one of Franklin Roosevelt's sons. They had never been able to keep the parts supplied for the cars properly, and sometimes there was a very long wait for parts when they were needed. I once had an accident with one of my Fiats and waited for several months for the parts for repair to be delivered. I owned a Fiat 850 Spyder, an unbearably cute little two-seat convertible. The top went up and down with ease. The little 850cc motor worked very hard but did manage over 40 miles per gallon on the road, and well over 30 in the city. It was a good little commuter car.

As I said, I should have known. I had asked for an AM/FM radio and one was duly installed in the dashboard. I proudly stowed the top behind the seats, buttoned down the tonneau, and drove off. After a few blocks on the way home I decided to enjoy a few tunes, so I turned on the radio. All I could hear was muffled voices and an occasional sound of a bass drum. I figured, well, the top was down and maybe I just needed to turn up the volume. The voices became louder but were still muffled. This was a mystery. In all my other cars, including the little Austin-Healey, the sound was clear. This was anything but.

I returned straightaway to the dealer and let my salesman hear the radio. It was still muffled, and nothing, no adjustment, no fine-tuning, could make it any clearer.

The salesman called over the mechanic who had installed it, an Italian man who spoke no English, but who looked at the car, gestured with his arms toward it, and said over and over, "Bella... Bella..." with loving looks.

The salesman explained in Italian the radio problem. The mechanic had the perfect solution. He had not been able to find an appropriate place to install the loudspeaker so he put it inside the glove compartment. Seemed perfectly logical to him that if I wanted to hear the radio all I had to do was drive with the glove compartment open. Yeah, sure. After he had repositioned it down in the bottom of the passenger foot well where a passenger could kick it, I drove off, promising to warn all my passengers not to stretch their legs out. Like I said, I should have known.

H.G. Peters had a commercial production company in Primos, Pennsylvania, on the "Main Line" near Swarthmore and other very wealthy towns on the outskirts of Philadelphia. H.G. himself had become wealthy by having a contract to do all the still photography for RCA, Whirlpool, and other RCA-based products. For this purpose he built a studio in Primos a block or so away from his home so he wouldn't have to walk too far to work. This was one of the most modern studios I had ever seen. Dick Clark used it regularly for his *American Bandstand*, among other local Philadelphia shows. The camera room alone was superbly equipped, with 16mm and 35mm cameras of every stripe, Mitchells, Arriflexes, even Maurers and Bach-Auricons, God knows why. Lighting and grip equipment, a full, stocked prop room, wardrobe department, the works. Full, modern makeup department with well-lit tables. He could afford it since he was still making stills, and good ones, for RCA. Personally he drove a new Cadillac El Dorado although in his garage there were both a Ferrari and a Mercedes 300SL Gullwing. He preferred the Caddy. His garage also had a lift and a full complement of tools, and a full-time mechanic to go with them. Can't remember if he had a gasoline pump but I wouldn't be surprised.

He phoned me the day after Christmas in 1968, said that he was producing a commercial for Gino's Pizza, and could I drive down to Primos to be the AD for Alessio diPaolo, a director I had known before. Of course I could. Could I come right now? Of course I could. I dressed quickly, put together a little care package with some snacks and water, my briefcase with my work items, heavy anorak, heavy boots; I didn't know what I would need so I was loaded for bear.

Walked downstairs to the garden leading to the parking lot to find out that it had snowed about three feet the night before. Drat. Snow is always so quiet. At least with rain you can hear the raindrops. With hail, even better. But snow? Not a sound. The parking lot was a beautiful white field with regularly spaced one- or two-foot high mounds of snow where the cars were. Now where had I parked the Fiat? And if I found it how could I possibly get it out to get to Primos? I returned to the apartment and phoned H.G. Peters to tell them I would be late. How late? I don't know but I hope I'll be there by this afternoon. I grabbed my shovel and started digging around where I thought my car would be. In the meantime the snowplow had driven past and had plowed the street, at the same time putting a six-foot berm of snow blocking in the parking lot. I might get the car out but I sure wouldn't get out to the street. Back to the phone. H.G. said don't worry, they would do what they could without me and I would get there when I could.

I found the car and dug it out as best I could without impeding its route to the street, then I dug a path out to the street. This took over an hour. Then I returned to the car to find that the door lock was frozen. If it ain't one damn thing... I searched the apartment for a small blowtorch I had bought for the purpose. Lit it up, thawed the lock, opened the car, turned the key, and it wouldn't start. The oil had gelled. After several tries it did start and I let it warm up for a few minutes before attempting the road to Philadelphia from Scarsdale, a drive of 2½ hours under the best circumstances. No help for it but to just go.

Luckily H.G. Peters had been prepared for the eventuality and had made reservations in a local motel for the night. However, this was really getting to be a big pain for this Los Angeles native and the thought occurred that maybe there was a career for me on the West Coast eventually. But for now I was bound for Philadelphia.

CHAPTER 31

GENERATION

Soon, in late January of 1969, I was called again to return to the feature film world, this time on *Generation*. George Schaefer directing. This time the UPM was Ben Chapman, another legend. An old Army Air Force pilot, he had had quite amazing adventures. Told me he had learned in old open cockpit Spads. His instructor told him to always keep a 50-cent piece in his pocket. If he was flying in a cloud and became disoriented he would take the half dollar in his hand and open his hand. If the coin fell upwards he knew that he was flying upside-down.

Filming revolved around a building in downtown Manhattan near Attorney Street. The script called for Pete Duel and his young wife, played by Kim Darby, to play a young couple trying to make their way in the world without much money. They lived in a run-down tenement with a few pieces of used furniture. He played a plumber. In those days the "555" phone numbers had not yet come into common usage, so I had the painter use my own phone number on the side of his panel truck. I expected people to phone me to come and fix their plumbing but nothing like that ever happened.

The building we had as a location was really a wreck. It had at least seventy-five years of paint, many layers of different colors, much of it peeled off. It was a fantastic array of colors. The building had been taken over by the City of New York so it cost us nothing for permission to film its exterior and interior. The set dressers had a field day populating the interior with the most run-down furniture imaginable from Goodwill. Really grungy stuff. But it was our set dressing and we needed to keep it intact at least until we finished filming.

The building was in a really rundown section of Manhattan. OK, it was a slum. Street gangs kept control of their home blocks. The police seldom went into that neighborhood for their own safety. Our building was one of the worst of the worst. The city had done nothing to keep it up. A few homeless people had camped on the upper floors in spite of the lack of plumbing and other conveniences, which gave the whole place a rather rancid aroma. The electricity worked only because we paid Con Edison to turn it back on. The surprise was that late at night a local street gang used our building as a clubhouse. That answered the question as to why someone had put a pool table and a few folding chairs into the back room, a room we did not need for the picture.

Even without knowing about the clubhouse situation I felt we needed to protect our furniture somehow so we wouldn't have to buy new furniture every day. I hired Burns Detectives guards to put one of their best men into the front room and stay there overnight. Around 2:00 am the next morning my phone rang at home. Burns informed me that a local street gang inhabited the building. They were so intimidating that the guard had run away from the building in fear for his life and returned to the office. They told me they could no longer guard the building. I thanked them for their work and phoned Pinkerton's. To my surprise the same person who told me that Burns and Pinkerton's were the same company answered the call. OK, where do we go from here? I asked the man if there were any group he could think of that might help us to guard the building, and who could stand by on the set while we filmed to ensure the safety of the cast, including Pete Duel, Kim Darby, and David Janssen. The man introduced himself as an off-duty member of the NYPD. Told me there was a group of off-duty police who handled just such cases and they would be happy to help out. I hired him and his buddies.

The next morning I went down to the building on Attorney Street to see what had happened. Our furniture was still there as were two very substantial off-duty policemen. One was the gentleman with whom I had spoken the night before. We chatted for a few minutes while I explained the needs of film production. He and his partner would stay during the day and be replaced at night by another set of guards until we were finished filming. They would act as public relations experts to help us with the neighborhood crowds. Filming was to begin two days hence.

The next day, the day prior to filming, we left the building alone except for a brief visit in the early evening to make sure everything was OK for the next day's shoot. It wasn't. The City of New York decided that the building did not represent their better side, so they sent a crew down to repaint the building in fresh paint, give it a spruced-up look. Exactly what we did not need. I called our scenic artist in charge and explained the problem. What we wanted as a rundown building had a nice, fresh coat of paint on it and certainly did not look any longer like the slum we needed for the film. We quickly found something else to film the following day and gave the painter the time to repaint the building into a slum, with the appearance of several coats of matte paint all peeling off, just like we needed. Whew.

Filming began as planned the day following. The people who lived in the neighborhood had never seen a film being shot before. Children stayed home from school, parents stayed home from work, it seemed like a thousand people all crowded around our location, around the motor homes used by the stars, generally getting in the way. Some of them approached David Janssen for his autograph, around seventy-five of them, on the way from the set to his motor home. All he wanted to do was to study his lines, which he could not do if he signed seventy-five autographs, and many people wanted two or three autographs for their mothers-in-law, et al. He disappeared into his motor home without signing any.

This did not please the neighborhood folk, who first started calling his name, then banging on the motor home door, then physically rocking the motor home violently from side to side. It was in danger of tipping over. I went to our guards and pointed out the situation. They had been watching the set, not aware that a block away this disturbance had happened. They quickly hurried over to the motor home and with the help of their batons dispersed the crowd in short order. They also called for backup from others of their group, and filming went on undisturbed until we wrapped.

It would not be the last time I called upon outside groups to help us with guard service.

CHAPTER 32

LARCHMONT

In the meantime I was moving our home from the apartment in Scarsdale to the house in Larchmont. This took three days even though it was only a few blocks. After we moved in we realized that we had only seen the house during the daytime, never at night. Now that we were there at night we quickly saw that in order to save money the family who sold us the house had only installed 25-watt bulbs everywhere. No wonder their children were squinting. We started replacing the bulbs with 100-watt ones and found that it blew the fuses. In those days there were no circuit breakers, only fuses. The house had been built in 1928 and the electric system had never been upgraded. We had to hire an electric contractor who had to break into the walls to replace all the house wiring, a lengthy and costly process. Eventually the work was finished and we had a fine little house in the country.

Except: I began to notice that the kitchen had a noticeable droop in the ceiling. The center was a couple of inches lower than the sides. I looked at the house plans and discovered that the upstairs bathroom was directly over the kitchen, and the bathtub was directly over the center. I checked around the bathtub and realized that the caulking had long since given way. The best I could do right now was to re-caulk the bathtub and hope that the pool of water over the kitchen ceiling did not eventually weigh down the structure to give way. Some religious ritual went along with this. By now there were two sons, Chris, who was doing just fine in a pre-school, and the baby Kevin, a strapping, insistent youngster, both blessedly healthy and both very alert, aware, and quick to learn. Many happy Sundays were spent on Jones Beach with the family, usually capped by stopping off at the Frieds for dinner and then the drive home to Larchmont.

CHAPTER 33

BANANAS

A few months later Milt Felsen phoned me and asked me if I wanted to go to Puerto Rico to work with Woody Allen. He was directing *Bananas* based out of San Juan. The producer, another New York legend named Jack Grossberg, needed a UPM to help handle the production tasks in PR. I was on the next plane.

Jack Grossberg was one of the most experienced production people in New York and had been acting as his own production manager. He was overqualified for the job, having managed such productions as *Requiem for a Heavyweight*, *Pretty Poison*, and every Woody Allen film beginning with *Take the Money and Run*. He would later manage the production of the version of *King Kong* that starred Charles Grodin and Jeff Bridges. We would later become close friends. I visited him in his condo in Marina del Rey, and later in Woodland Hills, just before he paid the final price for many years of heavy smoking at age seventy-three.

This, however, was a Rollins-Joffe film through United Artists. They flew me down to San Juan in style, first class on one of the first 747s to fly that route. What luxury. Excellent service, good food. I could almost overlook the fact that the serving tray on my seat was broken and dumped my lunch into my lap at a particularly awkward moment. We were housed at a Sheraton Hotel right on the beach. I had a car for my own use. My job consisted mainly of sitting in the office and approving bills that Jack Grossberg had already approved. I did get out to the set to watch Woody direct. He seemed to be a rather shy man who would retreat to a corner of the set between shots to study the script by himself. A very amusing visitor was the great sportscaster Howard Cosell. In the film he interviews the newly assassinated dictator of a banana republic. Howard improvised the interview almost entirely and it was hysterically funny. He was also one of the most amusing and literate lunch companions it has been my pleasure to enjoy. His stories of encounters with major sports figures were memorable, especially his encounters with Cassius Clay, later known as Mohammed Ali.

We had hired most of the crew from Puerto Rico and many did not speak English, which led us to hire a 2nd AD named Axel Anderson, a German, to translate from English to Spanish for us when necessary. I learned that in the Spanish-speaking world the expression for "roll it" was "el rollo," and when the camera ran out of film we had "el reloado."

Directing oneself in a film is frightfully difficult since one cannot watch the viewfinder as the film is being shot. Woody had to trust the cameraman, Andy Costikyan, to have gotten the shot properly, since instant playback had not yet been invented. His trust was not misplaced. Andy was superb, and knew intuitively what Woody wanted in the shot.

We worked with the Cinemobile, a new bus-like location filming truck that had a revolutionary design. In most location trucks we lower the tailgate and walk equipment into and out of the body of the truck. With the Cinemobile, invented by Fouad Said when he was cameraman on the TV series *I Spy*, all the sides of the vehicles had doors that opened outward to make the equipment much more readily available. It was a large as a city bus. Some of the vehicles even had a platform on the roof that could be raised on a telescoping stand and used as a camera platform. Its one big drawback was that it was as big as a city bus.

The streets of Old San Juan are narrow and without sidewalks. The buildings come right to the street. Navigation by auto is difficult. Navigation by bus or truck is impossible because the streets, designed for horseback riders, are so narrow that there is no room for a long vehicle to turn a corner. The best the Cinemobile could do was to drive a few blocks into the neighborhood in a straight line, park, blocking traffic, and then back out when filming was complete. This usually left it a few blocks away from where the actual filming was taking place.

For the few days we filmed in Old San Juan our solution was to offload the Cinemobile into small trucks and use those while we filmed. Even so they barely were able to navigate.

I only worked on the film while they were in Puerto Rico, not at all back in New York. I left the company when they returned. Jack could handle the production tasks, he and his hand-picked unit manager, Morty Gorowitz, who happened to be his brother-in-law.

CHAPTER 34

A SAFE PLACE

Immediately after I returned to New York I was called by the Guild to interview with Henry Jaglom for a film, *A Safe Place*. Tuesday Weld and Orson Welles were cast. Jaglom had written the script and was directing, and Bert Schneider, who had produced *Easy Rider*, was producer. His brother, Harold Schneider, was associate producer. UPM was Bob Barron. Jaglom was part of the social scene surrounding the *Easy Rider* group and had a small role in *Drive, He Said* and *The Last Movie*. Barron's only other credit was on *Godzilla*.

Jaglom was brilliant, creative, insightful, and entirely undisciplined. I was hired during the first week of filming. The company had signed their DGA agreement the day before. Sharon Sachs had been the 1st AD and had done an admirable job of trying to keep the job on schedule and on budget but Jaglom had defeated her at every turn, convinced as he was that his creative impulses were better than any written schedule. The producers felt that hiring a Guild AD would solve the problem.

I read, broke down, and scheduled the project. In classic film production process I then went over the schedule with Jaglom to make sure we were not scheduling too much work in any one day, or worse, too little. The idea of predicting what he would shoot in the future was a bit much for Henry, and we parted with him telling me to make the schedule and he would follow it as best he could.

Filming re-started the next day in an apartment in Manhattan. We had our actors, Tuesday Weld and Phil Proctor. The crew was ready. One of New York's finest cameramen was working with us, Dick Kratina. Suddenly, around midday, a crew from one of the network entertainment shows appeared to film us filming the movie. Henry immediately stopped his filming to film the crew filming us. He followed them around the apartment with Lou Barlia, the camera operator, saying how many layers of reality he could achieve by filming the filmers filming the filmers. It was all great sport.

Later on we were filming in Central Park. I had the cast Jaglom had requested for that day, although we were still unsure of which scenes he would film. I had tried to put every possibility on the call sheet the day before. Jaglom arrived and had us set up facing a rock in the Sheep Meadow. Presently a car drove up and Brother Theodore, a comedian who specialized in ranting, appeared. Henry greeted him effusively and led him up to the rock, where he spent the morning doing one of his trademark rants against society. The cast that had been called was remarkably patient and waited on the sidelines. After we broke for lunch Jaglom decided to have them work in a scene. Brother Theodore had left. He never appears in the film and is not on the credits. I have no idea to this day why he was there.

A few days later we had the pleasure of Orson Welles joining us to act in the film. He was trying to convince Bert Schneider, the producer and scion of the Schneider clan of Columbia Pictures, to help him to fund a picture of his own. However, being Orson Welles, he saw an opportunity to add to the production. Consequently the main character's name changed from Susan (Jaglom's script) to Noah (Orson's script). Every morning we sent one of the production assistants, Jerry Samet, to the Essex House Hotel where Orson was staying. He knocked on the door of Orson's room and a very large arm reached out the crack in the door and handed Jerry a pile of script pages. Jerry ran them over to the production office, where the secretary quickly typed them up, made copies, and sent them to the set for the cast to try to memorize before Orson appeared on location in Central Park.

While Orson was there Jaglom did not appear to have much to do with the production. He did consult with Orson from time to time but the rest of us knew who the real director was. While we were filming Orson entertained us with magic tricks at which he was expert. He also did a few tricks in the film but I was no longer working there to see them.

One day while Orson was directing, Jaglom looked around and saw that all the production assistants were away from the set, and only the equipment trucks were left, no station wagons or errand cars. Jaglom ordered me to take my car and drive his assistant to the cleaner's to pick up his pants, that he had a very important dinner that evening and he needed the pants. I answered that I had to stay at the location because I was supposed to run the set for him. He said, "But you're my assistant, aren't you?" "Yes, but for the production, not for personal errands." "But this is a professional dinner. I need the pants." "Sorry, Henry, I can't leave the set unless it is an emergency." "This IS an emergency. I need those pants." "Sorry, Henry. Can't do it. Now what is your next shot, so I can tell the crew?" "F*** you, Bob."

From that time on, no matter what I asked or said, Jaglom's answer was only "F*** you." At that point I told the producer, Harold Schneider, what happened. He told me that he had been an AD and he would take over for a while. I watched as he went to Jaglom and asked what the next shot was, and Jaglom answered "F*** you." My job on the film was finished. No point in my trying to run the set without the director's cooperation. I was replaced by Steve Kesten, who finished out the film somehow.

While I was waiting for another movie to come along I was hired to do a commercial for Nelson Rockefeller, who was running for Governor of New York in 1970. We filmed him for half a day in an office in Manhattan, not his own office, but one with large windows and the Manhattan skyline in the background. He didn't need it. He didn't need anything. Nelson Rockefeller was one of the most persistently charismatic men I have ever met. On his entrance he filled the room and dominated it until the moment he left, and somewhat after that. Tall, dignified, graceful, yet very warm and friendly, he immediately made us feel that he could be our best friend, or big brother. A person we could confide in and trust. I never felt that way about any other public figure except for John F. Kennedy. He was making a speech at UCLA in 1960 when I was a student there, and I stood in a lunch line immediately in front of him and had a few words with him. He was running for president at the time.

Now I was in a kind of limbo between commercial production and feature film and TV work. Except for one or two ADs in New York, there was not enough feature film production to keep everyone consistently employed, and commercial production houses were under the impression that I was now a "theatrical" AD and wouldn't work on commercials. When I worked I made enough money to carry us over the unemployed periods. I still made the rounds of commercial production houses but a new generation of ADs had come in and they were preferred over me, the old theatrical guy. The commercials were few and far between.

CHAPTER 35

JUMP

Presently I was called by The Cannon Group. This company had just been formed by Chris Dewey and Dennis Friedland, two young businessmen. They bought a Swedish film showing naked girls, distributed it in the United States, and made a killing financially. Their next project was a film directed by John Avildsen, *Joe*, starring Peter Boyle. This opened to excellent reviews and made a fortune for the company.

Looking around for another project they came upon a script by Richard Wheelwright entitled *Jump*, about a backwoods boy who buys a stock car and races it. Joe Manduke directed. Chris Dewey himself produced it on site. We filmed in Tampa, Florida. The film had a virtual who's who of excellent actors. Tom Ligon played the lead. Minor roles were superbly performed by Logan Ramsey, Colin Wilcox-Horne, Norman Rose, Sudie Bond, Conrad Bain, Paul Sorvino, and Judd Hirsch. This was a treat.

A few incidents during filming. *Patton* with George C. Scott had just opened and we wanted to see it. We were filming late but decided to go to the local drive-in theatre for their last screening. We arrived at about 10:00 pm and entered, finding a space near the screen. Adjusted the loudspeaker in the window. The three-hour long film ran for about an hour when suddenly the screen was blank and the lights came up. A voice came over the loudspeaker saying that as a courtesy to the patrons who had to get up early in the morning for work, the film would shut down now and the theatre would close. We, of course, were there to see the entire film and were understandably upset, but that was the company policy and the film was never finished for us. In fact I have never seen the rest of it.

I had driven my Fiat 850 Spyder down to Florida for the film. I used it during the production to get to and from the set. I also used it in one of several races shown in the film. We had hired a special racing shop to prepare the Chevy Malibu we used in the film. The Chevy started as a regular street legal car at the beginning of the film and in the last few scenes it had roll cages built in and special gas tanks, and the engine was anything but street legal. That car really went very fast. It appeared in a couple of street races at the film's start but later it only could run on one of several racetracks around Tampa. One of the street races also featured a Porsche, and BMW, and my Fiat. The Chevy won the race, so the other cars didn't really matter, but in the background the Fiat finished the race before the Porsche. I also got photos of the Fiat being rigged to carry a camera during the race. These would come in handy when the Fiat had structural problems a year later.

The Fiat's engine was partially behind and partially between the seats. It was muffled quite well but was still loud. It also tended to overheat even in the Florida winter, temperatures averaged in the 80s and 90s during our shoot. This made it uncomfortable to drive for any distance. I had to drive it back to New York, a two-day trip, and to enhance the engine cooling I had to leave the heater on to bleed more heat from the engine. Not fun.

The director, Joe Manduke, and I became friends during the filming. We usually drove to the set and back to the hotel together. Having been an AD and UPM himself he knew how to prepare a scene better than anyone I had ever worked with. We spent weekends together going to locations for the following week and making angle charts with complete descriptions of the action, where the camera would be placed and with what lens, actors movements, etc. This was especially valuable when we filmed the auto races with three or four cameras. I Xeroxed Joe's notes, made a descriptive booklet from them, and distributed them to the crew prior to filming. During the races I stayed in the announcer's booth. Besides announcing the race, I could also announce to the crew to "turn to shot 5 on page 3" and everyone knew what lenses were to be used, where the cameras pointed, etc. I also could direct the extras, in a manner of speaking: "OK, folks, now watch car #5 as it rounds the far turn"; 1500 heads all turned in the same direction. Worked like a charm. Without this kind of organization we could never have photographed the races we did in the time we had.

We had the usual location pains. The King's Inn in Tampa, where we were put up, had a restaurant-lounge with its own band. The bandleader fancied himself the master musician of Tampa and kept trying to impress us with his artistry on the saxophone. He would tell his band to keep playing while he came over to our table and played with great gusto into our ears at close range. Usually we were involved in discussing the day's shoot and our plans for the next day, the discussion of which had to be on hold while this saxophonist played. After two or three days during which we told him that we did not need him or his band for the film, and that we were trying to have discussions that he was interrupting with his loud music, further action had to be taken. I had already complained to the hotel management to no avail. Finally, the next time he came to our table and began blowing his horn, I poured a glass of water into the sax's bell. That shut him up. There was a minor kerfuffle the next day when the hotel management handed me a bill for a new saxophone to replace the one they claimed I had ruined. I explained the reason, the discussions we couldn't have, the loud playing into our ears, and the saxophone bill disappeared behind the manager's desk. The bandleader did not reappear while we were there, either.

One of the pleasures of Tampa was the presence of Ybor City, an area of transplanted Cubans. Not only were truly fine cigars manufactured there but also there were a number of excellent Cuban restaurants. Fried bananas is a specialty, and Cuban coffee is excellent if one wishes to stay awake for three days straight.

One of the characters in the film was supposed to be a really bad burlesque comedian. None were to be found in Tampa, or St. Pete, next door, but Miami had its share so we imported one. He did not disappoint. Everything from "This guy walks into a bar with a duck on his head…" to "I know you're out there, I can hear you breathing…." Joe and I amused ourselves by throwing back and forth lines like, "What is this, an audience or a jury?" Sometimes the simple things in life can be great fun.

The film came to an end toward the end of January, 1971, and I took three days to drive back to New York from Tampa.

CHAPTER 36

ALLEN FUNT

Almost immediately after I returned from Florida I got a call from Allen Funt of *Candid Camera* fame. He had a small success with *What Do You Say to a Naked Lady?*, and his network TV show was one of the most popular. Had been, at any rate. Now it was a few years later, and although Allen was certainly not wanting for income due to syndication, he wanted to get back into production with a new film about finance. I was called into his office for an interview.

I prepared myself, as always, by asking people I knew who had worked with him about their experiences. It seemed that the average professional career with him was a month or less. Crew people just didn't stick around. Allen's show was based on making people feel uncomfortable, and this seemed to extend to his own life as well. He never was happy unless someone around him was not. He also had all the symptoms of Tourette Syndrome, unable to control his tendency to swear at people for no good reason. Maybe he had a reason, I don't know.

I was ushered into his office, a large room with a huge desk at one end and nothing anywhere else except for a chair or two in front of the desk for visitors. On the desk was a battery of monitors. Allen ("Call me Allen. We're one big family here") explained that he had cameras in every room and he could watch the editors and writers at work, and hold two-way conversations with them at any time. Surrounding us on the walls were the worst possible paintings of landscapes and portraits, all displayed with lights on the frames to make them more visible. Unfortunately. He was proud of them.

Allen started with the expected spiel, "Bob, we heard good things about you. We need fresh blood here, new ideas. We know you will be a great addition to the team. We're one big family here. My door is always open. You can always come in and talk to me about anything." With that, through the door that was always open, I heard the phone ring on the secretary's desk and she said through the door which was always open, "Allen, your wife is on the phone."

With that, Allen picked up the phone. He turned beet red and started yelling into the phone at top volume, "You &^$#@%! I told you never to phone me here, you &%$#! When I get home I'll rip your $%## off and shove them up your @%$#!" He went on in this vein for maybe ten or fifteen more seconds before he slammed the phone down without her having said a word. Then, without breaking his rhythm, he sat back down, smiled his avuncular smile, and said, "Now Bob, as I was saying, we'd love to have you join our family…" This pattern would repeat itself to the point where I watched him ruin his own TV segments by swearing uncontrollably at the bewildered subjects.

I stayed with Allen for five or six weeks before he finally fired me in a rage. We were filming in Kansas City, Missouri, in a grammar school. We were asking fifth and sixth grade kids to explain the national debt. Naturally, all the parents and most of the school staff were standing around the room watching the great man interview the kids, who as always performed admirably. Children are easy marks for this kind of thing because they are guileless and always trying to please, even explaining things of which they have no understanding at all.

We had tickets to return to New York on a 5:00 pm flight from KC to JFK. Around eleven in the morning Allen asked me to change our flight arrangements to an earlier flight because we would probably be finished filming by noon and he wanted to return to NY earlier. Seemed reasonable enough. I went to the school office and phoned TWA, which had booked our flight. There were earlier flights than the 5:00 pm, but they were all connecting flights through other cities and landed in NY later because of layovers. The earliest we could arrive in NY was the flight we already had booked. I asked the agent to check the other airlines and was told that she already had done so. Of all the flights to NY, the one we were booked on arrived first.

I went back to the classroom where Allen was interviewing a ten-year-old. When he was through I called him aside and quietly told him that we could leave KC earlier, but the 5:00 pm flight was the one that landed first. I saw it coming. He turned red in the face and said to me in a very loud voice, "Bob, you're so full of #$%@! I don't know why I hired you in the first place!~ Now get back on the %$^#@ing telephone and get us an earlier flight to New York, you #$%()*#@!" He walked back to the table where he had been interviewing kids, to find that the parents and school staff, and the children, were quietly leaving the room to get away from this raging monster. Seeing that the show was over he turned to me, made reference to my heritage, suggested a physically impossible sexual position, and yelled, "You're fired!"

Unfortunately no effort on his part could get us to New York any earlier. Also unfortunately our seat reservations were in adjoining seats on the flight. I enjoyed a good meal and a glass of wine while Allen tried his best to squeeze himself into the farthest corner of his seat to get away from me. A real nut case.

There followed a dry period. I had little work in commercials any longer and there were few feature films or TV shows to be had.

I did have one commercial but it did not happen. I was hired by an advertising agency to scout a shopping mall in the heartland of America: Springfield, Missouri.

The idea was that in the middle of the country people shopped at such and such a store. The producer, director, and I landed in St. Louis and transferred to a small puddle-jumper for the flight to Springfield. We had been aware that the day before there was a tornado that had struck Springfield but we did not know the extent of the damage. Luckily it did not bother the motel we had booked so we had a place to stay. But the shopping center was severely damaged as was part of the surrounding neighborhood, hardly the sight the advertisers wanted in their commercial. So we returned to New York.

There was some talk about how lucky we were to live in New York where there were no tornadoes. The fact is that when I was working in Manhattan in a high-rise building, I looked out over Central Park in the midst of a storm and I did see a tornado, a small one. It was reported in the *Times* the next day. Oh well. There were also very minor earthquakes from time to time in Manhattan, which has a couple of faults running through Central Park, but none with enough energy to do damage.

I lived in New York for eleven years, from 1962 to 1973. I often asked New Yorkers why they wanted to live in all that heat and humidity in the summer and snow in the winter when they could live in Los Angeles and have much more pleasant weather for the whole year. The answer was usually that there are earthquakes in Los Angeles. I have been living in L.A. since 1973 and there have been earthquakes, yes. Two of them. I was in the middle of the Northridge earthquake in 1994, within half a mile of the epicenter, and what a ride that was. More about it later. But during my years in New York there were two hurricanes in which people died, crippling snowstorms in which people died, blistering hot summers with the requisite photos in the *Daily News* of kids playing in the fire hydrant sprinklers and eggs poaching on the sidewalk. People died every year from the heat. People died every year from the cold. New York is a very difficult city to live in. I began to look for a means to transfer back to the West Coast. This would come two years later.

This was a dry spell in which I had no work at all. Both Lucy and I went a little crazy making ends meet. She had a job with a publishing company in Manhattan which helped some, and we had some savings. The children were blissfully unaware of this, and they kept going to school and day care as necessary so Daddy could go to Manhattan and look for work.

There was one interview of note. Ralph L. Savarese, a producer, phoned to ask me if I were available to be UPM on his film *Jordi*. I drove into Manhattan on a Friday to interview in his office in Carnegie Hall. Impressive. He gave me the script and told me to return on Monday and we would discuss it. The script, by Yabo Jablonsky, was quite good, about an autistic child in a mental hospital and the doctor who treated him. I returned to the office on Monday, told Ralph that I was interested. He told me to pack because we would leave for Philadelphia on Wednesday and begin filming on Thursday. I realized that this was amateur hour. I told him I needed time to properly prepare the film. He didn't even have an assistant director yet.

Nothing had been done except for casting the major roles and finding a hospital, but beside that there was nothing. No schedule, no breakdowns, no crew, nothing. I left the office expecting to never hear from Ralph L. Savarese again.

Three years later I hired acoustic genius Fred Kamiel as sound mixer on a film. I had known Freddy since I moved to NY ten years before. His audio shop was on the ground floor of the building I had moved into on 60h Street when I first came to NY. Freddy had just finished building a super high quality sound system into the mansion owned by Leopold Godowski, Jr. Godowski Sr. was a noted concert pianist. Godowski Jr. was a noted concert violinist. He had married Frances Gershwin, sister of George. He and his fiddling partner, Leopold Mannes, unhappy with the state of color film in 1917, began to experiment with chemicals to make a better version. Darkroom timers had not been invented yet so the boys had to find a system of timing the photo development process. They did so by playing their violins in the dark, playing tunes whose exact time they knew. Kodak heard of their experiments and with the financial backing of Kuhn, Loeb, gave them their own lab for experiments. The result was Kodachrome. It gave the boys financial independence.

Leopold Godowski Jr. bought a mansion in upstate New York. He hired Freddy Kamiel to equip it with a super stereo system, speakers in every room, control panels, able to play different music in different parts of the house. Freddy spent a month taking acoustic readings in each room and designed a system built into the walls, each speaker in its optimal position. Freddy hand-built the preamplifiers, amplifiers, tuners, did all the wiring, and attached the world's best turntables and tape players to the system. It was a wonder.

Another job Freddy had was to repair the marginal acoustics of the Lincoln Center concert hall after the original builders rendered the first few concerts inaudible to part of the audience.

Having finished, Freddy specialized in building systems and designing amplifiers for select clients. My apartment was three floors above his store. I often went downstairs and chatted with him while he sat at his workbench. I promised myself that some day I could hire him as a sound mixer. I did so in the early 1970s.

At one of our lunches he told me that the year prior he had worked the sound on a film in Philadelphia. My ears perked up. Who was the director? Yabo Jablonsky. Producer, Ralph L. Savarese.

Ralph had hired a crew from New York and put them up in a five-star hotel in Philadelphia. There were two or three days of prep during which the crew and cast went to the special school to be used as a location. Then ensued one week of filming.

The filming went well. So well, in fact, that Ralph threw a party for crew and cast that Saturday evening. No expense was spared. There was a full bar, complete meal with choice of beef or fish, and a dance band had been hired. This had all been managed by the hotel. The food was devoured and the music enjoyed by all. The drinks flowed.

Sometime during mid-evening the hotel manager arrived. Was the food good enough? The dance band merry? The bar adequate? All was apparently in order. Good! Now here is the bill for the evening... Bill? Isn't Ralph handling that? No, sorry, Ralph checked out around six this evening just before dinner. Probably back in New York by now.

Ralph had left not only the hotel bill unpaid but also had not paid for the equipment rental, salaries—in fact Ralph had paid for nothing. Ralph was handsome, suave, well groomed, sincere. The kind of fellow you hope your daughter brings home. The ideal salesman. In fact if he had been honest he could have made millions as a salesman. He was excellent at that. He was also a compulsive liar, as the crew, cast, and hotel discovered. His kind still exist and give movie people a bad name.

One little item of amusement—the Fiat 850 Spyder died one month after I made the last payment. It was three years and one month old. Fiats in those days were excellent cars, beautifully designed and well constructed, but for Italian roads, not for New York. New York in winter in the early 1970s spread salt on the pavement to prevent ice from forming. Most American cars have an undercoating to prevent the salt from corroding the metal chassis. Not Fiat. The right front lower retaining arm tried to rust its way apart from the chassis, which was the car's body. This made it very dicey to drive the car. Sometimes the wheel pointed where you aimed it, sometimes not. It would be useless to bring the car back to the dealer so I somehow wrestled it across the Tappan Zee Bridge to Englewood, NJ, where Fiat-Roosevelt had its head offices. I learned that after World War II, the price for Fiat to stay in business and to sell its product in the USA was to allow one of President Roosevelt's sons to head up the company. Could be apocryphal.

I had armed myself with the publicity stills from the movie in Tampa, in which my Fiat won the race with the Porsche. Millions of dollars of free publicity. I parked the car in the parking lot of the headquarters building and went in search of the head of advertising. He was available and we met. I told him my sad tale of the broken chassis. The car had originally cost me $1750. New. You could do that in them days. Now, three years and one month later, the price had risen to an astronomical $2100.

I put on a pretty good show, explaining how this lovely little car had failed me, how I had treated it with kid gloves for all these years and made it a movie star. Mr. Kaplan opined how he could get me a break on a new one. It would only cost $1800, a special price for me. I showed him more photos of the Porsche race. The price came down to $1600. It eventually was reduced to $1400 for a new Fiat 850 Spyder. At that point I was not willing to settle for anything less than a real bargain. I pointed out that I could easily put the car back into a movie somewhere with mechanic trying to fix it, and make it a running gag throughout the picture. He saw the light. I drove off with a brand new, bright blue Fiat 850 Spyder for $200. Fully guaranteed.

Update: The new Fiat rusted to death in two years, not three, and I sold it for junk. Now that Fiat has purchased Chrysler Motors, one hopes that they have learned that lesson.

CHAPTER 37

GREASER'S PALACE

When work did come, it came in a very bizarre way. I got a call from the union that there was a job opening in Santa Fe, NM, working on a film with Bob Downey, Sr. In those days there was no Jr. yet, so it was just Bob. I would drive the Fiat down to New Mexico and begin work, and Lucy would load the kids and the cats into the Volvo and follow me down when she was ready. Since it was June the weather was good for driving, no snowdrifts or heat waves. Not yet anyway. I put the top down on the Fiat, put the pedal to the metal, and made it from New York to Santa Fe in forty-eight hours.

Of course, when I arrived, for a number of hours I could hear nothing. The Fiat's engine, rear-mounted, was halfway into the passenger cabin next to my right ear. Having that thing thrumming at me for such a long time made hearing hard for the first few hours in Santa Fe.

The film has since become a cult classic, entitled *Greaser's Palace*. It was the story of a town tyrant in the 1880s in the Old West and his efforts to overcome a bad case of constipation. Complicating this was the second coming of Jesus, who appears in town to help his flock.

The company was housed at La Fonda Hotel, the "Inn at the End of the Trail," arguably the oldest hotel in the USA, having been founded in 1607 or thereabouts. (For comparison, the Pilgrims' first Thanksgiving feast was in 1621.) The company office was directly across the street, just off the Plaza in Santa Fe. The sign on the door said, diplomatically, "The Palace." The producer was Cyma Rubin, whose main claim to fame was twofold: she had been the backer of the *No No Nanette* revival on Broadway, a wildly successful show; and her husband was Dr. Sam Rubin, who founded the house of Fabergé and then sold it for millions and millions of dollars. Backing a Broadway play, or a Bob Downey film, was pennies to her.

It wasn't a complete gamble. Bob had just released a film called *Putney Swope*, an outrageous send-up of Madison Avenue, which had taken most of the country by storm. Made for pennies, it posited what would happen if an African-American were to gain control of a Madison Avenue advertising agency. Bob, with his entirely offbeat sense of humor, had the new agency writers come up with such lines as "Use Preparation J and kiss your hemorrhoids goodbye."

Greaser's Palace was even further out in left field. In this film Jesus returns to Earth for the second coming. He thinks he is going to 1937 in America, since he has been practicing his boogie-woogie routine, and he is going to audition for "The Agent Morris," who expects to represent him as an actor-singer-dancer. But by accident he finds himself in 1837 in the West, in a small backwater Western town with cowboys, Indians, and all manner of cattle and livestock. But he still wears his zoot suit with a peg leg and a reet pleat, and the requisite watch chain at his pocket, along with a shocking pink hat.

The town is ruled with an iron fist by a tyrant named "Seaweedhead Greaser." His son, repeatedly being killed by his father and resurrected, is "Lamy Homo." So named because Bob Downey would much rather take the train than fly in an airplane. The Santa Fe railroad station is in a small suburb named "Lamy," hence the name of the character. Never mind that Lamy was named after Jean-Baptiste Lamy, first Archbishop of New Mexico. The character remained Lamy Homo.

Greaser's Palace was an eye-opener for me. I had never been involved with such a freewheeling production before. I drove, as I said, in forty-eight hours, to find that I had a total of three days to prepare the film before shooting began. At first I was apprehensive. Soon I fell into Bob Downey's rhythm of filmmaking, and everything went smoothly thereafter. Bob was, and is, one of the most inventive film artists it was ever my pleasure to work with. He taught me more about guerrilla filmmaking than any book could ever have. And trust me, I needed it.

The schedule, such as it was, allowed for considerable variation. Since most of our filming took place on Pueblo Indian Territory we could work on a daily basis with the tribe's governor and lieutenants, as well as the Pueblo police. I learned early that Bob was accustomed to filming a scene as written, sometimes, and sometimes he would send in an actor who was standing at the sidelines waiting for the next scene, or just visiting for the day. Sometimes he would allow the scene to play out and then not call "cut" just to see what the actors would do after the scene was over. Sometimes he would rewrite the scene on the spot, have the actors rehearse the new scene, and shoot. Sometimes he would not use the script at all, but improvise something on the spot.

He had also been told that filming with one camera was efficient, but filming with two cameras at once was even more so. One would film the master scene and the other would shoot close-ups or inserts while the master was being shot. It certainly helped with continuity and cut down on retakes. What we did, however, was film a good part of the time with five cameras at once. If two were efficient, just imagine what five could do! What five could do besides being super efficient was to use a huge amount of film. There were days where we used more than 30,000 feet of prime Kodak. This was expensive. Very expensive when measured against a daily use of maybe 5,000 feet for the average show. Not to mention the problem of watching dailies. Bud Smith, the film editor, solved the problem by hiring a Kem flatbed editing machine with three screens on which we could view three scenes at once. Bud did yeoman's service, many times over, on *GP*.

The script supervisor on a film is the editor's eyes and ears on set. He or she keeps accurate and extensive notes as to the length of each take, if it was not good (an "N.G." take), why it wasn't, which camera was rolling at the time and how much film was used, etc. What lines were spoken and which were said incorrectly, how long the cigarette was, and all the items that had to be matched to other takes. It is a very key position on set as it allows the editor to bypass the process of screening every foot of film to see what is there. He or she can just use the good takes and ignore the bad ones.

We had a really weird script supervisor. I learned later that she had been hired in New York when one of the film staff saw her in an elevator carrying a script, hence she must be a script supervisor. She was no such thing. Had never made a note in her life, didn't understand what was expected of her, did not know how to use a stopwatch to time scenes, could not understand continuity. Add to that the fact that we sometimes filmed with five cameras at once and she was supposed to track all of them regarding footage, angle, timing, etc. She was completely lost. Bud Smith was not happy about this at all and the rest of us were at a loss as to how to help her. She was entirely overwhelmed. The company had bought her a brand new state of the art stopwatch and a good typewriter for her notes. She left the typewriter outside in the rain where it rusted. She lost the stopwatch. After the first few days she did not even come to the set. She sat in the catering trailer and had the assistant cameramen run back and forth to tell her what the last shot was about. She never turned in any notes. Bud Smith was adamant about having her replaced, as was I. Bob Downey took a few days to decide and then hired a legitimate script supervisor from New York. That solved most of the problem.

Things then turned really strange. I had told the girl that her services were no longer needed. We gave her a couple of days to pack herself up and return to New York. You can imagine my surprise when two days later she showed up on the set sitting near the new script supervisor, notebook in hand, making notes of the shots. I asked her what she was doing there and she answered that she had a commitment to the film and wanted to finish it. I told her that her presence was not necessary but she was equally insistent that she was going to stay. I asked Bob what he wanted to do. Since she was now paying for her own hotel room and per diem, all it cost the company was one lunch. Bob said to let her stay. She remained on the set throughout the filming, determinedly making notes, looking over the shoulder of the script supervisor, and generally being very pleasant to the crew. Once in a while someone would ask her whether she had turned her script notes in to Bud Smith and she would answer that she was still writing them up. It became the company joke, one of many.

Postscript: She stayed in Santa Fe after the film, found herself a rich rancher and married him. Three years later, two years after the film had been released, I was in New York working on another film and I walked into a restaurant across the street from Lincoln Center. There was this fired script girl sitting at the bar with a friend. She was wearing what appeared to be very expensive turquoise belt and squash necklaces and rings, and sporting a very chic Stetson hat, along with Tony Lama boots. Top of the line all the way. She was relaxed and content. I got a table and sat down, and presently she recognized me and came over. I offered her a drink and she sat down. I asked the obvious question, "Have you turned in your notes yet?" She said with an entirely straight face, "No, I'm still writing them up. I should be finished in a month or so and I'll turn them in then." She was entirely serious.

Greaser's Palace was a marvelous goldmine of odd cinematic experience. For instance, Bob decided that we should have the world's tallest man appear as the barkeep in Seaweedhead Greaser's restaurant. Accordingly he contacted his agent in New York, who contacted Eddie Carmel. Eddie had become famous for being featured in the photograph by Diane Arbus entitled "Jewish Giant at home in the Bronx with his Parents." Eddie suffered from acromegaly, a disease of the pituitary gland. This causes abnormal growth of the spine and body, as well as the nose, eyebrow ridge, and forehead. The patients are usually far taller than normal. Eddie claimed to be 8' 9" tall, but in fact he was about 7' 8." Nobody was tall enough to repudiate him.

The corollary to gigantism is the fact that a giant's bones become weak and brittle, the more so the taller he is. Eddie, an intelligent, perceptive gentleman, well educated, died at age thirty-six in New York from complications arising from his disease. In 1971 when we worked with him he already had become so brittle that he was afraid to stand up unsupported. The scene in the movie called for Greaser to lose his temper at Eddie and hit him so hard he falls out the door and down the stairs. That was patently impossible since he could not or would not even stand up.

In fact he did not fit into an automobile. We had to send a pickup truck with a mattress in the bed to pick him up at the airport. Getting him from the airplane to the pickup truck was a study in logistics also. And this was prior to the current avalanche of security arrangements.

At any rate we managed to get him to the La Fonda hotel into a room on the first floor because he would not have been able to negotiate the elevator, and certainly not the staircase. His wheelchair was custom made and did not fit through a normal door. When he carried his crutches across the armrests on the wheelchair, passing him in the hallway was not possible. Getting him to the set in the morning and back to the hotel at night entailed using the mattress and pickup truck.

He was with us for three weeks before he flew back to New York. But the stir he caused in Santa Fe was remembered for weeks afterwards. His agent did not tell us that he would not stand up. This raised problems that nobody could anticipate. He was too tall to fit into the shower and too long to fit into the bathtub. His response was to not bathe for three weeks. This became obvious to us toward the middle of the second week. After that nobody would enter his hotel room, not even the room service staff. After he left the management left the room open to air out for a week before the cleaning crew would enter it.

Eddie had a sense of humor about his height. I remember one day in the third week we were going from his room down the hallway to the door and the pickup truck to take him to the set. Because of the length of his crutches across the wheelchair's armrests nobody could pass in either direction. As we walked down the hall toward the front door, approaching us in the opposite direction was an elderly lady, the kind with a flowered dress and a pillbox hat with a thin veil over her hair. As she saw us she walked more and more slowly, realizing that she could not get past us in the hallway. Eventually she stopped a few feet in front of us. Eddie didn't help much. Here was this bizarre looking giant in an oversized wheelchair blocking the hallway and exuding an extremely indelicate aroma. It looked straight at the lady and said the worst possible thing—"Don't be afraid, Madame. I've just been appointed the hotel's official lover!" With that she turned on her heel and ran away as fast as she could, back toward the hotel lobby.

Diane Arbus' ex-husband and business partner was Allan Arbus, who played Jesus Christ in *Greaser's Palace*. In the movie we called him "Jessy," and he danced a wicked boogie-woogie routine entitled "Jessy's Back in Town," celebrating the second coming, in Greaser's Bar. The song was written by Jack Nitzsche, the noted composer and arranger for everyone from The Beach Boys to Sonny Bono to the Rolling Stones, and also a friend of Bob Downey, who seemed to know everyone.

Unhappily in the middle of filming Diane passed away, and Allan had to return to New York to take care of their daughters until he found someone to care for them while we were filming. I had to take the news to Allan. He was in his room studying his lines for tomorrow. He had earlier shown great affection for Diane although they had been divorced for some time, but his spiritual side was still strongly connected to her. I sincerely hope that I never have to do that again for anyone. It took Allan some time to recover enough to be able to express himself clearly. I phoned the airport, made a reservation to New York, and drove him down to catch the plane. It must have been excruciatingly painful for him. But being the professional he was, he came back to Santa Fe the next week and we resumed filming his scenes. Bob Downey was able to accommodate his absence by moving some scenes around, rewriting a few, and giving us enough to do for the week that Allan was handling his New York situation.

Since we had the "tallest man in the world," Eddie Carmel, it stood to reason that we would have one of the shortest, Hervé Villechaize. Hervé was noted for playing the role of "Tattoo" in *Fantasy Island*. An accomplished photographer and artist, he was a wonderful sparkle of cheer and creativity to us all when he was with us. He played two roles in *GP*, one scene of which was included in the final cut. He

GREASER'S PALACE

played "Mr. Spitunia" to Stan Gottlieb's "Spitunia."

He also played in a scene that was not included in the final cut. This scene took place in Nazareth. Joseph, the carpenter, played by Stan Gottlieb, is in his carpenter shop working at his workbench. Jesus, played by Allan Arbus, has his own workbench and is trying to tie some sticks of wood onto the legs of a three-legged stool. All three legs are of different lengths and the thing won't stand up. Eventually Jesus gets frustrated and throws the stool into the corner where it joins a huge pile of broken furniture. The resulting crash brings out the Virgin Mary, played by Hervé Villechaize. Hervé had enough trouble speaking English with his thick French accent, so Bob helped by asking him to speak in a Jewish accent. That didn't work either. Joseph says to Jesus, "What's the matter?" Jesus answers, "I'm a burden." Joseph: "You're not a burden but you are the worst carpenter in Nazareth." Jesus goes to the front door, leans against the door jamb, and pouts.

Mary asks him what's wrong. Jesus answers, "I'm not supposed to be a carpenter. I'm an actor-singer-dancer. I have to go to Jerusalem where, it is written, the agent Morris awaits me." Mary grabs Jesus by the scruff of the neck and marches him back inside to confront Joseph. This wasn't easy because Allan was a great deal taller than Hervé. They go to Joseph, where Jesus repeats about the agent Morris. Mary wants Joseph to talk some sense into the kid. Instead, Joseph puts his hand on Jesus' shoulder and says sincerely, "Quick, go, my son, before you change your mind." Jesus does. Then Joseph starts chasing Mary around the carpenter shop, hollering, "He's gone, Virgin, and now you're gonna bleed!" Cut—end of scene.

We filmed this scene as described but I suppose it was too raw for the censors at United Artists back then. Or maybe Cyma herself vetoed it. Hard to say. Not the only scene that did not make it into the final film.

The following scene had Jesus asking God to be sent to Earth so he can meet with the agent Morris. God, played by Woody Chambliss, asks when Jesus wants to go. Jesus, who has been practicing his boogie-woogie routine and who has a freshly pressed zoot suit (with a killer-diller coat with a drape shape, a peg leg and a reet pleat. And an outsized watch chain hanging from the belt to below the knee and back to a side pocket) wants to go to Jerusalem in 1937. God, who is distracted at the time, instead sends him to the far west in America in 1837.

Our picture picks up with Jesus parachuting into the fields next to the Western town where Seaweedhead Greaser holds sway. This was an accomplishment all by itself. We hired a stunt double for Allan who was good at parachuting, and then we had to hire a helicopter to rise far enough above the field to enable the parachute drop to be effective. This was not easy since the field was just outside of Los Alamos in a valley called Valle Grande, a huge volcanic caldera. The floor of the valley was 8,500 feet above sea level and the helo had to go up another 2,000 feet or so. The air is so thin at that altitude that it took the helo a full half hour to make the climb. Then when the stuntman parachuted out, the air was too thin to keep the parachute inflated properly and he dropped much faster than we had figured. The result was no worse than a sprained ankle, but it was painful for him nonetheless.

Speaking of painful, we had a medic on the set, actually a lady who had taken some first-aid courses. She dispensed bandages, ointments, and advice. She did so after her accident also. She lost her footing and fell into a gully on location, spent the rest of the film with her leg in a cast. That didn't slow her up much when she had to get to an injured crew person.

We had a couple of them. One scene took place in Madrid, a ghost town about thirty miles south of Santa Fe in the middle of the desert. Maybe a few homesteaders lived in the abandoned buildings, but very few. The scene took place at the town church. The steeple was not set back from the front of the building so a camera in the steeple could point straight down and photograph people entering the building from directly above, one floor up.

One of the camera operators and an assistant prepped an Arriflex with a 10x1 zoom lens, grabbed a camera mount, and climbed the stairs into the steeple. When there, they attached the lens to the camera, attached the camera to the mount, and cranked the mount over until the camera was pointing straight down, directly onto the tops of the heads of people entering the front door of the church. At that moment, the wardrobe lady happened to be walking into the door. The assistant had not attached the safety mount to fasten the lens to the camera. When the lens fell it hit the wardrobe girl on the collar bone, missing her head by fractions of an inch. Even so, it broke her collar bone.

The medic was not prepared to handle an emergency of this kind. We put the injured girl into a station wagon and sent her back to the Santa Fe hospital where she could get proper treatment. I put the camera crew into the same station wagon. I told them that when we returned to town after filming that evening I sincerely hoped they would have left for New York or wherever they called home. We never saw them again. I can put up with a lot of things, but incompetence that results in injury has no business on any set of mine.

That was the only major injury we had during the filming. We got off cheap.

There were other difficulties. We wanted to film on top of a mesa at an old Indian ruin, called "Puye Cliffs." It was the remains of an adobe building created maybe 1,000 years ago. Originally it had been two and three stories tall and housed a thousand natives or so. Now only the first story remains and that is not in very good shape. However, the mesa top is sacred ground to the Santa Clara Pueblo. They hold religious rituals there.

We were assigned a tribal policeman whose purpose was to keep us from harming the structures. Seems that recently there had been another film company there, Filmways, making an episode of *Bearcats* with Dennis Cole and Rod Taylor. In that episode the director needed a low-angle shot of the men driving the car among the buildings. To achieve that he instructed the grips to take down a thousand-year-old wall which they left in pieces on the building floor. After that the Pueblo were not going to let anyone film there again, ever. We had to go some distance to convince the Pueblo Governor and his staff that we would maintain the integrity of the sacred ground. Even so we had a tribal policeman with us. Very nice man. I shared my lunch with him and he became a friend also. And we were super careful not to touch any of the structures.

By this time Lucy had driven out to Santa Fe to be with me for the filming. Our two sons were there as well, ages two and six. It was a big adventure for them. An even bigger one for Lucy. Our caterer was really struggling from the git-go. Lucy had taken courses in catering at Cornell, and she wanted to test her skills. Marriage made in heaven, right? Well, sort of.

Santa Fe itself is 5,800 feet above sea level and the air is thin. Because of the altitude, water boils at 180°. It takes a half hour to boil an egg. Lunch became a daily logistical amusement. Would it be ready on time? Would it be cooked well enough? And there was the fact that due to the nature of the film and the composition of the crew, many were vegans and many were organic fanatics. Lunch had to accommodate all these, as well as any visitors from the New Mexico Film Commission or even from the studio in Hollywood.

One of the more fanatic vegans was Marco Heiblim, a camera assistant who was constantly pestering the chef, Lucy, about how he wanted his food prepared and of what ingredients. Insisted on seeing the ingredient lists on the cans and bottles. Lucy had a short fuse anyway, so this lasted for a week or two until she chased him out of the kitchen trailer, threatening to bean him with a huge cast iron frying pan. He gave her lots of leeway after that. Marco was very verbal about his dietary requirements. That's almost all he spoke about at mealtime until we were really tired of listening to his organic rants, his constant complaints about the sorry state of store-bought foods, his insistence that his regimen was the best for all of us.

It was hot in the desert in July and we were usually filming outside. I tried to make sure that there was always ice cream or something frozen on the catering truck for the crew to snack on. We kept icewater buckets near the set with bandannas kept cold for the crew to mop their fevered brows. Once in a great while, when I knew it would take a while to prepare a set for the next scene, I got in my car and drove to the nearest Carvel Ice Cream shop on the highway to buy milk shakes for those crew folk who wanted them. Carvel wasn't particularly organic since it was made mostly of chemicals, but on a hot day it sure tasted good. On one of these trips I entered the Carvel shop, which appeared empty. I went to the counter and ordered the usual 50 milkshakes. From the corner of my eye I saw something moving along the wall of the Carvel shop. I turned to see Marco making his way to the door as quickly and silently as he could. "Marco!" I said. "How could you? This is almost all chemicals!" Marco replied, as innocently as he could under the circumstances, "I can't help myself. I love the stuff." He never bothered the caterer again.

The western town was peopled with western people, quite a few members of the local pueblo, some Hispanics, and a few actors from various troupes around Santa Fe and Albuquerque. We had a would-be western star with the redundant name of Rex King. He sang a song for Seaweedhead Greaser, after which Greaser shot him.

The town also had all manner of animals and birds. The local animal suppliers had a field day with us. There were horses, cows, mules, sheep, goats, ducks, cats, dogs, chickens. Oh yes, some different colored chickens. The wrangler who supplied the animals had asked Bob Downey what color chickens he wanted in the town, and Bob replied that he wanted a lot of different colored chickens. That's what we got, too. The man bought some white chickens and spray painted them green. Green chickens. We had our different colored chickens. They immediately went to the bottom of the pecking order, of course, and over the course of the film they became more and more ragged as the other normal colored chickens plucked at them. They still appear in the film and they are still green.

There were also dogs and cats in the village. One baby kitten struck my fancy especially. He was a little Persian mix. Didn't have the flat Persian face, but was entirely white with a long bushy tail and one green eye and one blue eye. He started following me around on the set. I called him "Moosa," which was the Tewa word for cat. Tewa is the language spoken by the Pueblo Indians of the Tesuque Pueblo. I asked José Herrera, the kindly old Pueblo native who made my headband for me. Their word was derived from the way they heard the cat speak. "Moosa Moosa." Like the Chinese call their cat "Mao."

Moosa followed me around enough that I took him back to my hotel room every evening and he slept curled under my arm. I fed him milk and some cat food. Took him back to the set every day so he could be in the picture. When Lucy came, he stayed in the hotel room permanently with the other cats. Eventually he came to L.A. with us.

One thing Bob Downey did was to keep a fully loaded Arriflex camera ready next to the main camera. If any crew person saw something he or she considered worthy of filming, they could pick up the camera and film it. Several of the shots in the film were taken by grips or sound men and they were left in the film. We even had a location manager, Forrest Murray, who began by helping Bob find some locations for the film during pre-production. The two got on so well that Bob kept Forrest on the film as a grip, and eventually he became one of the camera operators. Union niceties were not part of Bob's makeup. Forrest, still a good friend, is now one of Hollywood's more adept low-budget film producers. Has been a member of the DGA for many years and teaches film production classes at UCLA, last I heard. Took some excellent shots for *GP*.

Luana Anders played Seaweedhead Greaser's daughter, the indefatigable Cholera Greaser. A great gal, excellent actress, a bit buffaloed by the unstructured production occurring around her. Also a devotee of Nichiren Shoshu, she chanted

GREASER'S PALACE

in the morning and evening. Our hotel rooms were next to each other. The incessant "Nam-Myoho-Renge-Kyo" came through the wall separating our rooms. I have no problem with anyone else's religion, but if it wakes me up I do. This did. She would get up at 4:00 in the morning to do her devotional. I first asked her to chant a little more quietly, which she could not do. I finally asked the hotel to move me to another room. Absent that, Luana was a delight to work with. Unfortunately she died way too young at age fifty-eight of cancer. She sure was fun when we were filming. She was Jesus' love interest, and she played it to the hilt.

For a brief time we had the company of Toni Basil, a brilliant dancer and choreographer. At Puye Cliffs she performed an immensely creative and sensual dance that she choreographed herself. Mesmerized the crew and cast.

I should mention that Albert Henderson played Seaweedhead Greaser. An actor of Shakespearean bent, he was perfect in the role. His wife, who was also his agent, was with us for a while during the shoot. I worked with him three years later in New York on *The Supercops*. Both were satisfying connections.

"Greaser's Palace" was the name of a real building. It was the biggest building in town, built on top of a small hillock. It was three stories tall, made entirely of wood. There was a bar-restaurant occupying the first floor. The second floor had three or four jail cells. One of them held Lamy Homo from time to time. Another was Cholera's private apartment. Another cell held Bob Downey's mother, in costume. The third floor had a couple of other rooms, but the real attraction was the privy that was built out over the corner of the building. It was here that Seaweedhead Greaser would go to try to alleviate his constipation. The building was designed and built by David Forman, who was to become a composer-performer of some note in the mid-1970s. His building was a real work of art.

The ground floor bar was large enough to hold the crew, cast, and some of the equipment. That was handy because almost every day there was a drenching rainstorm. The air was so clear where we were filming that we could see the storm approach across the desert a half hour to an hour away. We had plenty of time to get the equipment and ourselves into the Palace. The storm usually lasted five or ten minutes before it moved off into the Sangre de Cristo Mountains. Then we would emerge from our wooden cocoon and continue filming.

These rainstorms were quite spectacular. They were usually accompanied by a spectacular rainbow, sometimes even a double rainbow. Bob fell in love with them and asked Peter Powell, the director of photography, to film one in the background of a scene. Peter was not certain that he could catch the moment, so he contacted Edmund Scientific and ordered a special prism that would create a rainbow in the camera lens. It took a week to arrive. The day we were to use it, we had the camera all set up, Peter had calibrated the prism to be at exactly the right spot in front of the lens, the scene was rehearsed, and the rainstorm was rapidly approaching. Suddenly, on cue, the most beautiful double rainbow anyone had ever seen appeared just behind the shot. Peter pulled the prism away and got the shot. We fled into the Palace, thanking the spirits for smiling on us in this way.

By that time, however, not only the crew and the equipment found refuge from the "Gully washers" but also many of the town animals thought the Palace was a good place of refuge from the rain as well. So we shared our space with chickens, dogs, sheep, a few mules. After a few days of this the interior of the Palace began to have a peculiar aroma. We learned to keep the animals out.

Santa Fe was a magical place, full of artists, rebels, lawyers, lawbreakers, sculptors, hippies, and homeless. Everyone seemed to tolerate everyone else. At any one time in the coffee shop of the Inn of the Governors on the Plaza one might see some State Highway Patrolmen at one table, some well-dressed major drug dealers at another, businessmen in suits, hippies in rags, native Americans with headbands and boots, and even filmmakers in all kinds of fashion. All leaving each other alone and minding their own business. Wherever we went it was like that. Our set was like that.

Producer Cyma Rubin was never certain of what we were doing. She usually did not stay very long when she visited. She was very nice and extremely tolerant of our madness. She never entirely understood why we named a house in the village "Seymour Tiffany." We did so because once when she was visiting we made reservations at a very upscale restaurant in Santa Fe called Tiffany's. She phoned to reserve a table under her own name, "Cyma." When we got there the reservation had been transformed to "Seymour." Hence, Seymour Tiffany. She did play in one scene, accompanying the Holy Ghost in the church window in Madrid, while the cowboy Gary Indiana tries unsuccessfully to mount his horse outside.

Gary Indiana was so named because Bob was not fond of the city, having spent a few weeks there once editing a previous film. In fact, Jesus himself refers in not very flattering terms to Gary Indiana in his stock speech to the faithful. Seems he is approaching a group of Greaser's Palace village denizens when the priest keeps insisting that he should give them a sign, some sign that he is really the Christ risen. In the resulting inspirational speech Jesus mentions Gary Indiana in not very flattering terms. Thus, Downey's revenge.

At any one time various crew members and a few cast members were involved in absorbing perception-altering substances. These were readily available in the Santa Fe of that era. It didn't matter. The film was made in spite of, and probably in some cases, because of this fact. I was as guilty as everyone else for imbibing, but never to the extent that it rendered me incompetent. Not true of all the crew, but we did get the job done. The film had its own logic which we followed to the hilt. What resulted is, I am convinced, a classic film of noble proportions in both its intent and its execution. Also one of the most delightful films it was ever my pleasure to work on.

All good things come to an end, and we wrapped the film in early September

1971. My job was finished. Lucy and I packed the kids into the car to travel to Los Angeles to visit with Dad before we drove home to New York. It was seasonably hot, like 115°F or so when we drove through the desert to L.A. The Volvo was air-conditioned, the Fiat was not. I drove the Fiat. But the Pacific Ocean beckoned, and I had not seen my father for years. I also planned to spend a few days visiting my half-brothers in San Francisco before driving back across the country. The plan was to drive to L.A. in two cars, then to have a tow bar fabricated for the Fiat and tow the Fiat back to New York behind the Volvo, using it more or less as a trailer.

CHAPTER 38

L.A. TRIP 1971

We tried to make the trip to L.A. in one long run, but as usual fate intervened. As we drove through Needles, CA, one of the hottest towns in the U.S., we decided to stop for lunch at a local Denny's. As we went inside I asked Lucy if the cats would be OK in the Volvo while we ate, and they just had to be. We were hungry, and more important, we were human and they were cats. We ordered lunch. Around the middle of the meal Lucy went to the car to check on the cats, and did not return. After a few minutes I went out to the car to see what was wrong. One of the cats had fainted in the heat. We paid our bill and found a nearby motel that took pets, checked in, and turned up the air conditioning full blast. It took two or three hours before the poor kitty began to breathe normally and show some signs of life. It was the first time, and the last, that I rented a motel room for a cat.

We arrived in L.A. the next day. Dad was waiting for us. He had prepared two rooms in his house for us to stay. At this point he lived in a large house at the top of the mountain in Pacific Palisades on Lachman Lane, up the hill from Marquez Avenue near the beach. It had a magnificent view of the ocean, Catalina Island, and a good part of the Los Angeles basin. On clear days, anyway. Dad no longer had a butler and maid, but Gaby Staabs, a very distant cousin, would come by and cook and clean for them. Normally Gaby and her husband lived in and managed the apartment house Dad had built on the corner of Crescent Heights and Santa Monica Boulevard, right in the heart of West Hollywood. But she had become almost a part of the family by hanging out at Dad's house, doing errands, etc. She was not very swift, even very slightly retarded, but had a good heart.

At any rate Dad welcomed us into his home with open arms. We parked Volvo and Fiat off to the side of the driveway so he and Peggy could drive out with their two Mercedes when they wished. Unpacked the cars and moved into the two rooms. While I was unpacking I saw the TV remote on the side-table next to the fold-out bed. Turned on the TV to watch the late afternoon news. Pushed the button on the remote but nothing seemed to work. Put the remote back on the table. Lucy came in and tried the remote also. It still didn't work. We continued unpacking and preparing the kids for dinner and bed. I looked over and saw another remote on top of the TV set. Tried it. Bingo. The set turned on as if by magic. Ah, the wonders of the modern age. In Santa Fe the hotel rooms did not yet have remotes for the TV sets. This was luxury. I remembered something I had left in the car, so I went back out front to the driveway to retrieve it, and there was Dad, his tool kit on the ground, every tool spread out over the driveway. "What's wrong?" "I don't know, but the garage door keeps opening and closing all by itself. I have to fix it." I never told him.

We stayed there for about a week. Side trip so the kids could be properly introduced to Disneyland. We won one of those ridiculous huge teddy bears around the size of a small child, which Kevin became attached to.

Dad and I never discussed my career. His was over. He had directed his last film, *The Singing Nun* with Debbie Reynolds, at Fox in 1965. His contract was up and not renewed. He had toyed with a few scripts but nothing concrete had turned up. He did not have to work. His agent, Paul Kohner, was not aggressively searching for work for him, and Dad accepted that. He had been working steadily since the early 1920s, had seen monumental changes in the cinema and indeed was an intimate part of most of them. I think he was relieved not to be in the rat race any longer.

I asked him why he felt his time was over, and he answered with a story. The painter Rembrandt van Rijn is hired by a very wealthy burgher in Amsterdam to paint his portrait. The burgher sets aside a wing of his house for Rembrandt to work. He has all the easels and brushes he needs, a special atelier to set up, even a small living room and kitchen should the master be tired or hungry. Rembrandt is being paid a princely sum. He gets his equipment in order and the burgher comes and sits for some sketches. Rembrandt begins to get a feel for the composition and mood of the portrait. The burgher leaves Rembrandt alone for a few days to attend to some business, and Rembrandt takes the time to start to sketch in the lines and fill in some of the colors.

Presently the burgher returns to see what progress has been made. Rembrandt proudly shows the unfinished work, and the burgher shows great delight at what has been done so far. But he says to Rembrandt, "Rem, sweetheart, baby, I just Looove what you're doing! Nobody could do it better! There's just one thing. Now please understand I'm not telling you how to do the painting. I'm not a painter, just a businessman, and I wouldn't want to impose. But the last guy who painted my portrait ordered way too much red paint. It's still sitting in a box in the garage. Now I noticed that you are using a lot of green paint. Now remember, Rem, sweetheart, baby, I don't know anything about painting. That's your business. But if you could just help me out here by using less green paint and a little more red…"

"That," said Dad, "is why I finally quit the business."

As for my own career, personal life, hopes and dreams, there wasn't much interest and I didn't offer. We had never been close in the past and there was no reason to grow closer at this point. After all we lived poles apart. He and Peggy enjoyed playing with their grandchildren and we enjoyed some very good meals together.

Presently it was time for us to return to New York so that I could return to work.

Adventures In Hollywood: A Memoir By Bob Koster

We had a great farewell dinner, and Lucy and I left for San Francisco with the Fiat towed by the Volvo. The drive took two days because we took the scenic Highway 1 up the coast, one of the most spectacular drives in the world. My brother Nick had a large house in Marin County where he put us up for three or four days. My other bother, Peter, came to visit as well, and we had a great reunion dinner. Really nice guys. Lucy, the kids and I eventually got on the road with the Volvo filled with ourselves, two children, and four cats. Quite a zoo. We stopped at Yosemite National Park, right in the Valley, and stayed in a tent overnight. Back on the road the next day, taking a more or less Northern route to New York. I wanted Lucy and the kids to have a view of some of the more spectacular scenery of Montana and Wyoming.

By now we had our driving down to a science. The Fiat, while not spacious, served to carry a few suitcases and Kevin's big teddy bear from Disneyland. The car seemed to be towing the Fiat, if not with great strength, at least not with sliding backwards downhill when we had just climbed up. Since the Fiat's steering wheel had to be free to move, the only thing we put into the driver's seat was Kevin's teddy bear. It did not get into the steering wheel's spokes and the wheel could turn as it wished.

We did not know that the company that welded the tow bar onto the car had not attached it to the chassis, but just to the weak, thin body panel under the front bumper. Starting and stopping the car caused the welded joint to stress back and forth, weakening it considerably.

As we drove gaily across the bridge over the Missouri River connecting Kansas City, Kansas, with Kansas City, Missouri, the tow bar broke. We were not moving very fast, maybe 40 miles per hour, but nonetheless the Fiat smashed itself against the railing and came to a grinding stop. I felt the Volvo lurch forward. One glance in the rear mirror showed what had happened. I quickly pulled over to the side to check the damage. The people in the car behind the Fiat had not realized that it was being towed, only thought that it was following our Volvo too closely. When the car smashed into the railing they pulled over behind it and approached on foot to see if anyone inside was injured. As I walked back they were discussing how a teddy bear could have caused an accident. Scratching their heads. I really needed the comic relief at that moment.

We stayed in a motel for over a week while the local Fiat dealer waited for the parts necessary to allow the car to roll. The frame had bent and needed straightening. The car kind of crabbed sideways but we still managed to make the rest of the trip to New York without incident.

We took the car directly to the Fiat dealer in Scarsdale, Big Dee Auto Sales, for repair. It took Fiat eight months to send the proper parts to fix the car from Italy, costing the insurance company a lot of money in loan car rentals. Eventually it was repaired. Well, too.

CHAPTER 39

AMERICAN TOURISTER

Not much work before the end of the year. A few commercials. One took place in Puerto Rico. This was welcome because it was a very cold winter in Larchmont. The product was American Tourister Luggage. They were making a series of commercials showing the hardiness of the suitcases. One famous commercial showed a gorilla throwing around a piece of A-T Luggage and generally treating it extremely impolitely. Ours had a piece of luggage dropped from a helicopter onto a grassy field and not breaking open. It was never used to my knowledge. We started filming with the helo at 1500', and the suitcase broke open and bent. Dropped to 1000', then 500'. Same result. Moved from the grassy field to a field of wheat, then to a marsh. Same result. Suitcase inevitably burst open and bent. I think we finally dropped from 250' with one or two very light items in the suitcase and then it remained shut, but it was so ludicrous at that point that it could not be shown. The "Truth in Advertising" rules prevented us from doing what we should have done, empty the suitcase entirely and weld it shut. Oh well…

CHAPTER 40

RED CROSS

A few commercials held me over to the next film. One memorable one for the National Red Cross. We filmed at their New York State headquarters in Westchester County. We had a station wagon filled with equipment and another with the crew. As we unloaded in front of the building, two or three limousines drove up and disgorged a dozen or so young ladies who entered the building. Hmmm. I asked the Red Cross rep if they were clients. No, they are secretaries. The story was that the headquarters was until recently in New York City. When it moved upstate, the Red Cross wanted to keep its secretaries. Take the train? No, then they would have had to pay. We hire limousines to bring them here daily from New York and return them in the evening. That way they can still work for us and keep their salaries intact. (N.B. That was the last time I ever donated to the Red Cross.)

CHAPTER 41

VIRGIN ISLANDS VACATION

Lucy and I did have a lovely vacation in Barbados and the U.S. Virgin Islands. Lucy's parents looked after Chris and Kevin. I had to become accustomed again to driving on the left side of the street, and shifting with my left hand. It became easier since I had done a few commercials in the Bahamas, which have the same peculiarity. Both islands are very beautiful and have a distinct rhythm that tourists can fall into quite easily. Barbados has in addition the finest rum distillery I have ever seen, the Mount Gay company. The distillery where they make their fine Eclipse Rum is located right in the middle of a sugar cane field. Doesn't get much fresher and purer than that.

The U.S. Virgin Islands, capital: Charlotte Amalie, was just beginning its infestation with Rastafarians. Rastafarians follow the teachings of Ras Tafari Mekonnen, the original name of Emperor Haile Selassie of Ethiopia. "Ras" means "Head" or "Prince." When he was elevated to Emperor in 1930 he took the name "Haile Selassie", which means "Power of the Trinity." But back to the present. The Emp was worshipped by the Rasta as the Messiah and followed his teachings. Some of their interpretations were a bit off, I fear. A few weeks before we arrived at St. Thomas some Rastas had attacked a local golf course and shot a couple of tourists to death. Injured a few others. I'm not sure that Ras Tafari would have approved. Lucy and I, however, had a delightful vacation without being in the slightest inconvenienced by the Rastas. And their music, Reggae, is highly admired around the world.

Rasta consider the act of smoking cannabis, or "Ganja" as they call it, a spiritual act. Many wear "Herb hats" above their dreadlocks, in which they keep their stash. Sounds like a good idea to me.

CHAPTER 42

RALPH L. SAVARESE PRODUCTIONS

After we returned to New York the phone rang. It was my old friend Al Rossman. We had studied at UCLA together and had kept in touch over the years. I was the best man at his wedding a few years before. His wife, Faith, Lucy, Al and I would go to dinner from time to time. He had finished a series of films for the USIA, and had come to NY to work on other films besides propaganda. Working for Allegro Films, an industrial firm, Al met one of their producers who had aspirations to produce and direct theatrical films. His name was Ralph L. Savarese.

Over lunch I told Al my story about Ralph. He listened with interest. Ralph had just produced and directed a film called *The Cage*. Al had been the cameraman. They became friends, and when Ralph decided to open his own company he called Al to be the head of production. Several projects were in the pipeline: a TV musical special with Sammy Davis Jr., called *Davis in Vegas*, a half-hour TV comedy series with Marty Allen and Steve Rossi, a feature film called *The Sword and the Switchblade*. And others. There was money behind Ralph this time. Teamster money. Ralph's uncle was involved with the Teamsters in NY, and they had managed to free some money, Ralph told us, from the union pension fund. The offices were in a small office building in midtown, but they were about to move to new offices on 55th Street. The office suite had been occupied by Sammy Davis' organization. Ralph had taken them over and refurbished them, as well as supplied them with the very latest in intercoms, phone systems, and other high-tech gadgets of the time.

Al offered me the job of production manager, in charge of the overall production of all shows. I insisted on meeting with Ralph prior to accepting the job. Ralph greeted me warmly and ushered me into his office. He had missed me, he said, wished I had been with them in Philadelphia. Well, those days were over now and we were about to embark on a brand new course of action, plunging head first into the mainstream of theatrical production. I would be a definite asset to the firm. Not one to mince words, I asked about the ultimate fate of *Jordi*. Oh that, he said. "We finished that film and entered it in several film festivals, where it won prizes." He showed me the parchments attesting to those awards. There were three or four of them. "And look here—we have an agreement with Sammy to do the Vegas show." He showed me Sammy's signature on the contract to appear. This certainly looked

RALPH L. SAVARESE PRODUCTIONS

better than when he was doing *Jordi*.

I accepted the job and was given an office. I was told not to bring much equipment into it because we would be moving soon into the new digs on 55th.

My first sign that something was askew was when Ralph came into my office on the first day with the book *The Sword and the Switchblade*. Told me he had just optioned it and wanted to make the film. Had a famous actor of the day lined up for the lead. Told me to budget the film. I asked him where the script was. He said it hadn't been written yet. With my vast experience in the film business I could easily read the book, imagine which parts would be scripted and which not, and make a budget. I told him that this was a very unorthodox way to budget a film, without a script, but he insisted. I read the book and made a generic budget for a film with a sixty-day shooting schedule. I never saw it again.

We moved to the new offices and I was given a rather spacious office of my own. We all shared a secretary for the time being because nothing was in production yet. A young man, Jeff Bleckner, was writing the script for the *Davis in Vegas* project. An old-time comedy writer, Snag Werris, formerly with the Jackie Gleason Show, was writing the Allen and Rossi project, to be entitled *Upp and Addam*. A singing group was to play second lead, the Sounds of Soul, with the lead singer, Jonathan Edwards. They regularly hung out in the offices and serenaded us with glorious song.

The projects seemed to be progressing nicely. The first to be produced was *Upp and Addam*. We actually had a script for that. I urged Ralph, who was to direct, to join the Directors Guild. We hired a casting director and an art director, and we rented a studio on 57th Street. A crew was hired to build the set, and soon we also hired a crew to film. Al would be the cameraman himself. Everyone was being paid properly.

From time to time Ralph's uncle, the "backer," would appear. He was a very energetic man, very businesslike. Spoke fast. You could trust what he said. He asked the right questions. He also had another gentleman with him, "Nickie," whose purpose was not obvious at first. He was 6'4" and ate cows for breakfast. Solid muscle. Dressed very well but never tied his necktie. He watched over Uncle like a hawk protecting its young. Ralph and the Uncle would disappear into the office for private conferences, and "Nickie" would walk around the office talking to all and sundry. Always stopped at my door for a good word. Spoke a little like Marlon Brando in *On the Waterfront*, however. I always answered him in kind.

Marty Allen and Steve Rossi also hung out at the office when they were in town. They were both very pleasant people to be around, especially so since this TV show would be their entrée into the wild and wacky, wonderful world of TV. Marty and I established a rapport right from the git-go, throwing terrible lines back and forth as I had with the burly cue comic in Tampa. Except that Marty was far more literate and far more funny. And when Snag Werris joined in, it became a real treat for me. This was often since there was always food and drink in Ralph's office. We always could come and go there as we wished except for the few times the Uncle was around. And even then, they only closed the door for a few minutes each time.

I made a schedule and budget for *Upp and Addam* that I discussed with Ralph, and also with Allen and Rossi. They had some commitments to appear in Vegas and other venues that we had to schedule around. It was uncomfortable but workable. In the meantime construction on the set was proceeding properly, the crew was coming in to discuss equipment rental, and the cast was being lined up for the shoot. We had an extras casting company handling the few background talent we needed, including the stand-ins for Allen and Rossi.

The week prior to filming was getting hectic. I instituted production meetings every morning of that week. All department heads were requested to join so we could all stay in touch as to progress. That part was going smoothly. I had hired a set decorator to help the art director in furnishing the set, and the property master was busy procuring all the necessary props for the show.

At the same time, we were discussing leaving two weeks later for Vegas to scout locations for the Davis show. Ralph also made reference to a couple of other projects in the offing. We would be busy for the foreseeable future.

There was a minor glitch. Allen and Rossi were giving more and more of their time away and our time with them, the leads in the show, was more and more restricted. We have a seven-day shoot and they were now down to two days. I asked Ralph to show me their contract, but Ralph couldn't find it on short notice. It must be in the attorney's office. I phoned the attorney but could not speak with him and the drone on the phone was of no use. The schedule was holding at two days, and they were going to be very full days. I mentioned it to Allen and Rossi. They just smiled and made a few jokes, and left the office.

On Thursday of the week prior to filming, the property master returned to me all the receipts for his petty cash and the remainder of the $3,000 he had drawn. This was at around 5:00 pm, and I didn't want to take the time right then to check over his accounting, so I handed the whole envelope to the accountant with the request that it be locked in the safe overnight.

Friday I was in the office by 8:00 am to handle the last day of pre-production. We would begin filming on Monday. Ralph wasn't in yet, and neither was Al. Al usually came in early too, but I usually beat him. He came in shortly after me. I answered the few calls that had piled up and went to the accountant for the prop man's petty cash envelope. She told me that it wasn't there. Ralph had come in last night after everyone had gone home and cleaned out the safe, including around $200,000 in cash from the Teamsters that had not yet been deposited as a payment for the show. It was gone. All kinds of red lights and sirens went off in my head. Was there any money left in the bank account? How much? Luckily Ralph had not gotten that, and there was just enough to pay off the crew through the end of the week.

When Al arrived a few minutes later I filled him in. Our order of business was to pay the crew off for Friday, keep the construction crew through Monday to strike the set, and then close the offices as soon as possible. I handled the Friday part and then went home. Ralph never showed up. There was speculation that he had fled to the Caribbean. Al stayed on with a couple of people for a week or so, finishing up odd bits and pieces. It had been fun while it lasted, and we all made a few dollars from it.

A few months later I worked with a producer who knew Sammy Davis Jr. I mentioned the Savarese affair to him, and a week later the producer made a trip to Vegas and saw Sammy. He phoned me to say that Sammy hardly knew Ralph, had never signed a contract with him. All the documents Ralph had shown me were forgeries, including the awards for *Jordi*.

I never saw Uncle or Nickie again. Three or four months later Uncle phoned me. He said that the FBI was investigating the whole affair. If they contacted me—and he was very explicit about this—I was to tell them absolutely everything I knew. They never called, and that was the last I heard about it. Except that Al and I once in a while refer to it even today in humorous terms.

CHAPTER 43

STICKS AND BONES

Not long after that Bob Downey Sr., a prince, phoned. He would be directing another show, *Sticks and Bones*, and would I be interested in being the production guy. Would I! It was originally the Pulitzer Prize-winning play by David Rabe about the return of a Vietnam War vet to his family in Yonkers. Joseph Papp had produced it on Broadway through the New York Shakespeare Festival, and now CBS had picked it up as a movie of the week.

Bob Downey now lived in a house in Greenwich, CT. I drove up to get him every morning and back to his home every evening, and I did so gladly. It gave us a chance to discuss what we would be filming that day. The large location house in Yonkers had four stories. We had rented it for the duration, and the art director had done a wizard job of filling the house with ultra middle class furniture. Exactly the kind the Ozzie and Harriet would have liked. In fact, in the show the names of the family were Ozzie, Harriet, Ricky, and David.

The first floor of the house had kitchen, living room, any room that the public might access. And the videotape room. Second floor had the bedrooms. Third floor had crew supply, wardrobe, electric, makeup rooms, dressing rooms, etc. And the fourth floor, actually a big attic, was our production office. Once again, Peter Powell was the cameraman and Bud Smith was editor. Lee Rothberg provided the video equipment, which in those days was like providing us with the battleship *New Jersey*. This was all very exciting because we shot entirely on location, and to my knowledge it was the very first movie of the week to have done so on tape. We used 2" "quad" tape in those days. The use of tape meant that some of us—Bob, myself, Peter, and of course the tape crew—had to wear headphones to stay coordinated with each other. We were not accustomed to this either, a film crew shooting with tape, but it took all of a day or so to become used to it. It also took me a while to get used to the fact that as the UPM and 1st AD I was also connected to a loudspeaker system throughout the house, so if I needed an actor I flipped the switch on my transmitter and said "Cliff DeYoung, please come to the living room for scene 102." Worked like a charm. Worked too well, in fact. At times I forgot that it was on when I made private comments. That happened once or twice before I got used to keeping a hand on the transmitter at my belt. For a month or so after the show was over, every time I spoke my hand went automatically to my belt.

Picking up Bob at his house in Greenwich was a trip. Bob had a dog, possibly a small terrier of some kind, named Sturges and a cat named Kubrick. I'd appear at the door at 6:00 am and ring the bell. Sturges would come barking to the door. Presently Bob would appear, shove Sturges out of the way with his foot, say to me, "Don't pay any attention to Sturges. He's full of shit." And we'd get in the car and drive down to Yonkers. This was a regular morning ritual.

Taping was on schedule and on budget. The actors—Tom Aldredge, Cliff de Young, Anne Jackson, and the rest—were all pros, and those who hadn't worked with Bob before fell quickly into the spirit of a Downey movie. The show was finished on time, the editing done. It was afterwards that things fell apart. Richard Nixon was president and his FCC was not partial to anti-war messages. We had a show of substance and CBS was scared to death to give it a normal release. To make matters even more dicey, POWs were returning to the U.S. under an exchange agreement and the government was understandably sensitive to the returning POW issue. Bob went to the first screening at CBS when the programming people were due to discuss when to air the show. After the lights came up there was a full minute of silence, probably longer. Then someone said, "That's important!" Nobody seemed to know what to do with the show. All agreed that it was a ground-breaking show but nobody wanted to take the responsibility of finally giving it air time.

The result was that the show was aired only once, at 12:30 in the morning, without any publicity at all. Few people even knew that it would be broadcast and fewer still watched it. Shame on CBS.

CHAPTER 44

CONCORD ELECTRONICS

I had another of those pesky dry spells at this time. I kept busy, however, with a very interesting project. Lucy's uncle, Joe Benjamin, was the owner of Benjamin Miracord, importer of fine stereo equipment. Among other things they imported the Miracord turntable from Germany, probably the finest, most accurate turntable available. Reliable, too. We bought one in the early 1970s and it is still going strong today, forty years later. He also imported the Swiss Lenco turntable, another premium brand. He manufactured Earth speakers, the finest of their kind.

My interest lay in his sales of equipment by Concord. Concord at that time was an offshoot of Matsushita, parent company of Panasonic. They were selling portable videotape units. This was a brand new field and nobody knew what to do with them yet. I remember telling the group head (no kidding!) that I could see easy-play cartridges in the future, and people would go down to the corner to a vending machine and rent a movie for a dollar or two, take the cartridge home, play the film, and return it the next day. Naturally I was laughed at. All us geniuses must suffer that fate.

The device consisted of a large-ish camera connected by a thick cable to a reel-to-reel videotape recorder. The lot weighed about forty pounds. The camera alone weighed in at around five pounds and it had to be plugged into the wall. Batteries were not available. Concord had a couple of demo reels showing the capabilities. One had a golf lesson, and the other was a sales training film. This wasn't much of a demo. I immediately saw the possibilities for commercial use. Even though this was a black-and-white model, incapable of photographing in color, it was portable and presaged all sorts of wonderful things. In the theatrical field, for instance, it might be used to record rehearsals or shows. It could be used for scouting locations, to show the producers back in the office what a house looked like. It definitely could be used for casting sessions. With a time-base stabilizer it could actually be used for broadcast-quality video. The possibilities seemed limitless.

I took a demo model and started making the rounds of movie production houses. As would be expected, few were interested. It was too bulky, they said. Too cumbersome. Too heavy. Camera was too large and could not be moved as easily as a film camera. Sound was scratchy. I did make one sale to one actor who wanted to photograph his own rehearsals, and that was my only sale. After about a month of frustrating pavement pounding I took the machine back to the shop and left, dejected. Not before I had taken some great video of my wife and kids, though. But with no means of replaying the tape it was useless. And with the Fiat it was a bear to haul into Manhattan and back. Took up the entire rear seat, such as it was.

Oh well, back to the unemployment line. I found in the movie business, for me, there was always another show somewhere. The next one was the last I worked in New York. I finally decided that if I wanted to keep working on theatrical films I would have to move back to California to do so. But in the meantime I had another film to do.

CHAPTER 45

THE SUPERCOPS

The *Supercops* was produced by MGM. Gordon Parks, a genius photographer and excellent director who had made his bones on *Shaft* and *The Learning Tree*, was directing. Producer was Bill Belasco, a diminutive fellow from L.A. whose primary qualification was a close friendship with James T. Aubrey, the studio chief. I was to be 1st AD and Dave Golden, a man of vast NY experience, was to be the UPM. MGM's production manager at the time was Lin Parsons, Jr., one of the most knowledgeable, experienced L.A. production people. I was given three weeks or so of prep, enough time to do a schedule and to see the locations with Gordon before filming began.

I had an excellent 2nd AD in mind, a street-smart fellow with a great sense of humor and a great talent for scheduling, as well as a very likeable personality. Crews loved working with him. Kurt Baker had been one of the production people at MPO Productions, NY's largest commercial production company. He knew just about all the crews, directors, and equipment there were to know. And we were a good team. This served us well in the next few weeks. We needed all the help we could get.

The movie was the true story of two NY policemen with an unorthodox approach to police work. The "Supercops" were Dave Greenberg and Bob Hantz, two of NYPD's finest. They had made a highly publicized reputation by making drug busts in the neighborhood. I got to know both of them during the course of the film, and developed a healthy respect and some affection for both. We broke bread several times together and kept in touch for a while after the show was over.

Two or three days after I began working, Bill Belasco managed to fire Dave Golden. This was almost inevitable. Dave had been one of the most experienced production managers, and Belasco was a newcomer to the business who was unsure of himself. His major purpose in life was to not have James T. Aubrey yell at him. He was around forty years old but looked sixty. You get that way if you are unhappy and afraid. Allan Funt looked around twenty years older than his actual age.

Belasco immediately promoted me to UPM and Kurt Baker to 1st AD. Kurt hired Joe Wallenstein as his 2nd. Dave had already done most of the pre-production work. We had a forty-five-day shooting schedule which I hoped we could hold, because I knew that filming was going to be very difficult. We were slated to film in Bedford-Stuyvesant, a real hell-hole of a neighborhood. There were numerous street gangs, and many block associations. Crime was rampant. So was homelessness.

The latter problem was made much worse by the Nixon administration. To win the election in 1972, Nixon had promised the poorest sections of town that the government would fund low-income housing. At the time people were living in Bed-Stuy, four or five families to a room, sometimes without electricity or running water. Most of the street stores were shuttered. Cars were abandoned on the street, so the streets were never swept. There was garbage all over the streets and sidewalks, which were not cleaned. Children played in the filth, having nowhere else to go. The police seldom went into the neighborhood. There was no point in doing so. Into this atmosphere Nixon promised to build low income housing. When we got there, about twenty square blocks of the worst part had been razed to the ground. In a few cases construction had begun and the foundations and a few walls were standing. In some cases the ground was absolutely bare. Just rubble. But whatever the progress of construction, the government had stopped as soon as the election was over. The buildings had been empty for a few months, and there was no construction happening there at all. It had utterly ceased.

So what happened to the people who had been living in the now-leveled buildings? They were living in cars on the street. They were living with relatives, now six or seven families to a room. They were living on sidewalks, in alleys, behind gutters. They were homeless for the most part. And for the most part they hated anyone white. After all, we had put them into this situation. To repeat, the police never came into the neighborhood. But we did.

The 22nd precinct had abandoned a 100-year-old building and moved a few blocks away to a new building with modern facilities. New radios, teletype machines, the lot. We took over the old building, which had the old-fashioned high sergeant's desk in the lobby, old globe-type lamps, antique furnishings. Worked well for the film. I had my office on the first floor of the building, but the rest of the building was basically one large set.

The building was so old, in fact, that while we were setting up, the police were bringing wheelbarrows out of the storeroom with old ledgers and records. As one trundled past me a ledger fell off onto the floor. The policeman did not notice it missing so I picked it up and began leafing through it. It was from 1863. One entry read that a man was discovered having dodged the draft for the Civil War. He was summarily hanged from a nearby lamppost. This was all written down very neatly, and that was the extent of the entry.

Since the neighborhood was really depressed we took advantage of as many local businesses as we could. We hired a local caterer. If we needed any construction or props we tried to have things built locally. We hired locals as extras and runners and production assistants when possible. We also hired a local chapter of the Black

Muslims to work with us as bodyguards. The local police had their hands full with other problems. Our lives and well-being were threatened daily. We were filming on the street when a member of the sound crew was hit by a heavy liquor bottle thrown out of the third-story window at us. From time to time, people approached the crew, demanded money, and pulled knives on us in broad daylight. It was a dangerous, nerve-wracking situation. Trying to film in those circumstances was crazy.

To further make the situation unforgettable, Gordon Parks and Bill Belasco did not bother to hide their mutual hatred. Add to that the idea that James Aubrey felt that discord brings out the best in people. He and Belasco, his friend, fomented discord whenever possible. This erupted into fistfights more than once, and the crew had to separate Belasco and Gordon.

We had a forty-five-day shooting schedule. At one point Jim Aubrey, back in his office in Hollywood, decided that this was really more of a movie-of-the-week than a feature film, and ordered Bill Belasco to shorten the schedule to twenty-two days. Belasco, who normally stayed in the MGM offices in Manhattan on 55th and 6th, phoned me and ordered me to tell Gordon Parks. I suggested that he come to the set and discuss it with Gordon himself. He agreed. Said he would be at my office in an hour or so and asked me to go to the street location with him. I waited two hours before phoning his office to see when he was coming. His secretary told me he could not be disturbed at that time because he was getting his daily massage. I forgot about the schedule change and it was never brought up again.

Belasco seemed to want to get in the way of production. If there was a chance to somehow cause a problem he took it. The police usually stayed inside their precinct house except for urgent emergencies. Our film company was a matter of minor curiosity and annoyance to them, but nothing they felt moved to help with. We had to develop our own methods of coping with the madness in the streets. The two "Supercops" were with us all the way, of course, but even they could not keep track of everything that could possible threaten us on the set.

To take up the slack, as there were daily physical threats to us, we made an arrangement with the Black Muslims in the neighborhood to provide security for us. This cost MGM a few dollars but it was well worth it. There was a caveat. The Muslims requested that we not publicize their presence in any way. No reporters, no articles, no TV. They were adamant about working in the background, so much so that they threatened to leave the show forthwith if they heard about themselves in the press.

They were a tremendous help to us in many areas besides security. They suggested local merchants we could work with for various supplies. They helped to provide the catering, and it was really good food. They acted when necessary as a buffer between ourselves and the many people in the neighborhood who tried to extort money from us. Many. At the beginning of the film we had visitors every day who claimed to be the real authority on the block whom we would have to hire for peace on the location. We were not street smart enough to know who was real and who was not, but the Muslim Brotherhood had insight it would have taken us years to acquire. At any time I noticed several recognizable brothers standing watchfully near the crew, and another few I did not recognize working through the crowds that gathered wherever we filmed. After the show had finished I learned through other sources that the Black Panthers, a radical Black Power party not above using illegal activities to further their own ends, had planned to hijack our equipment trucks, steal all the film equipment, and sell it to finance their work. The Muslim Brotherhood stopped that, thank goodness.

But there were complications beyond even that. Bill Belasco had befriended a famous movie gossip columnist of the time, Rona Barrett. He just could not resist telling her about the Muslims. Sure enough, within a day or two, several local newspapers that carried her column ran stories about our involvement with the Muslims, gave fanciful descriptions of their religion and rituals, and generally repeated Belasco's somewhat jaundiced view of the whole affair along with her own misinformation. Exactly what the Muslims did not want. The Muslims disappeared from our set. At first I didn't know why. I did know that now we were very vulnerable to street attack.

I phoned my primary contact with them and asked for a meeting. He didn't want one. I begged and pleaded. He relented. At the meeting he was very clear about being angry that we had broken our word to him and his group. He did not want his people working with such dishonest people. After some discussion he said he might consider going back to work protecting us if Bill Belasco himself came to a meeting and apologized. There was no chance of that. Belasco considered the Muslims some kind of weird cult that deserved no attention whatsoever. Furthermore he told me that I had completely exaggerated the danger situation. Nobody would get hurt. Nobody was in jeopardy. We needed to speed up the filming anyway because JTA (James T. Aubrey) wanted us to finish early. Forget the Muslims, they are only street fighters wearing suits.

I met with the Muslim representative alone. I was honest with him. I told him exactly what had passed with Belasco. I told him that we were just crew people trying to earn a living, and we needed his protection. I told him that his group would be paid properly for their work, if only they would come back and help us. We shook hands and the next day his group reappeared. We had no further trouble. I had them paid properly even though the company accountant, Chuck Ogle, was trying to get on Bill Belasco's good side and I worried that he would be telling Belasco about it. He never did, to his credit.

We lived in Larchmont at that time. It took over an hour to drive each way to and from the office. And I usually arrived around 6:00 am, because that's when the crew started to filter in. I parked on the street in front of the precinct house. Usually I had to step across people sleeping on the sidewalk, or just lying there, freshly awakened. A short time later, children would begin to filter down from apartments in the area, or out of cars on the street, and begin going through the many garbage cans looking for something to eat for breakfast. I usually ordered more food than we needed, not knowing who from the MGM ranks or from the city would join us on location, usually right at lunch time, and as a courtesy we fed them. Any leftover food was given to these neighborhood children. Some days we had more than others to give in this way. It was a practice that I carried out for the rest of my career, either giving our food to hospitals, or to police stations, or to churches or neighborhood organizations.

I seldom returned home before nine or ten at night, and seldom left for work much after five in the morning. It was a brutal schedule. My family seldom saw me. Many times I stayed in Manhattan and ate dinner before returning home because I knew that Lucy would not be happy having to cook an extra dinner at 9 PM. The kids had to do without Daddy except for the weekends, and then I usually tried to catch up on sleep. The company had given me a Chevy Camaro to drive back and forth, and at least I could listen to the radio on the way to and from work. The sound system was excellent, far better than in my Fiat. Sunday was family day and we inevitably ended up at Lucy's parents' house in Great Neck.

I did manage to help Moosa become a movie star. The scene in the movie took place in Sheila Frazier's bedroom in an apartment building in NY. I had shown a photo of Moosa to Gordon, who admired the cat's long, white, silky fur, and two different colored eyes, thought that he would be great as a lap cat in Sheila Frazier's bedroom scene.

Moosa behaved very well during the filming, sitting quietly in Sheila's lap and staring directly into the camera when necessary to show his green and blue eyes. A real pro. Then when we finished his scene he jumped right into the heater flue and couldn't be found for fifteen minutes. The whole crew was searching the house for him before he was finally dragged out, dusty but unbowed.

Lucy's mother, Doris, had passed away in 1969, and her father, George, remarried, another teacher, a very nice, portly lady named Gertrude. Gertrude had a son, Edward. Edward was a ne'er-do-well black sheep of a kid. No ambition, no goals. The reason became obvious quickly. Gertrude had mothered him to death.

Being the softy I am, I took pity on Edward and offered to hire him as a production assistant on the show, a position he gladly accepted. I told him to show up bright and early on Monday. He did. His job was to go to the film lab in Manhattan at 6:00 AM and pick up the dailies, which had been processed overnight. Then he was to bring them to the office, because Gordon wanted to see the preceding day's dailies after work. The editor was in the MGM building in Manhattan, and he needed to sync the dailies first. So Edward had to get the film, take it to the Manhattan office, then bring the synced dailies to our Bed-Stuy office. For the rest of the day he worked as an office P.A., that is, ran errands for us, got coffee, and did whatever other tasks nobody else wanted to do. He would be able to go home around six in the evening unless we needed him desperately for something else. He made a small wage plus overtime, but the possibility always existed that if this worked out, he would be able to work on other films after this one and eventually work his way into production.

Edward showed up at the lab on Monday promptly at 6:00 am, took the film and drove it to the Manhattan editing room. He came to our office at around ten or so. Had a little breakfast. Did a few errands. Drove in to Manhattan for us and back. At the end of the day's filming he took the film to the lab and then went home. It was a long day.

Tuesday was different. I expected Edward in our office around 10:00 am as on Monday, but he didn't show up. I phoned the film editor to see if he had left yet, and he had not seen him. Nor had the lab. Now I was worried. Was he in an accident on the expressway? I phoned his home to see if Gertrude had heard from him. She told me he was still asleep, that yesterday had really tired him out and he would probably be in around noon. I told her that he was expected at the lab at 6:00 am and we were now going to have our dailies late. She told me his sleep was more important. I told her he needn't come in today or any other day. I needed to hire people who were reliable. She hung up. Oh well, I tried. We hired someone else.

Another day about a week prior to finish, we filmed in New York City Hall, downtown. The building had a huge circular atrium with a second-story balcony that went all the way around the room. We were filming on the ground floor, and various city council members and other New York dignitaries would stop for a few minutes at the railing and watch the filming below. We had run cable all over the floor, always covered by rubber mats so people wouldn't trip, lights everywhere, sound equipment. It was a real show. Dick Kratina, our excellent cameraman, was just finishing lighting the set. Gordon was there, as were Ron Liebman and David Selby, our principal actors.

At this moment Bill Belasco appeared. He took me aside and quietly told me that he had just spoken to JTA. JTA decided, he said, that this movie was already too expensive and we should stop filming immediately, wrap everything up, and send the crew and cast home. I told him we hadn't finished filming yet. He said he knew that, and we should quit right now while we were ahead. At this point Gordon came over and overheard that last sentence. He said in a very loud voice, "At least let us finish today's shooting!" Belasco replied, "No, wrap it up right now. The crew is fired." Gordon started yelling at Belasco that since we had hired them for the day we should at least finish the day's filming. Belasco told him no, we couldn't do that, the picture was over. With that Gordon started toward Belasco. Belasco wisely said "I'm going to phone JTA right now and see." Gordon was breathing hard. We went outside to the production office motor home. We sat down. Gordon asked me if Belasco was crazy.

I didn't have to answer. The door of the motor home burst open and Belasco stood at the door and shouted, 'We have to wrap the picture now. The crew is fired." Then, as Gordon was going toward him, fists clenched, Belasco slammed the door, got into his limo, and fled back to the MGM office in midtown. Gordon, bless him, went back into the building and finished filming. I went to the phone and called Lin Parsons, the production head of MGM, to ask what he suggested. He told me to keep filming until he heard otherwise, then he would let me know. The subject never was brought up again.

Movies always have a wrap party. This is a way for the producer to thank the crew that had been spending so many hours and their invaluable talent to make his or her project a reality. True to form, Belasco left on a plane the day we finished filming. Asked about the wrap party he said some very unpleasant things about the crew and about New York in general. With that he left us. No wrap party. I went to Chuck Ogle, the accountant who was trying to stay in Belasco's good graces, who said that he was under strict orders not to have a wrap party.

Gordon Parks to the rescue. We decided to have a wrap party in a park in Westchester County. It would be a great relief after the heat of the city and the squalor of Bed-Stuy. We also decided to take all the kids who lived on the block where our office had been, bus them up, have plenty of food for them, some toys, give them a day in the country. We were in for a big surprise.

The buses left on time. We met an hour or so later in a wonderful wooded green park near Larchmont. The property department had outdone themselves with the settings, and the caterer had prepared an especially delicious meal, with the requisite hot dogs and burgers for the kids. On arrival the kids could choose games and toys to keep them amused while their parents enjoyed the plentiful food. It was too much for them. Within a few minutes all the toys had been broken. The kids had no idea how to play with them, never having had toys of their own. The food, for the most part, was taken, a bite or two eaten, the rest thrown on the ground. The squirrels had a field day. The children, unaccustomed to having too much of anything, much less enough of anything, could not cope. We quickly packed the food away from them and doled it out judiciously, giving the leftovers to the parents to keep for later. Even Gordon was surprised at this. The crew and cast at least had time to socialize for the rest of the afternoon.

It was time to go. I had been in New York now for eleven years. I had been given my choice of movies that happened into the neighborhood. I managed to work on several entire films but the majority of the films and TV shows I worked on were pieces of films that were shot mostly in Hollywood. There were some whole films, but except for *Supercops* they were mostly in other places, like Florida or New Mexico. Remembering that I am a member of a national organization, the Directors Guild, I decided to go back home to Los Angeles and work in the REAL industry.

CHAPTER 46

MOVING TO LOS ANGELES

I wrote letters to Joe Youngerman and to Morris Abrams. Joe was still the National Executive Secretary of the DGA, and Morrie was still the business agent for ADs and UPMs. Both had held their positions for many, many years and had been in those positions when I had left for NY eleven years earlier.

Lucy and I packed up our stuff. I sold the second Fiat to a crew member of *Supercops*. It was wrecked within a month. We put the house on the market. It was bought by a New York banking executive named Mr. Spiridon. I never did find out if he was related to the first man to win the marathon in the 1896 Olympic games. I should have asked. When we sold the house the buyer had an engineer go over the house thoroughly. I pointed out to him one very obvious fact. The kitchen ceiling was bowed. The house had been built in 1925 or so. The upstairs bathroom was directly over the kitchen so that the plumbing stack could be built easily. The grouting around the bathtub was never done properly, and for many years water had been seeping around the edges of the bathtub and into the space between the bathroom floor and the kitchen ceiling. This put a tremendous strain on the ceiling, which bowed downward from the weight of the water that had collected above. In fact I could easily reach up to the ceiling and feel with my fingers that it was not solid. Spongy. When Mr. Spiridon was first examining the house with a view toward buying it, I pointed this out to him. He bought the house anyway.

We were scheduled to move out on a Friday. I had phoned Mayflower Moving in New York. We would drive to Los Angeles and find and buy a home there before we could unload the truck. Mayflower agreed to store the furniture and other items until we had a place to put them. The movers were to arrive on Friday morning at eight, pack whatever had to be packed, load the truck, and get on the road by evening time. Seemed logical. Ever hear of Murphy's Law?

Lucy and I had packed what we felt we would need for a month or so until we bought a house and could have Mayflower deliver our goods. I bought a big luggage carrier for the top of the car, a big steel basket device, lots of canvas to cover it, and lots of bungee cord, hooks, and ropes. We were loaded for bear. We had plenty of suitcases. We put the essential items in the trunk, which was nearly overloaded as it was. We also had a spare 3-gallon gas tank because we were in the midst of one of

America's perennial gas crises. We were ready to go by 8:00 AM.

9:00 AM came and went. Noon. 6:00 PM. We didn't want to leave the house because the movers might arrive at any minute. We phoned the moving company several times but they were no help. They just told us that the truck had several stops to make that day and we were just one of them. The driver had not checked in and the company had no idea where they were. We ordered pizza and cokes. We found some blankets and slept on the bare mattresses.

Around 2:00 AM on Saturday the front doorbell rang. It was the movers. It was pitch black outside. No streetlights, nothing. All the houses in the neighborhood were dark, as would be expected. I turned on the lights to allow us to get the furniture moved into the truck, and found that the lights did not work. This was a huge truck, so tall that on the way in it had snapped off the power cables for the neighborhood. Great. For the next four hours we loaded the truck by flashlight.

The truck left around 6:30 AM or so. We bundled into the Volvo, started the motor, put the car in reverse, and tried to back out of the driveway. The car did not move. I checked the tires. They were inflated properly. However, the weight of the car had defeated the shock absorbers, and the body of the car was resting on the tops of the tires. The chassis was three inches lower than normal. We had piled too much weight on top of the car. We spent the next hour unloading the trunk and the top basket. Now the car rolled, but not well. The shocks were gone.

It rolled well enough that I could go to the local Volvo dealer and request new shocks, heavy duty if you please. The way the car was now I would never make it across the country without new shocks. I returned home, got the family, and checked into a motel. Locked the suitcases in the garage. Hoped Mr. Spiridon wouldn't be too upset.

I had the shock absorbers replaced and rented a U-Haul trailer. We were off and running on Sunday morning.

The trip across country was relatively uneventful, if you consider that we again had the Volvo with myself, Lucy, eight-year-old Chris, four-year-old Kevin, as well as Plippy, Tigger, Muffin, and Moosa, the cat box on the back seat floor, and a water bowl and small bowl of kibble. The cats were not used to riding in a car. I've had more exciting trips, but not much. "Are we there yet?" "Daddy, can we stop at a bathroom?" "Daddy, how much longer?" "Meow!"

I had phoned my father, who owned an apartment house in the middle of Hollywood, to see if there were any spare apartments. No, but someone was moving out and there would be one in two weeks. I could rent an apartment then.

We went to a motel on Ventura Boulevard in Tarzana, one that had a couple of suites with kitchenettes. Lucy and the kids would be less uncomfortable there. I could start looking for work and Lucy could begin looking for a house. For now there was a swimming pool. I got my swim trunks and jumped in. In a few minutes Lucy came running out of the room and yelled "Did you feel it?? Did you feel it??" Feel what? "There was an earthquake! Everything was shaking! The cats were scared!" I had been in the pool where earthquakes could not be felt. But Lucy and the kids had a fine welcome to L.A.

I remembered my old friend Mike Farrell. We had attended the West Hollywood grammar school together. He was now a well-known actor, having appeared in *M*A*S*H, Man and the City, Days of Our Lives,* and many other vehicles. He had a house in Hollywood somewhere. I found his number and phoned him. He was just leaving to spend two weeks at a house he had rented at the beach in Malibu. Would I like to house-sit for two weeks?

I drove up and we unloaded the Volvo. Tomorrow Lucy would start house hunting, but in the meantime at least we had a place to stay. And I had a base to operate from, with a phone, so I could go job hunting. But first there was the DGA.

The Directors Guild has a "Qualification List" of UPMs and ADs that had been accepted by the Guild and by the producers to be qualified to work sets on the West Coast. Since I had been living in New York I was not on the list. Fallen between the cracks. I didn't even know about it since I was living in New York when it came into existence, and in New York we had nothing like it. I drove to DGA Headquarters in West Hollywood to tell them that I was available. I found that Morrie Abrams was no longer the business agent for the UPMs and ADs. There was a much younger man there, Don Parker. I had never met him before.

I went into Don's office and introduced myself. Explained that I was the prodigal son returning from eleven years in the wilds of New York, and I wanted to be placed on the availability list to be able to work. Don was very apologetic when he told me that now there was the qualification list, and I wasn't on it. I needed a certain number of days' experience to be on the list. I had many multiples of the proper number of days, of course, in New York. There was something of a minor competition between the New York and Hollywood branches of the DGA. The New York people had street smarts, whereas the Hollywood people felt they had the history behind them. Much more experience in the studios, which did not exist in New York. I couldn't be on the list because I was a New York member. That meant I could not work. What to do? Move back? Let's try something else.

I left Don and went into Joe Youngerman's office. Joe had been National Executive Secretary ever since the Guild was founded in 1936. My father had been one of the very first members back then. I knew him as "Uncle Joe" since I was a youngster. Joe was a very distinguished looking older man with a great shock of white hair and a very pleasant disposition. He ruled the many members, who considered themselves artists and demanded appropriate treatment, with an iron fist clothed in a velvet glove. Generally the members deferred to his judgment and enjoyed being left alone to direct or otherwise manage pictures. There were the usual group who formed committees, and the negotiating committee was the most feisty of them all, but the Guild was still a fairly simple place even in those days.

Joe, the ultimate diplomat, was in an excellent post.

I entered Joe Youngerman's office not knowing what to expect. I hadn't seen Joe since he bid me a fond farewell back in 1962 when I left for NY. Now it was 1973, and as Sam Goldwyn said, "We've passed a lot of water since then." Joe rose when I entered the room, came around the desk with a warm, friendly greeting. We sat at his coffee table and chatted for a few minutes about my NY experiences, which amused him greatly.

I finally got around to letting him know that I had just moved back from New York and wanted to work. He called Don Parker into the office to discuss it. Don told him that I wasn't on the qualification list and so couldn't work until I had completed 400 days of credited work. Joe explained that I had joined the Guild in Los Angeles and never had legally transferred to the New York local, and that therefore all the work I had done in New York would be credited to those 400 days. They added up to several thousand, over the 11 years I was away. I was put on the list immediately.

Sometimes you just get lucky. I did. Within a week I got a call from ABC Circle Films. My old friend Marty Hornstein from MPO in NY had turned down a job with ABC Circle and recommended me for the job. I drove to their office on the 20th Century-Fox lot and was hired immediately.

In those days ABC Circle was managed by Marty Katz, with Herb Jellinek as VP/Production. Marty Katz was a very short person. I determined that a person's title in this business is inversely proportional to his or her height. Robert Relyea, for instance was 6'4", and was "Production Director" of MGM. Marty Katz was 5'2" or so, and was "Executive Vice President in Charge of Worldwide Production Management and Administration," or something like that. Marty was a pleasant enough man. He lived close to me in Woodland Hills so it was easy for him to bring his wife and children over to swim in our pool. This kept me employed for two years or so.

Pool? Yes, we bought a house up the hill near Topanga Canyon. Chris and Kevin each had his own bedroom. There was a spare bedroom that I turned into an office. The house had no pool when we moved in, but understanding that summer in Woodland Hills can easily reach 100°F and not infrequently 110°, it became almost a necessity. At home we were either indoors or in the pool during the summer. The kids loved it. I played "movie producer" quite often and floated about on a rubber raft in the middle of the pool while I read my scripts.

I needed a car. Couldn't leave Lucy alone without wheels, not when she had even more now to do, with the family shopping and cooking in between her duties as a real estate agent. Even though it was easier, I had even more responsibility in Los Angeles at work than I had in New York. Now that we lived on the West Coast I could be more confident in owning a sports car. No Fiats, but something more substantial. I went to several dealers in Los Angeles: Mercedes, Alfa-Romeo, MG.

I read up in *Consumer Reports* about reliability, comfort, economy. In those days gasoline was still far less than one dollar per gallon, so gas wasn't a big problem. I settled on a Triumph TR-6. Miller Motors in Van Nuys was the local dealer. The car went through the usual teething pains, a top that didn't exactly fit, rattles where there shouldn't be. These sometimes could be fixed by the dealer, more often I was told by the dealer that that was the way the car was built and if there were leaks during a rainstorm, well, that was the price of owning a swell sports car like this.

CHAPTER 47

OUTRAGE

The first show I worked on for ABC Circle was *Outrage*. Director was Richard T. Heffron, stars were Robert Culp and Marlyn Mason. Camera was John M. Stephens. This was a really big eye-opener for me. I had not worked on a film in Hollywood since 1961, *Mr. Hobbs*. I had not realized how easy Hollywood made it for you to work. In NY it was always a struggle, always an antagonist situation. Always us against them. In L.A., everyone seemed to be working **with** you. What a pleasure. Even the city made it easy to obtain film permits. Hiring the crew was a snap. ABC Circle already had a list of crewpersons who were "regulars" with the company. There was George Shanahan, who not only found and "cleared" the locations but also obtained the permits from the city or cities for production. He also arranged for the police who were assigned to our show for traffic control. There was always traffic control except when we filmed inside the studio, and then the studio police were there. The art director usually helped to scout locations. In this case we had Bill Malley who had also been art director of *The Exorcist* and was a master at finding and rearranging locations to suit the film.

    I didn't have to order the equipment. Fox Studios' arrangement, as with all major studios, allowed companies that rented office space on their lot to use, for a fee, the huge stock of equipment there. Cameras, lights, grip equipment, the lot. Sound equipment was traditionally provided by the sound mixer from his own personal supply, which was a good thing because he usually maintained it at peak performance himself.

    The location manager and the art director usually cooperated in finding and prepping the locations, another thing I was not used to. In NY I had to do that. Gee. This was really living!

    Richard T. Heffron was a very prepared director. He knew exactly what he wanted to cover in each scene, what close-ups and inserts were necessary for editing. But no matter what he did, Marty Katz and his assistant, Ron Fury, also a short person, seemed to try to bargain him down to something less, no matter what the affect on the final product. Richard finally turned to me after one of these budget-cutting sessions and proclaimed that "Working for ABC Circle is like being nibbled to death by a bunch of friendly midgets!"

Ron Fury was a character himself. The only show he had ever worked on before this was *Lance Link, Secret Chimp*. He insisted on regaling us with funny stories of how he had worked with chimpanzees. Not very inspiring. He did have membership in the Playboy Club so we had some interesting lunches.

Robert Culp was the ideal actor for this show. It required someone who was upstanding, professional, and displayed a cynical attitude and wry sense of humor. That was Bob. Not to say that he was difficult—just the opposite. But the persona visible on screen was a projection of himself.

A brief word about that. There are several classes of actors. There are performers, that is, those screen characters who project themselves or parts of themselves over and over again. Some are well known for this and audiences expect the same character from them no matter what the name of the character they are playing. Cary Grant, Humphrey Bogart, Tom Cruise, and Jack Nicholson all play themselves to a greater or lesser degree. Then there are actors, those screen characters who can assume the identity of another person easily and convincingly. Sir Laurence Olivier could just as easily play a Dr. Mengele villain, as in *Marathon Man*, and a Simon Wiesenthal Nazi hunter, as in *The Boys from Brazil*, or a besotted music hall comedian, as in *The Entertainer*. He was equally convincing in all these disparate characters. Sir Alec Guinness, Liam Neeson, Philip Seymour Hoffman are all as capable. Tom Hanks, as well. These are actors. They assume another person's character convincingly. Max Schell did a brilliant job of playing two diametrically opposed characters in *Man in the Glass Booth*. These are far fewer in number than the "performers" who play themselves, with minor variations, over and over again. In the movie industry there is plenty of opportunity for both to shine, and rightly so. But it is important that we recognize these two shades of actor.

Outrage was my first trial by fire in Hollywood, and it came with some authority. ABC Circle could not have been more supportive. However, they did hire me as both the UPM and 1st AD for the show. I worked my butt off. I was so anxious to do a good job that I stayed late at night, poring over the budget and schedule to make sure everything was perfect. I insisted in scouting the locations myself and clearing them with the appropriate authorities. I carefully crafted the schedule and then used it to make the lists of extras. This was very detailed as to gender, age, even a short physical description. I had never had the pleasure of working with Central Casting, the extras casting company, before, and they came through with no problems at all.

ABC Circle had hired a 2nd AD for me, an old-timer well familiar with the studio system who had worked on the Fox lot for decades. He turned into a dead loss on the first day of filming. I had given him my carefully crafted list of extras to order for the first day, and when they arrived at the location they were the wrong number of people, and the wrong descriptions. What happened? He had never even looked at the list I made but made up his own without consulting me. His list bore no relation to the schedule and daily extras requirements. He was just guessing. I replaced him with someone a bit more current.

ABC did its job when called upon, but in strange ways. A scene called for Marlyn Mason to ride on horseback through the neighborhood, with her daughter riding the same horse behind the saddle and hanging on with her arms around her mother. The daughter was about ten years old, very thin and lithe, and very blonde. The scene called for some neighborhood yahoos to come hot-rodding past the horse on the street, at which point the horse was to rear up on its hind legs, scaring Marlyn Mason and her daughter, who was now hanging on for dear life. The actress playing the ten-year-old daughter had never ridden a horse before and was quite scared. I phoned the office and asked them to find a stunt double for the little girl.

About an hour later a car drove up and out stepped "Little Angelo," a well-known midget. He had played one of the "Munchkins" in *The Wizard of Oz*. He was short, fat, and had black hair and a black moustache. Only his height matched that of the little girl, nothing else did. He announced that he was there to be stunt double for the girl.

I told him what we needed, someone with long, blonde hair who was thin. He told us that he was already contracted to appear the next day as himself, that his hair had to stay black and he refused to shave the moustache. I phoned the office and was informed that it was the best they could do and we would have to live with it. I asked him to please at least shave the moustache and he refused. Said his livelihood depended on it. We found a blonde wig and somehow altered the wardrobe so he just fit into it. The moustache was a problem. I told the director I could fix it. I borrowed some flesh-colored band-aids from the company medic, and pasted them carefully over Little Angelo's moustache. There. Now he was a short, fat version of our thin, lithe actress, but maybe in a long-shot from the back it wouldn't be that noticeable. In the final edit the shot is down to a very few seconds, so Angelo is not an obvious mismatch, but we who worked on the film know about it, and Richard Heffron never let me forget the Midget with the Moustache. It became a running gag between us when we worked together later.

I learned quickly that even if there was to be an hour for lunch I could easily inhale an entire steak dinner, with potatoes, salad, veggies, dessert, and coffee, in around seven to eight minutes. This was necessary because lunch time was the usual time when crew members could come to me for help with equipment needs, film stock, location situations, etc. without disrupting the filming process.

This is necessary too because a film crew can easily cost up to $20,000 per hour, including salaries, location costs, equipment rentals, everything all considered. There are costs for everything. Lunch: The food, tables and chairs or benches, paper or plastic plates, cups, plastic table settings, napkins. Then there is the cost of the cook and assistant, the gasoline for the traveling kitchen, any other maintenance costs. Not to mention the cost of renting the space to set up the tables and chairs, somewhere out of the weather if necessary, and with heaters if too cold during the winter. All these costs add up. Taken all in, the hourly cost can be surprising. That means that a delay of five minutes can cost a lot of money. The importance of the AD lies in the ability to keep the crew working as efficiently as possible to take advantage of every working minute.

We were filming in a private neighborhood in Palos Verdes Estates. A quite wealthy neighborhood, in fact. We had some night filming and we needed the approval of the residents to film past sundown. ABC threw a champagne party for the residents in a five- or six-square block area, so we could explain to them what we were doing and get their approval. This was given. We commenced filming.

There is, however, a law that states that there is always a malcontent. With *Hello Dolly!* it was the Peugeot owner. In this case it was a resident who lived about four blocks away in this quiet neighborhood. For a movie company to be entirely quiet is impossible. For it to try to curb the noise as much as possible is normal. This man wasn't complaining about the noise, he complained, loudly and at length, about the lights and how they disturbed his tranquility. From where he lived, four blocks away, he could barely see a glow in the distance, much less be distressed by our lights. But this did not prevent him from complaining to the local police, to the city council, and eventually hiring a lawyer to get a temporary restraining order preventing us from filming. By the time the TRO was in effect, however, we had finished the film and moved out of the neighborhood. But be warned. If the reader ever wishes to film in Palos Verdes Estates be sure to check for any TROs that might still be in effect.

The story called for Bob Culp, in a fit of anger against the young hoodlums who were trying to scare him and his wife away from the area, to go to their houses and spray paint over the front of one, tear up the lawn at another, smash the windshield of the car in a third, and so forth. We damaged about five or six houses. Restored them after the filming, of course. At the very end of the block was the owner of a chain of martial arts gyms named Chuck Norris. He was already famous as a martial arts expert though he had not yet starred in movies or TV. We had purposely bypassed his house when getting permission to vandalize houses just because we knew his reputation as a martial arts expert.

At least we did so until his wife approached us on the street and asked why we didn't want to vandalize their house. We agreed to do so with great relief.

The movie was finished on time and on budget. I spent a couple of weeks cleaning up odds and ends. ABC handled the entire post-production so there was no need for my talents after that. But Marty Katz kept me for their next project, *Children of God*. This was to be directed by Harvey Hart. It was the story of a girl who joins a religious cult and has to be deprogrammed. Its name changed later to *Can Ellen Be Saved?*

CHAPTER 48

CAN ELLEN BE SAVED?

Michael Parks played the religious leader, John Saxon the deprogrammer, Kathy Cannon played the girl. Leslie Nielsen played the father, a serious role for a very funny comic actor. At the time he was still considered a serious actor. In four years he would play the lead role in *Airplane*, which started him on a long and well-deserved career of comedy.

Our location was in Camarillo, where we used the Adolfo Camarillo Estate as our religious headquarters. This was appropriate since the Camarillo family had leased the house to the Catholic Church to use as a retreat for burnt-out priests and nuns. It was a beautifully constructed and well maintained old Victorian house with all the original furnishings. Don Adolfo had been a very short man, maybe 5' tall, so the house had certain concessions we had to accommodate. For instance the doorknobs were two or three inches lower than normal, forcing taller people to stoop to open the door. The furniture, which we did not use, had shorter legs than normal as well. We replaced it with our own furniture for the film.

The house that stood for the family home was on a wide, upper-middle class street in Santa Monica, California. We filmed there for two days. While we were filming, my cousin, Micha, drove down on my brother Peter's motorcycle for lunch. Then ensued the only time in my life I ever tried to ride a motorcycle. I was not terribly successful. I didn't fall off, but I scared myself enough to know that four wheels are better than two for me.

We finished the show in time to celebrate Christmas. ABC had other films to do and they asked me to stand by. Marty Katz and his wife, Angelika, were frequent guests at our house, and we had many dinners and shared other events together. My work at ABC was there as long as I wanted it.

Around this time Bill Belasco popped up once more. He knew that I had moved to Los Angeles. He was about to produce the life story of the gossip columnist Rona Barrett, the columnist who had broken the story of the Muslims and their work with *Supercops*. Bill had commissioned a script. He told me that if I made the budget and the picture were approved I would be the associate producer. He strongly implied that this was a foregone conclusion since his close friend JTA was still in charge at MGM. I told him that I would only do the budget if I were paid on delivery, and I set my fee outside the norm by half again in order to dissuade him from hiring me. It didn't work. I was soon doing the schedule and budget. It took two weeks.

I delivered the documents to his home on Stone Canyon Road, an exclusive area of West Los Angeles. I was prepared to go over the figures and the schedule with him but he hadn't the faintest idea of how schedule and budget were constructed, so any discussion would be a waste of time. I asked him for my fee. He told me that he would mail me a check.

I picked up the schedule and budget and started to leave. He asked me to leave them. I reminded him that I was always paid on delivery. He appealed to my happy memories of our work together on *Supercops*, and that of course was the wrong thing to do. He finally disappeared into his office and returned with a check drawn to the full amount.

I took the check to my bank and deposited it, but asked the teller to phone Belasco's branch and as a courtesy put a hold on the amount. The teller then informed me that the check was no good. Insufficient funds.

I phoned Belasco. He said to wait a day and then redeposit the check. I suggested that I would go to his house and hand him back the check as long as he gave me cash for it. I told him that if he did not do that I would take the check to the police department and discuss it with them. I had the cash two hours later.

A few months later I read in the paper that Belasco had dined at one of West L.A.'s better restaurants and picked up one of the dishwasher lads. He let the boy drive them both back to Belasco's house where, I suspect, Belasco was going to treat the lad to an evening of poetry reading. In any case the boy managed to crash Belasco's car against a tree in Beverly Hills, killing them both instantly.

CHAPTER 49

JUDGE DEE AND THE MONASTERY MURDERS

One of the pleasures of the film business is the variety. Unlike a job at General Motors or IBM, every show has a different set of personnel and different problems. Different opportunities. Many have vastly different subjects that cause one to research widely differing subjects. In New York, on Supercops, I learned a great deal about New York City police work. With Can Ellen Be Saved?, the research involved religious cults and the process of deprogramming. On Greaser's Palace we learned much about Native American life. The Pueblo tribes still live much the same way they did a thousand years ago, given cars and electricity. But their habits and mores are the same. The next show would be a real treat.

In the seventh century CE in China there lived a judge named Judge Dee. His real name was Ti Jen-chieh (狄仁傑). Lived in China 630-700 CE. He was a magistrate at the court of Wu Zetian (武則天) in the Tang dynasty. In those days a magistrate was empowered to travel the country acting as a court system. He could investigate crimes, prosecute the criminal, and pass sentence. The caveat was that if it were to be discovered later that the criminal was sentenced unjustly, the same sentence would then be applied to the judge. Now why didn't we think of that?

In the mid-1900s the Dutch consul to Chaing Kai-shek's (蔣介石 / 蔣中正) government was Robert van Gulik. Van Gulik discovered the history of Judge Dee and wrote a series of novels around his adventures. These became as popular overseas as Ellery Queen novels were here. There is still a hard core of Judge Dee fans among the mystery novel followers around the world.

Jerry Isenberg, a producer at ABC with an excellent record of hits, commissioned Nick Meyer to write the script for *Judge Dee and the Monastery Murders*. Jeremy Paul Kagan directed. He was ideal because his father, a rabbi, had been a scholar of Oriental history. Jerry determined that our cast should consist of only Oriental actors. This was accomplished, with one exception.

Khigh Diegh was a well-known Oriental actor. He had played the role of Wo Fat in the *Hawaii Five-O* series, Dr. Yen Lo in *Manchurian Candidate*, Four Finger Wu in *Noble House*, Warlord Sing Lu Chan in *Kung Fu*, and so forth. A gentle, distinguished man, the founder of the Taoist sanctuary in North Hollywood, author of several books on Taoist philosophy, he was the essence of Oriental.

His birth name was Kenneth Dickerson and he was Anglo-Egyptian-Sudanese in heritage. But he had recreated himself as an Oriental and that he remained. We were approached by an Oriental actor's group who checked our cast for authenticity. They told us about Khigh, but by that time the contract was signed and we couldn't negate it. Khigh performed admirably, as he always did, and the subject was never mentioned again.

In fact Khigh was also an expert in herbal medicine. I have been asthmatic ever since Lucy got that first kitten. I have used inhalers, pills, all sorts of preventatives and remedies. All worked to some extent but none were perfect. One day Khigh showed up on the set with a small vial of herbal fluid, mostly of eucalyptus scent. He suggested that I coat the entrance to my nostrils with it. It would open up my breathing passages without affecting anything else. This would be good because the medicine I was taking generally opened up blood vessels and everything else as well as breathing apparatus. It worked, and I have used it off and on ever since.

I met several exceptional people on that show. The makeup man was Stan Winston. He would later win Academy Awards for makeup and special effects, especially for the *Jurassic Park* series. On our show he did the makeup, which was considerable. Chinese actors, Chinese circus performers, horror creatures, all kinds of weird and amazing people, and Stan did them all. Further, one evening the cameraman was having trouble lighting the immense *Lost Horizons* set on the back lot at Warner Bros. Studio and the crew was bored out of their minds. Stan put on a musical comedy, all by himself, acting out all the roles, singing and dancing all over the block-long set, jumping up on walls and down curbs, all extemporaneous and of course not captured on film. More's the pity. Stan and I became more than acquaintances. He helped me later in life and I helped him.

Another extraordinary man was Jeremy Paul Kagan. Now something of an honored old-timer at the Directors Guild and in the movie industry in general, he guides the Directors' Track at the USC Film School. On *Judge Dee* he approached the subject with such unbounded infectious enthusiasm that the whole crew immediately loved the project. It was one of those few "magic" shows I worked on where everything worked just right.

The cast was exceptional. Everyone from James Hong to Keye Luke, from Mako, Yuki Shimoda, Frances Fong, to Miiko Taka and Irene Tsu. I have never before or since worked with a group as consistently professional and eager to work that extra bit to make the scene just so much better.

Tony Brand, the 2nd AD, became a friend. We worked together again on other projects.

There was also Charlie Jumps. Possibly the most misnamed man I have ever met. Of course he was very accomplished. He had a "Class A" radio license, which means that he was adept at Morse Code. He was an old steam railroad buff who not only delighted in traveling around the West riding nostalgia trains, such as the Cumbres and Toltec in New Mexico and the Heber Creeper in Utah, but also made model railroad cars from scratch, with the wiring and all. Painted them, too.

In China in 700 CE it was customary for parents to show their children "Devil Scrolls," specially painted scrolls showing what would happen to them if they disobeyed. If they picked their noses their noses would be cut off, that kind of thing. There were also statuary displays showing statues of people in various stages of dismemberment, the results of various bad behaviors. We needed some statues showing people being punished. We already had hired one lady for a scene that called for a lady whose arm had been amputated. Since she was supposed to be naked, we hired a lady whose arm had been amputated at the shoulder. She appears in long shot and very blurry, and only for an instant in a window across a courtyard. But we were going to dwell on the statues for a few moments, so we needed a man who had no arms. Maybe a double amputee?

I phoned Central Casting, spoke to Carl Joy who was in charge at the time. Between Carl and Jim Green, key casting agent there, we were able to handle almost any problem. Need a man without arms? No problem. Give us a day or two to dig one up for you.

Charlie Jumps appeared on the set at the call time, 6:00 am, accompanied by his wife. He had driven himself in his Thunderbird. He was about 5' tall and had no arms. One leg was much shorter than the other. Besides that he was normal. Had an active social life, was a delightful companion, if a bit bizarre. He and I became friends right away. His day job was as a customer rep for a cable TV company. He worked mostly on the phone. I found that he could write by placing a pen between the toes of his left foot. Very lovely script, too. Lunch was an adventure. He always asked for a straw, even for wine and beer. He kept a napkin folded on the edge of the table so he could wipe his mouth. When in company or in a restaurant he was usually fed by someone nearby, but alone at home he could use his feet. He drove his car. He had a steering wheel mounted on the floor where he could reach it with his left foot, and he worked the brake and accelerator with his right. The door had an extra extension on the opening lever so he could reach it with his foot.

We needed Charlie to be a statue, which means he needed to be in a gray makeup to look like an old statue, and to stand very still while the camera was rolling. He did so with aplomb. I would work with him in the future.

The filming went smoothly. A few little glitches as there always are, but mostly nothing to disturb the flow of production. We had built a two-story set on the sound stage at Fox Studios and the walls were stored for later use in other productions. I stayed in touch with several people on that show, the Oriental casting people, some of the crew. Tony Brand.

ABC did not have anything for me to do immediately for a month or two, so

I rested and recuperated from three shows in a row. In the meantime I was doing schedules and budgets for prospective shows, earning a little money each time and building an ever wider group of companies that knew me. Every time I did a budget it was with the understanding that when the picture was funded I would have the right of refusal, that is they would give me first choice of being the UPM or 1st AD or both. 1973 drifted into 1974.

CHAPTER 50

KADOKAWA BUNKO

I did have a brief foray into the Los Angeles commercial world, in a very strange way. I was called by Dr. Akiko Agishi, a Japanese lady who produced TV commercials in Los Angeles for Japanese TV. Seems that American film stars and sports figures could command exceptionally large fees from Japanese TV for endorsing their products. Yul Brynner and Jack Nicklaus could be paid as much as several hundred thousand dollars for one commercial, since whatever they endorsed was bought by millions. Ours was a commercial for a Japanese publishing firm named Kadokawa Bunko, an upper-class publisher of classic literature, much like Penguin Books here.

The director was, well, several people. In Japan, I learned, decisions were by consensus. The main actor, Minoru Terada Domberger, spoke no English, and he also was considered a director. I spoke no Japanese. We both spoke enough German to be able to communicate. The cameraman, Noriaki Yokosuka, spoke neither English nor German, so I spoke with him through Minoru. Also the art director, Eiko, a lovely lady from Tokyo. This was a whole new experience for me.

Minoru Terada Domberger? He is a Japanese director, actor, and jazz singer. My understanding was that he was sent to live on a farm in Germany during the war, and the family adopted him. He graduated from university in Germany and appeared in many stage performances there, then returned to his home land and flourished even more.

Our commercial had a Japanese man with a large sack filled with books. An American policeman asks him, curiously, what is in the bag, and the Japanese man dumps the bag onto the hood of a nearby auto. The policeman, delighted, lets the man go on his way. I had worked on *Police Story* and knew maybe two dozen American actors and extras who owned police uniforms at home. They all appeared properly official and would have made excellent policemen. We held a casting session, and about twenty men showed up in uniform. After the director(s) had seen all of them, I asked them which man they would cast as the policeman. They told me they would answer the following day. Consensus.

The next day I asked again, and they said they wanted me to play the policeman. I didn't even have the regulation haircut. They said it didn't matter. So I went down to the Western Costume Company and had myself fitted out. In the meantime we were trying to find a proper location. Again by consensus, they chose a car wrecking yard in Pacoima. This was becoming more bizarre by the minute. However, they were all very nice, easy to get along with, and certainly open to any suggestions I might make even if they did not follow them.

We filmed in the evening. I quickly learned the folly of trying to be an AD and actor at the same time. As the policeman I had to drive the car into the shot with the lights blinking on the roof, stop at exactly the same place every time, exit the car and approach Minoru. I had to stop at a certain spot and ask him what he was doing. There was a line drawn on the ground where I was told to stop. I would be out of focus if I were a few inches behind or in front of the line. Then after I spoke I was to walk to the hood of the car and stand with Minoru as he dumped the books onto the car hood. When I saw the books I was to smile at him.

What actually happened: I made sure everyone was ready, then called "Roll it!" When the assistant cameraman clapped the slate, I jumped into the police car and turned on the lights. The director called "Action" in Japanese, at the same time waving his arms wildly for me to drive into the shot. I drove in, stopped where I should, exited the car, and walked to the line in the dirt. Gave my speech. Walked to the car hood, watched Minoru dump the books, smiled at him. The director yelled "Cut" in Japanese. I got back into the car and backed it into its off screen position for the next take. There was only one camera angle, one shot, no intercuts, so it had to be perfect.

After about the first five takes it began to rain, softly at first, then more and more heavily. The crew scrambled to put rain shelters up over the camera and crew. Minoru's hair started to hang down. My hair started to hang down. The police uniform was soaked. This was becoming not very comfortable. I asked the director/cameraman if he wanted to continue, and he just smiled. He was happy with the rain. He said to me, through Minoru, "Feel the rain." I said, "You didn't have to remind me of that." No, no, he explained, it is a friendly rain. It makes me smile to be in the rain. I smiled because I was in the rain. We did several more takes, in the rain, and then wrapped up the production.

The next day I returned the uniform to Western Costume, vowing never to allow myself to be cast in anything ever again.

Two months later I received in the mail three copies of the commercial on 16mm film and a big poster of the major scene, rain and all. I had it framed as a monument to my own folly in trying to act.

Four months after that Dr. Agishi phoned me. A group of visiting Japanese businessmen from the Tokyo movie industry had toured the Hollywood facilities and were holding a farewell banquet in the New Otani Hotel in a private banquet room. Would I be interested in joining? I didn't know what I could contribute as a production manager. There were people from the major laboratories, the major equipment suppliers, and a couple from the studios. But after all I was in the movie industry and it was a free dinner.

I arrived at the appointed hour and was shown to a seat at the head table, along with a couple of fellows from Fox and Universal. Glad I thought to wear a suit and tie. Glad I had a smattering of facility with Hashi (chopsticks). Especially glad I really did like sushi, sashimi, and teriyaki this and that. And the inevitable sake. This was really good sake. Must have been for heaven's sake.

Just as we were finishing up our meals the host stood and called for attention. He introduced all the visiting American people, the Fox and Universal people, Image Transform, CFI Labs, and so forth. These introductions were all made in Japanese. We picked up on who was being introduced because the MC mentioned them by name along with a brief introduction. At each announcement there was applause, broad smiles; we were made to feel most welcome in this company. When the man introduced me, he spoke a few sentences and the room burst into frenzied whistles, applause, foot stomping, I've never been so heavily applauded in my life. I turned to Dr. Agishi and asked what the man had said. She explained that I was introduced as the man in the Kadokawa Bunko commercial, which had become wildly popular and had won every commercial award Japan had to offer. I was a celebrity in Japan. The next day my poster moved from my office wall to the living room.

Still hanging on my living room wall.

CHAPTER 51

DARKTOWN STRUTTERS

I received a phone call from my old friend Joe Viola from New York. We had worked together on TV commercials at PGL Productions. He had come to Hollywood and was one of the head writers at a very popular TV series, *Saint Elsewhere*. Now he had been hired to direct a film for Gene Corman, brother of the famous Roger Corman. The picture, *Darktown Strutters*, was a comedy about an Afro-American girl motorcycle gang.

The UPM was Jack Bohrer, who had been UPM on a couple of dozen Roger Corman features. Plenty of experience with low-budget filming. The actresses were largely inexperienced but learned quickly how to maneuver the three-wheel motorcycles. There still were stunts to be done and an Afro-American stunt man was hired. He was unable to find enough Black stunt ladies, so he hired as many Black stuntmen as possible.

I finished my breakdowns and strip board, and went over the schedule with Joe Viola, who made a few small changes and then approved it. I took the schedule to Jack Bohrer and asked him to approve it, then have the secretaries publish it for the crew. I asked him when the production meeting would be. Normally the production meeting, lasting several hours, is the opportunity for all the department heads to go through the script in a conference room with the director, to make sure everyone knows what happens when, and who is responsible for what, and what the director expects to happen. The UPM, AD, and usually the producer are present. Sometimes even the editor and the extras casting people. The more people who communicate about this, the better the pre-production period will be. I asked Jack Bohrer when the production meeting would be and he asked me what it was. I explained it to him. His response: "Why that's a marvelous idea! Let's do it!" He had been UPM on over a dozen productions and had never had a production meeting. Hmmm…

I only had about ten days to prepare, not really enough time to work out proper extras lists, schedules, and so forth. But Gene Corman's system was to try to press everyone to work as fast as possible without much concern with the quality of that work. Just get it done somehow.

The first week we were held up for some time because nobody had thought to get proper fitting wardrobe for the big, muscular stunt men who were supposed to look like the lithe, slim little girls playing the leads. Seams were ripping everywhere and the wardrobe people were hard pressed to try to resize the wardrobe that had been fitted to the girls. We needed this for the stunt shots. There was no help for it except to wait for the wardrobe to be refitted. Couldn't have the stunt men appear naked, now, could we?

For this reason and others of similar ilk we started falling behind schedule. The production department had not done its work, and the UPM was more interested in having lunch with the producer than in proper prep. We paid for that. On Thursday or Friday of the first week I was replaced, as was the director, Joe Viola, and the script supervisor. The producer made no secret that he felt that I should have yelled at the crew more. I was too "soft." Personally I disagreed with him. I always found that working with a crew rather than cracking a whip over them made them prouder of their work, and consequently we got more work done in a shorter period of time, and it was of better quality than if I were a slave driver. The producer, however, was panicked at being behind schedule. He paid dearly for that the very next day.

I was no longer there, but a member of the crew phoned me to tell me. I wasn't happy to hear it but I wasn't surprised. The next day, with the new AD and director, neither of whom had any time to prep, they filmed the big bank robbery scene. In the street outside of the bank, the robbers were to exit the bank holding bags full of money and brandishing Tommy guns. The AD started to set up traffic patterns to accommodate the scene, but the producer insisted that they not waste time with that. Anyway the unpaid extras driving by saved him even more money. They rolled the camera, the bandits exited the bank with machine guns, and the traffic kept rolling on the street. One lady driving past saw the scene and panicked because of the guns. Tried to put on the brakes and kicked the accelerator instead. Her car jumped the curb and knocked over several passers-by, none of whom were connected with the film in any way, but who now would be connected legally. I was very happy not to be working on the film any longer. If the film would have made money, now it would be tied up in lawsuits that would prevent any profit.

CHAPTER 52

THE MAN IN THE GLASS BOOTH

I spent about a week relaxing at home, trying to get to know my wife and sons again, when the phone rang. It was Jim DiGangi, an old New York hand. He needed a UPM/AD for a new show. He was working with Eli Landau's American Film Theatre, an attempt to put really high quality films into movie theatres, paid for by subscription. The films were movies made from plays currently or recently on Broadway. *The Three Sisters*, *Rhinoceros*, and *Long Day's Journey into Night* were all produced this way. We were to film *The Man in the Glass Booth*, from a book and play originally written by Robert Shaw, yes, the same actor who was in *Jaws*.

I was interviewed by Jimmy DiGangi and by Mort Abrahams, the line producer. Mort would be given the title Executive Producer and Ely Landau would take the title Producer without the Executive, so that if the film won an Oscar he could go on stage and collect it. In those days they were trying to limit the number of people on stage during the Oscar ceremonies, so only the producer could claim the statue. Jimmy wanted me. We had known each other in New York. I had never worked with him but we had known each other from Guild meetings and other events. Mort Abrahams, an old-line producer who had worked for Harry Cohn at Columbia Pictures, had many years of experience under his belt and did an exceptional job on this film.

Arthur Hiller, director of such hits as *Love Story* and *The Out of Towners*, was the perfect choice for this. He is a "people" director, an actor's friend. He chose Maximilian Schell, as well as Lois Nettleton, Luther Adler, and other accomplished actors to play the major roles. We moved into offices at 20h Century-Fox Studio and began preparation.

The main character, Goldman, was played on stage by Donald Pleasance, who wanted to play the same role in the film. Arthur Hiller, however, had chosen Max Schell for the lead. Charlie Cohn had been played on stage by Larry Pressman, who played the same role in the film.

Max Schell did a very difficult job of playing two entirely different characters, Arthur Goldman, a millionaire Jewish building contractor in New York, and Nazi SS Colonel Adolf Dorff, commander of a concentration camp. We hired Stan Winston

Adventures In Hollywood: A Memoir By Bob Koster

Front row: I, scriptwright Edward Anhalt, director Arthur Hiller, producer Mort Abrahams.
Second Row: Dir. photography Sam Levenson, chief electrician Les Everson.
Behind Arthur Hiller, editor Dave Bretherton.

Larry Pressman, Max Schell (as Goldman), director Arthur Hiller.

for the makeup and he did a brilliant job. He varied the makeup very slightly between the Goldman character and Dorff, and it was just enough to help make the character difference. Cameraman was Sam Leavitt, who had filmed *Exodus* and *Guess Who's Coming to Dinner.*

Lee Rafner joined us as 2nd AD. He had had a long and distinguished career in TV, having directed coverage of the manned space flights for NBC. Now he wanted to try his hand at theatrical features. He couldn't have been a better choice. He was, and is, superb in his work.

Art direction was by Joel Schiller, creative visual force behind *Lenny* and *The Buddy Holly Story*, among others. A man of singular creative intent, he is also a fine artist and a good impresario. We have remained friends ever since.

This might seem strange that I would mention this, but it is unusual for people to stay in touch after a film is finished. We go on to other films and new sets of filming companions. We travel from one social world to another. Working with the same group, even for only four or five months, creates a kind of family feeling amongst the crew. If one works on a TV series that lasts four or five years, even more so. But there is always another show and a new set of temporary companions. These then become the new family. This life can be disturbing to those unaccustomed to it. The one constant is always the family at home, and this must be nurtured and cherished. It is after all the reason for all the other things. You put up with a lot of nonsense at work in order to have a decent home life. Luckily I didn't have that much nonsense and if I did, it was over soon and another job came along with less nonsense. I was lucky.

The Man in the Glass Booth marked itself with artistic excellence and delightful working conditions. Very little went wrong. There were minor roadblocks but nothing major. For instance, we wanted to cast two well-known European actors in the court scene. These gentlemen had actually spent time in concentrations camps. We wanted them to portray camp survivors. They declined the roles because what the script called for was too close to their own experience, and the memory was too painful. Entirely understandable.

I lost several relatives in the camps myself. I did not know them in person. The memory was still there, however. There was a scene in which Goldman goes to his "Treasure Room," filled with artifacts from the camps: camp pajamas, gold teeth, menorahs, mezuzahs, defaced Bibles, other belongings like eyeglasses and wallets. A potpourri of camp detritus. Joel had borrowed the actual items from the Holocaust Museum in Los Angeles. These were real, not props, not costumes. Actual prisoners' clothing. I had never considered myself very sensitive to such things, but I had to leave the set and ask Lee Rafner to take over for that day. I just couldn't handle it. I have always found it difficult to see movies of the camps and the bodies, but having the actual artifacts in front of me was just too much. I remember watching *Judgment at Nuremberg*, a really wonderful film. When the prosecution in that trial was showing the Holocaust footage I always shut my eyes. I know that horrid things happen in the world, but there are some things that are so horrible that I cannot bear to witness them.

Luther Adler, playing the chief justice, was a delightful person. Most of the time, between takes or scenes, he was just Luther. Told stories about his family and about the early days of the Yiddish Theatre in New York, where his family played such a big role. He was gay and ribald, a wonderful lunch companion. However, when he donned the robe of the chief justice in the film, we would always refer to him as "Your Honor" and pay him the respect due a justice. With the robe on he really *became* the judge. Different manner, everything. The consummate actor.

Lois Nettleton, likewise, was completely at home with us. So was Lloyd Bochner. In fact everyone connected with the show was with us 100 percent. It was one of those magic experiences we all live for in show biz, where everything from the script onward is fine. We get one of these every few years and it helps us to suffer through the bad ones. I was lucky in that I had very few "bad" ones, just a number of "not magic" ones. This one was magic.

Arthur Hiller and the cast had worked out most of the action in rehearsal before any film went through the camera. It was almost like photographing a stage play. Maybe it was because that was what it was. Robert Shaw had written the stage play as well as the book. The screenplay however was written by Edward Anhalt, writer of *The Young Lions* and *Becket*. He went back to the book for his inspiration and expanded it in minor ways, but he also added some psychological and emotional content missing from the stage play. Robert Shaw was not happy about this so he requested that his name be removed from the credits, which it was. Later, when he saw the finished product, he was impressed enough to request that his name be restored. By that time all the release prints had been distributed and it was too late.

We had a week of filming in New York. I duly wrapped the company in Los Angeles, hired my old friend from CBS, Tony Alatis, as the NY AD, and got on the plane. We had cleared an apartment on the corner of 5th Avenue and 55th Street, one with a large terrace around it so we could put lots of great statuary around it. We had already filmed the interior of the apartment on the sound stage. In fact we found the apartment in New York before we filmed the interior in Los Angeles so that we could see the statues through the windows on the sound stage, and the doors opened in the proper direction. It all worked like a charm. We took the same statues with us to NY on the plane as overweight luggage. The TWA rep managed to bypass the luggage payment for us in return for a film credit. We hired an almost complete crew in NY. Sam Leavitt came, and the gaffer, Les Everson. But almost everyone else was drawn from the list I had worked with in NY for so many years. Good people, all. Tony Alatis and I worked that out to perfection.

THE MAN IN THE GLASS BOOTH

Filming went smoothly in NY with a couple of small, understandable glitches. In one scene Max Schell is on his terrace with a telescope. He looks down fifty stories to the street below and sees his father, an old Hasidic Jew, pushing an ice-cream cart. He looks away, rubs his eyes, and when he looks back the father has been replaced by a black-uniformed Nazi SS officer in full regalia. This meant an extra standing in full Nazi regalia on the corner of 5th Avenue and 55th Street, in plain view of the terrace across the street, and of course, in plain view of all passers-by. And we couldn't have anyone there to guard him. I realized quickly that we had to have someone there to tell people that this was for a film. People were buying ice cream cones, milk shakes, candy cones, vegetables, all sorts of things to throw at him. I had to quickly send a P.A. downstairs to stand with the extra to tell the street passersby that it was for a movie. Even that did not stop them all from soiling his uniform. Five minutes later we finished the shot. I radioed the P.A. downstairs to cover him with an overcoat and get him upstairs before someone really hurt him.

The crowd was considerably kinder to the man playing the Hasidic Jew. They kept trying to buy ice cream from him, and he kept explaining that he did not have ice cream, it was only a movie. He had almost as much trouble as the Nazi.

CHAPTER 53

THE BARONY

After a couple of weeks of sleeping and being lazy I put out the word that I was available. I did this as always by calling the DGA and putting my name on the "availability list" which the Guild distributed to all signatory producers. And in those days nearly every producer in Hollywood was a signatory. It wasn't long before my old friend Marty Hornstein called. He was working at Warner Brothers for Paul Heller and Fred Weintraub. They had hired Bob Clouse to direct a bleak film called *The Barony*, about a post-apocalyptic world. Max von Sydow and Yul Brynner were the leads. Since it was post-apocalyptic I was able to give Charlie Jumps a few days work as a mutant. He did well.

With Marty Hornstein.

Max and I.

Yul Brynner and Max von Sydow were delightful characters. Both Max and Yul had motor homes to hang out in between scenes. Max was definitely one of the boys. He always had lunch with us, told great stories of the movies he had done in the U.S. and abroad, and his work with our idol Ingmar Bergman. Max usually stayed on the set unless he was being made up.

Yul was different. He stayed in his motor home unless called upon. He always ate alone. His contractual demands were unusual. His contract stipulated to a particular kind of cut crystal glassware, Orrefors, very simple and elegant. Into these glasses would be poured a particular year of a particular estate-bottled vintage wine for his pleasure. Never during work, only as a little pick-me-up after the wrap. His contract further stipulated that he was to be housed in a suite at the Bel-Air Hotel, and that he be given the use of a white Lincoln Continental convertible for the length of his stay. That car was a point of contention because we had to rent one for him, and we never did get one in which the radio worked well. He kept returning the cars to us and asking for another with a good radio. The Teamsters were amused at first, then later became exasperated with his demands. Of this Yul was blissfully unaware.

Sometimes Yul would startle us by wearing the silver contact lenses he used in *Westworld*, just to see our reaction. Not often because it was very difficult to see through those and he would sometimes bump into doorways.

Max kneeling next to front camera, Yul standing behind.
Back row, third from left, Robert Clouse, director. Extreme right, I.

But on the plus side he was a great storyteller and delighted us by relating stories of *The King and I* and his other triumphs. He had a huge well of knowledge and experience from which to draw. Of his background he was a bit obscure. He may have been part Mongolian, or part Japanese, or part Rom, or all of those. The story changed from week to week. He may have been an aerialist in a circus on the island of Sakhalin, or in Ulaan Bataar, or in China. He may have had an accident and fallen fifty feet off a high wire and broken most of the bones in his body. He did limp rather markedly except when the camera was rolling. Then he was as straight and sure of himself as any of us. But it was obvious that part of the time he was in pain. Might have been arthritis. He still kept smilin' through. And although he was distant he was more than kind to the crew and his fellow cast members. He just wasn't one of the boys like Max was.

Bob Clouse, the director, was stone deaf. I doubt that hearing aids did more than occupy his ears. I was the first assistant director. I would call "Roll it," the sound man said "Speed," the cameraman said "Marker," the signal for the assistant to clap the slate, the slate was clapped, and then we sat there. After a few seconds, Clouse would look at me and say, "Why aren't we rolling yet?" Eventually he watched the camera assistant to get his cue when to say "Action!" Marty Hornstein had worked on Clouse's previous film, *Golden Needles*, in Hong

Kong, and was familiar with his peculiarities. Clouse did know film, however, and was a wonderfully professional director to work with on the set. One just became accustomed to his asking the same question several times, and repeating the answer more and more loudly until he got it.

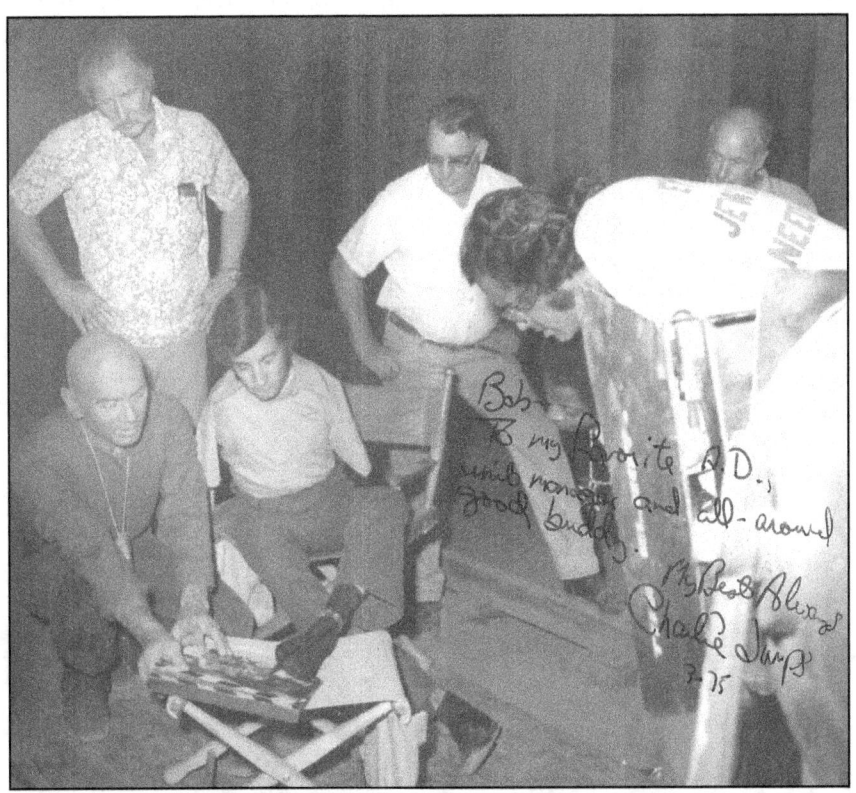

Charlie Jumps, the incredible armless man,
autographs a photo for Yul Brynner with his foot.

We filmed in Warner Studios in Burbank. Some location work was filmed downtown Los Angeles in a very depressed area. This was supposed to be post-apocalyptic, and this street looked the part. We also filmed in the old, closed Desmond's Department Store on Wilshire. Once the most upper-class store in Los Angeles, it had been closed for a number of years. The interior was appropriately filled with broken display cases and cobwebs, saving our effects people some time. We built our own NY subway station on the sound stage. There was a pit set into it where the stunt man Bill Smith would drop. At the bottom of the cage were hundreds of rats, all crawling around and making rat noises. It was only when we actually filmed the scene that we found that Bill, a stunt man with many years experience putting his life at risk, had an innate fear of rats. But being the pro he is, he did the scene and lay down with the rats at the bottom of the pit until the shot was over. Being professionals themselves, the rats crawled over him on cue.

The good guy in *The Barony* was played by Richard Kelton. In the movie he is able to grow fresh vegetables, giving the Barony residents a reason to think that there will be a future after all. Richard was a good actor, very professional. He died three years later aged thirty-five when he went into his dressing room to study his lines, and a gas leak in the heater asphyxiated him. A tragic end to a short, brilliant career.

CHAPTER 54

TRILOGY OF TERROR

We were still socially connected to Marty Katz. He was still in charge of production at ABC Circle Films. I was rehired by ABC Circle Films, this time for a horror show, *Trilogy of Terror*. The producer-director was Dan Curtis. Curtis had made a career of doing horror shows—*Dark Shadows* and others. A good director, he knew what he wanted. At 6'4" he was also very intimidating. He was also selectively hearing impaired. Wore hearing aids and only heard what he wanted to.

The movie was to consist of three short horror stories, all starring Karen Black. The script had been written by Kit Carson. The main story had a girl receiving a present from a friend. The present turns out to be a voodoo doll. The doll chases her around her apartment.

I hired an old friend of the family to build the doll. Erich von Bülow was a very distinguished Czech gentleman. When he lived in Prague he had worked with the legendary puppeteer and puppet animator, Jiri Trnka. For his beliefs, however, he had been imprisoned by the Communists. He escaped and walked out of East Europe to freedom. Made his way to the U.S., where he started working in animated puppetry again. His most famous creation on film was the Pillsbury Doughboy. His second most famous was the voodoo doll for our film.

Erich did not disappoint. He built four identical voodoo dolls for the show. One was just a doll. Another was animated and its legs were attached to wheels, so it would appear to be running across the floor. There were two others for other purposes. After the show was finished I was given one of the four. It was later stolen by movers when I moved from one apartment to another. While I still had it I kept it on the mantelpiece.

Dan Curtis knew exactly what he was doing. We needed a motel for one scene in the show. I scouted Westwood and Westchester for good motels, in quiet places so we could record sound. I found four of them, different styles. One was faux Spanish colonial. One was Tudor. One was modern. I took photos of each along with shots of the interiors and showed them to Dan. He said, "You choose. People don't watch my movies to see the motel style." So I chose.

The production meeting was unique in my experience. During a production meeting, normally, the director goes through the script page by page. The department heads, cameraman, key grip, chief lighting technician, prop master, et al., have the opportunity to ask questions and to talk with each other about how certain effects are to be achieved. The best kind of communication. A production meeting for a movie of the week might take four or five hours. For a feature film it usually lasts for an entire day and lunch is brought in.

In this case, we all were seated around the conference table. Dan Curtis appeared exactly at 9:00 am. He placed his script on the table. Said, "Any questions?" Nobody raised their hands or asked anything. So he took the script and left. The meeting lasted maybe fifteen seconds. I asked him later why he did it that way. His answer was that he had already met with everyone individually and saw no reason to duplicate what he had already said

Karen Black was very easy to work with. Very professional. Her most difficult role was that of the girl with the voodoo doll since she was the only actress in the piece. The only other character was the doll. She carried it all by herself, very well. A single-character show is very hard on the actor. Tom Hanks certainly earned all the applause he received for his performance in *Cast Away*.

We did some filming in a very exclusive neighborhood in the Wilshire Area of Los Angeles called Fremont Place. Several foreign consulates were headquartered there. The houses were, well, mansions. One expected to see original Picassos and Breughels on the walls. We had arranged to film exterior and interior of one of these. The house had recently been acquired by a rich importer from Idaho who had not yet moved in. This made our lives easier since we did not have to move anything out before we put our own set dressing in. Good for the art department.

Filming was trouble-free. We finished as usual on time and on budget. I guess I was lucky. Almost all my shows were that way. I tried to pick the very best people in each department, and they all delivered for the show. Over the years I built up a crew that I could rely on, and in turn I kept them working as much as possible. They never let me down.

CHAPTER 55

INCREDIBLE MELTING MAN

About this time I received a phone call from a writer/director, Bill Sachs. I had known Bill from my New York years. An overly talented man who had not yet quite found the right way to channel his creativity. He had been the "film doctor" who fixed the film *Joe* with Peter Boyle. The Cannon Group had hired him when John Avildson finished his cut. What they had was a standard troubled-youth film in which Susan Sarandon argues with her parents, then leaves home, then the father searches for her. There were several films on the market like that. Cannon wanted to make it exceptional, and they hired Bill to do it. He suggested that they cut off the entire front story with Susan and her parents, and shift the focus of the film to the character of Joe, who had appeared around halfway into the picture. Peter Boyle was far more interesting than the family was. They didn't have much footage on him, however, so Bill shot an extra few minutes with Boyle and reedited the film.

The company had no money for a big splashy premiere so the film was released in a theatre on 57th Street in New York. The critics came to the first showing. The next morning papers trumpeted the greatness of the film, the terrific character of "Joe," the editing, the whole shot. John Avildson was suddenly a big success and the Cannon Group was on the map in a big way.

Bill Sachs had also directed a film that was little seen in the U.S., but which won prizes at the Berlin Film Festival. *There Is No Thirteen* is almost avant-garde in its presentation. A little like the more contemporary *Being John Malkovich*. But even the Berlin prizes did not catapult Bill to the big time the way it should have.

Now he was directing a film from his own script, with independent financing, called *The Incredible Melting Man*. It was about an astronaut who contracts a mysterious disease in outer space that slowly melts his body. As the film progresses his features become more and more distorted until late in the picture he is little more than a walking blob.

Bill wrote a scene into the film in which the melting man, late in the picture, is walking near a gully at a railroad track. Two winos are drinking from a bottle in a paper bag at the bottom of the gully, and they look up and see the melting man passing. One turns to the other and says, "Look at that guy." The other says, "And we thought we were in bad shape." Bill needed someone to play the drunks so he

221

asked me, and also another assistant director named Jimmy Inch.

To prepare for the role I let my beard grow for five days or so; I looked very scruffy. Jimmy already looked scruffy. We were filming out in the Sepulveda Basin. Bill had several other scenes to film that night before he got to us. I had a room in the dressing trailer. I knew that it was going to be a late night; I just didn't realize how late. I had brought a bottle of brandy with me to help keep the chill away.

Needless to say, when Bill got to our scene around 4:00 the next morning, there was no need for me to try to act drunk. My role came off perfectly. So did Jimmy's.

CHAPTER 56

FOOD OF THE GODS

In the mid-1970s there was a film company known as American International Pictures. It specialized in making sensational films of a violent/sexual/horror nature. Roger Corman produced through them. James Nicholson and Sam Arkoff were the owners. Their movies almost always made money because they featured scantily dressed girls in terror for their lives, being rescued by superhuman good guys of some kind. It was all in good fun, and the kids loved it.

One of their most consistent director/writer/producers was Bert I. Gordon. He had made several films for them, including *Earth vs. The Spider*, *The Mad Bomber*, and *Necromancy*. His films usually featured civilization being threatened by oversized insects and animals. The effects were usually done with matte shots, leaving the actors to battle creatures they could not see and would be placed on the screen in post-production. Sometimes rear projection was used, in which the actors played in front of a screen on which the monsters were projected from the rear. Movie magic.

Bert's next film was *Food of the Gods*, taken from an H.G. Wells novel about oversized rats and wasps that attack a small town. Stars were Marjoe Gortner, Ida Lupino, Ralph Meeker, and Pamela Franklin.

It would have been simple enough to film in Piru or some other town close to Los Angeles. Save a lot of location money too, hotel bills, airline expenses, etc. Bert's wife, Flora, was AD and UPM. AIP wanted me to work as production consultant, make sure they were on budget and schedule. From the outset Flora decided that I was superfluous and she could handle the entire thing herself, trying to prove to her husband that she was a worthy partner. They were divorced soon after. They decided to film near Vancouver, Canada, on Bowen Island, a resort island just off the coast of Horseshoe Bay, about twenty-five miles north of Vancouver. The only way to get to the island was four times a day on the ferry. There were no bridges. There was no town on the island, per se, just a general store, a gas station, and a Canadian Legion Hall. And an absolutely gorgeous resort built on one of the most spectacular inlets on the island, managed by the CNIB, Canadian National Institute for the Blind, for people who couldn't see. We were to film from early December to mid-January.

Why were we there? Because Bert's daughter was in school in Vancouver and he hadn't seen her for a while. I mentioned this to the AIP folk and the only result was that Flora now had more reason to hate me. AIP didn't care where it was shot or how much money they spent. My job became very simple.

We checked with the Vancouver Film Commission to see if and when it snowed in Vancouver. Filming outside during a snowstorm was not called for in the script, and the majority of the film was exterior. The Film Commission reassured us that it never snowed in Vancouver before mid-January. We were home free on that score at any rate.

We scouted the island for likely locations and found one that was picturesque and available. It was the summer retreat of the family that owned the largest sugar refinery in British Columbia. The father had just died and left the business to his twin sons. Their mother was secretary, accountant, and oh so much more. We arranged to have dinner in Vancouver with the three of them to discuss renting their summer mansion for the film. This was one of the more bizarre meals I have ever attended. The twins sat on either side of their mother. They hated each other and had not spoken for years. If they had to discuss something, one would say to the mother, "Ask my brother if it's OK to do so and so." The mother would turn to the other brother and say, "Your brother wants to know if it's OK to do so and so." The other brother would say to the mother, "Tell my brother that I feel it's OK except for this difference." The mother would then turn back to the first brother and say, "Your brother feels it is OK except for this difference…"

Eventually, through the good offices of the mother, we made our arrangements.

The only place on the island we could put up the crew was at the CNIB resort, and those arrangements were made. Since there was no other option, several summer homes were leased for the cast and the director, and myself. I shared a house at first with Marjoe Gortner. He shared his quarters with his secretary. When he saw the facilities at the mansion we were filming for location, he decided that was where he wanted to stay, so he moved. Next, Mr. and Mrs. Ralph Meeker moved in with me. Delightful company, and a good actor. When his role was finished, Elliott Schick moved in. Elliott was VP Production at AIP and he wanted to know what was going on. He saw right away.

Among other things, Flora and Bert had asked me to negotiate with the local IATSE for the crew. It took two days, but they finally agreed to be put up at the CNIB facility instead of being bused back and forth, and ferried, to and from the island each day. That would save us three hours a day. I agreed to cater breakfast, lunch, and dinner for everyone, with plenty of leftovers for snacks. There were no restaurants on the island. The caterer would need two station wagons to resupply every day from Vancouver. The local general store was not equipped to provision a company of over 100 people.

The evening came when the Gordons were to meet with the local IATSE and

FOOD OF THE GODS

Teamster business agents to sign the agreements. We all sat down after having met and greeted everyone. The Gordons, without even looking at the agreement I had negotiated, said that I had no authority to speak for them and they wanted to negotiate their own agreement. I asked if I could speak with Bert and Flora in private.

I told Bert that the agreement had already been hammered out with the IATSE and the Teamsters. He went into paranoid mode. "If we don't sign they are going to send their goons after us, aren't they?" "No, Bert, they don't work that way. They will renegotiate with you if that's what you want. But please believe me when I tell you that this is a far better than average agreement." Flora: "It's no good. You don't know how to negotiate. We can do it ourselves." "But Flora, you haven't read it." "I don't have to read it." Bert: "They are going to sneak into our hotel rooms and beat us. They are going to strand us on the island." And on and on.

We returned to the meeting room. The business agents looked at me questioningly, and all I could do was shrug my shoulders, wish them the best, and leave the room. I phoned L.A. to tell the AIP staff what had happened. Sent a memo, too. Gee, I sure wish there had been email in those days.

This set the tone for the rest of the film. The Gordons would ask me to do something to help them, and when I had done it they would immediately undo it and redo it, almost always with a worse result.

Bert Gordon was a man of infinite self-assurance and little talent. His films made money but were usually made at a ridiculous and unnecessary cost. They could have made much more money.

Bert and Flora made a few mistakes in the production, mistakes I could not correct for them. They had cast Pamela Franklin as the romantic lead opposite Marjoe. Pamela had forgotten to tell them that she was pregnant. Bert didn't want to release her and hire someone else, so she played the entire film, ludicrously, dressed in an overcoat.

Bert had a favorite special effects man, a big, happy fellow from Los Angeles. He came to Vancouver and hired a local FX man to help. I phoned a friend in L.A. to check on this big guy's credentials. I was told under no circumstances to let him have a book of matches. He was the most inept FX man in L.A.. Don't trust him to light a cigarette.

The giant wasps needed a giant wasp nest. We commissioned a local FX shop to create a five-foot high wasps nest out of Styrofoam. One scene calls for Marjoe to place a small charge of dynamite inside the access hole in the bottom of the nest, place a wick into the hole, and blow it up. Our FX man rigged the device. The camera rolled. Marjoe ran into the shot, placed the wick up into the access hole, then ran out. The wick burned up into the hole, then—nothing. No explosion, not even a puff of smoke. We left the camera rolling for five minutes then cut it.

The FX man prepared another wick. The camera rolled. Marjoe ran into the shot, placed the wick up into the access hole, then ran out. The wick burned up into the hole, then—nothing. No explosion, not even a puff of smoke. We left the camera rolling for five minutes then cut it. The director was getting nervous and the crew were not happy either.

The L.A. FX man ordered his Vancouver assistant to stick his head up inside the hole to look inside the wasps nest and see what the problem was. The crew quite volubly argued against it, but the L.A. FX man was adamant. It had been ten minutes since the wick had been placed in the hole and nothing could possibly go wrong. He told the Vancouver FX man to stick his head in the hole, and he did.

There ensued the damndest explosion you've ever seen, pieces of wasps nest all over the place, and the Vancouver man lying on the ground, his face bloody. He was alive and conscious but in intense pain. The explosion had driven shards of Styrofoam into his face, especially into his eyes.

There were no vehicles available. The company runabout was in Vancouver getting provisions for the caterer. The only available car was Pamela Franklin's limousine. I quickly got the FX man into the limousine and told the driver to go back to Vancouver to the nearest hospital as quickly as possible. The Gordons had not sprung for the money for a radio to shore, so we had no way of letting anyone off the island know about the accident.

Pamela Franklin stopped the limousine from leaving the set. Where were we taking her car? I told her what happened. She ordered the FX man out of the limo. She needed it to go to Vancouver to get her some bananas. She was pregnant and needed the bananas as soon as possible. I ignored her and got the limo and FX man away from there as fast as possible. Pamela was very unhappy that we had foiled her banana errand, but I was insistent. The Gordons said nothing. Now I had Pamela against me too. I just couldn't do anything right.

I kept in touch with Lucy by phone. By now I was obvious that I would be spending Christmas and probably New Year in Canada. She could take some money and buy the kids presents and put my name on them. We would have some kind of celebration when I returned. Nobody was happy about this arrangement but there was nothing to be done.

On December 15 it snowed for the first time that season in Vancouver. Two feet. Nothing could move, least of all our equipment trucks. I contacted the one gas station on the island to find out if there were caterpillar tractors there that could haul our equipment trucks and motor homes to the location. Luckily there were some, and just as soon as they were finished clearing the road, maybe in three or four hours, they would come and help us. Could they come a little sooner? No, after all, we were only a movie, and they had to do important things like plow the roads for the residents. Nothing to do but wait. Elliott Schick suggested that maybe a few strategically placed dollars would help. They did not. Somewhere around noon we saw our tractors appear, slowly they pulled the trucks up to the location, and then they returned to the gas station. We would have to leave the trucks at the mansion and be shuttled by whatever means to and from the CNIB.

But at least we accomplished the important thing. Bert and Flora got to visit with their daughter.

I had known for some time that I could do nothing for this group. With a sense of relief I heard from Lucy that she was going into the hospital for a minor operation. An excuse to get away from there!

I asked Eliot to be relieved. After all, he was there to help out on behalf of AIP, and I had some kind of medical emergency back home. He gave his permission and I was gone the next day.

In fact it was a very minor operation. Lucy was home two days later, and I was able to be the stay-at-home dad until she was well enough. I did make a trip in to AIP's offices on Doheny and Wilshire to report on the progress of the film. They production chiefs were remarkably sympathetic. At that point, however, they had little choice but to let the film be finished.

CHAPTER 57

FUTUREWORLD

I spent a few weeks at home before the next call came. It was AIP again. This time it was Marty Hornstein. He had signed on as UPM of *Futureworld*, Michael Crichton's sequel to *Westworld*. Director was Richard Heffron, the director of *Outrage*, the film with the midget with the moustache. The producer was James T. Aubrey who had retained the rights to the *Westworld* series from Crichton, and had brought it to AIP when he was forced out of MGM as production chief. It was probably the biggest budget film AIP ever produced.

We would film on the lot at MGM for a week or so, and then go to location at NASA's Manned Space Flight Center just south of Houston, Texas. We would spend a few days filming in Houston itself, majorly at the Rice University Medical Center, where we would use Dr. Michael DeBakey's operating room as a set. Then we would go to NASA HQ at the Johnson Manned Space Center for the remainder of the filming.

I had always been fascinated with the space program and here was a chance to go to the headquarters of it all. We would be filming in NASA's facilities, the anechoic chamber, the anaerobic chamber, master control, the space shuttle, the whole nine yards. Sure, I'd be up for that.

Peter Fonda and Blythe Danner starred. Arthur Hill, John Ryan, Yul Brynner, and Stu Margolin also played in it. Good, solid actors all. And I knew that with Dick Heffron directing we would be on schedule and on budget.

I read the script and began to schedule the film. There were a few little worries. There was a two-day shoot at a big auditorium in Houston. There was the problem of moving easily around at NASA, which was highly guarded by military police. There were the logistics of getting the entire crew, and set dressing, and props, and wardrobe, to Houston and back. Since I was to be the 1st AD these worries were Marty Hornstein's but I always tried to help when I could.

There were minor glitches. We filmed a scene at MGM studios that was supposed to be inside the "Space Bar" in a space station floating above the Earth. Through the windows could be seen some astronauts in pressure suits floating in space. The production designer, Trevor Williams, and the director of photography, Gene Polito, were not on the best of terms. Consequently they did not discuss everything as thoroughly as they might have prior to filming.

The windows of the Space Bar looked out over a black curtain which to the eye seemed like outer space. Through the window could be seen astronauts floating, which was accomplished by putting them into pressurized NASA space suits and hanging them from wires from the ceiling so they could seem to float past the windows. The windows had smoked glass in them that made the view from the windows very dark. Hard to see the space men. Gene had to bring out the super hot lights to get the image necessary through those darkened windows.

The stunt men in the space suits had no air conditioning and the suits grew hotter and hotter. Both men eventually fainted. There was no way for them to let us know that they were in trouble as their internal radios were not activated. But after all they were stunt men, and they had no permanent damage, only discomfort. Negotiations then took place between the camera and art departments. Nothing should go wrong when we filmed at NASA.

Of course it did. When in Houston we stayed at the Hyatt Regency, one of those grand Hyatt hotels with an elevator visible from the atrium. Crew members would sit at the bar after work and bet on which elevator would reach the ground floor first. Great fun. Marty had made a really great deal with the hotel since it was off-season and he had given them over 100 rooms for a set period of time. We also would stay there for a day or two after we finished filming at NASA.

One thing about the Hyatt, its restaurants close at 10:00 pm. Not even a coffee shop open. So when we wrapped after 10:30 we were SOL. We came to be fond of the Eggs 'n' Things five blocks away down the street.

We had some scenes that took place inside a hospital operating room. We had the pleasure of filming inside the operating room of Dr Michael DeBakey. He had actually six operating rooms arranged round a central control room. In one operating room his assistants would prep the patient. Then Dr. DeBakey came in and operated, while the assistants went into the next operating room and prepped the next patient. When DeBakey had finished his operation he went into the next room and operated there, while other assistants sewed up the patient in room #1. DeBakey was operating in room #2, while the prep assistants were working in room #3. It was a very efficient system.

We filmed in one of the rooms and tried not to touch anything anywhere else. Didn't matter. After we left, the hospital staff had to disinfect everything near us anyway.

Funny about operating in hospitals. They seem to think that their precious patients are more important than our film. If we were filming in a hallway and they had an emergency, they would just wheel their patient right through the shot to get to the ER or the OR. We were accustomed to being catered to and not used to such cavalier treatment. Seriously, a few of the crew did not like this arrangement, but it was necessary.

We still had that two-day shoot at the Houston auditorium, known as Jones Hall, home of the Houston Symphony Orchestra. The script called for a very complex shooting plan and we needed the time to accomplish it. We also had about 600 extras, cast for us by Gary Chason, Houston's premier casting agent at the time. There would be two or three cameras filming simultaneously to save time, and the schedule still called for two days filming because of the coverage.

James Aubrey told me to reschedule the scenes for one day. I replied that the way the script was we could only do it in two days and that would be very tight. He ordered me to reschedule for one day and he would have the script adjusted to accommodate, reducing the time necessary to shoot. I did the reschedule as ordered, informing Dick Heffron and Marty Hornstein as to what had happened and to be prepared for script changes.

The script was never changed, and we filmed for 26 hours straight to get the work done. At wrap time Jim Aubrey appeared on the set and grandly announced that he was giving us the rest of the day off. He was greeted by stunned silence. Nobody knew what he had expected. He appeared rested and refreshed, obviously had a good night's sleep while we were working through the night. We had filmed from 6:00 am on one day to 8:00 am the next, and we are all completely exhausted.

The results of this: The company spent a great deal of money on overtime, meal penalties, "Golden Hours"—far more than an extra day would have cost by two or three times. Fully a third of the crew became ill and had to be shipped back to Los Angeles and replaced. Extra air fares and hotel bills, as well as various medical expenses. We also lost Marty Hornstein. He came down with pneumonia. He struggled with it for a week or two and then went home, to be replaced by the indefatigable Elliott Schick. Cameraman Gene Polito was replaced by Howard Schwartz, and the problems with the art department disappeared.

The local press covered us while we were at Jones Hall. CBS, NBC, and ABC all had affiliates here, with reporters giving commentary and interviewing the stars and the crew when possible. Anyone connected with Hollywood was fair game. One TV reporter approached me with a question. He was a member of the Screen Actors Guild. Where would he go to get a small part in the film? Silly me. Gave him Gary Chason's phone number. That evening on TV, this reporter announced that if anyone wanted to be in the film they should phone Gary Chason, and he showed the phone number on the screen. Within a minute it put Gary's phone out of commission. There were thousands of phone calls at the same time.

The company moved to NASA, about a half hour south of Houston on Galveston Bay, almost without incident. Oh, yes, there was an incident. We had had a papier-mâché rocket ship built at a prop house in Houston. It was strapped to the back of a truck for transport to NASA so we could use it. It fell off the truck.

NASA was an interesting place to film. Being a government facility, the U.S. government charged us nothing for permission to film. The problem was with the individual buildings. For instance, we filmed in Master Control, the big room with the big screens on the wall that you always see whenever the news broadcasts show anything about space exploration. There are maybe thirty workstations there as well as the big displays on the wall. Behind the operators, there is a glassed-in room for observers, family, etc.

Although we paid the government nothing for the ability to film there, there were several subcontractors who operated the facility. For instance, Northrop managed the building itself at that time. IBM managed the master control room for the computer facilities. Ford Aeroneutronics managed the displays. There were two or three other subcontractors who managed various aspects of Master Control. We also had to make a contract with KB Janitorial which handled sweeping the floor and cleaning up. These subcontractors had no qualms about charging us for the use of their facilities.

We planned to have maybe twenty extras sitting at the consoles, with displays on their individual screens, speaking into their microphones as if something important were happening. We had a wonderful graphic designer, Brent Sellstrom, with a fine knowledge of computers to handle all the displays, large and small. That part was taken care of. But another problem arose. Or another opportunity, if you will. Richard Heffron wanted to see the operators at the consoles speaking into the microphones on their headsets. What would they say? Richard asked me to make a few dozen 3" x 5" cards with terse announcements on them for the extras to read. That was easy. I spent an evening at my desk making out the cards. It was obvious that many of them would have "Begin .... on my mark; three, two, one, mark!" No problem inventing things for the people to say either. "Begin countdown on my mark…" "Begin blast-off sequence on my mark…" "Begin escape pod launch sequence on my mark…" "Begin vertical and horizontal screen adjustment on my mark…" Then I began to run out of brilliant ideas. So we started "Begin archeological studies on my mark…" all the way down to "Begin proctology studies on my mark…" I also had one operator saying over and over again into his mike, "Ground control to Major Tom…" from a well-known rock song. Since these people could barely be heard, and since the audience would be concentrating on hearing the dialogue anyway, we got away with it. The only difficulty was in keeping the speakers from laughing while they spoke into the mikes. Of course we gave out the cards with the more serious statements to the operators closest to the camera, just to be safe.

NASA had not yet been taken over by the Department of Defense so we had reasonable freedom to come and go as needed. Our only stopping point was at the main gate, and we had ID badges allowing us on the property. Once on the property we drove ourselves right to the location building, parked, and went in without any further ID checks. The PR people were more than willing to help us as well. We received press kits left over from former space efforts. Recently there had been the first international hookup between a Russian and an American space capsule, with a great deal of press in attendance. There were press kits available from this and I managed to take one home, in both English and Russian.

One of the buildings housed the "anaerobic chamber." This was a huge ten-story high structure that could be made completely airtight. Space capsules were placed in it to test their space worthiness. If the air was pumped out and the capsule was filled with air, if any air escaped from the space capsule when it shouldn't, it would be obvious. Astronauts' lives would depend on this. This chamber would never be pumped out when we were there, but we could place our space ship (yes, the fallen one) inside and photograph it from the top down. Worked like a charm.

The room operators told us that the chamber was so big that it had its own weather patterns inside. When the room was evacuated there was a near-vacuum inside. After the vacuum experiments air was allowed in. As it entered the empty chamber it tried to expand to fill the space, and this cooled it considerably. The result of this was usually a snowstorm inside the chamber. It startled the scientists the first time and then they became accustomed to it.

We also filmed inside the "Anechoic Chamber." This room was completely isolated from the world as far as sounds were concerned. It was designed to test radio signals from the satellite. It was important that no signal be reflected from the walls, so the room was soundproof and had large Styrofoam cones pointed outward from the walls and ceiling to prevent echoes of any kind of waves, sound, microwaves, anything. It worked beautifully. It was like being inside the famous "Dome of Silence" from the *Get Smart* TV series.

Our lives after work were just like usual. We slept fast, spent the weekends doing laundry. Once in a while we had dinner together with some others. A gal from very high in Houston society invited some of us over for dinner one evening and it was just as stiff and formal as one would expect with someone in the upper society atmosphere of a big Southern city, with all of us lower-class film folk. But it was kind of jolly nonetheless. I think she was curious as to what kind of people we were. She seemed nice enough but I certainly wouldn't have invited her for dinner in my house in L.A.

We finished the film and I drove back to Los Angeles. I had had my TR-6 in Houston, a good city for sports cars. I wasn't able to drive it to Houston myself because there was not enough time, so Ron Underwood, one of our AFI interns, drove it for me. Ron later became a really good director, doing *Tremors* and the remake of *Mighty Joe Young*. But now I had the time to drive myself back, and it was a pleasure. Also gave me the time to decompress after the film.

About half the distance from Houston to Los Angeles is in the state of Texas. It's roughly 1,500 miles from L.A. to Houston, and 750 miles of that is in Texas. Driving in Texas in those days was like driving in Germany. The speed limits were not observed really by anyone. I usually cruised at 85-90 MPH, radio blaring. This all came to a halt at the New Mexico border. I could not have been five miles inside NM before I saw the old highway patrol flashing red lights in my rear view. I pulled over. The officer said, "Just in from Texas, eh? Better keep the speed down. We're stricter here." He gave me a warning, and I drove in a more relaxed manner from there on.

While I had been in Houston I received a phone call from Bob Rolsky at Columbia Pictures Television asking about my availability. They wanted me to come there and work on the TV series *Police Story* when I was finished with *Futureworld*. I told Bob that I needed some time to relax before the next assignment. He agreed.

I had heard of a very exclusive resort in Acapulco, Mexico, called Las Brisas. Their signature pink-roofed jeeps were ubiquitous in Acapulco. One could rent a little bungalow, with bedroom and sitting room/kitchen, as well as a private swimming pool with large wall separating it from other bungalow/pool areas. We could go skinny-dipping if we wanted to. And every morning when the maids made up the room, the pool cleaner spread fresh hibiscus petals on the pool surface. It was really a kind of honeymoon place. I wanted to be as far away from the movie industry as possible.

Naturally, as we were checking in, one of those pink-roofed jeeps drove up with Paul Lazarus, the line producer of *Futureworld*. "Hi, Bob! Good to see you here! Let's get together for dinner!" Sure, Paul. Love it, baby. Have your girl call my girl and we'll do lunch.

The rest of the vacation was similar. Sure, we rested, ate some good food, and I had the chance to go scuba diving, which I always enjoy. Acapulco Harbor has a shipwreck at the bottom of the bay, and I was able to dive into the ship, swim down the corridors, look into the cabins, and generally see what was down there. It was enjoyable. We also saw the fabled cliff-divers of La Quebrada, diving off a 95-foot cliff into six feet of water. Dinner at El Mirador hotel while watching the cliff divers was a treat. And the bottled water was great, as were the tropical drinks. I stayed with bottled water when away from Las Brisas since I knew of horror stories of people who drank the local water and paid dearly for it.

Not us. We were very careful, in restaurants and any public area. Only bottled water supplied by the hotel, which we carried with us. In restaurants I usually ordered something with tequila in it because I figured that the tequila killed whatever was bad in the water.

The vacation was not without little setbacks. I got a traffic ticket for running through a green light. Like I said, the pink-topped jeeps were flags. "Sucker here!" I was taking Lucy to dinner at a local restaurant. We had stopped at a red light. When it turned green we started out, only to be rewarded by the familiar flashing red lights in the rear view mirror. I pulled over and the policeman, very fat and very friendly, approached the car, ticket book in hand. "What is wrong, officer?" "Sorry, señor, you went right through the light." "But it was green, officer." "Sorry, señor, you went through the light."

No dummy here. "Look, officer, I know that I have broken the law and I apologize sincerely. I know that there will be a fine." I handed him $10. "I would sincerely appreciate if you would take this to the judge and pay it for me." "No problem, señor. I'll take care of it." The red flashing lights stopped flashing. I proceeded to take Lucy to dinner and I have no doubt that the policeman went directly to the courthouse to pay my fine for me.

A minor annoyance was that on the very first morning there, Lucy was sunning herself at our private pool when an unfriendly local bee stung her right in the middle of her derriere. Lying by the pool was OK, but sitting anywhere like in a restaurant in a normal position was a problem for her. Somehow we finished the vacation with no further incidents. I received another phone call from Bob Rolsky (How the devil did he find me in Acapulco???) to ensure that I came to Columbia Pictures when we returned.

CHAPTER 58

POLICE STORY

When we returned I had a meeting with Richard Learman, the UPM of the TV series, and Liam O'Brien, the producer. Then I met with Mel Swope, line producer. Approved, I was to start next week. I took the first script home to break down and schedule it. In those days it took about a day to make the break down sheets for a one-hour episode. Each hour episode actually took about forty-seven or forty-eight minutes of film time, the rest being used by commercials and promotional announcements. Usually the next morning I would bring in the breakdown sheets and the schedule, go over it with the director, and then hand the breakdown sheets in shooting order to the secretaries, who then typed up the schedule and printed copies for the cast and crew.

On the set of Police Story, UPM Richard Learman just behind the lens.

In this case the director was Michael O'Herlihy. An Irish nobleman, brother of the actor Daniel O'Herlihy, he was one of the most well-organized directors I have ever worked with. He had his peculiarities. One was to give the assistant director as little information as possible. We never knew exactly what his next shot would be, so we had to be prepared to film in two or three directions at once. We did not know when he planned to finish filming during the day, but we did know that it was usually around 3:00 pm. The producers and crews loved him because he finished early every day like clockwork. But he never gave us a warning.

He did have a silent agreement with the property master. When he was on the last shot of the day he would sit in his chair and put out his arm. The prop master would place in his hand a glass of wine. We knew we were on the last shot by that; no other signal was necessary. The crew could begin wrapping up and loading the trucks with all the equipment we did not need for that last shot.

Police Story was a TV series in which there was no running cast. There were new stars every week since each week we showed the story of a new set of policemen. It made it very interesting. I was one of two first assistant directors. We alternated shows with each other while the company kept filming. The other AD was Carl Olsen, an old-line gruff AD, very experienced, but with a great feeling for people. I grew to be very respectful of him.

The director of photography was Emmett Bergholtz, an elder distinguished man whose career stretched back to *Abe Lincoln in Illinois*, 1940, on which he was camera assistant. He could light almost any set within a half hour. This endeared him to directors and producers alike.

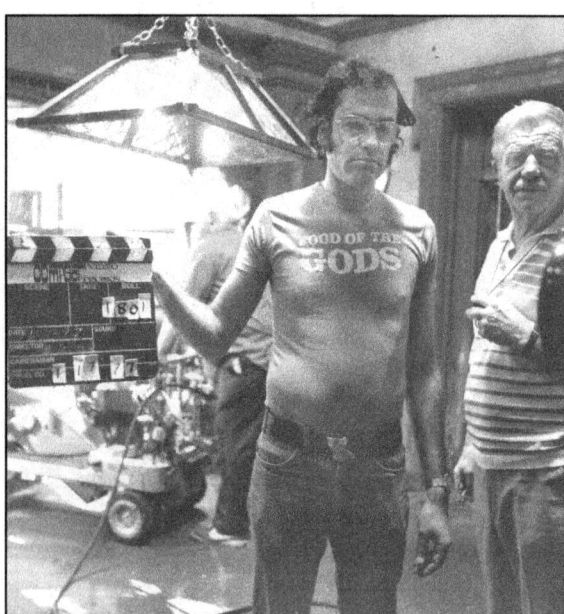

Emmett Bergholtz, an amazingly fine director of photography.

We usual filmed for three days on location and four days in studio. There was a standing set of a police department, and we had other sets as necessary. Ross Bellah, the art director, was very good at staying just ahead of us in construction.

One of the directors I was particularly fond of was Barry Shear. He had directed a number of films but had never had a great success until he directed Across 110th Street. As he put it, it gave him "f*** you" money so he never had to work again. Now he could pick and choose his projects and enjoy himself. He had a truly horrid reputation with ADs. I learned quickly why. We were of course on a strict budget. We were limited in the numbers of extras we could hire for each episode. I told Barry the limits, and we were able to design the budget and schedule to make maximum use of the extras we had, if some brought changes of clothes with them they could appear in more than one scene. It would appear as if we had many more extras than there were. We stayed with that figure. It seems that some ADs would just listen to what Barry wanted, took his extras order down, and then on the day of filming there might or might not be the number Barry had wanted. My way was easier and more manageable and Barry did not feel as if he had been lied to.

One of our directors was a big problem. Vince Edwards had been the star of his own TV series in the 1960s, *Ben Casey*. His main claim to acting ability was his use of an expression that indicated that he had eaten something bad very recently and his digestive system was rebelling. But he did have a screen presence. He was also, in his own mind, a star.

One weekend we wrapped on Friday evening, and he told me that he was going to spend the weekend in Las Vegas. I suggested that if he did that he might not be back in time on Monday morning. He said he would, and he was going anyway. He drove off in his Mercedes-Benz. Monday morning crew call was 7:00 am and he missed it. Wasn't at work at 8:00 am either. Finally showed up around 10:30, after the crew had been standing around for three and a half hours waiting for him. He drove on the lot in a brand new BMW. I asked him what had happened. He explained to me, with a completely straight face, that the valet in Las Vegas had left a burning cigarette on the passenger seat of his Mercedes. He couldn't be seen driving around in such a car. So first thing Monday morning he went to his BMW dealer and traded it in on a new BMW. Had to wait for the car to be ready to drive off the lot, and then he came to work. I noted all this on the production report. Edwards was not pleased.

I had spoken several times with the executive producer, David Gerber. I found him to be eminently approachable. He was always interested in listening to other people's ideas. Well respected on the Columbia lot. He told me that he preferred to have lots of extras in any given scene, lots of movement around the actors in offices, in hallways, on the street. Gave the show life. I concentrated on doing that for most of the shows.

In Edwards' show there was a scene in an office building. As usual, I put lots of extras, walking back and forth, populating the scene with activity, giving it life. Edwards saw the rehearsal and told me that he wanted the scene to be bare, that he wanted one extra or at the most two, in the shot. I explained what David Gerber wanted. He told me in no uncertain terms that this was his show and that he wanted very few extras. I did as he asked.

The next morning, after David Gerber screened the dailies from the day before, he phoned the set. Asked to speak with Vince Edwards. I went to the phone with Edwards and stood nearby. I heard Edwards tell Gerber, "Well, if you wanted lots of extras why didn't the AD tell me?"

Then an amazing thing happened. There were a few moments of Edwards just listening. Then he turned to me and said, "I'm sorry. You were right. There should have been more extras." The phone was still connected and the mike was open. I suspect that Gerber told Edwards that I never would have agreed to less extras and he owed me an apology, which he gave immediately. One of the more satisfying moments in my career.

Working on a TV series is, again, like paddling a leaky kayak upstream against rapids. You just hope you survive. We had an excellent crew, none better. The directors were for the most part right on top of the shooting plan. The producers, from Gerber to Swope, were adept and supportive. We never had to wait for a script; unlike many series our scripts were always delivered on time and they changed very little. For production, it was a good situation all the way around.

The head of production for CPT was Seymour Friedman, an old-time director/producer who had studied well under Jack Fier. He had a switch at his desk by which he could close his office door by remote control when he wished. More than once I appeared in his doorway to ask a question and suddenly the door closed in my face. But he probably knew more about production than I ever would and once in a while he would favor me with some advice. He also constantly tested my knowledge and ability in scheduling and budgeting. In the production department we were used to his constant badgering and took it with humor.

It was a pleasure to work with some of the actors, not so pleasurable for others. In the main, the older more established actors were easier to work with than the younger ones who were just entering the movie star mill. The older ones were far more tolerant, secure in their careers, understanding the exigencies of filming, able to change schedules when necessary, always prompt and professional. Some of the younger ones were far less confident and treated every variation from the norm as a threat to their career, and to their existence. There were not many in between those two extremes. Our show did not have regular stars. We changed from one episode to the next. One week we might have Hugh O'Brian starring, the next Steve Lawrence and George DiCenzo. Al Onorato, our casting director, did a superb job of finding the right character types for the roles. It was a well-oiled machine.

One of the younger actors came to me often to ask how to pronounce certain words in the script. I had been an English major, after all. I usually referred him to the director unless the director told me to help. I tried not to speak to the actors about anything but their time on the set. Anything else was the director's purview. I could speak to the director about things I saw in the scene that he didn't, but I never addressed the actors directly. Only assistant directly.

One of our episodes was on videotape, the first episodic show to do so.

CHAPTER 59

SPACE FORCE

Right after *Police Story* was finished, Columbia assigned me to be both UPM and 1st AD on a half-hour comedy pilot entitled *Space Force*. John Boni and Norman Stiles were the writer-producers. They had just finished working on Mel Brooks' *When Things Were Rotten*. Their kind of comedy was not mine necessarily, but lots of what they did was very funny. And we had Fred Willard in the cast, a comedy master. The entire action takes place on board a spacecraft.

I was able to cast my sons as green-skinned extras from the planet Algon who are transported up to the spacecraft for a tour. Chris and Kevin loved every minute of it. They were already very avid fans of *Star Trek*. The idea of actually being aliens was just wonderful to them. When the set was being lit they were able to sit in the commander's chair and play with all the switches and dials.

In order to make the set look much larger than it really was we had the art director build a corridor with a room at the end of it with crew men walking around in the room. Since there wasn't much room on the stage to build it, the art director used forced perspective. Built a corridor that became narrower with distance. Central Casting found us three or four midgets. We put them in space suits and had them walk around in the room. From our camera they looked like normal sized people much farther away.

Peter Compton directed. He had a great sense of humor. The cast really had trouble not laughing at the situations Boni and Stiles had written them into. It was not a bad show, but it was up against another show, *Quark*, and would soon be up against another, *Space Balls*, all space comedies. Sometimes you can't win. *Quark* was also produced at Columbia. The UPM/AD on that was a friend from earlier days, Maximilian Bing. He and I would get together at lunch and tell terrible jokes to each other.

At the time Fox was in development on several projects, one being *Roses Roses*, scripted by Frederick Raphael. Mark Rydell was to direct. I was hired to budget and then manage the project, and Ted Haworth would be the art director. Alan Ladd Jr., studio head, was personally interested in this project. I worked with Gareth Wigan, Ladd's associate, on the budget. Mark, Ted, and I scouted locations all up and down the California coast to find just the right vistas for the film. We rented a car in Eureka and drove the entire length of Highway 1, possibly the most spectacular drive in the world. Along the way we found several possible venues. I went back to the office and with Ted Haworth we made a budget for the show. Alan Ladd Jr. wanted us to be able to make the film for $3 million "below the line," meaning without the stars, script, or director. I budgeted it as tightly as I could, and still was unable to get it below $3.2 million. The Fox staff told me that I could make it anything I wanted to, and they were right. I could make the budget $2.5 million. But when we shot it would still cost $3.2 million and then they would blame me for going over budget. I refused to manipulate the budget.

Perhaps I should have. Fox canceled the film and it was never made. Mark Rydell went on to direct two very successful films, *The Rose* with Bette Midler, and *On Golden Pond* with Kate Hepburn and the Fonda family.

CHAPTER 60

BUTCH AND SUNDANCE

I was told to stand by on the lot. Fox had another film for me. *Butch and Sundance, the Early Days* was to be the sequel to *Butch Cassidy and the Sundance Kid*. The director was Richard Lester. Lester coined the term "prequel" to describe the film. It was produced after the first film but took place in history before the first film. The producer was Gabe Katzka and the line producer was Steven Bach. William Goldman had written the original *Butch Cassidy and the Sundance Kid*. The actual script for our film was written by Alan Burns.

Gabe Katzka as executive producer had gotten the script and director and brought the package to Fox for production. Fox agreed to finance it. After that, Katzka disappeared and we never saw him again. Steven Bach was the acting producer. A highly experienced, perceptive man, he was able to thread the minefield of studio politics to get the best possible picture made. He was a great backstop for me.

The picture was a little difficult. We were to film in Santa Fe, NM, Chama, NM, and Telluride, CO. We had rented a studio in Albuquerque, where we filmed the major dance-hall sequence. We found original locations we could film where possible. Butch and Sundance had actually held up a bank in Telluride. Richard Lester, who had turned into a demanding director, wanted to film inside that bank. It was now an Elk's lodge but it still had the teller's cages. The platform, where the bank officers had sat, was now a bar. We had to make it over entirely. In order to get permission to do so I joined the Elks Club. I stopped just before the initiation ceremony and never completed my membership requirements. I did it for the film. I keep telling myself that, anyway.

Richard Lester was a brilliant director. He worked well with Laszlo Kovacs, our director of photography. The crew was mostly of Laszlo's choosing. When he interviewed for the job he gave me a list of crew members with their weekly salaries, and made it clear that if we did not hire them he would not do the film. Not being one to knuckle under to blackmail, I told the Fox production staff that we could get another cameraman. They told me to go ahead and hire Laszlo's crew no matter what the cost. In those days Ray Gosnell, a well-experienced, old-school UPM, was the production manager of the studio. His assistant was John W. Rogers. Rogers' father, Charles Rogers, had originally hired my father at Universal. John was in production because of family connections, not talent. His manners were East Coast prep school. He hadn't studied very hard because he kept embarrassing himself by mispronouncing words and speaking ungrammatically in obvious ways. Also, while the film was in production, he was fired from Fox and given four hours to clean out his desk and leave the lot. He had been caught taking kickbacks from crew members for hiring them, down to 50 cents a week from secretaries. It was sordid and messy. He had never asked me for anything so I wasn't personally familiar with the system, but the word got around the studio very fast. He had trouble being hired anywhere after that. The movie industry can be a small world sometimes.

At the same time that we were preparing the *Butch* project, Fox released a minor B-grade sci-fi picture called *Star Wars*. Suddenly the whole studio was in an uproar. That picture had made the covers of both *Time* and *Newsweek* magazines in the same week, and the attendance was going through the roof. The studio was gearing up for a major publicity push. Phones in the studio offices were ringing off the hook. Local stock brokers were offering to buy stock options from anyone at the studio who had them as salary compensation. Fox stock had just soared and was going higher by the hour. The production department wasn't paying as much attention as they would have normally to the *Butch* team.

This was unfortunate because Richard Lester was taking on the role of tyrant, with me at any rate. Steven Bach informed me that Lester had wanted his own production manager from England, Denis O'Dell, for the movie, and that Fox had turned him down. From then on he did everything in his power to show Fox how incompetent I was. I had contacted his favorite stillsman to work on our picture. The fellow was currently employed on another film but would be free to take ours when it was over. The two did not overlap. He did not want to sign a deal memo yet until he was finished with his other film. I was in Telluride when Lester phoned from England to see how the stillsman was coming along and I told him. "What??? You couldn't even get a deal memo from him??? Get one immediately!!! We can't afford to lose him!!! Now what other bad news do you have for me?" No matter what I said or did it was wrong. I managed to clear all the locations for him because he had convinced Fox that we did not need a location manager, standard Hollywood procedure. I had to do it. I was shuttling between Hollywood and budget meetings, and Santa Fe, where I was clearing locations. Lester seemed to know what buttons to push.

It was a huge job in any case. Our locations stretched for literally hundreds of miles across desert and mountain. We had to build five villages in the desert of New Mexico that we could rob. We rented the Cumbres and Toltec Narrow-gauge railway. This was during the winter, and the railroad crew had to take the locomotive out of storage and prepare it for travel. The first trip it had to push a snow plow to clear the tracks so that we could film it. All this had to be arranged for by me personally since I was also the location manager. Furthermore, Lester wanted to film on the property of two or three pueblos. These areas are the property of the natives themselves and the American government has no authority there. I had to appear before tribal councils to get permission to film.

To add to this confusion I was in the midst of a divorce from Lucy, my first wife. Trust me—filming in New Mexico and trying to manage a court case in Los Angeles is neither easy nor fun. I do not recommend it. Lucy and I were too different in character, and this was gnawing at us. In any case I was too much of a libertine and she was too conservative. The movie industry is the wrong business for this combination. The divorce was probably inevitable.

I finally hired Booth Gallett, a local film producer, to help with the location work. The two of us were run ragged anyway, but at least it was some relief.

I had to arrange for locations on Jemez Pueblo land. Red Rock Canyon is one of the more spectacular sights along the trail from Los Alamos, down through Bernalillo to Albuquerque. The tribal council called me to a meeting. I had never been to a tribal meeting before and did not know what to expect. The Pueblo governor brought Booth and me into the council room and introduced us to the council, some six members, along with former governors and council members who acted as consultants. Booth and I sat off to the side. Booth was enjoying this, an old hand with the Native Americans.

The pueblos respect silence. One person may speak at a meeting, then there might be silence for five minutes before the next person speaks. This gives the next speaker a chance to weigh his words carefully and prepare his speech. Those silent stretches grew to dominate the meeting, which lasted maybe two hours for fifteen minutes of actual speaking. I respectfully kept silent. Maybe they have the right idea. If more of us contemplated what we were to say before spouting…

I was able to clear up some confusion. I mentioned that we wanted to film from the top of Red Rock Canyon. The top of the mesa had witnessed a terrible slaughter by Mexican troops of native forces. In the seventeenth century the Mexicans had literally thrown the Indian braves off the cliffs to their death during the battle. In Pueblo tradition the spirit of the brave was kept in an earthen pot. These pots were taken to the top of the mesa and broken, releasing the spirit to rise to its reward. The top of the mesa was sacred ground to the Pueblo, filled with shattered pots, and we were only permitted up there infrequently and for exceptional reasons, not for a casual visit. Remember, Pueblos are not part of the United States. Their laws apply, their police have absolute authority, and their courts are not related to ours. It's as close to a foreign country as can be imagined.

I had told the council that we wanted to take a few shots from the top of the mesa. There was silence. Each member of the council said a few words, spaced by a few minutes until the next council member spoke in his native language, Tewa. After about twenty minutes they answered me. The governor asked me if I meant "shots" from a camera or from a rifle. I told them it was a camera. He translated into Tewa for the group, to audible and visible affirmations. There was more silence, then more discussion, and then we had our permission.

Booth and I sometimes had to drive overnight between Santa Fe and Telluride to get permission for something. Flying from Santa Fe to Telluride was not possible since there was no airport at Telluride. The closest airport was in Montrose, about three hours away in the snowy landscape of the 1978 winter. The drive took about six hours, about the same time as a flight, and much less expensive if more tiring. The Telluride city council was not very interested in having a film company come up and disrupt their skiing season, so we were not very welcome there. I had a great deal of public relations work to do, appearing on their local radio station, visiting council members at their homes, hosting local dinners, and so forth. It wasn't easy but eventually they reluctantly gave their permission.

I was also able to secure the Cumbres and Toltec Railroad, a magnificent scenic railroad that trundled though the high forests of the Uncompahgre Mountains from Chama, NM, out onto the plains surrounding Antonito, CO. It was perfect for the film. Art Director Jack de Govia and I saw how obvious that was immediately. We went to Chama, NM, where the railroad was headquartered. The train was in its winter sheds and nowhere near being ready to take to the tracks again. We found someone at the shed who referred us to someone else who referred us to someone else. At length we found the owner. Earl Bell lived on a large ranch in Arizona. I phoned him. This was in January, and the roads were next to impassable because of the snow. Jack and I were lucky to find two spare rooms at the Chama Inn to stay overnight. Earl was to drive up the next day and meet us at 5:00 pm at the Chama Café.

The next day, 5:00 pm came, then 5:30. No Earl. I phoned the Arizona number (no cell pones in those days, remember?) and spoke to Mrs. Bell. (Ma Bell?) She told us to be patient, he would arrive. He was in his station wagon and she had packed some sandwiches and coffee in a thermos, and he should arrive any minute.

He did arrive a few minutes later. He would be hard to mistake. He was a short man, wiry, wearing a railroad engineer's striped coveralls and carrying a lunch box. It was obvious that he was somehow connected to the railroad. He shook off the snow and came and sat down with us. Introductions all around. We concluded our negotiations in about ten minutes, shook hands, and settled down for a good Chama dinner. His attorney would send me a paper to sign within two or three days as soon as Earl could get back to his office in Arizona.

I saw his station wagon outside the window. It was about ten years old and not in the best shape. I couldn't resist asking the obvious—how come you own the railroad?

Well, he said, he had always been fascinated by railroading. When he heard about the railroad being sold for scrap he decided to rescue it as an historical object, so he asked a few of his friends, raised some money, and bought the thing. They didn't expect to make any money for a few years but eventually they would have some return on their investment.

OK, I guess the ranch in Arizona is a much better investment, for you to afford to buy a railroad and rebuild it. No, it does OK, but it supports itself, that's about all. I happened to be fascinated by astronomy. I had a copy of *Astronomy Magazine* with me. On the cover was a photo of a telescope in Arizona with a laser pointing at the receiver on the moon. It could measure the distance to the moon within a few feet. Earl saw the cover and pointed to the laser. "See that? I invented it." That explained the ranch and the railroad. This unassuming man in the engineer's overall could certainly afford to buy a railroad.

Unbeknownst to me, all the time I was doing this, Lester was working behind my back, telling the Fox staff how inefficient I was, how I was ruining his picture. I got little hints of this from time to time when the brass would ask me to do something completely outlandish.

One of these things was when Lester had gotten a message that there was a full-size railroad in Utah, the "Heber Creeper," that had vintage cars and locomotive that we could photograph for the picture, instead of the Cumbres and Toltec. I had already made the agreement with the Cumbres and Toltec people, and they were about to take their locomotive out of its winter storage and begin to refurbish it for us.

Suddenly Fox phoned and told us to catch the next plane for Salt Lake City to see the Heber Creeper. I was to go with Jackson de Govia. There followed a slapstick comedy as I have seldom seen in real life. First of all we had to fly from Santa Fe, NM, to Salt Lake City. This entailed getting on a small local airline at the Santa Fe airport, and flying to SLC with two or three stops between. The first was at Farmington, NM, the second was at Moab, UT, or someplace like that, and finally we landed in Salt Lake City. Each leg of the flight was about a half hour. There was one stewardess, and she was hard pressed to do her job properly. Every time we took off she had to make the legal safety announcements including that there were life jackets under the seats, and the oxygen masks would come down from overhead compartments, complete with demonstrations. In addition she had to pass out little bags of peanuts to all the passengers. After she made the safety announcements she would grab a large bag filled with the small peanut bags, and practically run down the aisle giving each of us our peanut bag. Then she would start at the rear of the airplane with a garbage bag and collect the empty peanut bags. By the time she returned to the front of the plane we were on our landing path, and she had to make sure all our seat backs were straight, seat belts fastened, trays returned to their places, and then she sat down in her little seat just in time to land. Then she rose, stood next to the front door, thanked departing passengers and welcomed new passengers, helped them to their seats, and did the safety spiel again. She managed to do this three times in the hour-and-a-half flight. It was the only time I ever tipped a stewardess, but she certainly earned it.

When we landed at Salt Lake City, we were greeted by a member of the Heber Creeper PR department. He offered to carry our luggage out to the limousine they had arranged for us. Part way to the door we were stopped by a member of the Salt Lake City Film Commission, who wanted to show us his state for filming. He had just heard that someone from Fox was arriving and he didn't want to waste the opportunity to beguile us to film there. He wanted us to ride in his limousine, which he had arranged just for us. He also wanted to carry our bags. The Heber Creeper guy and the Salt Lake City guy then indulged in a tug-of-war with our suitcases. We finally settled by having Jack de Govia in one limo and me in the other. We didn't bother to sort out whose luggage was whose at that point; we could do that at the hotel.

The two Utah folks took us to dinner at one of the better restaurants in Salt Lake City, at which we were the only guests who were not wearing ties and suits. I had forgotten that Mormons did not like alcohol, coffee, even Coca-Cola. In the restaurant the waiter asked us if we wanted a little drink before dinner, and I sure did. I wanted a gin and tonic. He brought the tonic. He also pointed out a threadbare little wooden room, almost like a garage, off to the side of the restaurant, where if I wished I could buy little airline-size bottle of whatever alcoholic beverage I wished. Naturally, to get there, still dressed in my location clothing, I had to walk the length of the restaurant down rows of finely dressed ladies and gentlemen whose expressions indicated that they felt I was there by mistake, to put it mildly. I bought two bottles of gin and returned to the table. We ordered our meal. The waiter asked if we wanted any wine with dinner. When I answered "no" a bit quickly, he explained that the restaurant served it at the table. I didn't have to go to their special store for this. OK, we can have wine.

The best wine on the wine list was a Mondavi generic. We ordered it. The waiter reappeared shortly with a silver wine bucket filled with ice, the requisite towel, the works. He showed us the wine bottle. We approved. The waiter then unscrewed the screw-on top and placed it before me to sniff. I had trouble keeping a straight face. To their credit, the rest of the meal was superb. Afterwards I found out that the restaurant had been built in a former Jewish temple. There is a social comment there somewhere.

The next day we were treated to a grand breakfast and then hustled out to the Salt Lake airport where we boarded a Cessna business plane for Heber City, to see the sights. One look at the train showed us that it was altogether too large for the scenes we needed to film. And anyway the Cumbres and Toltec went through far more spectacular country, ending up on the plains near Antonito, CO, where we could stage the robbery properly. So back into the plane to see some small towns in Utah that we might be able to rob. Most were built in the 1930s and '40s and could not possibly be rebuilt for the film. Those that weren't, we met the "bishops" of the towns and they were not very thrilled to have a decadent film company there. The saints were not to have our company on this trip.

We returned to Santa Fe to begin preparations at the locations we had already arranged. We were building five separate villages, refurbishing an historical ranch site, and building the dance hall set in the studio in Albuquerque. It was quite a job.

On one trip back to Los Angeles I was introduced to the new associate producer of the film, Jack B. Bernstein. I had met him in New York when he was an AD there, and since then he had moved to Hollywood to work on feature films. He had worked on several films at Fox, and the word on the street was that once he was on a film there would be changes in the production department. Immediately Jack took me into his office to discuss any problems the film might have. I told him what I felt was going on with Lester. He did not comment.

I knew that my days on the film were numbered, but I kept on working as long as I could. The show must go on. Back in Santa Fe I finished all the prep for the film. Jack Bernstein asked me how it was going, and he helped with the Telluride city problems, but mostly he kept to himself and stayed with Richard Lester on the set. Bernstein had brought his wife with him to the location. He insisted that she needed the very finest accommodations. The crew was put up at the Hilton Hotel so I arranged for the presidential suite for Jack. The day after they arrived, Jack told me that it wasn't good enough for his wife and that we should arrange for a local apartment. I had to take a production assistant off the set to search for an apartment, which we found the next day. That day Jack and his wife moved in. The next time I saw him was the day after that. We pulled into the parking lot at the Hilton, which also had given us production offices and storage space. He exited his rented car, pulled out an armful of Hilton sheets pillows, towels, soap, everything moveable from the hotel. As he walked back to the hotel from his car, he turned to me and said, "Can you imagine? They called me a thief!" I could imagine very easily.

Not long after that Jack informed me that a new unit manager had been hired, Wilbur Mosier, and that he would finish the film. I was to return to Fox in Hollywood. I was both depressed and relieved. It had been a very hard film. Nobody could have done a better job at setting it up than I did, saving the studio money in location fees time after time. I had made an excellent deal with the Hilton Hotel to house the crew. I had arranged for all the housing for the crew in Telluride. I had made all the arrangements with the New Mexico and Colorado film commissions. I cleared all the locations that Lester had wanted and hired the crew he had preferred. There was not much left to do but finish the film. Will Mosier did that very well. I still don't know why Jack Bernstein was there except to replace me.

An amusing note. At a dinner at Booth's house I met a young man who was the self-styled astrologer of Santa Fe. I had always suspected that astrology was a less than perfect science. The concept that 1/365 of the entire world population acts exactly the same and has the same destiny still doesn't make much sense. I had brought my telescope and on odd evenings was able to look at planets and stars, far brighter in Santa Fe than in Los Angeles. I had it at Booth's house that evening. Mars was in Gemini, right next to Castor. Or was it Pollux? Anyway it was a tiny red dot in the sky, and I trained my telescope on it. It was a small red disk, no visible details but interesting nonetheless. I went into the house and asked Booth and the guests if anyone wanted to see Mars. This astrologer fellow came out. I pointed Gemini out to him, showed him where Mars was. He didn't even look through the telescope. He told me in no uncertain terms that Mars was in Taurus at that time. Asked him how he knew that, since he needed only to look upward and see where Mars was. He told me that in the charts he used it was in Taurus. I asked what charts he used. He told me that they were Ptolemy's charts, made in the first century CE, state of the art 2,000 years ago.

    I arrived back at Fox the next day, collected my stuff, went out to the parking lot where my car had been parked for three months, and in keeping with the terrible Lucas electric equipment, it wouldn't start. AAA came and helped.

CHAPTER 61

FLESH AND BLOOD

I received a phone call from Paramount. They were about to start a four-hour novel for television called *Flesh and Blood*. Director was Jud Taylor, a well-known Hollywood pro. Tom Berenger, Susan Pleshette, John Cassavetes, and Denzel Washington. It would have about an eight-week shooting schedule in Hollywood, New York, Chicago, and Las Vegas. I accepted right away. I had three days to make the schedule since we were leaving for Chicago immediately. I went to work. Got the schedule done in record time, quite an accomplishment since we had no computer programs for that kind of thing in those days.

We went to Chicago and set up offices in the Ambassador East Hotel. Our first filming was to be in New York for some drive-by shots and background. No real scenes with the actors. We had three or four days to do the work. Since I had worked in New York for so long, George Fenaja, the UPM, gave me the job of managing the entire NY shoot. I hired John Starke on the recommendation of Paramount to be the NY UPM. A good choice. The shoot went very smoothly.

During the first week in Chicago one evening I finished filming around 10:00 pm, and I went to the famous Pump Room, in the hotel's ground floor, and asked for dinner. The maitre d' informed me that one needed a reservation well in advance. The implication was that we movie folk were not good enough to dine in the Pump Room. I found the maitre d's name and gave it to our casting people. He was called in for a bit part in the film. We never had a problem eating there after that.

Denzel Washington was an exceptional actor. He played Tom Berenger's sidekick and manager in the story. A very serious actor, he usually studied his role in the car on the way from the hotel to the location. Unfortunately he was in our car, in which the script girl, the 2nd AD and I rode, and our driver. We usually discussed the production on the way, and also indulged in the usual showbiz levity. This disturbed Denzel's study time. He rightly requested that we try to stay quiet on the drive so he could study. Eventually he got his own car to the location. Actors need their time. It only makes sense.

I had known Tom Berenger from *Butch and Sundance*, and we shared several dinners together. A very bright young man and a good actor. Not quite as serious as Denzel, but he had his own bridges to cross. He actually went into very heavy physical training to be buff enough for the boxing scenes. The shots of him jogging through Chicago were taken during his actual jogs through Chicago. They were not staged.

Then there was Suzanne Pleshette. She was only serious when the camera started rolling. Her husband was always with her, Texas oil millionaire Tim Gallagher. They were an obviously wonderful couple. He put up with her outbursts, and she with his quiet demeanor. She was never angry or demanding, but she did have an odd sense of humor. Her affectionate nickname for me was "F***face." I never learned what she called me when she was upset. As far as I know she never was.

Chicago went well and Las Vegas went well. We spent a few days in Carson City, NV, filming at the Nevada State Prison, maximum security section. Filming inside a prison is not easy. There are numerous checkpoints and guard gates that have to be gone through, with appropriate ceremony. Some of our tools were not permitted, especially anything with sharp edges. A necessary piece of equipment forgotten in the truck could mean a fifteen-minute delay while someone worked his way through the security gates to get it, then returned through the security gates.

John Roselius played one of the boxers in the fight scenes. John and I liked each other immediately since we were both old-time radio fans, and both had a good healthy respect for Bob and Ray. We went around imitating "...ly Ballou, winner of seven Peabody Awards for diction" in imitation of Bob and Ray and their silliness. John was also an expert on life inside prisons, not because he had spent time in one but because he was involved in teaching prisoners useful occupations for when they were released. Had spent quite some time in prisons and had gotten to know prisoners and their habits well. He was a kind of informal technical advisor in that area.

Unfortunately because I had worked on this one film, somehow Hollywood started looking at me as the "prison guy." Any film that had prisons in it became fair game for me. We had a taste of it in Chicago when we filmed in the Clark County prison, and a much bigger dose in the Nevada State Prison in Carson City. While we were in the exercise yard we were approached by a youngish inmate with an arm full of stuffed animals. He told us that he had made them in the workshop and wanted to sell them. There were little teddy bears and puppy dogs. We had little need for this at the time, but a couple of the female crew people took pity on the guy. They asked me to ask the guards if this was permitted. The guards informed me that this innocent-looking fellow was in fact a mass murderer who had killed and dismembered several girls and left parts of their bodies scattered around the forests near Lake Tahoe a few years before. We steered clear of him after that.

We returned to Los Angeles. On the lot at Paramount was the original *Squaw Man* shed, which was being used as a gym. It has since been removed to the parking lot opposite the Hollywood Bowl where it stands as a museum of Hollywood history. But when we filmed *Flesh and Blood* it was still the Paramount studio gym, with appropriate reference to Cecil B. DeMille. The scenes in the script that occurred in the prison gym were staged there. Tom Berenger had spent considerable time and effort to develop his body into that of a boxer for the film, going into training as if it were to be his career. He was also protective of his acting ability, as was Denzel. Tom requested that when we filmed fight scenes we close the set to visitors. Accordingly I told the 2nd ADs to allow only crew and cast members into the gym when we were filming. I also kept my eyes open.

The studio brass almost never showed up on the set unless there was a distinguished guest visiting, and then they always phoned ahead. One day a neatly but casually dressed man appeared at the side of the set, watched the action for a couple of minutes. I didn't recognize him, so I approached him. "Beg your pardon, but are you part of our filming company?" "No, not part of the company." "Do you work here on the lot somewhere?" "Yes, I work at Paramount." "Our actor has requested that we keep the set closed, only crew and working cast allowed in here. Could you kindly go to another company's set? That would be very kind of you." "Yes, of course." He started to walk away. As he strode away, he turned back to me. "Do you know me?" Oh-oh. Trouble ahead. "No, I'm afraid I don't." "I'm Barry Diller." Barry Diller was CEO of Paramount. "Mr. Diller, do you know me?" "No, I'm afraid I don't." "Thank God." Mr. Diller laughed and left.

I know that we finished the film on schedule. I never saw the budget so I didn't know if we were on budget or not. Paramount seemed to be happy with my work, and I remained friends outside the business with the executive producer, Herb Hirschman.

CHAPTER 62

MORE THAN FRIENDS

Seymour Friedman called and asked me to handle UPM/AD duties on a new MOW for Columbia, entitled *Love Me and I'll Be Your Best Friend*. It was to be filmed in both L.A. and New York. I was ideal for it since I still knew the NY crews and filming conditions. The writers were Phil Mishkin and Rob Reiner, who would later become one of Hollywood's most honored directors. The director was Jim Burrows.

The title caused more than a little hilarity. In a production office, the secretary who answers the phone usually gives the name of the production. Hence: "Good morning, *Ben-Hur*, can I help you?" or "Good afternoon, *Avatar*, how may I direct your call?" In this case it was *"Love Me and I'll Be Your Best Friend*. May I help you?" Lots of amusing responses to that.

The show went smoothly. The shoot in New York was less so.

There were a few instances when filming was held up for a time in the Bronx, where Penny Marshall went to school. She was a national celebrity, and nowhere less than in the Bronx at her old school. Kids crowded around her. She was as gracious and accommodating to the public as anyone I have ever seen. In private she could be hilariously funny and inventive, as was Rob Reiner.

CHAPTER 63

UNIVERSAL INTERLUDE

Universal called me to work on *Quincy, M.E.* with Jack Klugman. I only worked on one episode when the regular UPM was ill, but I watched as a well-oiled machine made my job almost entirely superfluous. Ron Martinez, the AD, knew what everyone, especially Jack, wanted so well that he was able to anticipate far better than I, the newcomer. Also, the show was produced by Maurice Klugman, Jack's brother, who also had the routine down cold. It was like riding a horse who already knew the way, how fast to go, and when to stop for lunch. Universal was like that.

I stayed there for about a year or so, working on shows and pieces of shows. What they were does not matter much since they all blended together somehow. When you worked at Universal those days you worked for the studio and did whatever they asked. You may be assigned to one show or several. You may be in prep on one show while shooting another while wrapping a third. The machine was designed to make it as easy as possible for the UPM. All the departments had been set up years ago to service the productions with a minimum of difficulty, and it worked admirably.

Sometimes it worked even when the communication did not. I was sitting in my office working on a budget when the phone rang. It was the insert stage, telling me that the pool table and the wardrobe jacket had arrived for the pool shot. There were a rack of balls and a cue. The last two shows I had worked had no pool table scene so I was stymied. I went to the sound stage where the AD there asked me where the actor was. I looked at the call sheet and saw my name down as the UPM. I understood that what was needed was just an extra with a good arm, to wear the jacket and take the pool shot. Face would never be seen, only the two arms in the jacket. I asked the size of the jacket. I went to the makeup department where a long line of extras was waiting to get into makeup for a crowd scene. I found one who looked like he would fit the jacket, and took him to the pool set. He slipped the jacket on. They did the shot. He took off the jacket and I returned him to the makeup department, having signed his extras voucher so he could be paid. Then I returned to the office to work on the budget again. To this day I have no idea what that shot was for.

I was assigned to work on the "*MacArthur* Stretch." The two-and-a-half-hour long movie about the life of Gen. Douglas MacArthur had been made with Gregory Peck in the lead role, but NBC had bought it for a four-hour time slot. Extra footage was needed. It was decided to add the story of the Japanese General Tomoyuki Yamashita, the "Tiger of Malaya." He had been unjustly tried and convicted for the Manila Massacre, an event over which he had no control and over which he protested. It was carried out by the Japanese Navy, had nothing to do with him. MacArthur needed to show his mettle and Yamashita was the fall guy.

Jimmy Shigeta played the main role. We shot an extra forty-five minutes of film to fill in the four-hour time slot. Joseph Sargent directed, as he had the main movie. The producer was a studio employee named Harry Tatelman. He was one of those Universal folks who hung around at the studio waiting for an assignment. The studio regularly gave him work to do. He usually found someone else to do the work. That was I, in this case.

The first thing Harry did was come into my office to discuss the project. He told me immediately that because he had hired me he expected certain things. One was that he had a favorite charity, something about orphans in Burbank, and he expected me to donate at least $5,000. I don't remember anything else he said, and none mattered anyway. I put the shoot together, handled the crew and location problems, worked with the casting department, arranged for the equipment, did the whole job, in fact. Harry, however, was the producer, so he was able to sit in his office and try to collect money for his charity elsewhere, I guess. If the penalty for not donating was that I never had the pleasure of working with him again, well, so much the better. He never did a thing to produce the picture anyway.

The shoot went perfectly smoothly. We filmed in the studio and on location. Huntington Library in San Marino, just east of Pasadena, has a perfect Japanese garden and teahouse. We turned it into Yamashita's estate for the show. Jimmy Shigeta was a delightful performer. He had appeared in one of Dad's films, *Flower Drum Song*, and we spent some time reminiscing together. We also did some filming on the back lot, and some stage filming as well. A real plus was that our AD at Joe Sargent's request was a real old-timer named Jimmy Nicholson. Jim was already in his late sixties when we hired him, and had well over 100 titles to his credit as UPM or AD, or both. Could have done both our jobs with a hand tied behind his back. We became friends and remained so until his death in 2004 at age ninety. A delightful lunch partner and a true gentleman.

In the original film MacArthur's adjutant was played by another fine actor, Nicolas Coster. I had a brother named Nicolas Koster who was also an actor. I introduced myself to Nick and we had a lot of fun with real and imagined mix-ups of family names from there on. "I'd like to introduce you to my brother. Wait a minute he's not my brother, just has the same name. How can he have the same name if he's not my brother?" The fact is that he has hundreds of credits, well over

400, and has had a long and distinguished career. And he began acting after my brother's last appearance, so it's legit.

Next I was assigned to a pilot, *When the Whistle Blows*, about a crew of redneck blue-collar workers and their lives and wives. The only actor I remember is Michele Phillips. She was a delight to work with. The script called for a building skeleton, three stories tall, to be so badly constructed that it falls down on cue. This is not easy, since it must be built properly to begin with so that it can stand up properly until it fails. Then it must fall down in a predictable direction so it won't hurt anyone. It was an impressive undertaking for a movie construction crew. Nevertheless, I read the script and phoned Universal's special effects department. The department head came on the line immediately. He had read the script, he said, and knew what to do. Asked me the address where this construction was to be built. That's all he needed to know, and all I had to do. Universal was like that. If this were New York I would have hired an art director to design the thing, hired the crew to build it, bought the steel and lumber, rented the construction materials, done most of the prep myself. At Universal I just had to tell them what the address was, and voila! A building skeleton that would fall down on cue. It was all so easy.

On the other hand I went daily to the construction site to check on the progress. Each day I went I drove onto the property and not a soul was in sight. The minute one of the crew saw my car, the trucks emptied of men and they began working very diligently. Inside the trucks were tables with playing cards on them. Hmmm…

However, things were not ideal in paradise. Universal had the habit of trying to see just how much work you could handle. While I was working on *When the Whistle Blows* I got a call from the production head in TV that a TV film called *Condominium* needed a UPM for a few days just for a scene or two. Asked me if I could handle it. They sent a script over to my office. I read it and asked which scene needed help. The UPM was on his way to New York to handle some scenes there and they just needed someone to fill in for a week. The show I was already working on was considered a "light" one so I maybe could handle two? I told them that even though it seemed "light" I'd prefer to stay with just the one.

The next day in the TV daily production meeting I found that I had been assigned to *Condominium* as well, and that the shoot was for two days hence. The scene was the biggest special effects scene they had, the one in which the apartment is flooded and all the people in it are drowned. There was a huge dump tank brought into the sound stage with thousands of gallons of water. Stunt people had been hired to play the condo residents, all certified for underwater work. Five or six cameras would roll since it would be impossible to have a second take. And this was in addition to managing *When the Whistle Blows*. I really gave it my best try, but it was late nights and adroit time management that got me through that. Just before the big day of the drowning scene, the production head called me into his office and suggested that since I was doing so well with those two shows I could handle a third, just a

UNIVERSAL INTERLUDE

couple of days shoot, a simple thing out on the back lot. I told him I couldn't handle any more, that I was working practically 24/7 on those two shows and there was no possibility of another. I just couldn't.

After we got through the drowning and the whistle blowing, I decided to have a vacation by working somewhere else for a while.

CHAPTER 64

GIDEON'S TRUMPET

I received a phone call from Robert H. Justman asking me to come for an interview. Anthony Lewis, the legal correspondent for *The New York Times*, had written a book about Clarence Earl Gideon. The Gideon vs. Wainwright decision of the Supreme Court mandated that anyone on trial for a felony is entitled to legal counsel. Clarence Earl Gideon was a ne'er-do-well rootless vagrant in Panama City, Florida, when he was unjustly accused and convicted of burglary and sentenced to five years in prison. He was no stranger to prison, having spent years there off and on for petty theft and larceny; this time he was innocent. Because of Florida law he was denied counsel and ordered to represent himself, which he did unsuccessfully.

He spent enough time in the prison library that he was able to draft a petition to the U.S. Supreme Court, handwritten on yellow pads, stating that he should have been provided counsel.

The Court elected to hear his case and decided that he was right. Gideon's case was argued by none other than Abe Fortas. Over 2,000 convicts in Florida alone were freed because of that decision, but not Gideon. He was, however, granted a second trial with an attorney, and then he was found innocent and freed. Public defenders came into existence because of that decision and the entire course of U.S. trial law has changed.

The film was made under the aegis of *Hallmark Hall of Fame*. The guiding influence of the show was John Houseman. Gideon was played by Henry Fonda. Fortas was José Ferrer. Lane Smith played the lawyer who defended Gideon in the retrial, and the great Fay Wray, the beautiful wraith of *King Kong*, played Gideon's landlady. Not unusual as David W. Rintels, who wrote the script, was engaged to marry Fay's daughter. Rintels is one of Hollywood's foremost screenwriters. His TV series, *The Defenders*, was a landmark in legal television production, the precursor for almost all the lawyer shows that followed.

But the spark, although a quiet one, was Robert Justman. Bob was the guiding light of the original *Star Trek* TV series. Another old-timer, he went all the way back to the original *Superman* TV series with George Reeves. Told some very funny stories about shooting with Reeves. Reeves apparently enjoyed a drink or two at lunch. He had to be photographed jumping out windows or into bushes before lunch therefore, because he was just as likely to jump into the wall or into a tree after lunch. He had to be sewn into his Superman suit before lunch as well, since after lunch he was unable to stand still enough to avoid being stabbed by the seamstress' needle.

Remembering the fine work of Jimmy Nicholson as AD on *MacArthur*, I brought him again out of retirement to work the set on this show. We also were able to put together an exceptional crew. The director, Robert J. Collins, had been the creator of the TV series, *Police Woman*. He also wrote and directed *J. Edgar Hoover*, and *The Hijacking of the Achille Lauro*. The cameraman, Don Birnkrant, had been director of photography on *Attica*, an exceptional accomplishment in itself. The sound man was my old friend Jimmy Pilcher. Jimmy started in the biz as a singer/dancer at Universal, one of the Jivin' Jacks 'n' Jills, of which my stepmother, Peggy Moran, was also a member. So were Donald O'Connor, Peggy Ryan, Jane Withers, and dozens more familiar faces. Our art director was Eddie Carfagno. The Supreme Court was a veritable who's who of classic actors. John Houseman himself played the Chief Justice. In the film he was called the Chief Justice, but in real life it was Earl Warren. Our attorney told us not to give the justices their real names. Among the associate justices were Sam Jaffe, Dean Jagger, William Prince, Liam O'Brien, Ford Rainey, and Emmet Lavery. There were nine justices.

(N.B. The tradition when the justices sit down to deliberate a case is that each shakes hands with all the others. How many handshakes are there? Answer to follow.)

We filmed in several interesting locations. For the courtroom we filmed in the old courthouse in Santa Ana, California. Wood-paneled walls, old, high judge's bench, old-fashioned jury box and chairs, the lot. Beautiful and perfect for our purposes. Our prison was Chino Men's Prison in Chino, California. It had the dormitories, exercise yard, everything we needed. There was a processing center where prisoners are admitted, take their showers, are issued their prison clothing, etc. There was no library that we could use, however. For that we went to the library at the VA hospital in Westwood,L.A. It was in an old wooden building on the campus. Not used very often, but we were able to put our own law books into it, the books that Gideon used to draw up his petition.

Eddie Carfagno, our art director magician, managed to construct enough of the Supreme Court for our use, the bench, two walls, part of the audience, and the attorneys' stands—$9,000 all in. We filmed at the Culver City Studios for three or four days to show the arguments pro and con Gideon's petition.

Henry Fonda was not a very well man when we filmed. He had had a quadruple heart bypass, a hip replacement, and was suffering from cancer in his lower torso. The insurance bill for him alone was $50,000. We gladly paid it for the talent of this great man. There was a $250,000 deductible on the policy as well. But Bob Justman was able to convince the insurance company that if we finished the film without incident they would refund $25,000, so that was a big plus on our small budget.

Not only was Hank on time, even early, every day, but when we were on location in Chino and Santa Ana he stayed gladly in a local motel. He had a hot plate with him and food, and he always made his own breakfast, and sometimes his own dinner. He was always more than prepared. He knew his own lines and was able to help other less experienced actors with theirs as well. His place was within an arm's length of the camera, even when lighting was taking place, so he could jump in when needed. A very shy man in person, he always had a ready smile for the dozens of fans who approached him when we were in public, even in the prison. Always willing to give an autograph or pose for a picture. He understood well where his loyalty lay, in the spirit of this audience. He was a model that many other actors could pattern themselves after.

All the actors on this show were pros. Not a bad egg in the box. There were idiosyncrasies, there always are. Sam Jaffe, the grand old man of film, was now eighty-nine years old and still had a tremendous presence on screen. His wife, the noted actress, Bettye Ackerman, brought him to the sound stage every morning and took him home at night. Most days she stayed with him during the filming. Sam had memorized his lines. He had them down to the finest twitch of an eyebrow. But he was, after all, eighty-nine years old, and he couldn't always remember where the lines went. So we photographed him over several of the actors' shoulders. He repeated all his lines from each position, and we trusted the editor to edit them into the film properly.

Dean Jagger did not have an easy time of it. His speech was affected by a stroke. We had to dub some of his lines. He also was not walking well, so we photographed him, and all the rest of the Supreme Court justices, mostly sitting down.

José Ferrer was also a pro. I had seen four of the films he directed, *The Great Man*, *I Accuse!*, *Cockleshell Heroes*, and *The High Cost of Loving*. I admired his directing ability as much as I did his acting. At heart he was a shameless ham. I had seen him in two episodes of *Your Show of Shows* with Sid Caesar. In both he acted in mock operas, entitled "Il Marriaggio del Fausto" and "La Forza del Gravity." He played a devil type in both and he was screamingly funny. I think he missed his calling.

Bob Justman and I complemented each other quite well. He was another wonderful old-school UPM who liked to double-check everything and I welcomed it. He gave me enough leeway to be able to run the show as I saw fit, and it apparently was to his liking because we agreed on almost all the choices. Further, he introduced me to several new crew folk whom I kept in my book, excellent people all. To add frosting to the cake, our makeup man was the same as he had on *Star Trek*. Frank Phillips gave me a couple of sets of "Spock ears" to give to my sons who were avid fans of the show and loved the idea.

Our transportation coordinator was Chuck Hansen, a man whose habit it was to keep the crew working no matter what. The common image of Teamsters is that they drive to work, then play cards or snooze all day, then drive home. Not on Chuck's crew. They washed the trucks. Then they washed the cars. Then they checked the oil and fluids on all the vehicles. They neither slept nor played cards, not that I saw anyway. Chuck and I made several shows together. He and the famous Norm Honath of ABC Circle were two of the greatest transportation coordinators in the city.

As a movie of the week we had a twenty-day shooting schedule. We finished on schedule and on budget. This was one of the magic shows I enjoyed working so much. Everyone got along well. There were no major disruptions. We were all firing on the same eight cylinders all the time. Even when the days were long, and they were from time to time, it was still a pleasure to work on this worthwhile project with these gentlemen.

The show was broadcast to rave reviews and is still shown regularly on the cable channels. The DVD sales are also respectable. I have since worked with the Ventura County Sheriff's Department. We have contact with the Public Defenders office. They show the show normally to all new inductees.

CHAPTER 65

HUSTLER OF MUSCLE BEACH

Furia-Oringer Productions then hired me as UPM for a movie of the week entitled *Hustler of Muscle Beach* about a young man who joins the body building crowd in Venice and enters in competition. Jonathan Kaplan was the director. The producer/writer, John Furia, had written the script for Dad's last film, *The Singing Nun*, with Debbie Reynolds. The line producer was Neil Maffeo, former head of production for *The Waltons*, a landmark series in Hollywood. He had the reputation for being a very tough producer indeed. I was curious so I accepted the job.

It turned out that Maffeo, an old UPM from the early days at Lorimar Productions, had already done all the UPM work. I was only there to fulfill a DGA requirement for a UPM presence. There was little to do. The budget had been made, the crew and cast hired. I was at best a caretaker, and even that was modified because Maffeo would remain on the set for the run of the picture. I was just, well, there. Oh, I signed the bills, but they couldn't be paid unless Maffeo signed them also. Well, I must say this was far easier than doing two shows at once at Universal.

Director Jonathan Kaplan had a gruff manner about him. One of the scenes called for a muscle-man contest at Venice beach, with some other events to surround it and give it more substance. One of these was a beauty contest, another a gymnastics exhibition. There were several good gymnastic studios in Los Angeles at the time. There was another gymnastic studio much closer, in El Segundo, a few miles down the coast. We went there to see what they had to offer. It was gym mostly for children, but this could be visually interesting if they were willing. We went into the practice room where the owner greeted us. Jonathan Kaplan, the director, explained that we were concentrating on muscle-building, Mr. Universe style, but that "we need some junk sports to fill in the competition." End of their involvement. Gymnasts are rightfully proud of their sport, and did not enjoy being called "junk." We finally found some members of the Carreiro Gymnastic Studio in Hollywood who were willing to help.

This show was not easy because we were filming in January, 1980, one of the coldest, rainiest, stormiest winters Los Angeles had ever seen. Filming at the beach was an interesting exercise because there were absolutely none of the usual denizens on the boardwalk. It was bare. And Maffeo didn't want to hire extras just for the beach scenes. He had budgeted to use background people who were there anyway and would work for a release, or a free lunch, but not for union minimum.

Around seven or eight blocks down the beach was a senior center catering to elderly Jewish people who wanted to spend their days at the beach in a nice warm place where they could eat, play cards, paint, do senior things. And walk out on the beach if they chose. Most of the time this was an idyllic situation but for now it was really raining and storming every day. There were the traditional mudslides in Malibu, a few houses washed out to sea, the canyons became roaring torrents and the news broadcasts were filled with crying residents bemoaning the loss of their homes or belongings. And the forecasts were not better. It would keep raining.

We made an agreement with the Jewish Center that if their members would come out to the boardwalk and act as extras we would provide hot lunches for them on the days they did. We also donated to their general fund for equipment and supplies. We asked them to pray for sunshine.

In fact it was too rainy to film. The script called for sunny California beach weather and it just never came. We held the competition inside a tent with the rain pounding on the roof. During the brief periods when it wasn't raining we ran outside to squeeze off a few shots, then back inside the tent to escape the deluge. During one of the dry periods our extras had walked from their senior center down the six or seven blocks to our location. At lunch time the rain was pouring down in sheets. We had several buses to transport the crew from the location down the boardwalk to the senior center for lunch. I told one of the bus drivers to keep his bus available for the seniors who were our extras. They were all in their mid-seventies to nineties and I didn't want them to walk back to their shelter in the rain. Maffeo immediately countermanded my order and told the bus drivers not to take the extras back to their shelter under any circumstances. They would have to walk in the rain. Neither the bus drivers nor I could believe that he would say that, but he had. And the extras had heard him. With that he drove away in his Cadillac. As soon as he left the site we opened the bus doors for the extras to be able to have transport back to their home. The AD, Ray Marsh, was there and told me that was typical of Maffeo. I didn't do any more than one show with him.

One of our scenes on the boardwalk involved showing the filming of a TV commercial featuring body building. We hired an old UCLA friend, Paul Bartel, to play the commercial director. Franco Columbu played the body builder for the scene. He was a well-known body builder of minuscule height, around 5' 5." One of Arnold Schwartzenegger's best friends. Arnold himself visited our set while we were filming but he wouldn't appear as a walk-on. I had a chance to talk to him briefly and was most impressed by his perception and wit. At 6' 2" he towered over Columbu, but Columbu had tremendous screen presence in the film. Arnold was already a recognizable celebrity and when we walked down to the Muscle Beach part of Venice, the body builders there all gathered around him as the reigning king of body building. Still is, I imagine. After all, he was Mr. Universe five times and Mr. Olympia seven times. He retired from competition in 1975, but changed his mind and won the Mr. Olympia title one last time in 1980 just to prove that he could do it. Very impressive indeed.

The rest of the filming was mundane, and there was little I could do except collect money and stay out of Maffeo's way. I succeeded at both. Funny how different shows can be in tone and importance to one's career. Contrast this to *Gideon's Trumpet*. No comparison, none at all. I never even saw this show when it was broadcast, and I don't have a copy of it. Not interested.

CHAPTER 66

THE RETURN OF FRANK CANNON

When I was attending UCLA, I was friends with Cal "Buzz" Naylor, son of the famed restaurateur "Tiny" Naylor. Cal chose movies instead of cooking. Probably a good choice. In any case he had a long and distinguished career in movies and TV, mostly as a UPM or AD. We had known each other since the early 1960s. When I moved back to Hollywood we reestablished our connection and had kept in touch. He was working as the UPM/AD on a TV movie of the week entitled *The Return of Frank Cannon*. William Conrad starred, just as he did in the original TV series years before for Quinn Martin Productions. This was Quinn Martin's last gasp. The UPM was, ostensibly, Fred Ahern, who had been with QM for many years. Freddy had retired but agreed to lend his name to the show as UPM. Cal Naylor, with both UPM and AD work on his shoulders, finally convinced Matt Herman, the new production head of QM, to hire a UPM to help out. I came in four days before filming started. The crew had been hired. The director was my old friend Corey Allen. Everyone was staying at a motel in Del Mar, right across from the racetrack. Thank goodness it wasn't racing season. The director, producer, and stars were staying at a more upscale hotel/resort on Balboa Bay, around twenty miles from the crew.

Cal phoned me at home and asked for help. It was eight at night. I said I might be able to drive down in the next day or two. He told me that I was needed at a production meeting tomorrow morning at 8:00 am in San Diego. I packed quickly, got in the Triumph, and drove down.

Nothing had been done. Four days from filming and only a very sketchy schedule. The art director, George Chan, was just building sets without knowing when they would be shot. Casting department was tearing their hair. Crew didn't know what equipment to order because nobody knew what was going to be shot. Fred Ahern was not there, Cal was busy trying to get the extras lists done for the show and at least prepare for the first day. Chaos reigned.

I took George Chan, Corey Allen, and Cal aside with the schedule and asked what, if anything, would be ready to film the first day. George had prepared one or two sets, so we settled on those. After that we stayed about three or four days ahead of filming in our preparations. This kept our heads above water. After a week or so

Matt Herman replaced Fred Ahern entirely. He showed up and wanted to go over the budget with me. I did the best I could, but after all a budget was dependent upon a schedule, and there was no schedule as yet. I explained that to Matt, but being a more corporate-minded guy, he wanted a budget. It became guesswork.

At least by keeping in close contact with Cal we were able to prep as we went along. This kept the show from arriving at a set with nothing to do. Corey Allen generally went along with what we had decided, knowing that we would cover his trail when at all possible. At least the script was completely workable and needed no revisions.

We did have a few very pleasant dinners with Del Mar residents and discovered a few excellent restaurants, mainly seafood. But the workdays were long and hard. Corey Allen, one of the most adept directors in Hollywood, was constantly publicly criticized by William Conrad, who was convinced that he knew much more about the show than Corey did. And there was another annoying factor. Conrad had never memorized a script in his life. One of his entourage was a splendid fellow named Mike Audley. Mike was the nominal dialogue coach for the show. He was part of Conrad's contract. His actual job was to make up "cue cards" and hide them from the camera but leave them visible to Conrad.

In fact, Conrad had been a legend in the radio world, where scripts were read on the air, never memorized. The individual pages were always kept in transparent cellulose sheets so the paper didn't make a crinkling sound when the pages were changed. But memorizing? Radio artists never heard of it, never had to. And during all 121 episodes of the *Cannon* series Conrad never memorized a line. We knew it from the start. If we wanted Conrad to act in the show he would do so gladly, but Mike Audley would be there to make the cue cards.

Other than that Conrad was very professional, always on time, always happy to help other actors. And fun to chat with between scenes. He owned half of the state of Montana to hear him tell it, and his hobby was sailplane flying. He could talk about that for hours, the peacefulness of it, the thrill of soaring about on the wind. Whenever he was upset about something, however, he took it out on the increasingly stoic Corey Allen.

We used quite a few locations in the city of San Diego and a few on the outskirts. The story revolved around horses and the horsey society. Our location was convenient to Rancho Santa Fe, an upper-class community where people usually owned horses and appeared in horse shows in *dressage*. There was also Del Mar racetrack, former haunt of such as Jimmy Durante and other racing fans. Tiny Naylor, Cal's father, was also a fan who owned several horses. Cal told me that his dad had died of a heart attack while writing a check to buy a horse in Del Mar.

Also while we were there the North San Diego County Fair was in progress, held at the fair grounds right next to the racetrack. That was fascinating. I had not been to a good old county fair for years, since going to the L.A. Fair while attending Pomona. There were children showing off their pet goats, other kids with bottle cap collections, and an amazing display of electric model trains. There were roping competitions and horse races, chickens and ducks and sheep. The smell alone was overwhelming.

We kept filming. Somehow sets were built on time. We lost a couple of cast because of the unreliability of the schedule, but all in all the picture went very well. It had a handsome, professional look to it that entirely belied the chaos that was rampant while we were filming. The professionalism of the crew cast, and staff saved the day.

I drove back to Los Angeles in my Triumph. Triumph was always called Triumph, even when the company first began to make bicycles in 1897. Its presence led to a very odd situation. Quinn Martin already had an agreement with the San Diego Teamsters who controlled all rolling stock. And the horses, too, by the way. Teamsters are so called because they originally were the drivers of horse teams that took the wagons and stagecoaches across the country. Their logo still has two horses' heads. In any case I had my Triumph car. The Teamster contract provided that anyone who went from the office to the set and back had to be driven. I was assigned a driver, Rigoberto Gonzales, and a Chrysler Imperial to drive me around. I thought this a big waste of gasoline and money. I suggested to Michael Rhodes, the producer, that I use my Triumph and save the company some gas. Also they could use the Chrysler for one of the stars. They thought that was a grand idea. I suspect I am the only person to have had a chauffeured Triumph TR-6 for a month. Rigo was a great driver and he came to be a good friend.

One incident on the last day of filming. Corey Allen had a fine appreciation of good cinema. He taught acting and stage presence in acting schools in Los Angeles, and his directing was a masterpiece of well-thought work. On our last day we had two scenes to film in a hotel in North San Diego. We had secured the penthouse suite and were filming in the living room area. There was a bedroom off the living room, and the bathroom was off the bedroom, requiring crew and cast to walk through the bedroom to get to the bath. We also kept the unused lights and grip equipment in the bedroom while filming in the much larger living room.

It was around eleven in the morning when we were on the last shot of the film. We had already checked out of our motel early that morning. There was nothing left to do except to pack our equipment and drive back to Los Angeles. Someone had turned on the TV set in the bedroom. A film was showing, *No Highway in the Sky*, and the crew was watching it off and on whenever someone went into the room for a piece of equipment. It had just started screening when Corey went in to wash his hands. He saw what was playing, and came back into the living room where the crew and cast were. He first asked my permission, and then announced to the crew that a very special film was showing in the bedroom and he urged everyone to watch it. We stopped lighting the set and went in to sit down and watch. When the film was over he remarked to all that this was one of the best constructed films he had ever seen, spoke a little about the story and the editing, and we went back to work. Finished an hour later, wrapped up, and drove back to Los Angeles with time to spare.

As we went out to the trucks for the drive I asked Corey if he remembered who had directed the film, and he did not. He was delighted to find that my father had directed it.

CHAPTER 67

FANTASY ISLAND

Shortly after this Seymour Friedman called from Columbia Pictures TV. He needed someone to help with *Fantasy Island*. They had fallen behind schedule and needed to manage two units at the same time to shoot two shows simultaneously. This was not that difficult since Ricardo Montalban and Hervé Villechaize were not required for every scene. The stories were mostly about the guest stars. We could shuttle Hervé and Ricardo back and forth from one show to the other.

Leslie Martinson was the director of the episode I was assigned to. The stars were Eva Gabor, Craig Stevens, Gene Barry, and Mike Connors.

I thought this would be easy and in many ways it was. The production machine ran very smoothly for being episodic. I did re-make my acquaintance with Hervé, whom I had known on *Greaser's Palace*. Ricardo Montalban was always the perfect gentleman. Our two location days were spent at Palos Verdes at a very posh mansion overlooking the Pacific Ocean. Everything worked very smoothly and very quickly.

There was one unusual aspect to the film. The script called for Eva Gabor to attempt suicide by driving her car over a cliff. My first thought was to buy an old used car, have her rev it up, and let it sail over a cliff at Palos Verdes or somewhere near. Maybe put a Gabor mannequin in the driver's seat. In fact we did the reverse and saved a lot of money in the process. We found some stock footage of a car driving off a cliff in long shot, and we bought a matching car and painted it the same color. Had Eva drive our car up to the cliff and cut to the stock footage. Our car was never damaged. We sold it after the show.

After the show Hervé and I kept in touch, and within a week or so he invited me over for a barbeque. Actually, he told me to phone his social secretary and make an appointment for a barbeque. I did so, for the next weekend. The secretary informed me that I was to bring seven oversized "butcher cut" steaks from a private butchery, with the fat removed. Also some corn on the cob. Seven steaks? Yes, for Hervé, his wife, his ex-wife, my two sons, my wife Sandy, and me. Seven. And to be there at 5:00 pm sharp. Off-putting? Yes, but Hervé was an old friend and I went along with it just to spend the evening with him. Not sure what that would bring.

We arrived as instructed. Hervé met us at the door wearing a .44 magnum revolver, Dirty Harry style, on his hip. He explained that his house was formerly a halfway house for drug addicts. Some of these had not heard that the house was sold and was now a private residence. They would show up at his door all hours of the day and night, and were usually under the influence. When a midget answered the door they would freak out, and Hervé was understandably in fear for his life. Once in the house he removed the pistol from its holster and put it on a table near the door, in easy reach for when the doorbell rang again.

The remainder of the afternoon was fairly normal. I had brought some 8mm film from *Greaser's Palace* behind-the-scenes which we showed, and it brought back amusing memories for us both. Hervé's wife and ex-wife were both very accommodating and very nice. His ex was his manager, accountant, confidante, secretary. His wife was, well, a wife. Hervé was an excellent chef and the food was delicious. It bloody well better be for what it had cost. Chris and Kevin enjoyed meeting Hervé again, and he, them.

CHAPTER 68

DARK NIGHT OF THE SCARECROW

The next call was from Joseph Wizan. He had been an agent for many years, and a good one. He was branching out into producing. We met for a while and were very compatible. He was about to start a new project. Frank de Fellitta was going to direct a script by J.D. Feigelson, *Dark Night of the Scarecrow*. Frank had written *Audrey Rose* and was a master of suspense and horror. *Scarecrow* was right up his alley.

I pulled together my usual team. We hired Vince Martinelli as director of photography. The AD was Daisy Gerber, a Hungarian girl with whom I had attended UCLA in years past and who was the first female graduate of the DGA Training Program in the early 1960s.

We set up offices at Lion's Gate Studios in Westwood and went into preproduction. Locations were needed. We hired a super location manager named Kool Lusby to find and clear them. She went way out of her job description when we found the ideal farm near Piru, in Ventura County. The owners had just been burned by another film company that had stiffed them on the site rental and they swore they would never rent to a movie company again. Kool, a superb baker, made them a cake to die for. Problem solved.

We set up offices in a shopping center in Valencia, just on the Ventura County border. The union contracts provided that the crew could drive themselves to the location if it were less than ten miles from the production office. If not, the crew had to report to the office and be bused the rest of the way. Piru was just inside the ten-mile limit. The crew took to this with wry smiles. I was visited by the union reps who demanded that we bus the crew to the location. I showed them the map, with the mileages, and they reluctantly agreed that we were within the legal limit.

It was dreadfully hot when we filmed. Worse, there was a "red flag alert" warning of brush fires, and all non-essential work had to stop, including our film. That lasted for one day, then we went back to work. Our cast was excellent, all pros. Charles Durning lead, with Larry Drake, Tonya Crow, Lane Smith, and Jocelyn Brando. I was in the film also.

Larry Drake, playing the tragic victim, hides in a scarecrow costume and stands out in a field to prevent being found by the vigilante group led by Durning. They find him anyway and shoot him, killing him in broad daylight in the scarecrow costume. Problem was that Larry Drake was already somewhat portly. If he wore the metal protective shield, special effects squibs, and the electrical apparatus necessary to show the bullet hits he would be fat and grotesque. And his eyes had to be visible inside the scarecrow mask. It was not the ideal situation.

Bob in costume without scarecrow mask.

I, however, was quite slim in those days and about the same height as Larry. I could easily wear the scarecrow outfit and all the effects accoutrements and still appear as if he were inside the costume. I got wired up and walked out into the field. It was another hot summer day, but not overly so, when I was shot. I jerked around on the scarecrow frame convincingly in my death throes. The show became a cult classic and is played regularly around Halloween every year on TV. The cognoscenti know that I was the scarecrow, and I have been hailed as a horror classic actor in a few circles.

One of the vigilantes, Claude Earl Jones, knew that he was going to be on location for a few days at a time, so he brought his motor home and lived at the location when we were there. He could sleep in his own bed, make his own breakfast and dinner when he wished, and he was right there for filming when necessary. Neat. A few of the crew put themselves up in a local motel in Valencia, a few miles away from filming.

The final scene has the little girl, played by a young and very talented Tonya Crowe, in the wheat field with the scarecrow. The scarecrow reaches down and hands her a flower. Larry Drake had already gone on to work on another show, so once again I got into costume, this time with padding. Let's face it, I played the title role.

The show finished on schedule and well under budget, enough so that I received a bonus check from Joe Wizan. It was a welcome surprise.

And with mask.

CHAPTER 69

McCLAIN'S LAW

I had kept in touch with Dick Birnie, who had been production head at Universal TV and was now in charge of MGM TV. He called me in for an interview for a new TV series.

Bob Justman had kept in touch. He and his wife, Jackie, and my wife and I had dinner from time to time. He usually brought a bottle of fine wine from his cellar. He was an oenologist of the first water, a member of *Les Amis du Vin*, and a regular at local wine tasting parties. And a fine gentleman to boot. He had been hired by Eric Bercovici to line-produce a new TV series, just bought by NBC and produced by MGM, called *McClain's Law*. The star was Jim Arness, who at the time held the record for having had the longest-lived dramatic TV series, *Gunsmoke*.

Big Jim was 6' 8." He was certainly a great presence. He was also one of the gentlest men I have ever met. Big men are like that since they do not need to be otherwise. We named the series *McClain's Law* because Jim had been given his first big role in the movies by John Wayne, playing the Duke's assistant in a film called *Big Jim McLain*. This was his homage to the Duke. It was also a darn good series, written mostly by two experts in the field, Steve Downing and Frank Abbatemarco. Both were former policemen. The executive producer was Eric Bercovici, who had just written and produced the blockbuster mini-series *Shogun*. At MGM he acted as the executive story editor of *McClain* as well as the other series he was doing, *Chicago Story*.

I had a connection to Eric Bercovici. His father, Leonardo "Nardo" Bercovici, wrote one of my Dad's best films, *The Bishop's Wife*. Nardo came in to the office one day and we had a chat. Great man.

We hired two ADs: Carl Olson, with whom I had alternated on *Police Story*, and Mack Bing, with whom I had shared some laughs at Columbia. Seymour Hoffberg was cameraman. All the crew people were excellent and we became something of a family. Working day in and day out for six or seven months will do that to a crew.

Jim Arness told me that he had met with the programming head of NBC. They wanted to capitalize on his popularity as star of *Gunsmoke* and were going to give the show lots of publicity and a good time slot. There would be no pilot. Our first show would be a two-hour special and there were eleven further hours of show contracted. We would be busy for several months.

I was assigned a production secretary named Deirdre LeBlanc. Her father had been one of the truly great matte artists in the painting department at MGM. He had been married to Dolores Costello, a film star from the 1930s, whose previous husband had been the great John Barrymore, "The Great Profile." Deirdre, nicknamed "Sam," had grown up amidst Hollywood royalty. She was not only an excellent secretary, but also an exquisite artist, a fine painter, an expert in leather work, and a writer of no mean ability.

The cast included Big Jim, Marshall Colt, a 6'5" actor who came close to Jim Arness in height— Jim dwarfed everyone else. Conchatta Ferrell played the inevitable restaurant/bar owner where the boys hung out after work. The sergeant was George DiCenzo. Carl Franklin had a running role as another cop in the system.

It worked like clockwork. We had put together a great team. We had our equipment trucks all stocked for our particular show.

The truck subject brings up another odd incident at the show's beginning. We needed certain trucks for the show. One was a wardrobe truck that was already rigged with clothes racks, dressing rooms, sewing machines, ironing boards—in fact it was a complete rolling wardrobe department. Our wardrobe master owned such a truck and was willing to rent it to the company for a pittance.

In order to put this into effect we had to first clear it with the MGM transportation department, to see if they had an equivalent trailer that we could use. MGM always had first choice of vehicles if they could supply. As it turned out, they did not have anything like it so I was able to rent the trailer from the wardrobe man. However, an odd thing happened during the vetting process.

I phoned the transport department to get the permission. The secretary told me that the head of transport at MGM was out at a meeting and I should phone back in a half hour. I did so, and she said, "He still isn't here. Just call back... No, wait. I see him coming now. He's coming up the steps. In the door. He's going to his desk. Now he's cleaning out his desk, putting things into his briefcase. Now he's leaving again." He had been fired. I listened to his last moments at MGM on the phone. He had been caught taking largesse from various studio suppliers such as paper towel and soap vendors. Transport was responsible for keeping the MGM janitorial service stocked with supplies and this man had apparently availed himself of that. A day or two later the president of MGM was also let go, David Begelman, the only man ever to be fired because of an unpublished book. *Indecent Exposure* documented Begelman's record of embezzlement and check forgery from Columbia Pictures when he was president. What was worse, he had claimed on his resume that he was a Yale graduate. Yale had never heard of him. He left a few days after the transportation head did. The shame of it was that Begelman was a very good producer.

Transport was then headed by a caretaker who cleaned up the department. Eddie

Saeta was another old-timer with a long history of production management. At one point he had been head of production for RKO. Eddie told me to go ahead and hire the wardrobe truck from our wardrobe master.

Jim Arness had an excellent manager, Richard St. Johns, who fashioned his contract after the one he had on *Gunsmoke*. There was a specific clause providing that Jim was not to film beyond noon on Friday. At the nearest airport to where we were filming a private plane would stand ready to fly him to his ranch in Arizona. It would fly him back on Sunday evening so he would be ready to film on Monday morning. The studio would pick up the cost of this. After a week or two of pre-production Jim let us know that he no longer owned a ranch in Arizona and we were free to use the money set aside for the airplane in other areas of production.

We learned Jim's habits as applied to production. He was a wonderful man to work with and a thorough professional. We also learned that if he began a statement with "It seems kinda funny…" what followed was something he didn't particularly like. These were few and far between. But one really big one was when NBC scheduled the show opposite *Dallas*, the highest rated show of the season. It did not give *McClain's Law* much of a chance at good ratings and we were canceled after one season. We were extended however, from thirteen to sixteen episodes. It seemed like a waste of good talent not to have scheduled the show in a better time slot. Jim still had a following but it was mostly male. Their wives wanted *Dallas*. The expected thing happened.

An amusing incident. One of our shows, a two-part show broadcast on successive weeks, dealt with the Aryan Brotherhood, a frighteningly vicious prison gang with members outside the walls as well as inside. There are three large gangs behind bars. The AB, or Aryan Brotherhood. Call themselves "The Brand." They hate anyone not white, Christian, and American. Sometimes they kill just to prove that it can be done. Behind bars they are feared. Another is La Familia, the Hispanic gang, with the same characteristics, except as applied to Hispanics. The Third is the BGF, or Black Guerrilla Fraternity, made up of black prisoners. The BGF and Familia were born primarily to protect their members from the AB but have since expanded their activities into other endeavors. This is where most of the troubles behind bars begin, with racial hatred.

Our two-part episode centered on the AB. Members have a very distinctive tattoo. Mike Hancock, our makeup man, fashioned that tattoo in removable form. The tattoo could be applied and would remain for about three days, and then quickly wear off. For the actors a new tattoo had to be applied then. Mike made a few dozen of these decals. He asked me if I wanted one, and of course I said yes, not thinking of the consequences.

That weekend I went to Palm Springs for a little break. I stayed at the Palm Springs Resort and Spa to take advantage of the steam baths and maybe get a massage. Checking in was no problem since the tattoo was hidden under my shirt.

But getting into the steam bath and sauna was a problem. I had this violent tattoo on my shoulder that included Nazi swastikas and the numbers "666" outlined in red, marking me as a member of the AB. If there had been a real member about he probably would have killed me just for wearing the tattoo. As it was, a few of the attendants there held a huddle in the corner during which they kept an eye on me and were obviously discussing what my possible connection was to the AB. Just after that I went into the massage area for a rub down. The masseur asked me outright and I told him about the TV show and the makeup. He seemed relieved. He left the room for about two minutes, and when he returned the rest of the staff were much more friendly toward me, tattoo or not. By the following day the tattoo had faded and I never asked for a tattoo again.

Our last show also had a wrap party right after the filming. It was bittersweet. The producers were still hoping for a pickup for the next season and the crew would have gladly returned to the show, but after a month or so we were all informed that the show had been canceled.

CHAPTER 70

GAVILAN

MGM was not finished with me, however. After a brief respite I came back to interview with Nick Corea and Steve Caldwell for a series with Robert Urich, called *Gavilan*. If ever there were a troubled series, the opposite of *McClain's Law*, this was it. "Gavilan" was a former CIA agent who specialized in underwater work. He was now out of the service, but they kept calling him back to handle special assignments, many of them involving scuba diving or underwater work. He had a butler, played by Fernando Lamas.

The "Gavilan" location house rented for the show was owned by Julie Payne Towne. Daughter of John Payne of *Miracle on 34th Street* fame, wife of the renowned writer/producer Robert Towne, she owned a house on the beach at Malibu known as the Rindge Estate. It was the original house in Malibu. Gavilan, being a water person, would be right at home here. We rearranged the furniture and added some things to the living room, mainly a 75-gallon aquarium. This was managed for us by David Grober of Motion Picture Marine. Caretakers had to go to the house every day to feed the fish, check the pH of the water, and so forth. Furthermore, parking on the beach was always a problem. The people who lived here were mostly film people themselves and did not want to be inconvenienced by other film people.

Fernando Lamas was a wonderful actor and a real gentleman from the same school as Ricardo Montalban. But after the second or third episode he contracted cancer. He lived only for about a month after that. We not only had to recast but we had to reshoot all the scenes he had been in, and there were many. A British gentleman took his place, Patrick McNee, formerly of *The Avengers*.

From the start, Robert Urich was pressing the writer/producers to write roles in for his wife, Heather Menzies. We had already hired his brother, Tom Urich, who was a little embarrassed about it. He was also one of the best production assistants I have ever known. Sharp and perceptive, he probably would have made an excellent AD if he wanted to go in that direction.

The producers, Nick Corea and Steven Caldwell, were hyper characters who brought immense creativity to their jobs. Nick had been producer and executive story editor of *The Incredible Hulk* TV series. He brought a sense of the bizarre and absurd to what could have been a mundane show and made it exceptional. Naturally

MGM decided that they should be replaced after the first episode or two.

I was called into the production office where Dick Birnie informed me of the change. I suggested that I had plenty of experience and could be the line producer. He agreed. He got permission from Leonard Goldberg, MGM-TV Head of Production, who approved. The only approval necessary was by Bob Urich. I made an appointment to see him. Entered his office, explained the situation. Bob Urich started laughing. He thought the idea was hysterically funny. Me, produce? Got to be kidding. He dismissed me from his office, still laughing. What a diplomat.

Eventually a new line producer was hired, John Cutts. I had met him when he was line producer on *Chicago Story* while I was working on *McClain's Law*. An extremely cultured British gentleman, also very pragmatic. The very essence of stiff upper lip production.

We were supposed to take the crew somewhere exotic for two episodes, and a special budget provision was made for that. After researching several locations we settled on the U.S. Virgin Islands, St. Thomas, centered on the town of Charlotte Amalie. There were absolutely no filming facilities there, not even a decent movie caterer. Caterers, yes, but they did parties and had no idea how to feed a hundred people in a half hour. We would have to bring everything—crew, cast, equipment, caterer, everything.

Everything was wrong with the Virgin Islands. The roads out of Charlotte Amalie were primitive. Cars lasted on the island maybe three years before the suspensions surrendered to the inevitable. Even the hardy VW didn't last long. There were numbers of resort hotels, but none were geared toward the business traveler. The town of Charlotte Amalie itself was built long before cars were invented and the streets were narrow and barely navigable. The food and all supplies for a movie crew had to be brought in to the island. Also—and this was crucial—there was no native water on the island. There were no springs, no brooks, no streams. All the water either had to fall from the sky or be shipped in. Buildings by law were built with roofs shaped like funnels that emptied all the rainwater into tanks beneath the houses.

The Virgin Islands Film Commission, of course, welcomed us with open arms. Hotels? No problem. We can arrange them for you. Caterer? We have several on the island. Weather? We have mild temperatures all year around. Haven't had a hurricane in decades. Locations? Name it and we'll help you to find it.

The script called for an abandoned hotel on the beach where a rebel army was building a force to take over a fictitious Caribbean nation. Abandoned hotel? Right here in Hull Bay, next to Magen's Bay. We went to see it. It was abandoned, all right. A shell of a building and pieces of lumber scattered around the trees near the beach. Beautiful site, and probably perfect for our use. Oh, and by the way, what happened here to the hotel? Oh, that. It was blown down by the hurricane here a couple of years ago. Oooops. Thought you said there hadn't been a hurricane in decades. Well, it never actually hit the island. It was 100 miles off shore. And it did this kind of damage? Well, it was a very strong hurricane.

Oh, and look here! This is a very historical island. We have the oldest Jewish temple in the Western Hemisphere. Yes, but we don't have anything in the script about that. Well, why don't you write something?

We returned to Los Angeles. How about the Dominican Republic? After all, they have water. Well, we are MGM, and the Dominican Republic is basically managed by Gulf and Western, which owns Paramount Pictures. Not very good for us.

We prepared to make the trip to the Virgin Islands. Everything had to be packed and catalogued. The exact contents of every box had to be carefully catalogued, down to the last cable and filter. We were using a carnet. Normally when one brings goods from one country to another one must pay import taxes. If one is only bringing in material to be used for business, and that same material will be taken out of the country when the job is finished, as long as it is catalogued properly it can be brought in and out without any import fees. That's called a carnet.

We carefully packed a 45-foot trailer and had all the papers ready. It would have to take three trips. First to Jacksonville, FL, to be loaded onto a barge. From there to San Juan, Puerto Rico, and from there by another barge to Charlotte Amalie. We contacted several airlines that flew to the Caribbean but none would give us complementary flights in exchange for screen credit. Guess we'll have to pay. We determined that it would cost us little more to charter a jet to take us down and bring us back, and we wouldn't have to worry about reservations or stopovers. Fly on our own schedule. Take all the luggage and extra equipment we needed and not worry about overweight. That's what we did.

We also had to barge down a catering truck so the crew could eat. Oh, the hotel had plenty of food, but who wants to eat conch salad very day? Barry Shapiro, the caterer from Unique Catering, arranged to ship down steaks and chops and seafood, anything we wanted. He even spent some time on the island himself to make sure that his crew was treating us properly.

The equipment truck driver got to Jacksonville and barged the truck down to San Juan. There it was offloaded, ready to be barged to Charlotte Amalie. And there it stayed. The driver phoned us to say that Puerto Rico Customs wanted to open the sealed truck to make sure there was no contraband inside. They were going to open every box and inspect the contents. This would hold us up for a couple of weeks. My assistant, Scott Murphy, flew down to San Juan to discuss this. He had with him some petty cash. It cost three or four cases of rum for the customs folks and the truck was freed to go on its way. Whew. Another lesson in international relations.

The crew was housed in Bluebeard's Castle, an old and revered structure on the island that had become a tourist resort. It had everything we needed; a good restaurant, room service, a suite we could use for a production office, our own telephone system. Plenty of room to park the trucks. What it did not have was television in the rooms. MGM had to contract with the local cable company to get TV in the rooms. Even today the tourists who stay at Bluebeard's Castle benefit from our TV series.

We had our huge truck with us but moving that behemoth around the island was not practical. We had to rent several smaller trucks just for the equipment in most cases. That meant hiring local teamsters. Another annoyance was that a local caterer felt that he was entitled to cater our show. He had catered a few government parties but had no experience with movie companies. He appealed to the VI Government and tried to get a restraining order preventing us from filming unless he catered the show. It took a day or so to handle that matter. The poor fellow so badly offended the government with his complaints that they stopped hiring him for parties and he lost about half his business.

A much more serious problem arose with the automatic rifles we had with us as props. We did not realize the danger from the Rastafarians who lived on the island. It was a real and immediate danger. These were revolutionaries whose purpose was to take over the island eventually and turn it into a Rastafarian utopia. In fact a couple of months before we arrived a few Rastas came out of the forest next to a well-known golf course on the island and shot a few golfers to death, then disappeared back into the bush just to prove that it could be done.

We, innocents abroad, had brought a few automatic weapons and several dozen automatic pistols with us along with plentiful blanks. We did not want to keep them in our hotel rooms, and the hotel did not have a large enough safe to handle them. We went to the U.S. National Guard Armory to see if we could store them in their gun safe. Surprisingly, we were refused permission. They wouldn't allow us to store our guns there because not even the National Guard stored their guns there. "Are you kidding? If the Rasta rebel this is the first place they will attack to get our arms! We can't keep any guns here!"

A few phone calls showed us that of all the private investigator services on the island only one had a large enough gun safe, and it only allowed us to park our guns there if we told absolutely nobody about what we were doing since they were afraid of being raided by the Rastas also.

The next big problem came up as soon as Nick Corea and Steve Caldwell left the show. They were replaced by David Levinson, an old-timer with many series under his belt. Suddenly Dave Levinson was burning a lot of midnight oil to revise some of the scripts that had been approved before the change. Then another spanner was thrown into the works when Bob Urich, the star, decided that he wanted his wife, Heather Menzies, to be written into the episodes in the islands, presumably so that MGM would have to pay for her travel rather than he. He refused get on the plane until he knew that she would be traveling with him as a fellow actor. Writing her into the script took a couple of days, delaying production until the rewrite was completed.

One of the scripts, left over from the Nick Corea days, called for a small one-man submarine. Our special effects man, Bill Schirmer, managed to construct a workable submarine on the island out of spare parts for around $9,000. I never knew how he managed it. It was essentially a steerable torpedo with a steel saddle on top and controls. Didn't go very fast, maybe two or three knots, but Bill designed into it a funnel in the rear of the tube that shot bubbles out the back, making it appear as if it were traveling much faster.

Many scenes required the characters to work underwater with scuba gear. This would be just fine in the Virgin Islands, well known for their crystal-clear, brilliant, blue-green waters. One could see miles underwater, just like in the Bahamas.

Unfortunately a hurricane, one of those that had never struck the islands, had just struck a couple hundred miles off shore. The water was roiled up to where one could see perhaps two or three feet in front of the face, and from then it rapidly petered out to a murky brown. (Say, wasn't there a TV series by that name?)

About a hundred yards off shore or so was a sunken hulk of a DC-3 that had been there for a couple of years. Just perfect for our show about the drug smugglers. We found it, eventually, but at most we could see only one of the cargo doors. In the murk the entire plane was hidden and we could only see small views of it. Nevertheless we staged a scene with the door being wrenched open and crates of contraband tumbling out to the ocean floor. We were able to get the shot. Our underwater cameraman, Jack Cooperman, did yeoman's service. We never did see the entire fuselage but we saw enough of the airplane to show where the door was in relation to the cockpit, etc. The picture was still murky, however.

At the time the MGM head of production was Leonard Goldberg. The big feature film at MGM at the time was *War Games*. John Badham had just replaced Martin Brest as director. Goldberg was busy running back and forth to the set, the "War Room," the most expensive set ever built in Hollywood up to that time. During this he was also watching our dailies and sending us messages daily as to what he hoped to see. The day he saw the underwater footage of the plane, he had seen maybe two minutes of it when he was called back to the set of *War Games*. He never saw the end of the dailies, never saw the scene where the door of the plane opened and the contraband tumbled out.

We received a message from MGM that the footage was not acceptable and we were to reshoot it. This was a considerable undertaking. The plane was not in very deep water, maybe 40 or 50 feet. But underwater filming is not easy. There must be a dive master, a chart kept as to how long each person stays underwater, to ensure that nobody runs out of air. There must be a dive boat or two to supply the crew with scuba gear. Filming underwater can only take a few minutes at a time because the crew has to rise to the surface gradually to prevent the "bends," a terrifyingly painful, and many times fatal, consequence of rising too suddenly. So the "bottom time" is limited by the safety factor. Unless one has a huge crew with several underwater cameramen one is necessarily limited to filming just a few minutes of usable footage each day.

Goldberg was not aware of this when he asked us to reshoot footage that was already acceptable. He just gave the order and expected it to be carried out. Had to be redone. Cost us two extra days of filming.

While we were filming on the islands, MGM wanted to begin preproduction on the episodes that would be filmed on our return. They hired another UPM, Ron Grow, to manage that preproduction back in Hollywood. I had known Ron from my Universal days, a good workmanlike UPM, very thorough.

We finished two episodes on the island and then packed all our stuff and returned to Hollywood. At least we somehow had gotten the footage they needed. The day after we returned, filming began on the next episode. At that point MGM informed me that Ron Grow was taking over the series and that I was to be let go. Ron had prepped the show and it was just easier to leave him on it.

CHAPTER 71

RIPLEY'S BELIEVE IT OR NOT

Seymour Friedman at Columbia called me yet again. He was doing a TV show called *Ripley's Believe It or Not*. Mel Stuart was the producer-director. I went to the office where the production manager for the show, Bob Anderson, hired me. The office was in the Wolper building on the corner of La Cienega and Third Street, very near to where I used to live. There were a number of decent restaurants and lunch places in the area, all of which I took advantage of eventually.

I was only assigned to the show for about three or four weeks. I worked on a few segments. One was about the last home and grave of D. H. Lawrence, the famous author who lived outside of Santa Fe, NM. He had died there in the 1920s. His grave was on the property. At some point in the 1940s grave robbers stole the body. It was found days later, and the robbers prosecuted. His widow then had the body dismantled, and had the floor of the mausoleum filled with concrete, and the body parts scattered throughout the concrete. The only way to get the body now is to take the entire building apart. Hired a local TV crew to tape the grave site and the mausoleum. Holly Palance, daughter of the actor Jack Palance, narrated the segment. There was much unusual about Santa Fe, but Mel Stuart didn't know about it so we didn't shoot it. I managed the entire segment on my own. A director came out just for the one day of filming.

Another segment was filmed in the Los Angeles area. The very oldest living thing on Earth is said to be a creosote bush in the middle of the desert near Palmdale. I had to find it and lead the crew out there. I traced down an archaeologist at the University of California at Riverside who had the information. "King Clone," as it is known, is an unmarked bush in the desert, and has been dated at around 11,500 years old, far older than the oldest giant sequoia trees. I did not mark it either since the scientist who entrusted me with the information asked that we not do so, for fear of having souvenir hunters destroy the thing. We did photograph it, however.

One of the more interesting items we handled was the Big Bang Theory of how the universe was born 14 billion years ago, give or take. We photographed that segment at the Mount Wilson Telescope on top of Mount Wilson, near Pasadena. At the time the telescope was built it was the largest telescope in the world with a diameter over eight feet. During the first part of the twentieth century it ruled supreme amongst telescopes. There was little enough civilization around it to disturb the atmospheric conditions. By now, however, the lights from Pasadena and other nearby cities have ruined the chances for deep-space visual astronomy. The telescope is still used for interferometry among other things. Jack Palance himself narrated that segment.

I only stayed with *Ripley* for four weeks or so. The production manager and I had entirely different ideas about how the show was to be managed. Seymour Friedman understood that and released me with an honorable discharge.

CHAPTER 72

TRAUMA CENTER

At this point Mark Evans, head of production for Twentieth Century-Fox TV, called and asked if I could production-manage a new show, *Trauma Center*. A repertory company show, produced by Bill Phillips, with Lou Ferrigno and Jim Naughton. Naughton was an accomplished stage actor who was beginning to make his name known on the TV screen. Lou Ferrigno was already a famous bodybuilder who had starred in *The Incredible Hulk* TV series as the muscle-bound persona of Bill Bixby, Dr. David Banner. Anyway, Lou was 6'5" and solid muscle. He played an ambulance driver—EMT. Naughton was the doctor at the trauma center who cared for the injured after Ferrigno brought them in.

Bill Phillips, the producer, would later become head of production at Columbia after Seymour retired. He and I did not see eye to eye about many things and my tenure there was short. It would probably have been longer except that we had budget problems. Mark Evans had his own ideas about how budgets should be made, and had asked me to cut certain areas that I knew we would need for the show. No matter how I explained it, he was adamant. After I left the show he added the items back into the budget and let it be known that I was the person who had left them out. Oh well. Those producers who knew me knew what had happened as did I. The others did not matter. I was able to provide work for my old friend Maximilian Bing as 1st AD. That was a plus.

One other point of difficulty was that Lou Ferrigno wanted to have an exercise room set up so that he could work out between scenes. Mark Evans was categorically against that. It was an extra-budget item. Lou was insistent, and I was visible to him while Mark was not. Again, after I left he got his gym.

CHAPTER 73

PASSIONS

I was called again by Joe Wizan, for whom I had done *Scarecrow*. He had another film to do, *Passions*, written and directed by Sandor Stern. This would star Joanne Woodward, Richard Crenna, and Lindsay Wagner. Sandy Stern had done most of the writing, although Janet Greek, Joe's wife, had a hand in it also. Filming was to take place 100 percent on location around Los Angeles and Malibu. There was almost no studio filming at all, which was fine with me. I had the title of associate producer on the film, and I also directed the second unit drivebys. First AD was again my friend Daisy Gerber.

This was another of those shows in which so little went wrong it was almost boring. The cast and crew were exemplary. Nothing exciting happened on the set. I had heard rumors that Lindsay Wagner could be difficult, would be late, would be hard on the crew, all kinds of bad rap about her. Nothing of the kind happened. She was there on time all the time, never late, always worked easily with the crew and other cast members, was very serious about playing her role properly. We were all delighted with her.

Daisy kept everything going at a good pace. Sandy Stern had the time he needed to work with the actors, who responded in kind.

One very minor incident. We were filming the second unit driving shots in Malibu. I had the camera on top of a hill overlooking the Malibu colony and was directing the car. From where we were standing I had a clear view of all the Los Angeles beach communities, all the way down to Palos Verdes, around thirty miles away. I had the camera set up and we were ready to roll, when I suddenly heard "Action!" on the walkie-talkie. I keyed the mike and said, "Who said that?" Then someone said, "Bring the car!" I quickly said, "No, don't bring the car yet."

Another film company was shooting on the beach in Santa Monica and we were receiving each other's transmissions. After we had that sorted out we arranged with each other to use non-conflicting frequencies, and we went back to filming. But for a minute there it was confusing.

I was called by Morris Abrams to work on a film as 1st AD. I can't even remember the name of it. Morrie was the UPM. I had known Morrie since childhood. He was one of the very earliest members of the DGA and had been a mentor when I joined in 1961.

His film had not yet been funded although a director was chosen and was waiting in the wings. I did a schedule on spec for them, went into the office a couple times a week, but the money never came through. I needed an income.

CHAPTER 74

THAT WAS THEN, THIS IS NOW

I got a call from Chris Cain. He had directed *Stone Boy* with Robert Duvall, great critical reviews and a little income, not much. He had been hired by a company in Minneapolis, MN, to make a film in St. Paul. *That Was Then, This Is Now* was taken from a book by S.E. Hinton that became a best-seller, especially among high school students. Emilio Estevez, the actor, liked it so much that he wrote the script, which was accepted by Media Ventures, the Minneapolis company. Chris Cain was excellent with young actors, and he was an ideal choice of director. I had interviewed with him for *Stone Boy* and we had been very compatible. I was hired as UPM. The line producer, Alan Belkin, told me to start the next Monday. I took the script home, phoned Morrie Abrams and told him I couldn't wait any longer for a show that might not happen. Morrie asked me not to take the other job because his film was about to be funded any day now, but since "any day now" had been going on for two weeks I told him that I had to take the other job. I started breaking down the script to schedule it. In those days we did this all by hand. Computerized scheduling and budgeting programs had not yet been invented except for one.

FilmTrax was the very first computerized budgeting system. Since nobody yet had a home computer, the user was required to go to the Santa Monica office of FilmTrax to work on the budget. It still cut days off the process, although the result was one of those wonderful foot-wide computer printouts generated in one long strip by a dot-matrix printer. Bring your ear plugs. The man who invented the system won a Technical Achievement Award from the Academy for it and it was the only "Oscar" he won, despite a monumental body of work in other areas: Michael Crichton.

I finished the schedule and budget, and returned to the production office in West Los Angeles. The producers and Chris Cain were waiting for me. We sat down at the conference table and I opened the schedule. At that point they informed me that I was no longer the production manager. They would not tell me what had happened. I was stunned. I had the job, I had begun the work. Why suddenly? They never told me until the film was over. I asked Chris Cain privately and even he would not discuss it. He did understand my dismay and as a kind of second prize he offered me the job of 1st AD. I accepted.

The producers, meanwhile, had intimated that I had had a bad report as a production person. When I accepted the assignment of 1st AD, I asked them as a courtesy that if I did a good job for them, they would inform the people who told them that I was as good as I said I was. They agreed to do so.

What happened was simply that Morrie Abrams had called them and told them that I was not a good production manager so that I would be free to work on his show. His hope was that they would let me go altogether and I would work with him. It did not work out that way. I did *That Was Then, This Is Now* anyway.

Morrie retired from the industry soon after, and a few years later I learned that he had died when he was hit by a bus while crossing a street.

I packed and left for Minneapolis where the film was to be shot. The crew was entirely non-union except for the DGA, WGA, and SAG. The department heads came from Los Angeles, but the crew members were recruited from the Minneapolis production pool. They were not at all experienced in making theatrical films, having only worked on commercials before this. This show would not be simple.

We all stayed in the Holiday Inn in St. Paul. It was less expensive than in Minneapolis, even if farther from the locations. The new production manager, Scott Rosenfelt, and I got along well. There were a few things I would have done differently, but by and large he did a more than adequate job for such a distant location. He had hired a company, for example, that provided both the electric and grip equipment, and the catering service. The catering service was not very good. The equipment was very good. The crew took to ordering in pizza for lunch instead of eating for free off the truck. Sometimes we ordered from McDonald's or Blimpie's. The caterer didn't care; they were paid anyway. Scott Rosenfelt couldn't do anything about it because he had a contract with them and if the caterer quit, the electric and grip equipment would also disappear. Oh well...

The electric and grip crews in Minneapolis were very good with commercials. Feature films, and being prepared for the next shot, was something they did not know much about. I watched them work for a couple of hours and then I determined that things were dragging.

Example: whenever a light is positioned at the side of the set so that the camera lens is visible from its place, a grip always puts a flag, stand, and sandbag there to shield the light from the lens. Otherwise there would be halation. The lens might not directly see the light, but if it shines anywhere near the lens it can fog the film anyway. So it must be shaded from the lens. In Hollywood it is standard that when a light goes up, a flag and stand go up next to it, and a sandbag appears to weigh down the stand so it doesn't topple over.

This process usually takes no more than five minutes. If it is done at the same time the light goes up it takes no minutes. But to collect the light, stand, and sandbag after the light has been raised could take five minutes. This is not much time, but it can add up over a day's work.

The average number of set-ups per day is twenty. Some shows have more, some less, but twenty is a good average for TV. Suppose five minutes were wasted on each setup because the grips did not put stands and flags where the lights are. Let's see, twenty times five, we have wasted 100 minutes. That is an hour and forty minutes. And it is overtime hours, not normal hours, because that's where we will pay for it. Over a week we will have wasted almost a whole day's work, just waiting for the grip stands.

What to do? I explained to the key grip what we usually do in Hollywood with the lights and stands. He told me that in Minneapolis they did it their way and it was perfectly good, and I should just pay attention to running the set and not tell other people what to do. I sympathized with him. If I had been doing something for several years one way and then someone from out of state comes and tells me that another way is more efficient, I would probably resent it too.

I went to Gary Lindberg, one of the Minneapolis producers, and explained the problem. I saw him watching the set while using the stopwatch in his wristwatch for a couple of hours, then he went quietly to the key grip and spoke with him off to the side. From then on whenever a light went up, a flag, stand, and sandbag appeared next to it immediately.

Several other situations arose in the same way.

Minnesota has its own peculiar climate. When we arrived there it was still summer. The temperature went up to 90 degrees during the day and dropped into the 60s at night. I was dressed accordingly. Then suddenly after about four weeks of filming, over one weekend the temperature dropped down into the 30s and 40s during the day, and freezing rain began to fall. I was cold. Luckily there was an Eddie Bauer store nearby so I got a good anorak. I asked the desk clerk at the hotel when autumn was in Minneapolis, and he told me it had been on Saturday.

Another incident pointed up the need for good safety procedures on the set. One setup had Morgan Freeman coming out the back door of a bar. A waiting rifleman shoots him. The way the scene was filmed, the rifleman was standing directly next to the camera so that the rifle barrel protruded into the left side of the frame. He shoots, and Morgan drops. Just before we rolled the camera the property master passed out earplugs for the crew. Gunshots, even quarter-load blanks, are extremely loud and can be damaging to the ears. The crew accepted the plugs, rolled them up and stuck them in their ears as protection, all except the camera operator. He was macho and no little gunshot was going to scare him, by golly. I showed him the shot, explained that the rifle chamber was right next to his left ear in order for the shot to work. Nope, he didn't need any wimpy earplugs. I told him it wasn't a suggestion; it was standard motion picture procedure. He argued about it briefly, then put the plugs into his ears. Just after I called "roll it" I saw him remove the earplugs even while he was looking through the camera. We took him to the hospital with a broken ear drum.

Adventures In Hollywood: A Memoir By Bob Koster

The picture actually went remarkably well for being a distant location. Very few problems. We did most of our casting locally. All our minor roles and extras came from the Minneapolis-St. Paul area. One little problem did come up. We filmed outside a house on a quiet street in St. Paul, supposed to be the home of Craig Sheffer and his mother, played by Barbara Babcock. Great actress. The master shot lasted around seven minutes with Emilio, Craig, and Barbara sitting on the porch. Checked the lens, the camera, everything was fine. Chris Cain was so happy with the master shot that he felt that we needed no further coverage. The shot was finished. We released Barbara to leave. She was due to fly to Greece right after filming to meet up with relatives. She had packed and her luggage was in the station wagon so she could go straight from the set to the airport.

She left. It took us a half hour or so to set up for the next scene. The next scene was also a long one. The assistant cameraman carefully packaged the film we had just shot and put it on the camera truck. He then took a roll of film and loaded the camera for the next shot. We did the shot. By now it was an hour since Barbara had left the set. The script girl was not experienced enough to have kept track of which roll of film was used for what, so she didn't mark down the serial numbers. Each roll has its own unique serial number. The assistant cameraman came running from the camera truck holding a fresh roll of film, the roll he thought he had just loaded into the camera. What he had done by accident was to reload the original roll back into the camera, the one that had the one shot we needed for the porch scene. We had just photographed the next scene over it, double-exposing the roll.

But Barbara was already on the plane headed for Greece. A phone call to the airport confirmed that she had left, but there was a stopover in New York at JFK airport. We left word to page her at JFK to turn around and return to Minneapolis to do the scene over again.

She took it with great good grace. She returned, repeated the scene, and left a day late for her rendezvous in Greece. The assistant cameraman couldn't stop apologizing for it. I am sure that he never did that again.

One of the extras we cast was a real slam-dancing, peacock-haired, nose-ring-chained wreck. Always showed up wearing a ratty leather jacket, half of his head shaved, a small gold chain running from his left nostril ring to one of his four or five earrings. His hair stood straight up. He had a perpetual sneer. Tattoos on his arms, what we could see of them. But he was always on time and always did exactly what was expected of him. Just weird, that's all. I never spoke with him except to let him know when he would be needed on the set. We had nothing in common at all.

After we wrapped the film we had the traditional wrap party and all our regulars attended. Not Barbara; she was in Greece. But John Ondov and Gary Lindberg bought out a restaurant for the evening, with open bar, plenty of really good food, a small dance band, the works. Some of our regular extras also showed up. One fellow didn't fit in. He was well dressed, wearing a dark suit and tie, well mannered.

Something about him was familiar… It was our slam-dancing delinquent. I asked him and he explained that he was studying at University of Minnesota. Major was nuclear physics. So what was he doing in that outrageous getup? He always wanted to act in a movie, and this was his chance not only to play but to stand out. Now that it was out of his system he would go back to being an atomic physicist. He was bright, intelligent, and the diametric opposite of how he portrayed himself in the film. Just felt he had to do it, that's all.

Soon after I came back to Los Angeles I discovered why I had been demoted to AD, what part Morrie Abrams played in it. I again asked Alan Belkin, the producer, to help me to get another job as a UPM and he said of course he would. Of course he didn't. I should have expected that.

Work was becoming more and more difficult to come by. I was passing the age of forty, had not kept up as many of my contacts as I should have, and was beginning to show gray hair. This was not good. The film industry was more and more a business for younger people. It was a social thing. I had plenty of experience. I could manage a production or run a set with the best of them. But many producers were looking not for experience or for expertise, but for a buddy they could go out drinking or wenching with in the evening. A pal. I had never been very adept at the Hollywood social scene. I had so much work that I didn't feel it necessary. I was awkward in crowds, except when being paid. I didn't play tennis with the right people. I didn't play tennis at all, in fact.

My car died and I needed a car. I had been out of work for a few months and my finances were low. In fact, I needed to move to a less expensive apartment.

A friend drove me to Van Nuys Boulevard in the San Fernando Valley, home to many car dealerships. At Keyes Motors I found a 1978 Ford Thunderbird. The sign in the windshield advertised the car for $2,750. Just about what I could afford. The salesman (The car is definitely you!") gave me a test drive, enough to see that the radio and windshield wipers did not work. I told him that I expected those to be repaired by the time I picked the car up the next day. He agreed. I also negotiated the price down to $2,500 for the inconvenience. Sounded like a good deal. It wasn't the kind if car I was used to but it ran, was reasonably reliable, and was comfortable. The salesman and I shook hands on the deal. He left to bring the sales manager to finalize the arrangement. That gentleman appeared, tried to give the impression that he was doing me a big favor by repairing the radio and windshield wipers. He also congratulated me on having made such a good deal at $2,750.

Wait a minute--$2,750? We just agreed on $2,500. Oh, he explained, the salesman wasn't authorized to make a deal like that. It was $2,750. I restrained my Hungarian temper but my German logic took over. I turned around and began to walk away. "Where are you going?" "To another dealer. I made a deal, shook hands, and to me that is a contract." "Wait. Let's discuss this." "There's nothing to discuss."

I turned back anyway. The manager said, "Well, OK, we'll stay at $2,500." "No we won't." "We won't?" "No, now the price is $2,250." He started sputtering. I said, "I'm going to cheat you out of the same amount that you tried to cheat me out of." "B-but you can't do that!" I started to walk away again. "OK, $2,250, but that's our final offer." I said I would be back tomorrow with the money as soon as the radio was fixed.

I had the money in a savings account, but I was still really annoyed at the nerve of these people, trying to bamboozle me out of $250. I had to go to the bank to get the money anyway. I got it in $1 bills. I mixed in some $5 bills just to keep it interesting. I unwrapped all the bills so they were not bound together but loose, and I put the lot into a shopping bag. It came to about $2,400 with taxes and everything else. They tried to charge me for insurance but I had my own.

I showed up at the dealer at 3:00 pm the next day. They had phoned to tell me the car was ready. I came in with my shopping bag and a book. The salesman was there, shook my hand warmly, ushered me into the finance guy. That worthy asked if I wanted to finance the car. No, I was paying cash. Do I want insurance? No, I have my own. Ours is better. No it's not. OK, it's $2,415.43 or something like that. I reached in my pocket and got the 43 cents. I asked him if he was ready to receive the cash and he agreed to do so. I opened the shopping bag and dumped the money out onto his desk. It went all over his papers, fell on the floor, went into his desk drawer, it was a mess.

He wasn't happy, but it was cash, and now he would have to count it. That's why I brought the book. I sat in his office for about two hours, reading my book, while he and an assistant counted the bills. The walls of the office were glass, and the salesmen were standing outside looking in and snickering at his plight. The sales manager showed up too. Asked me why I had done that. I told him it was because he had tried to cheat me in the first place, and maybe he wouldn't do that anymore. I doubt it, but at least he would never do it to me again. A couple of hours later I left with the car. Keyes Motors, remember it, dear reader.

With my car I was able to canvass the neighborhoods in the San Fernando Valley. I quickly settled on a two-room apartment with a loft in Tarzana. Walking distance from supermarkets and drugstores, cleaners, all close at hand. The apartment was on the second floor, making it uncomfortable for prospective burglars. A friend with a pickup truck helped me to move my meager belongings from Bronson Canyon to Tarzana.

That having been done, I still needed a job to support myself.

CHAPTER 75

BETWEEN THE DARKNESS AND THE DAWN

Directly after that John W. Rogers called. He had landed on his feet after being fired from Fox, and was now working as a production supervisor at Warner Bros. TV. He seemed to feel that we had some kind of connection since his father and mine had worked together so he called me to work on this show. The producer was Doris Quinlan, and the director, the suave, sophisticated Peter Levin. Other than that it was basically my show to manage as I wished. Rogers wasn't around to supervise very much.

He did startle me with one thing he did, however. I didn't give it much credence at the time, but it rebounded on me later. When he hired me, we were sitting in his office. He opened his top desk drawer, smiling, and said, "Now don't forget, every Friday one-tenth of your salary goes here." I started laughing and he laughed as well. I thought he was kidding. With his reputation I didn't think it was a very tasteful joke, but he wasn't a very tasteful guy either.

I made the schedule and budget. The studio accepted it, and we started hiring crew. This was another 100 percent location film. The locations were different than the last time, however. We found a large family house in Monrovia, home to a Mormon family. As soon as the mother found out that I was divorced she tried very hard to get me to date her daughter. I did secure the house for filming without that requirement and all was well.

We also needed a high school football game with the crowd in the bleachers. The Labor Department required that whenever minors were on the set welfare workers were required to ensure their well being. The mandated ratio was ten to one, one welfare worker for each ten kids. The school had a set of bleachers that easily held over 1,000 students. I had to appeal to the state labor board for a variance, since the regular school teachers would be there anyway. The alternative would have been to hire well over 100 welfare workers for those scenes.

The actors were exemplary. I must have been lucky. So few bad eggs in the talent department. Elizabeth Montgomery played the lead. Her male counterpart was Jimmy Naughton, and her mother was played by Dorothy McGuire. All wonderful people. The show went off without a hitch.

CHAPTER 76

THE SKY'S NO LIMIT

When I was living in NY, one of my friends was Bobby Schneider. We had never actually worked together but he lived nearby and we shared dinner many times. He was also an AD/UPM. He had been one of the production heads of the old VPI productions in the New York days. I would report to him on numerous commercials. We had discussed working together many times but it never had come to pass until now. David Lowell Rich was directing a TV movie called *The Sky's No Limit*, about the lives of three potential lady astronauts. Sharon Gless, Anne Archer, and Dee Wallace were the stars. Barnard Hughes was also in evidence. We would shoot in Houston, Texas, at NASA, and in the surrounding areas.

Since I had already filmed at NASA, although years before, I was somewhat familiar with the territory and turf. NASA, however, had changed greatly in the meanwhile. Now the Department of Defense was in charge and nobody could go anywhere without a guard. A couple of degrees better than working in a prison. At least we didn't need checkpoints in order to enter or leave.

Bob was the production manager and I was the 1st AD. Since David Lowell Rich had successfully directed and produced so many movies of the week for CBS he chose Harry Ackerman, an old CBS hand, as the line producer. Harry was great. So was David.

The three girls were as different as could be imagined. Dee Wallace is a method actor. She does breathing exercises, and sometimes physical exercises, before the camera rolls. Since we were all on her side we waited patiently while this was going on. Anne Archer is a good solid performer who slipped into the part like wearing an old cherished overcoat. No problems there at all. Sharon Gless was the humorist of the trio. Always full of fun. A serious actress who doesn't take her work seriously, but she really delivers.

Filming in the areas around Houston was very hot, humid, and physically uncomfortable, but very pleasant in every other way. Texas summers can be quite oppressive. We kept a bucket of iced water spiked with Seabreeze on the set at all times and lots of bandanas to soak in it to wear around our necks. That helped a great deal when we were outdoors.

Our crew was mostly non-union. A few union members worked under assumed names just for the income. We were visited by local union representatives who were joined by Hollywood union staffers, looking for union members working sub sombrero. We held out for three weeks like this, with the union members hiding behind flats and trees when the union reps arrived. It was awkward to say the least. In the fourth week the company finally signed a union contract, and everyone on the crew became a member. The union reps disappeared. Work in Hollywood had begun to suffer from the runaway production syndrome and jobs were becoming scarce. Unions were hurting for work, especially for the pension and health plan payments that were missing because of the non-union work.

Runaway production happened for several reasons but mostly because it was possible. When I first began working in the early 1960s cameras and lights weighed hundreds of pounds and required large dollies and stands to be able to handle them. Arriflex began importing very lightweight soundproof cameras in the mid-1960s. Mitchell tried to keep up but were too little too late. Panavision developed what was for a long time the industry standard, a very lightweight soundproof camera, even more facile than the excellent Arriflex. Eventually Panavision dominated the industry to the extent that they bought the Mitchell factory and began building Panavision cameras there. Arc lights were replaced by quartz lights, far lighter and easier to carry. Lowell Kits, developed by cameraman Ross Lowell, became the choice of documentarians and industrial producers. The old Western Electric sound trailer was replaced by the Nagra portable tape recorder, shrinking the sound crew size and making the equipment much more portable. The Nagra was about the size of an attaché case, a far cry from an entire trailer. At this point it was obvious that instead of building a ballroom set on a sound stage it would be easier to take all this portable equipment and film inside a real ballroom. Various state and foreign film commissions competed for Hollywood's business, offering tax incentives to film in their locations rather than on the tired old Hollywood streets. Living for a month or so in another city, or better yet in a foreign country, became very attractive to producers who enjoyed being far away from the restrictions of the Hollywood studios. Movies ran away. Hollywood crews bemoaned the loss, had meetings, petitioned their congressmen, and did what they could to stem the flow, but it had begun and could not be stopped. The backlash is still being felt.

Soon after we wrapped we all returned to Hollywood. It was actually better for me not to have been the UPM on the show because I could return sooner and start another project.

CHAPTER 77

CODENAME FOXFIRE

My next project was really part of a film. Corey Allen my old friend asked me to be his AD on a TV movie called *Codename Foxfire*. It finished filming on location in the Bahamas and returned to wrap up on the backlot and in the sound stages at Universal Studio. He only needed me for the Hollywood part. In those days Universal was halfway between the well-oiled machine I had known and the independent it was to become. It already had a non-union subsidiary, the Arthur Company, and everyone turned the blind eye toward it. It existed from the mid-1980s to the early 1990s. Offices were on the Universal lot. It produced entirely non-union films even though it was headquartered and funded by the biggest union company in town.

To go back a couple of decades, the studio had been purchased in 1958 by the Music Corporation of America, Hollywood's huge agent. Control of the studio was given to MCA chief Lew Wasserman. Wasserman and his partner, Dr. Jules Styne, ran the studio with a personal touch. Many of the stars were MCA clients. Wasserman had immense power and immense control. For a time he was the most respected, feared, and hated man in Hollywood. When the union contracts came up for renewal he did the negotiating for the studios, and the studios generally fell into line behind him to back his decisions regarding salaries and working conditions. There was a ritual every three years in which the studio chiefs from all the major studios would gather in the big theatre on the Universal lot. Lew Wasserman was on the stage with the heads of the unions. Lew would read the major conditions that he and the unions had agreed upon, the studio chiefs would sign, and everyone went home. This lasted through the time when the unions began to lose their power in Hollywood due to runaway production, and due to the immense pool of non-union talent available in Hollywood because the unions had excluded them. This change occurred in the mid to late 1980s. Universal, by now no longer the sole supplier of TV programming for NBC and was sold to Matsushita of Japan, manufacturers of Panasonic products among other things, and Lew's reign was over.

But by now Lew had built the studio into a money-making powerhouse. It produced a large percentage of the TV shows that appeared all over the world. It made blockbuster feature films like *Jaws* and *American Graffiti*. The backlot was turned into a studio tour with gaily decorated tour trams, guides, and staged entertainment such as a stunt show, a western shootout, and a lake with the *Jaws* shark jumping out at boat riders. It was said that Wasserman sat in his office on the top floor of the "Black Tower" building with binoculars, counting the tram riders.

The important thing is that the studio was beginning to lose its production focus, concentrating on public displays such as the studio tour. Films shot on the lot had to inform the studio tour days ahead of time so the trams could be rerouted. This is where I came in.

Foxfire was begun with Bob Jeffords as the 1st AD. He left the show when it returned to the U.S. from the Bahamas. That's when I took over. I had no prep time at all, but didn't really need it since I was just a caretaker for a few weeks while we finished. But other things were going wrong.

I learned this on the first day of filming. We had a scene at "Golden Monkey Pond" on the back lot, with Joanna Cassidy, the star, arriving by a float plane. Our float plane was identical to the one they had already filmed in the Bahamas. There was also a Jet-ski that Joanna was to ride out into the harbor. The ride had already been photographed, but she was to get on the Jet-ski and pull away from the wharf at the studio lot. She had appeared on time, as always, and hustled into makeup and wardrobe. Cameraman Robert Collins started setting up for the scene on the wharf. The float plane was there, as was the Jet-ski. Both had been painted to match the ones in the Bahamas, down to the registration numbers on the hull. Corey Allen called the actors out for a rehearsal. Joanna came out, as expected, with Kleenex around her neck to protect the makeup, and in her work clothes, she had not yet changed into the wet suit she wore in the scene in the Bahamas. The rehearsal went well. I sent Joanna back into wardrobe, and she just never emerged.

Corey asked me what happened. I called Gary Strangis, the 2nd AD, who was at the wardrobe trailer to see what the delay was. He said, "Bob, you'd better come back here and see for yourself." I went to the wardrobe room. There the wardrobe supervisor told me that the wet suit was still in the Bahamas. It had never been shipped along with a couple of other boxes that should have been in L.A. by now. We couldn't shoot the scene, which we had just spent an hour setting up. I ran back to the set to tell Corey and to figure out what else we could shoot. We were able to cobble together a couple of other scenes that should have occurred in other locations, and we shot those. In the meantime I went to the Universal production manager and asked why the wardrobe wasn't there, and how could something be scheduled for today when the wardrobe was missing. I got a very blank stare for an answer. The scene had been scheduled two or three weeks in advance, and it was the job of the production department to ensure that all the elements, from cameras to wardrobe, were available when needed. The producer, who had witnessed this entire debacle, gave me a perfect imitation of Oliver Hardy, "Another fine mess…"

Seems this kind of thing had been happening regularly during the production. That was Universal.

Three or four days later we were filming on a sound stage where Joanna was hanging from a parachute harness in front of a sky background. That scene was to take place from eight to around ten in the morning, then we were to go to the sound stage next door and film a yacht scene in a mockup the art director had built for us, so we could dolly from cabin to cabin. I wanted to make sure that the yacht set was ready, so while Bob lit the parachute scene I wandered next door to see the yacht. It should be nearly complete by now and the set dressers should be putting the finishing touches on the cabins.

No yacht. Nothing. Bare stage. Not a stick of wood. Thinking that the stage had been switched I phoned the art director and asked on which stage he had put the yacht. "Yacht? What yacht?" "Oh, you know, the one we're filming in around a half hour." "Filming?" "Did you see the call sheet for today?" "No, I've been busy." "Did you read the schedule?" "No, not recently. I've been preparing your show."

I convinced the gentleman to get to work on the yacht set right away so that we would have something, anything, to film this afternoon. He managed to cobble together something like a yacht cabin but it could only be photographed from one angle. In the meantime the crew waited for the set to be built. We lost around four hours that day. Corey was furious but nothing could be done. Another fine mess...

I had also noticed that when we were filming dialogue scenes in a quiet set, there was talking in the background. Soft voices. I began looking around while the camera was rolling and discovered that the sound mixer himself was talking into his microphone, giving instructions during the shot to the mike boom operator. I had never heard of this before. He was obviously recording his own voice as well as the dialogue. He must have been aware of it. I mentioned it to him. His answer, "You are not the first AD who has told me that. It doesn't bother the post-production people, so why should it bother you?" I told him that I had never seen that before and I would appreciate his not talking during the shot any more. He ignored me.

I called the production office and asked for the mixer to be replaced as soon as possible. The production head told me that this man had been at the studio for many years and the company was loyal to him, and he would stay on the production. They were willing to risk the expense of post-production sound replacement, a considerable sum, not to hurt his feelings, apparently. I dropped the subject. Another fine mess...

A few days later, Bob Collins was replaced as cameraman by another cameraman, a Universal regular. This man was a real charmer. He was a salesman for Herbalife, and his station wagon was filled with his product. He spent part of his time between setups trying to convince others on the crew to a) use Herbalife products, and b) to became salesmen themselves. What kind of a zoo had I gotten into here? What had happened to the smoothly working Universal I used to know?

I found out with great authority in the next few days. We were scheduled to film in a mansion in Agoura Hills, about twenty miles west of the studio. The mansion had all the space we needed but not much space to park cars in the driveway. With the huge Universal equipment trucks the parking area was filled. The mansion was built on a side road off Mulholland Highway on which parking was not permitted. The location manager had forgotten to arrange for a place for the crew cars to park. We arrived at the mansion in a driving rainstorm. The parking area was already filled with trucks. The road was about 200 yards away, and the crew, not knowing where else to park, had begun to park at the side of the road in spite of the "No Parking" signs. Then they had to walk through the very heavy downpour to get to the house. Soon there were fifty or sixty cars parked on the roadside.

The crew began lighting the interior set when the Sheriff's Department showed up. They did not come in to inquire about the cars; they merely began writing parking tickets. The crew noticed quickly, and within seconds, it seemed, the set was abandoned and the crew were in their cars, circling the block, waiting for the location manager to find a parking lot. Production had ground to a stop.

Being a man of sharp perception, the location manager realized that something had to be done. I suggested that he do it immediately since we could do nothing without a crew. However, he was involved in a conversation with the home owner concerning what kind of lunch was to be served, and to him that was more important than the fifty or sixty cars circling the block. After about fifteen minutes of this, I was able to persuade him to find a parking lot convenient to the location. This took another half hour, and the lot he found was about two miles away. It was being used by a construction crew that was building another mansion, and it was a dirt lot. Right now, because of the rainstorm, it was a mud pit. Cars could barely make their way across it without spinning wheels and kicking up mud in every direction.

To make matters even worse, since the crew had not been provided with a bus for the location, we only had two small mini-vans to transport them back to the mansion. This took another half hour, and eventually the mud-spattered crew arrived back at the mansion to go back to work. They were tracking mud through the house, making the owners very upset at Universal. The location manager had his hands full keeping the owners happy and worrying about where lunch was to be served, since he had forgotten to arrange for that also. About that time the studio sent out a bus. But by now we were easily three hours behind schedule. Another fine mess…

The art department was responsible for another small glitch. One scene called for a character to go to the wall, swing a painting out of the way to reveal a safe embedded in the wall, and open the safe. We had a mockup of the painting and the safe door on a stand so we could place the camera behind it and photograph the actor through the door as if the camera were inside the safe. Seems simple enough; it's done all the time. We finished the first part of the scene from the room. The actor swung the painting out; the safe was open. Now we needed the reverse shot. I radioed the 2nd AD to tell the set dressers to bring up the mock-up painting and safe door on a stand. The set dressing truck had been taken to the parking lot, two miles away in the rain and the mud. The set dressers knew we needed the mock-up painting for the next shot but didn't think to keep it handy.

It took a half hour for them to get a van, drive to the parking lot, cover the painting and door to keep them out of the rain, bring them over to the mansion, and set them up in front of the wall so we could place the camera behind them and photograph through them at the actor and the room behind. They had the piece set up when we realized that they had made a mistake. The real painting and safe door were both hinged on the right side, but the mockup was hinged on the left side. The door and painting would swing the wrong way. They could not be used. A phone call back to the studio resulted in the set dressers taking the door and painting down to the van, driving back to the studio in the rain, an hour each way, and spending an hour in the shop there changing the hinges over to the other side. Three hours wasted. We scraped together a couple of other shots we could do in the meantime, but it was a stretch. Another fine mess…

I had duly noted all these hold-ups on the production reports to explain why there was so much overtime each day. After the show was finished I had a talk with the production head of Universal TV and was told essentially that he was sorry I was so unhappy at the studio and perhaps I would be better off somewhere else. I said that was not the case, but I would be happy to work at the studio, understanding that some things go wrong and cannot be helped. It became obvious that my writing the mistakes on the daily report was a problem for them. They were accustomed to production delays but they were not used to being told why they happened. I never worked there again.

CHAPTER 78

THE GLADIATOR

I was called by my old friend (?) John Rogers to help out on a production that he wasn't working on. His friend, Bob Lovenheim, was producing a TV show that he hoped would become a series. *The Gladiator* starred Ken Wahl. Its subject was a fellow who owns a really big pickup truck armed with lots of gadgets that he uses to exact revenge on the evil people of the world. The director was Abel Ferrara, a New Yorker used to directing street films.

First thing when I got there I realized that the major players had been recommended or hired for the production by John Rogers. Claude Lawrence, an old pro, was one of Rogers' boys, as was the totally incompetent transportation head. This man costs us lots of money in trucks not being in the right place, cars not being prepared properly, and so forth. But I guess Rogers got his 10 percent from these folks. He sure didn't get it from me. This became a problem. I noticed from the start that the production staff was looking askance at me. Like I was doing something wrong. No matter what I did or in what manner, Abel and Jim were not satisfied. I was doing an excellent job but I was not good enough. I can only guess that Rogers was working behind my back to have me fired because I was not coughing up his 10 percent. Two weeks into principal photography I turned my walkie-talkie over to the 2nd AD, Michael Kennedy.

After I got home from leaving the show I received a phone call from Rogers. He explained that I had really embarrassed him on the show and he would never call me again for any work. I asked him specifically what I had done to embarrass him and he told me that I already knew. He also said that since we were old friends he hoped we would continue to have lunches and dinners together even if we did not work together.

I saw him around ten years later at a dinner party. He had become a frail old man who could barely walk with the help of a cane. We did not speak to each other.

CHAPTER 79

THE MAN WHO BROKE 1000 CHAINS

Bob Schneider called. He was UPM on a film in which the 1st AD had to leave for personal reasons and he had to make a switch. There were two weeks left for filming. He called me and I met with the director, Danny Mann, with whom I had worked back in the 1960s on *For Love of Ivy*. He didn't make many films but the ones he made were good ones. *Butterfield 8* was one of his. He specialized in working with good actors, developing character. Why he accepted this show is beyond me, but he was in the middle of it and needed help.

The Man Who Broke 1000 Chains was the autobiography of the man who wrote the book *I Was a Fugitive from a Chain Gang*, from which the famous film with Paul Muni was made. The script was written by Michael Campus, a man of no mean talent. All that was left to film were a few scenes between the two main actors, a kind of surrealistic scene with some period cars, and a very large battle scene. Simple enough, right?

It would have been but for the help we received from the star, Val Kilmer. A man of considerable talent, he also had considerable nerve. I would give him the call sheet for the following day on which he was to be in makeup at 7:00 am, and he would tell me that he might come at 9:00 am instead. I explained that we needed to save the sunlight for the scenes and he said that he would arrive around 9:00 am. I asked the producers to discuss it with him, and they ended up calling his agent. His agent told us that if we couldn't get him to arrive on time, what could an agent do?

I went to his motor home to call him to the set for a scene. He replied that he wasn't finished working on his lines and would be out shortly. The crew had to wait, sometimes for a half hour or more.

This was habitual. It was not isolated incidents. He may have changed his stripes by now, but at the time I worked with him he was indeed painful.

The biggest problem was our battlefield location. Danny Mann and the crew had chosen a field at Indian Dunes, just outside of Piru, lots of space, flat with a little stream to one side of it. The terrain was perfect to recreate the battle of the Argonne. The art director immediately put the crew to work digging trenches and bomb craters and building a couple of ruined houses. We were almost complete when Kilmer informed us that we should be using his parents' farm in Newhall. As a courtesy, Mike Campus and the art director went up to scout that location. There were several problems. There was a field, all right, but it was surrounded by high eucalyptus trees that could easily catch fire from the explosions in the scene. The field was barely large enough to handle the scene at any rate. The farm was within the Newhall City limits, making it subject to city laws. Those laws specifically prohibited fireworks of any kind. There was no way we could legally film there without getting a variance from the Newhall city council, and they were not in session. In any case, we had already built our set in Indian Dunes, and that worked very well for the film.

With that, Kilmer announced that since we were using the wrong location, he would not act in the scene until we had recreated the set on his parents' property. Nothing we told him would change his mind, and we had a two-day scene to film there. All night shooting. He was adamant.

The producers negotiated with his agent and himself but he would not relent. On the day prior to filming the scene he finally agreed to act in the scene, but only for one day, not two. We made the crew call for 2:00 pm to give the crew time to set up the lights and equipment while it was still daylight. We finished filming at 7:00 am the next morning costing the company dearly in overtime and meal penalties for the crew, even though the producers brought out a large professional barbecue and made ribs for everyone for dinner. But we did finish that scene in one day.

One other scene was problematic. We had contacted Lin Bothwell, a well-known provider of antique cars for filming. He rented us around a dozen cars from the 1920s and earlier. Electric starters only came into common use in the mid to late 1920s. Prior to that cars had to be cranked to start.

The scene called for these cars all to be facing inward, with Val Kilmer standing in the middle of the circle. It took a few minutes to set the scene up and by that time a couple of the cars had overheated and stalled. I ran in and cranked to restart them. When they started turning over, a few other cars had stalled. We decided to stop filming that scene, turn the cars off and let them cool down for a few minutes, crank them all again, and try to get the scene before they stalled again. We failed. We could only get about half of them running at one time. It took around three hours of cranking, stalling, restarting, cooling, and re-timing to get the scene shot. I had such a backache for the rest of that day from cranking. Thank goodness a few of the Teamsters decided to jump in and help or we would have never gotten the shot.

My part in the filming lasted only two weeks or so and I was certainly glad when it was finished.

CHAPTER 80

❖

HARDESTY HOUSE

Marty Katz was no longer at ABC Circle Films. In fact except for Herb Jellinek and the head of transportation, Norm Honath, few people were left that I remembered. But I had met one of their production supervisors there before, Dennis Judd. He and Michael Joyce were working as heads of production for the time being.

Michael Joyce phoned to offer me a job as UPM/1st AD on a new TV pilot they were shooting, called *Hardesty House*. It was a modest effort, a half-hour TV sitcom about a group of attorneys who had all been students of a master lawyer teacher named Hardesty. He willed them his house at the beach in Santa Monica to use as an office. The main lawyer was played by Bob Ginty, ably aided by Paul Rodriguez and the magnificent Susan Anton. There were two or three others.

Los Angeles has been described as a bunch of suburbs in search of a city, and it is true to an extent. The heart of Los Angeles is the downtown area. But within the Los Angeles County limits there are dozens of little cities, each individually chartered with its own mayor and city council, its own police department, in many cases its own newspapers and even TV stations. Between these cities the area is a patchwork quilt of incorporated Los Angeles City jurisdiction, and where that does not apply, the Los Angeles County Sheriff's Department has jurisdiction. When one applies for a permit to film one must apply at the appropriate city, or the county. The Los Angeles City Film permit office cannot handle permits for Beverly Hills or Malibu, for instance.

Santa Monica City requires filmmakers to canvass the area for permission to film, and unless there is prior permission from the city as well as from the neighbors, filming can only take place between 8:00 am and 10:00 pm. Filming in commercial areas is severely restricted by date. And—get this—a police officer is required for most filming, at $120 per hour, eight-hour minimum. That's $960 per day. Parking is also severely restricted and requires signed permission from the residents. Sounds like fun to me.

Filming went smoothly. ABC was a far cry from Universal. The locations were properly handled, the parking was a half block away for the crew and trucks. The neighbors had all signed the consent. The cast and crew were all pros. The director was very knowledgeable.

There was one little contretemps. The script called for one character to own a white 1964 Mustang convertible with a red leather interior. I didn't realize why this was so specific until the wife of one of the ABC staff approached me to say she owned such a car and it would be available for the laughably low price of $600 per day. I had already discussed it with transport coordinator Norm Honath, who located an identical car for $250 per day. I told the wife thanks, but we already had a car. Next thing I knew I received a phone call from an ABC vice president demanding that we use the wife's car. I explained the financial differential, and he explained that he had to keep peace in the office. We rented the wife's car.

Filming was completed with a minimum of fuss. While this was happening, ABC Circle was engaged in two other projects that were both monsters. One was *Amerika*, a futuristic fiction about what the United States would be like if Russia had won the cold war. This was in 1986, remember, before the collapse of the USSR. The Berlin Wall still stood. Donald Wrye, a gifted writer-director who had made some very interesting films and TV shows in the past, and who also had been at UCLA at the same time as I had, was the writer-director. A second unit UPM/1st AD was needed. I mentioned my old pal Cal Naylor, who had just finished several years work on a TV series. He was hired and worked with Don to finish the show in fine style. Mike Joyce was production supervisor of *Hardesty House*.

CHAPTER 81

WAR AND REMEMBRANCE

I didn't know it then, but ABC had big plans for me. The biggest. Besides *Amerika*, ABC was also in production on *War and Remembrance*, the single largest production of all time up to then. Thirty hours of TV mini-series, filmed all around the world, in Europe, the East Coast, West Coast, Hawaii. A monumental effort. It was the story of one man's view of the second world war. It took longer to film (five years) than it took to win the war (three and a half years). Dan Curtis, with whom I had worked previously on *Trilogy of Terror*, was writer-producer-director. There were over 600 speaking parts, including Churchill, Roosevelt, Hitler, and a cast of thousands of extras. The main characters were played by Robert Mitchum and Polly Bergen. It was actually the sequel to another monumental mini-series, WINDS OF WAR, which had been produced over the previous five years and had at the time of its release been the highest rated mini-series ever produced. ABC hoped to repeat the performance with another blockbuster show.

The story was born of a trilogy of books by Herman Wouk, of *Caine Mutiny* fame. He never completed the third book, but the first two were best-sellers. Perfect for their time, they told the next generation what their fathers had suffered in what was believed to be the last great battle between good and evil.

Dan Curtis was the producer-writer-director. He had some help with the first two tasks. Earl Wallace and Herman Wouk himself aided in the writing. Branko Lustig, Oscar-winning producer of *Schindler's List*, was the 1st AD, also had associate producer's credit.

The budget had been fashioned by Justin Buerlin, a legendary accountant working at ABC. It was something like a thousand pages long with all the backup material. I had never seen a budget so large and detailed before or since. It was done on a mainframe computer since at the time, 1986, no regular PC could have handled the job. I actually joined the company after they had been filming in Europe. I worked on the pre-production for the U.S. filming, both West and East Coast, and Hawaii, and I managed most of the West Coast filming before I left. I was there for a good eight or nine months and traveled far and wide for them.

My immediate superior was Michael Gallant, who held the title of production supervisor at ABC. The overall production manager of ABC, Ted Butcher, seeing what problems might develop, had disassociated himself from the production when it first began. Considering the magnitude of the production Gallant must be complimented for having even attempted the project, much less for shepherding it through all the possible pitfalls.

We had the advantage of technical support by two experts; Captain Dale Patterson, a thirty-year Navy veteran, was a member of the Naval Public Affairs Office. John Semcken had just retired from the Navy. He had gone through the U.S. Naval Academy at Indianapolis, from there to Top Gun school at Miramar Naval Air School, the actual home of Top Gun. He had been a carrier pilot. He had been the Technical Advisor and Navy rep on the movie, *Top Gun,* as well. He knew what was necessary, and he had the connections to help. Between him and Captain Patterson we had all the help we needed.

All the armed forces have public affairs offices in Hollywood, mostly in Westwood. It is in their interest to have Hollywood present them in a positive light. This pays off in dividends. After *Top Gun* was released, voluntary enlistment in the U.S. Air Force doubled. All the services, including the Coast Guard, hoped for such a response.

I read the book, all 1,056 pages of it. Fascinating. I began to read the script when it became obvious that this was a complete transformation of the book. Every scene, every line in the book was in this thirty-hour script. The script came in several volumes and dropping any of them on the foot would result in fractures.

Most of the crew had already been hired, as is ABC's way. I was a glorified caretaker. I soon realized that I had very little responsibility and almost no authority. I signed bills for payment but they were always countersigned by Gallant, so my signature was there to satisfy the DGA requirement.

The original budget was for $60,000,000. This is because the pattern budget for ABC movies of the week was $2,000,000 per hour. This was estimated at 30 hours so 30 x 2,000,000 = 60,000,000. Makes perfect sense. Except that we were going to make use of extensive filming abroad, working on U.S. Navy vessels, traveling around the country, etc. All this added up. At that point Justin Buerlin was brought in to do the budget. His eventual total was around $110,000,000. Due to unbelievable waste and other factors this ballooned to $125-130,000,000.

When I came on board the company had just returned from Europe where they had filmed the European part of the war. They did this without the benefit of a DGA production team, but they did have Michael Gallant and Branko Lustig. Lustig managed to withstand the daily lambasting that Dan Curtis favored him with. His reward for this is a long and successful career in Hollywood. Michael Gallant seemed to be able to stay out of the line of fire for the most part, although some things did bother him.

We had to build a White House set as it had been in Roosevelt's day. We rented a huge warehouse in Northridge and constructed the East Room, the Oval

Office, the front portico and driveway, Roosevelt's private office, and his private apartment upstairs. Ralph Bellamy, of course, played Roosevelt. We used the rest of the warehouse to store wardrobe, to build sets, to do makeup. There was plenty of room. There was a large parking lot on which we were able to build the upper deck of our submarine, roughly 100-feet long, and the miniature of the White House for the Christmas scene for Churchill's visit in 1941.

Furthermore the studio was now eight miles from my apartment, an easy bike ride. Took about forty-five minutes each way and gave me a good workout.

We filmed in other locations in Los Angeles as well. For the previous miniseries, *The Winds of War*, Dan Curtis had filmed in a particular house in Hancock Park, an exclusive neighborhood in the Wilshire area of L.A.. The house was still there with the same owners. *Winds* had been broadcast in 1983 and this was 1986, and our show probably would not be broadcast for another two or three years, so none of the audience would possibly make the connection if we were to find a new house. Anyway, the characters may have moved. Dan Curtis, however, insisted that we use the same house.

The owners saw us coming. They knew that Curtis wanted to use the house. Their price for rental went up to an exorbitant amount, something like $5,000 per day. And this would be for three weeks or so. We needed the time to replace their furniture with our period furniture and redecorate, then film for a few days, then return their house to the condition it was in before we came, all at that daily rate. Not only that, but it would of course be impossible for them to live in the house while we were working there, so they insisted that we relocate them. To Hawaii. Pay for their travel, hotel, and other expenses while we filmed in their house. I told Curtis that this was a holdup, but he was insistent. Michael Gallant couldn't convince him otherwise either. The ABC brass decided to give the man anything he wanted and went along with it.

The show had many costly, unnecessary oversights. Some of the ABC brass, seeing the expenses balloon to ridiculous heights, treated the show as a wonderful money tree that they could shake at their convenience and money would just flow down out of the sky into their pockets.

One highly placed ABC staffer owned a summer cottage at Big Bear Lake, around two hours by car east of Los Angles in the mountains. An idyllic spot. It was his habit to inflate the construction budgets of the shows he was associated with. Then after the sets had been built he would have the construction crew go to Big Bear and build a new wing onto the house, at ABC's expense.

Dan Curtis saw no reason to spare any expense of his own for the show. When we were in Hawaii, an entirely useless trip, he stayed in a penthouse suite at a five-star hotel on the beach, while the rest of the crew stayed at the Outrigger, where they soon discovered cockroaches in the rooms. To be fair, Bob Mitchum stayed at the same hotel as Curtis.

The entire trip to Hawaii was a waste of money. The islands never appeared in the show, only the submarine we found there and the open sea. We could not photograph the shore front which had changed radically since the war, with high-rise hotels galore and multi-storied office buildings. Photographing the city would have been a terrible anachronism.

At that time *Magnum P.I.* was the main production on the islands, and almost every decent local crew person was working on that project. There were no crew available for us. All the local equipment was also in use on *Magnum*. If we went to Hawaii we would have to fly our entire crew and cast, and barge over the trucks full of equipment.

Dan Curtis gave two reasons for filming in Hawaii, neither of which was valid. The first was that we could not film off the coast of California because the water was too cold. One scene called for the American submarine to torpedo a Japanese troop ship, and the troops would be marooned in the water. This would require 300 or so extras to swim in the water as if having been torpedoed. No land was visible in this scene; it was on the open sea. I did some research and at the time we were to film the water temperature off California was 68°, whereas off Hawaii the temperature was 75°. I told Curtis that and he said, "Well, that settles it. We're going to Hawaii." He wanted to go to Hawaii. We could have bought wet suits for the cast and crew for a small fraction of what the trip cost.

The second reason was that we needed the submarine that was anchored in Pearl Harbor. Beached is the proper term. On a beach opposite the Arizona Memorial is the attack submarine *Bowfin*. It is now a tourist attraction. One can rent a small tape recorder and take a tour through the inside of the submarine, listening to the narrator describe the different rooms, etc., as one does in a museum. The *Bowfin* had not been seaworthy for many years and none of its systems worked. The electric system was rotten. Power had to be brought in from the shore. The periscope would not extend or retract. It was owned by the U.S. Navy, but managed by the National Maritime Historical Foundation.

In contrast, in San Francisco Harbor is the *Pampanito*, a fully functioning submarine. Its electrics work, the periscope works smoothly, and it floats. Far better maintained than the *Bowfin*. We could have towed it down the coast, photographed it off Long Beach, and shipped it back to San Francisco for a small fraction of the cost of moving the entire film company to Hawaii for a submarine that did not work. But Curtis wanted to go to Hawaii and that was that. It was also important to the ABC brass, because they would all have to visit Hawaii to ensure that the show was being produced properly.

The *Bowfin* was a disaster. It had been beached many years before. Its hull was covered with barnacles. None of its operating systems worked. It was reasonably clean inside as it must be for the tourists, but everything else was in a shambles. In order to put the sub into the show it had to be seaworthy since we would be towing it out to the open sea to be photographed. When we first considered it we knew we would have to do some restoration to be able to accomplish that. We could tow the sub a few miles up the coast to Waianae Ship Yard to have it raised on the dry dock and to see what would be necessary to restore it.

Waianae did lift the sub out of the water and began to sandblast the barnacles off the hull. That's when we discovered that the barnacles were actually holding the rotting hull together. The sandblasting stopped, but not before we realized that the rear compartment of the ship had been weakened to the point that it could have split off the ship. Now we had the problem of towing the sub back to its beach without sinking the thing. The answer, we were told, was to pour cement into the last two compartments to stiffen the hull so it wouldn't break. Sounds good to me.

The cement was duly poured. The sub was towed back to its beach. We still intended to use it, so the fact that the rudder was frozen in a starboard position was a problem. When it was towed it kept trying to turn right. This was no good. We appealed to the National Maritime Historical Association for help. They were clueless. But we were, after all, in Pearl Harbor, the most modern Naval installation in the world, with the finest naval engineers anywhere. We contacted the Navy and they sent some experts to examine the sub. The hope was that we could somehow get the steering system to work, and if anyone could, they could. Or at least they would know how.

They duly descended into the sub and did a full investigation. When they emerged they were hard pressed to keep straight faces. Yes, they said, the steering could be fixed easily. If only we hadn't poured all that cement all over it.

The NMHA told us that our other options were not possible. We were not permitted to alter the exterior of the sub by either welding on a second rudder pointing to the port side to counteract the original, nor could we cut the rudder off altogether. We were stuck not only with a sub that turned right, but also with a ship that was considerably lower in the stern than it was in the bow due to the cement in the hull. Visually very interesting, and unique in submarine history.

I would estimate the extra cost of shipping the entire crew to Hawaii and back and the added expenses of the submarine, hotels, and everything else, probably raised the cost of the show by a million dollars. All this without ever photographing the shore. Any stretch of open sea would have been just as good. But what the heck.

In the meantime, we were filming in Los Angeles. Odd things kept happening. We were approached by a company that manufactured half-sized WW2 fighter planes. They thought we might buy a few of their plane kits for Japanese Zeros to use in the film. Recommended a fellow in Modesto who had built one, if we wished to see it.

We agreed to meet and film some test footage of the plane at Fox Field in Palmdale. He flew the plane in after we had set up the camera. We photographed his plane making several passes toward and away from the camera, and from the side. It looked exactly like a Zero, no question, and at speed it looked like it was going at the same speed a Zero flew. But when we saw the footage a huge problem became apparent. Since the plane was half-size, the pilot's head, clearly visible in the cockpit glass, was twice the size it should have been. Looked like the fellow either was suffering from a terrible tropical disease, or was holding a bizarre child's balloon with a face painted on it. The plane could not be used.

One of the camera assistants on that shoot was an old acquaintance from New York. Very nice Greek gentleman. We had worked on commercials in New York more than once. When we finished filming that day he invited me over to his house for dinner. Told me his wife was cooking a special Greek meal. I always loved Greek food so I accepted. Of course, I should have known better. In the middle of the meal he brought up the fact that he had bought twenty or thirty walkie-talkies, and he was just itching to have us rent them for the show. They were not inexpensive either, costing around $1,000 each or so. Not wanting to disturb a perfectly good Greek meal I told him to phone me in the office the following week.

When he did, I explained that we already had all the walkie-talkies we needed, rented from our electric/grip supplier. He became insistent. I told him that we would not rent from him, because we already had our own. Forget it. Not going to happen. He hung up on me. Ten minutes later he phoned back and told me that he was about to phone a vice president of CBS, a close personal friend of his who was also Greek, and he would have me fired if I did not rent his walkie-talkies. I did not bother to tell him that I worked for ABC, not CBS. I did ask him not to phone me anymore, and luckily he has not.

At another time we were filming on the property of Fort Irwin, near Barstow, CA. This is where the Army trains for desert warfare. The weather is almost always brutally hot, and the terrain is similar to that of the Middle East. We were to film two events here. One was a flyover by WWII aircraft in the "Missing Man" formation to honor the dead in battle. The other was the aftermath of the Battle of El Alamein.

The Missing Man formation consists of four fighter planes in a "Finger-Four" formation. When the planes fly over, the lead plane pulls up out of the formation and flies upward to the sky while the other three planes remain flying level. This indicates that the dead pilot being honored is flying to heaven. Somehow we found two working Spitfires and two P-51 Mustangs for the shot. They flew in to Palmdale airport, near Fort Irwin. On cue they started up, took off, and flew over the camera and crew at Fort Irwin. Unfortunately they had no radio contact with us, so they could not tell us that two of the four planes would not take off and were grounded. Didn't stop us from filming though. We filmed the Missing Man formation with two planes, one leaving the formation and flying upward. Looks strange, and certainly is not the Missing Man Formation, but one does what one can with the materials given one.

The Battle of El Alamein took place from October 23 to November 5, 1942.

Churchill said, of it, "This is not the end. This is not even the beginning of the end. This is, however, the end of the beginning." General Montgomery decisively whipped Rommel. After the battle was fought the battlefield was strewn with wrecked tanks, ferrets, armored personnel carriers, tires, dead bodies, motorcycles, the detritus of war.

Curtis and the staff went to Fort Irwin, a three-and-a-half-hour drive from the studio. We got into a couple of Hummers and drove out to the desert battlefield, a good simulation of the area around El Alamein in terrain and climate. Curtis designed the shot to have Montgomery standing in a personnel carrier, driving down the road toward the camera in a right-to-left direction. As the vehicle passes the camera, the camera pans with Monty to show the devastation across the battlefield, destroyed tanks, jeeps, dead bodies, etc. The camera finally sees the vehicle disappear in the distance down the road. This way we could see the entire battlefield and all its tragic finality, much like a Matthew Brady print from the Civil War.

This had become a major undertaking. The transportation coordinator, Norm Honath, was up to the task of finding all the vehicles and machinery necessary for the shot. We needed dozens of vehicles, uniforms (wardrobe department), many gallons of desert paint (set dressing), manikins for the dead bodies (props). It would not be easy. I had made arrangements to lodge the crew in two or three local hotels in Barstow. One hotel wasn't large enough for this one. No big hotels in Barstow like we had in Honolulu. Also, Norm had to arrange for buses to transport the crew and cast thirty miles to the location from Barstow, as well as the extras. Not much in the way of local talent in Barstow either.

That wasn't the biggest problem. The biggest problem was finding the World War II vehicles in running condition, or in any condition for that matter, to photograph. Norm contacted World War II clubs across the country and orchestrated an amazing logistical performance. People brought in their tanks, personnel carriers, motorcycles, and all the other vehicles. Mostly they were carried in on trucks. Hard to drive a World War II German Panzer tank down the highway without attracting attention. On a flatbed truck these could be covered. We needed German, British, and Italian vehicles. These were somewhat hard to find as most collectors in the U.S. had American vehicles, but Norm managed to find enough to fill the battlefield with the appropriate machines.

Once they had arrived at the location, and there were dozens of them, the owners had to be paid for rental. They had to be put up in local hotels, fed, given money for gasoline for the trip, and something for expenses. Those vehicles that had to be mobile needed some mechanical service also. We had to hire some mechanics familiar with the machinery, although mostly the owners tended to their own machines quite well.

Then we had to hire a paint crew. Almost all the vehicles were painted in the wrong kind of camouflage colors for the desert and they had to be repainted to appear authentic. This required a crew to paint them, and special paint. We used "peel-paint," a special paint that dries into a removable skin. It peels right off, revealing the original colors beneath the skin. This was far less expensive and easier than repainting the vehicles back to their original colors. It took time, however, so the vehicles had to arrive a few days earlier to be painted, and the owners and drivers had to spend more time in hotels locally. It added up.

Then the vehicles had to be scattered about the battlefield authentically, which means being driven or trucked into position. After that they needed to be rigged by the special effects team to appear as if they were on fire, or had been gutted by an explosion or damaged in some other way.

The mannequins had to be dressed in their proper uniforms. Wouldn't do to have an Italian soldier hanging out of a British tank. Our tech support people were more than helpful with that. The wardrobe department had done their homework also, so we had the proper uniforms for the various armies for desert warfare. Many of the uniforms had been rented from European wardrobe companies and shipped over just for this scene. Add to that the extra makeup needed to make the mannequins appear wounded or dead, even from a distance.

It was a monumental effort and it worked perfectly. The battlefield was set the day before we were to film the scene. The next morning Curtis and the camera crew were out on the location bright and early to catch the mid-morning light. Curtis had a brief discussion with Dietrich Lohmann, the cameraman. Branko called "Roll it!" and Curtis said "Action!" Montgomery's vehicle started down the road toward the camera. As it drove past the camera "Monty" waved at his troops. The camera never moved, never did the planned pan across the battlefield. Most of the carefully prepared vehicles were never seen. Norm Honath, who had arranged all of this, turned to Curtis and asked why he didn't pan across the field. Curtis said, "I changed my mind." That's the way it stayed.

Michael Gallant managed to keep the filming flowing properly and Dan Curtis kept spending money. The ABC brass kept finding new ways to put more of the budget into their own pockets. Many of the bills for non-production items crossed my desk. I was under the impression that I was there to save the company money, and the ABC people thought I was there to help them fatten their bank accounts. I refused to sign the bills.

One of the production heads for instance bought a brand new BMW sports car in Europe and had it shipped back to the U.S. Then he billed ABC for renting his car as a picture car, to the tune of $1000 per week. Picture car? A 1986 BMW appearing in World War II? Didn't make sense to me. I refused to sign the rental bill. The fellow protested, saying that he was being given the car "in lieu of salary" because I made so much more money than he did, being a DGA member. The ABC brass had OK'd it. I told him if they had done that, they would of course sign his bill and pay it, because I couldn't.

This was the same man who insisted that all our airline miles we were credited for flying back and forth to Hawaii must be added to his account, not to ours. He wanted to take his family on a vacation and we were to pay for it. I'd hate to see what he had done with the wardrobe budget for the show, since he was always dressed so nattily.

This sort of thing went on regularly at ABC. Ted Butcher, production executive, was not involved with this but just about everyone else was. Needless to say, after about eight or nine months I was replaced by another production manager who was more willing to sign bogus bills. And very soon after that, ABC was bought by Capital Cities under Bob Iger.

Cap Cities almost immediately instituted a thorough audit of the financial records of ABC Circle. Several people were allowed to resign from the company "for personal reasons" so as not to harm their reputations. The fellow with the sports car had a very bad week. He had to raise the money on short notice to repay ABC for the car.

I went home. It had been a long hard grind. I never spent so much time on a show in my life, except maybe *McLain's Law*, and even that didn't match this for longevity.

CHAPTER 82

COMPUTER

At this time I realized that many other production people were beginning to use personal computers for scheduling and budgeting. Personal computers had been around for a few years but were just beginning to gain great headway with the public. It was a brand-new technology and few people understood it. It was hard to comprehend a system that could do a myriad of tasks in many different areas. We were accustomed to one machine, one task. Car,—drive somewhere. Typewriter—write something. Slide rule—calculate. Steve Wozniak and Steve Jobs seemed to have the easiest system to use but it was still expensive. The IBM-based systems were less. There were three or four commercially available scheduling and budgeting systems.

Film Production Toolkit was started by Don Asquith, a DGA UPM who designed probably the most workable system. Many production people knew it and worked it. Don spent a great deal of time working out the bugs in the system and it showed. He also gave personal attention to his clients. Over the next few years however, he became ill, did not support his system properly, and it fell out of use. It was bought by another company, who transformed it into a good, workable Macintosh based system that worked for many years.

Movie Magic was probably the most usable system. It worked on either Mac or PC, and the data were interchangeable. It was more primitive than Toolkit though, and the company heads, Steve Greenfield and Chris Huntley, were not as open to change as others. Probably because of the difficulty of working on both platforms at once.

Turbo-Budget and Turbo-AD was designed and built by Emil Safier, a man who held a Ph.D. in Physics. His system was also workable but somewhat idiosyncratic. I liked Emil. He was a funny, cheerful man. His downfall was that he was also a graduate of the AFI program and felt that he knew what was best for the industry better than anyone else did. His system worked only on the PC. He did not consider the Mac a viable project. He also did not listen to UPMs when they suggested changes to his system.

I realized that I would have to adopt one of these systems in order to keep up with the rest of the ADs and UPMs in technology. I bought a computer, state-of-the-art in those days. It had 640k of RAM and a 10 MB hard drive. I thought it was just fine. As big as a large suitcase, it weighed thirty pounds or so, and had a handle that made it "portable." Kind of. It had the odd habit of overheating and losing all the work I had just done when it unexpectedly shut down two or three times a day.

However, that was what happened with all computers in those early days, so I put up with it. I bought Emil's Turbo system and installed it. It took a day or so for me to learn it. My next show would be easier and quicker to schedule. I hoped. Since there was no industry standard yet it did not really matter which system we used as long as it worked.

This began the next phase of my career. Little did I suspect how thoroughly computers would infiltrate civilization. I don't think anyone did at the time. It was just a rather expensive toy, too often troublesome. There was no internet as we know it, and just the beginnings of bulletin board systems. Communication by computer was still far in the future.

CHAPTER 83

SUPERCARRIER

I soon received a call from Chuck Fries Productions in Hollywood. They were about to begin production on a new TV series, *Supercarrier*, about the amusing adventures of various members of the crew of a fictitious aircraft carrier in the U.S. Navy. It was like a repertory company. There was the crusty old Master Chief Petty Officer, played by the indefatigable Richard Jaeckel. In the old WWII movies he always played "The Kid" because of his young face. Still had a young face but now it had much more authority. The ship's captain was played by Capt. Dale Dye, a former Marine, who has since made a well-deserved career of technical support for military movies. Also had a part in *Saving Private Ryan*. Good actor, and a real gentleman. Marie Windsor played the lovable owner of the bar/restaurant where the crew hung out in shore leave. The two main characters were Ken Olandt and John Bland, playing the flyers.

The executive producer was Steven De Souza who previously had produced and written *Die Hard* and *Die Hard 2* among other films. Of course, those were megabucks films with huge budgets and we now had a TV series to make. The line producer was Chuck Bowman, usually a director, and a good one. We built sets in a warehouse in Valencia near Magic Mountain amusement park. We had all our facilities here also, set building, wardrobe, makeup, everything. The sound stage was one of several in that industrial complex. Several shows were filming there. Since there was no convenient café we catered lunch and, when necessary, dinner, as if it were a distant location.

I was one of the two 1st ADs. The other was Bob Bender. The UPM was Gary LaPoten. Gary had been the DGA trainee on *The Barony* many years before and we knew each other well. He kept bowls of candies on his desk in a ragged semicircle so that they were always within his reach. The crew affectionately called him "Jabba the Hut" because he reminded us of that character in the *Star Wars* films, always munching on something interesting. He had made something of a name for himself when for two years he had listed himself with the DGA as "Gary AlaPoten," so his name could be at the top of the availability list. Like most good UPMs he cut budget corners when possible. On the plus side he was very pleasant to work with, had a good sense of humor, and could be reasoned with.

I became closer to Chuck Bowman and to the executive in charge of production, S. Bryan Hickox. We all seemed to work together well. They certainly gave me more support than a great many producers. We remained friends after the show. I was treated to several directors with whom I had worked before, Corey Allen, Michael O'Herlihy, and Jackie Cooper. Jackie Cooper had starred with my stepmother, Peggy, in a film in the 1930s entitled *The Big Guy*. I borrowed a poster from the film and put it up in the production office. Jackie and I were friends after that. He had been in the Navy, so he also played a Naval Officer in the film. Having been a child star from the age of seven in 1929, he has had one of the longest careers in show biz of anyone. By the time Jackie was a teenager he had little concept of a normal life. When the war broke out he joined the Navy and rose to the rank of captain, where at the time of our filming he still retained his rank in the Reserves. The uniform he wore in his role in the show was his official uniform.

Capt. Dale Patterson was our tech support man and liaison with the Navy, since we had permission to film on actual Naval vessels when they were in harbor. We also had some cooperation with the Navy fliers, especially from Point Mugu. In fact the Navy loved us until one episode. In that De Souza had written that a Russian submarine approached close enough to see the carrier in its periscope. In fact that would have been impossible. Our carriers are protected by surface vessels, but also primarily by submarines. No enemy sub can get anywhere near one of our carriers and are usually kept at last 300 or 400 miles away. The Navy got so upset by the idea that they withdrew all their support and we had to use built sets from then on.

We only did the nominal eleven series episodes. The show did not have enough ratings to last longer. It wasn't a bad show, just not spectacularly good. Probably could have stumbled on for another year or two, but what for? Chuck Fries was nothing if not a master of improvisation. After the contractual two showings by the network, the rights reverted to him. He released it in Europe and the Far East. South America. He even re-edited two shows into a feature film and released it theatrically. Eventually he made his money back. The show did not cost that much to begin with.

Even with the drive up to Valencia from Tarzana every day I enjoyed working on the show. The crew became a family and we had fun. There were moments of unexpected levity. Steven De Souza came to the set one day and began rewriting scenes we had just finished, then handing new script pages to the director. I had to phone Chuck Bowman to come and rescue us. Steven was accustomed to much bigger budget shows in which such rewrites are possible. Not to mention that the network legal department had approved scripts, after which revision was not permitted. Chuck took Steven out for lunch and then back to the office and we continued filming.

George Wilson, the writer of the book *Supercarrier* had contractually been given the title of associate producer although he did not have any direct involvement with the program. He just wrote the book. His fate was emblematic. When we began filming he had an office, a telephone with two lines, and a secretary. Presently one of the phone lines was removed. Then he had to share his secretary with someone else. Last we saw of him, he was sitting alone in the lunch room with a yellow pad, making notes about something. Fries figured out that he was being paid a salary for doing nothing and therefore he should cost the company nothing beyond that.

Steven was using a new script formatting program called "Scriptor." It was devised and sold by Screenplay Systems, same group responsible for "Movie Magic" scheduling and budgeting. It was really inconvenient at best, but with all still far more convenient than trying to format a script on the typewriter. Not to mention the possibility of just pushing a button on the computer and just printing out the script, or the necessary pages, all properly formatted with scene numbers, page numbers, etc. Screenplay Systems, Steve Greenfield and Chris Huntley, won an Oscar that year for having invented this program.

By this time I was bringing my computer to the office daily. Lugging a forty-pound suitcase full of delicate electronic gear back and forth was not my favorite activity, but I wanted to be part of the new generation.

At the same time, I was working in two different directions outside of filming. I was using Emil Safier's "Turbo-Budget" and "Turbo-AD" programs. One weekend, without asking or warning me, Emil went out of town for two or three days, and left my home phone number on his answering machine as the tech support number. Sure, Emil and I had been discussing enhancements to the program, but this was an imposition. It was also a serendipity. I suddenly became an "expert" on computer scheduling and budgeting. Not long after that Emil had been invited by the Film Accounting and Finance organization to lecture for an hour at one of their seminars. He couldn't go and asked me to.

One of the attendees was Charles Swartz, head of UCLA Extension Entertainment and Motion Picture Studies Division. After the lecture he asked me if I had ever lectured on the university level and would I be interested. Of course I would. Off and on for the next few years I gave classes at various schools, usually in the evenings, so that I could keep my day job. Charles and I became dinner companions. My teaching career had begun.

At the same time I saw the need for a textbook that incorporated the manual for using the computer to budget, and the essential financial information for budgeting at the same time. I began to sketch out the essence of the book.

Sarah-Jane Futch, my childhood sweetheart, had reappeared in my life. She moved back to Los Angeles from Pueblo, CO, where she had been living, and moved in with me. She was tolerant of my working hours, an angel when we were together, kind and understanding to her children and mine. A good cook. She was pretty, bright, and funny. At least my home life had become what I had always hoped it would be.

Adventures In Hollywood: A Memoir By Bob Koster

After the *Supercarrier* series was canceled, Chuck Fries kept me on, doing schedules and budgets for prospective projects, much like Universal had a year or two before. One of these programs was *K-9000*, a TV show about a super bionic police dog. The writer-producer, again, was Steven de Souza. A scene in the script took place down at the docks in which a minivan is parked on the deck of a large yacht. The dog gets into the van, starts the engine, and drives it off the yacht, leaping over the railing onto the dock and speeding away. I had budgeted that one shot alone at tens of thousands of dollars, to prep the car, to train the dog to drive, and so forth. Bryan Hickox agreed with me that this would put the cost of the show out of reach of the network, so the scene had to be changed. Bryan left it to me to tell Steven.

I did. Steven said he would write something much less expensive. His answer to the problem was to have the van already on the dock, eliminating the jump off the boat. The dog would still be driving. In the revised scene the dog drives away down the dock. An approaching semi-trailer truck, a big one, is passing in the other direction. The truck driver sees the dog driving and is unnerved by the sight, so he dives his truck off the edge of the dock into the water. That's how Steven saved money. At that point I started another show for Fries so I never saw how *K-9000* turned out. I know it was completed and actually shown on TV, but I missed it, darn it.

CHAPTER 84

PHANTOM OF THE MALL

Instead, I was given a new movie, *Phantom of the Mall*, to produce. Actually, Tom Fries, Chuck's son, produced it and I was line producer. Sort of a glorified UPM without the title. This was my very first non-DGA film since before I joined the Guild and I was quite uncomfortable about it. In fact it turned out that it was my only non-DGA film. Richard Friedman directed. His forte was horror films.

The film was a predictable programmer, nothing spectacular. The tech work was adequate. The actors were adequate. One, Pauly Shore, was a bit nuts but likeable and professional. The mayor of the town was played by Morgan Fairchild, a really beautiful member of the jet set and a good actress to boot.

The cameraman and I became friends. Harry Mathias was an excellent cameraman who also was a computer genius. In fact he built computers as a hobby. Showed me his own, and it was so neat and so obviously superior to anything I had seen that I asked him to build one for me.

This was my first really portable computer, and it was powerful and reliable. Had plenty of memory, was quick. I could easily hook it up to my large monitor on my desk in the loft, or I could use the plasma screen on the device itself. This was long before the days of flat screens and LCD technology. It also used both the floppy 5¼" disks and the new 3½" ones. CD technology had not yet come into its own. And it only weighed maybe ten pounds. I quickly adapted it to use Turbo-Budget and Turbo-AD, and I started writing my book on it. In fact I kept it for several years.

Harry was a little nervous about allowing the word to spread that he built computers because he wanted to be known as a cameraman first and a computer guy afterwards. I never told a soul until years later.

Phantom had little to distinguish it from others. A few little incidents arose as they will. We did quite a bit of filming in the Sherman Oaks Galleria shopping center, the same mall featured in *Fast Times at Ridgemont High*. Our trucks were parked along the back side of the main building to make it convenient for the crew to access their material. We hired a guard service to watch over the trucks and company cars when we were inside filming. One day the wardrobe lady mentioned to me that some of the wardrobe was missing. I went outside with her in time to see one of the guards emerging from the wardrobe truck with an armful of clothing and disappear into the garage. I followed him as he put the clothing into the trunk of his car. While he returned to the trucks I called the police and the guard service headquarters. The head of the guards appeared a few minutes after the police. The thief took the police to his car and opened the trunk to show them what he had stolen. The head of the guard service started to apologize but I cut him off. I phoned another guard service I usually use and they had guards covering us in a half hour. I then fired the previous guard service. In the meantime the police had the thief sitting on the steps of the truck. He was holding his head in his hands. He was really perceptive at that moment, because he said to me, "I guess I'll lose my job, huh?" I suspect that he has found another line of work by this time.

This was almost entirely a non-union show. We had contracts with the Screen Actors Guild, but that was about all. All our drivers were non-Teamsters, but with the proper drivers license ratings. This did not make the unions happy at all. Chuck Fries felt that he could do whatever he wanted to without any interference, and he thought that non-union talent was every bit as good as union craftsmen. The unions disagreed. They sent representatives to the set to try to catch any union workers using assumed names but there were none. The Teamsters sent representatives to the set to discuss the situation with producer Tom Fries but the eventual decision rested with Chuck Fries himself.

There suddenly were several men around the trucks whom I did not recognize. Then our lights started to flicker and go out. The power source seemed to somehow be intermittent. The generator operator repaired it and it again failed. This time there was nothing wrong with it, but the main power cable to our set had been cut. This annoyance lasted a day or two and then stopped. We had only another week left to film in any case. The unions appeared to have left us alone.

There was one more excitement while we filmed inside the Galleria. There is a rule in Los Angeles that whenever there is indoor filming in a public place the Los Angeles Fire department has to be notified, and if they deem it necessary they will assign a fire marshal to the show. In our case they deemed it.

The atrium of the Galleria is three stories tall inside. We staged a town meeting on the floor, a large open space. We could only film after they mall closed and before it opened the next morning, which limited our filming to between 9:00 pm and 7:00 am the next morning. Our big scene required a large number of big lights placed on the second and third levels of the atrium to light the main floor area. Since lights would be placed on the topmost level, we needed some advice from the fire marshal.

Every mall is equipped with an automatic sprinkler system in case of fire. At each sprinkler head, and there are many in a mall, there is a smoke and heat detector. If this device senses the presence of smoke, or if its thermometer registers above a certain temperature, it automatically triggers the sprinkler system. Our movie lights generate a lot of heat. Our fear was that the resulting rise in temperature would set off the sprinklers.

We asked the fire marshal how to handle this. The lights would be placed close to the sprinkler heads so that they could light the scene properly. The fire marshal had a very simple solution. If we cover the sprinkler head with a Styrofoam cup, the heat will not penetrate and the system won't go off. When we finish filming we remove the cups from the sprinklers to restore the system. Simple? You bet.

The Styrofoam was useless. When the system was triggered, at two in the morning, it went off with great authority. There was an unbelievable flood. The water was cascading down the escalators like rivers. Water was pouring off the second and third floor balconies like waterfalls. Our movie lights were popping their bulbs merrily, and the crew scurried for cover. We ran for the main water valve for the building but nobody could find it, so the water kept on a-comin'. The building engineer had left long since. Finding him and getting him out of bed to come down was not easy. Eventually, maybe a half-hour later, the water slowed and stopped but by that time the damage had been done. There was a good foot of water covering the floor of the mall. Opening the Galleria would be a problem the next day.

Of course the stores themselves were in terrible shape. The sprinklers went off not only in the atrium but also in the stores, drenching clothing, books, paintings, paper goods. It would take days to restock.

First thing the following morning I phoned our insurance company. They sent a representative down. He walked in the door and burst into laughter that didn't stop for an hour. He was laughing so hard he was crying. Then came the problem that the original advice was given by the fire marshal, a city employee. So who has to pay for this? The question still had not been settled a week later when the picture wrapped, and I never did find out. I went back into the Galleria a year later and voilà, it seemed like we had never been there.

Fries Productions kept me working on budgets after the show was over. Shortly I was assigned to another show. Al Nicholson had been the UPM of a show that was about to start filming, *The Case of the Hillside Stranglers*, a true crime drama set in Los Angeles. Just before filming he became ill and had to be replaced. I happened to be sitting in the office and Bryan Hickox slid me into the UPM slot. The show starred Richard Crenna, with whom I had worked before, and Dennis Farina and Billy Zane, both excellent actors. Al had done a superb job of pre-production so I had little to do except baby-sit the show. We filmed some of it in the actual locations where the bodies were found, a chilling idea, but good for the film. Stephen Gethers was the writer/producer. An old pro, he was a pleasure to work with. So was the cameraman, Ron Lautore. I had worked with him before also, as an assistant cameraman.

I am always amazed at the art of acting. Dennis Farina played an absolutely despicable murderer in *Hillside Stranglers*. With very little variation in his manner, he played a remarkable detective on *Law and Order* TV series for three years. Same guy, but I felt differently about him in each case. Good actors can do that. Billy Zane certainly did it in this show, and in *Titanic*, in which he played an insufferable snob, both with equal verve.

The real hero of the piece was Detective Sgt. Bob Grogan, a much larger than life character. He was on the set a good part of the time to give tech support, but also to watch how Crenna was playing him. In fact, Crenna played him down a bit. Grogan himself was boisterous, large, and of immense presence. Crenna, not short or slight but not huge like Grogan, was a little less commanding than Grogan. Both were wonderful for their roles. Had Grogan played himself the show would not have succeeded. He would have overwhelmed the other players.

At the same time as we were filming this, Fries was producing a piece of fluff entitled *Troop Beverly Hills*, about a fictitious Girl Scout-type group of Beverly Hills brats and their adventures. Shelley Long played the lead. Toward the end there was a huge scene at a fund-raiser dance with a few Hollywood celebrities along the lines of Pia Zadora and Frankie Avalon. The script was written by Ava Ostern-Fries, Chuck Fries' brand-new wife. She always wanted to be in the movies, and Chuck spared no expense to make this a memorable occasion. During the party scene she appeared and danced with a few movie stars. I had the feeling that was the whole point of the film.

Fries Productions was really a family-run organization. Chuck's three sons were involved one way or another. Chuck Jr. was a producer, as was Tom. Tom, unfortunately, passed away soon after we did *Phantom* together. There was a daughter Diana. She worked in the office. Eventually she left and went to work at the American Film Institute.

The AFI is a strange mixture of school, historical preservation, and self-congratulation. It thrives on its annual AFI awards. There have been a few notable graduates of the fellowship there, but quite possibly that was for their own talent rather than for anything the school gave them. I gave a few lectures there to the students when I was still giving classes on computer use on film. Sometimes they gave me a free lunch for my efforts.

Dad had retired in 1965, moved to Camarillo, Leisure Village, in 1980, and was enjoying relaxing and painting. Sarah and I visited him often. At this point I realized that he had a treasure trove of film memorabilia. He decided to make a record of his life and he had all the tools to do so. The still photos dated from about 1900. He had bought an 8mm movie camera in 1934 in Austria and had photographed himself directing from then onwards. The film is priceless because no other home movies exist, to my knowledge, of behind-the-scenes of filmmaking during that period of time, especially during the early years in Europe.

Dad set out to edit nine hours of 8mm film down to a manageable two-and-half hours. Then we took the film to Lee Rafner's home, where Lee had set up a film chain that could transfer the 8mm to Betamax. That having been done, we sat Dad down in front of his Betamax at home with a microphone. The machine had the ability to record a soundtrack over the video. Dad then narrated the resulting footage. It is a wonderful historical record of the movie industry during that period of time. There are the requisite garden parties and altogether too much baby-on-the-lawn footage of my brothers and me, but there is also so much film on actual sets and scenes from Dad's career and his commentary that it is a really fine historical document. I made several copies so that we could keep the original pristine. When we were finished Dad edited the footage back into its original form on the 8mm reels.

I had learned that Diane Fries worked in the AFI library. I contacted her and asked if they would like to have a copy of this Beta tape. Of course, she said. I told her that this was copyright material and in order to have a copy they would have to supply me with a letter of agreement accepting the video, and agreeing that they would never use the footage for anything except showing the students. They could not copy it or use it in any way for any commercial venture. Diane agreed.

I took the tape over to the AFI library and gave it to her. And where is the letter of agreement? Oh, that. Never mind. The office is working on it, and we'll have it ready in a few days. Not to worry. I didn't worry. Two weeks passed. I phoned the AFI library but Diane did not return my calls. Two more weeks passed. I phoned again, and again Diane did not return my calls. This was getting silly. I explained to the librarian about the letter. Now that a month had passed without any word, I assumed that the AFI did not agree to my requests. I went to the library and asked for my tape back. The librarian did not acknowledge that Diane worked there, claimed never to have seen or heard about the tape, and did not know what I was talking about. I phoned Fries Productions and left messages for Diane but that had no result either. To this day I have never heard from the AFI, Diane Fries, or what had happened to my tape. It probably vanished into someone's private collection. Thank goodness it wasn't the original.

Hillside Stranglers was my last job for Fries. I was beginning to lecture nights at UCLA and at Columbia College in Hollywood. I also had written a book, *The Budget Book*. This was a mixture of wisdom about how budgets are constructed, and tech manual for the use of Turbo-Budget. After I finished the book I sent a copy to the Copyright Office in the Library of Congress to register it. They phoned me. They had received my application for copyright, but who was Emil Safier? I explained that he was the author of the software shown in the book. They told me that he had also applied for a copyright in his name. They asked me who wrote the book and I told them that I had. Emil even had written my name in under "author" on his application. The copyright attorney told me that she was whiting out his name and inserting mine as the copyright owner. As it should be.

Emil? My friend? Trying to copyright my book? No, that can't be. I went to his office and asked. He felt that he had more right to own the copyright than I did because he was, after all, printing the book and he had made some suggestions as to the wording. His suggestions were far less than useful. His degree was in nuclear physics, not English. I told him that he was guilty of copyright infringement. I told him not to sell any more books until this matter was settled. I suggested that he call the Copyright Office in Washington to see what the legal guidelines are for copyright. He never did. He believed that he was right and nothing could sway him. I left the office and did not see him again, not on purpose, anyway.

CHAPTER 85

TRACEY THURMAN STORY

At this time I was working for dick clark productions. For some reason he does not capitalize the name. I had been hired to work on a show entitled *Under the Law: The Tracy Thurman Story*. It was a true story about a girl who married a really bad man. After the divorce he stalked her, and eventually caught her and nearly beat her to death even though there was a restraining order keeping him farther than 100 yards from her. The police ignored her complaints about him. After the beating in which she suffered permanent injuries, Tracy Thurman sued the city and won $2,000,000 in damages because the police did not protect her. The ex-husband was sentenced to twenty years in prison and would have been released for good behavior two or three years after the show aired.

For this reason Dick Clark kept his name off the credits. He was afraid that the husband would search him out and beat him up. We didn't even use "dick clark productions" as the company. We formed a separate corporation so Dick Clark's name would not be associated with the show.

One of the more interesting things about the show was that it actually took place in Torrington, Connecticut. We had to change the name for the movie to "Weddington, CT." Dick Clark was afraid that the town would sue him to get its $2,000,000 back. We did most of our filming in Alhambra, CA, a town with much use of Eastern Seaboard architecture. Looked like a Connecticut town. Problem was it also had numerous palm trees all over the place, not at all native to Torrington. Or Weddington. We had to pick our camera angles very carefully so as not to see the palms in the background, and we carried many bushes with us to cover the lower trunks of the palm trees in the foreground.

We also did some filming in Santa Paula, CA. It definitely had the look and feel of a Connecticut village. Fewer palm trees, too. One scene there I will never forget. Dale Midkiff played the ex-husband, a man with a violent, uncontrollable temper. One scene called for him to stop Tracey's car on the street and smash his hand through the windshield in an effort to hurt her. Modern cars are built with shatter-poof glass, specially strengthened and tempered not to break during an accident. I personally have taken a baseball bat to a windshield with no effect at all, on *Outrage*. Dale Midkiff managed to get himself so worked up and angry that he actually smashed his hand through Tracey's windshield without our using special effects glass, or scoring the glass that was there. Quite an accomplishment. Didn't even break any fingers doing so.

We had an extra day of filming in Pasadena (There are those palms again!) and then we finished within reasonable distance of the budget. Certainly within the contingency, although we went over the actual budget slightly.

CHAPTER 86

THE BOOK

I had written the original *Budget Book* almost as an afterthought. Now I had a call from Lone Eagle, a publisher of film books in Los Angeles who wanted to publish the book and give it wide distribution. I would have to rewrite it and expand on the explanation of the budget part of it. It would be a proper budgeting textbook. This worked fine for me, because I needed such a book for my classes at UCLA, where I was now teaching regularly.

At this point I knew that Turbo-Budget would not be on the market for very long so I switched my software template to the new industry standard, Movie Magic. The new book would be based on that software.

I took a couple of months rewriting it and presented it to Lone Eagle. Ralph Singleton, a producer, had written a similar book a few years prior, and wanted to update his book. His wife owned Lone Eagle Publishing. They made it clear to me that they would only publish the book if we gave Ralph the credit for writing it. I would get credit for editing it. Oh well, it was better than nothing and I would still make a few dollars. I submitted the finished product to them. They kept it for a few weeks and then returned it with notes. The editor, for instance, took umbrage at my use of the title "cameraman," as some cameramen were women. Her note said that she wanted me to stop using these outmoded sexist terms. In fact I knew cameramen who were women, and all of them were proud to be called "cameraman" with no exception. Just like "actors" are actors whether men or women. We use the same term for both. This note ran through the manuscript. Seemingly random, whimsical edits that only reflected the wishes of the publisher without having any useful value. I wasn't happy, but I wanted the book to be published.

Then came the big problem. I explained to Mrs. Singleton that I had had a dispute with Emil Safier over the copyright but that the Copyright Office had ruled in my favor and I am entirely free to do what I wished with the book. Mrs. Singleton immediately contacted Emil Safier to discuss the matter, and Emil told her that he owned the copyright. I told Mrs. Singleton to check with the Copyright Office to see who was right, but she said that she could not afford to publish the book for fear that Emil would sue.

Nothing I said after that would help. Mrs. Singleton decided that she would pay

331

me off for the work done and not publish my book after all. She promised $2,500.

I contacted a copyright attorney willing to work *pro bono* and we instituted a campaign to have Emil give up any pretense to ownership of the book. It took around one year, but eventually he had to pay me some money and write a letter agreeing to abandon any rights, legal or otherwise, that he felt he had in my book. He settled the day before we were to go to court. To this day he thinks I am a dishonest swine and I think he is an idiot. Or maybe it's the other way around.

An old friend from New York, Jerry Brandt, was working as publisher of a magazine *On Production* for the same publishing company that published *Hollywood Daily Variety* and a unit of Reed-Elsevier, the publishing giant that also owned the largest film reference publisher, Focal Press. He said that he would arrange to have the book published through Focal Press if I would retitle it *The* On Production *Budget Book* to reflect his magazine. Hey, no problem!

I was assigned an editor. She read the book and sent me notes, none of which had to do with the outmoded sexist terms. At the same time the company sent me a publishing contract, very professional, and very boilerplate. I read it carefully. Buried in one of the paragraphs was an innocent sentence: "The publisher shall have the book copyright registered in the copyright office in the name of the publisher." Ooops. Here we go again. I phoned the editor, a very nice girl, and read the sentence. She said that if I did not agree to that sentence just cross it out and initial it. I asked her to send a whole new contract without that sentence in it. A week later it arrived. I read it carefully, signed, and I was an author again.

Sometimes the book had an effect opposite to what I intended. I remember one interview I had with a producer. He had my book on his desk. I sat down and we chatted for a few minutes, then he asked me if I knew anything about budgeting. I said, "I wrote the book." He laughed good-naturedly and said, "Sure, but how much experience do you have?" "I wrote the book." I pointed to the book on his desk. He picked it up, scanned the cover, and said, "You mean you're Robert Koster?" I nodded humbly. That ended the interview, and I never got the job.

At this point I found the job offers were coming less and less frequently. I was heading toward fifty years old and had a little gray hair around the temples. The producers were growing younger. They wanted someone they could relate to for a UPM, not an old duffer. Someone they could bend the elbow with. I was old school. I never went to business college. I didn't have the right credentials.

Luckily I had a little savings and if I wanted it, a new career. I was teaching regularly at UCLA and at Columbia College in Hollywood, a media school. Al Rossman was Columbia's president. Another UCLA friend, Frank Zuniga, was the dean of somethingorother. Ron Waller, another UCLA buddy, was in charge of the equipment room. It was comfortable. I enjoy lecturing to a group of students. The students at Columbia were nowhere near the caliber of the UCLA crowd but they were serious. Many had come from foreign countries. And I was beginning to get jobs teaching at companies, such as Fox and Warner Brothers, and giving private lessons on Movie Magic and other programs. I started a company, StarComp. I also gave private consultations to producers and directors who wanted to learn the software. It made a little money, not much, but it was satisfying.

I had stayed in touch with Saul Kahan, my old friend from the Webb School. He had become a publicist in the movie industry, dealing with some major productions and favored by such as Mel Brooks and John Landis. He had a talent for a good turn of phrase. I asked him to think up a catchy name for my new company, and he immediately said "StarComp."

CHAPTER 87

FAMILY FILMS

I did two more films, both for the Catholic Church. Family Films was founded by a priest, Father Patrick Peyton, who gained fame for coining the phrase, "The family that prays together stays together." He then founded Family Theater that first had a weekly inspirational radio show and later made TV productions. These always starred famous Catholic Hollywood stars. The company now wanted to make a series of small films showing modern life value stories. They had hired Corey Allen to direct and he asked me to be his UPM. Couple of Jews doing Catholic films.

Even here there were odd events. Sarah's niece, Missy, was working as an extra in films. She was a regular on *Dr. Quinn, Medicine Woman*. My son, Kevin, was working on the show as a trainee for a time and the two had a chance to talk. When I worked for Family Films I was able to give Missy two or three days' work as well.

Missy's father, from whom her mother, Ann, had just obtained a divorce after about twenty-five years of marriage, was a French war hero named Jean Marillac. He was about ten years senior to Ann. They lived at Squaw Valley, near Lake Tahoe, where they raised their children. Through his contacts Jean helped to bring the Winter Olympic games to Squaw Valley in 1960. Ann, influenced heavily by her mother, was also enamored of the numbers of movie stars who frequented the valley for skiing in the winter. Ann enjoyed telling us stories of the dinners she had with these movie stars and how they had accepted her into their number. She was glamour struck. Missy lived out Ann's dreams by appearing as an extra in movies. And Ann lived out her mother's ambitions by hobnobbing with the stars as well.

Jean, Missy's father, was a direct descendant of St. Louise de Marillac, founder with St. Vincent de Paul of the Sisters of Charity. Her missionary work is famous, and she is venerated throughout the Catholic community. She lived from about 1590 to 1660 in France and her body can be seen in a reliquary in France.

I made a mistake. I shouldn't have done it, but I did not anticipate the results of my own actions. In every organization there is one person who knows all the inner workings of the group and without whom the organization would probably be paralyzed until a replacement was found. At Family Theater it was a lady named Mary. I told Mary that we were hiring my niece, Missy, as an extra, that her father was Jean Marillac, and they were direct descendants from St. Louise de Marillac. Mary immediately got up from the desk, fell to her knees in front of me, and began kissing my hand. People were standing around. I was very, very embarrassed. I lifted her up and explained that we were not blood relatives, but Missy was. I thought it would be a curio for them the next day when Missy showed up. Anyway, I was Jewish. That didn't make any difference to Mary. I was now the relative of a revered saint in the church, and to Mary, an object of reverence myself. It remained that way for the duration of my stay at that company.

The next day we filmed on location. We were visited very often by various bishops and church dignitaries, and that day was no exception. But this time all the priests and bishops were whispering among themselves and looking at Missy, who was becoming uncomfortable with the attention. After a while the attention focused elsewhere and Missy relaxed somewhat.

CHAPTER 88

TEACHING I

There were no production jobs after that. I had to concentrate on teaching. I held regular classes at Columbia College in Hollywood where I taught film production, computer basics, and computer use for scheduling and budgeting. At that time the 400-pound gorilla of scheduling and budgeting computer programs was Movie Magic. I met with Steve Greenfield, who ran the company along with Chris Huntley. I arranged not only to teach the program but also to sell it. With no income from the usual sources I had to scramble to pay the rent and to buy food every month. I was very thankful that my landlord appreciated my loyalty.

Sarah and I made one memorable trip to Palm Springs to see Sarah's former mother-in-law, Oma Foster. She was living in a trailer, and her elder remaining son, Seth, was staying with her until he was able to find a job, which he didn't. The younger son, David, came up from his home at Lake Elsinore to meet me also. David was a building contractor, but for right now he was living with a very rich lady who was supporting him. He was handsome, and his table manners were foul. I was disgusted with him but kept my own counsel since I did not want to offend Sarah. On the drive home Sarah told me that he had visited the family when they lived in Clancy, MT. They asked him to help to build a barn on their property. He agreed to do so, and instead he built a two-story house. That wasn't what they wanted, but Sarah's husband was unable or unwilling to stop the construction. Apparently the three brothers never got along at all. In any case, while David was in Montana the family discovered that he wore false teeth. These popped out of his mouth and fell into the septic tank. David picked them up and put them back into his mouth without washing them. It figures. When it came time for us to leave, Oma bid us a fond farewell, while we watched as Seth and David rolled around on the living room floor in a full-on fistfight. Didn't even stop to bid us goodbye. I told Sarah that I hoped we would never see these people again, and she understood.

I became the technical support person for two companies, Scriptware of Boulder, CO, and Truby's Storyline. I sat at my computer for most of the day, answered the telephone, and helped people with their computer and program problems. Most of the time I was successful. There were some clients I just could not help at all. One Scriptware user was a blind quadriplegic. That person knew nothing about computers and trying to change the memory configs was beyond him entirely. I finally had to tell him that I could not be of any help.

I also gave private lessons to movie directors and producers who wanted to learn about budgeting and scheduling. It became a cottage business for me. I taught several well-known directors, and a few actors and actresses who wanted to produce their own works.

To her credit, Mom was a big help. Every two months or so Mom and I would have lunch and she would slip one or two $100 bills into my pocket. I am not sure that Ronn knew about this, but it was most welcome. I do remember the only lunch we had in which Mom and I were alone together. She did that purposely to ask me if I was still Jewish. I had married Sarah, who was very religious, and Mom was afraid I had converted. The fact was that I was not wedded to any religion. I was Jewish by birth but had not set foot in a temple in many years and had no desire to do so. Mom also told me, during that one lunch we had alone, that when they were living in Switzerland they had deposited some money in a bank in Berne, and she gave me a contact name and number should anything happen. I wrote it down and forgot. She also gave me explicit instructions as to what to do in their apartment if they were both gone. I kept the notes in my safe deposit box. I suspected I would never need them.

CHAPTER 89

EARTHQUAKE

On the morning of January 17, 1994, Sarah and I were asleep. At 4:31 am we were awakened by a sudden jarring movement; then the whole building began shaking up and down violently. It just never stopped. It lasted forty-five seconds, but to us it was an hour or two. We could hear things falling off the shelves in the kitchen. The TV fell off its shelf in the bedroom. We were violently bounced up and down on the bed as if inside a cocktail shaker. The bed was literally hopping around on the floor. There was no way we could even consider standing in the bedroom doorway for safety. We couldn't get off the bed. Standing on the floor was impossible. After an eternity it stopped. We checked our persons and were unhurt, just shaken, not stirred. The electricity was off. Nothing in the apartment worked since it was all electric. The phone did work, however. After things had settled down we phoned our families. Everyone was OK, just a little shaken up. The quake had been felt as far as Ventura and Oxnard, even knocked down a couple of houses in Oxnard. Peggy and Sarah's family were OK, as were my two sons. We phoned Sarah's children, living in other states, to reassure them.

The electricity was not restored for a week. A local transformer had blown and the electric company had their hands full repairing the main lines before they could get down to individual homes. The damage was widespread. We were lucky. The condo buildings across the street were condemned and the tenants had to move out while they were rebuilt. One apartment house three doors down the street had come entirely off its foundation and had moved about four or five inches in a western direction. All the tenants there were evacuated and the building torn down and rebuilt.

Our building had a few cracks, nothing more. We grew to be proud of them. The owner, a Palm Springs resident, was too cheap to have them fixed so they are there still. He was a nice man in person but a nut case financially. He asked the manager to get prices on eight or ten plastic pool chairs. The least expensive ones near us were about $7 each. He found some in Palm Springs at $6 each, loaded them into his car, and spent around $30 in gasoline bringing them to Tarzana.

One young couple, newly married, had moved into our building from their home in Minneapolis. They had never been in an earthquake before and never wanted to be in another. The aftershocks went on for several days, some of them quite strong, and with every one these kids became more and more nervous. They moved into their car and eventually fled back to Minnesota.

We lost a lot of dishes and glasses. We were dispossessed for a week while the electricity was out. We slept at home but ate elsewhere. Couldn't stay in the evenings either unless we wanted to be romantic with candlelight. That worked. The worst part was the books. The water heater for the entire building was just outside of the loft in our apartment. It burst, flooding our apartment with a couple hundred gallons of water. The bookcases, not anchored to the wall, came tumbling down, dumping the books into the swimming pool that our living room had become. Many good books were ruined.

Sarah and I took refuge in the fact that we were luckier than most. We were healthy, had a roof over our heads; the only damage was to things, not people. We shook ourselves off and took stock. The carpet was a mess. The landlord had just replaced it two months before. Now it was multi-colored because the wet books had bled their different inks into it. The landlord understood but didn't replace it again.

CHAPTER 90

TRAVELING AND LECTURING

In my own world things were picking up. I was teaching regularly now both at UCLA and at USC. I was getting more consulting work. Disney World in Florida hired me to come down and teach their production department how to create a budget on Movie Magic. They put me up at the Disney Yacht Club Hotel in Disney World, a five-star accommodation. Everything was first class, from the food to the room service. I was there for five days. Three days I lectured and consulted, and the other two days they treated me to free days at Disney World. I had the run of the place, for free. Disney World is huge. It would have taken me at least a week to see all of it, but I covered quite a bit in the two days I had. Loved every minute of it.

An added pleasure during this Orlando trip was that my old CBS friend Tony Alatis had moved from New York to Sarasota. I phoned him. He drove up and we spent a marvelous evening together, had a splendid meal in a Disney restaurant (Yes, they do have a lovely wine list!), and rehashed old times at CBS Documentary Unit so many years before.

Another time I was flown to New York to give the production departments of Viacom lessons in Movie Magic. Viacom is a huge conglomerate, and some of its tentacles are MTV, Nickelodeon, CBS, Paramount, etc. etc., ad nauseam. I was there for a week. Each day another group came in to learn the program. An added attraction for me was the prospect of selling Viacom the Movie Magic program. They bought thirty copies from me. The fees I would earn from this would pay my rent for several months. Everyone was perfectly wonderful. I had a few dinners in some of my old haunts in Manhattan. Looked up some old friends from years gone by. Flew back to L.A.. With the orders in my pocket, I went to Movie Magic's offices in Burbank, where they fulfilled the order with great glee. That's when the trouble started. Viacom did not want to pay for the software. I think they expected to get it for free. They took over six months to pay Movie Magic. No matter whom I phoned at Viacom, no matter where Screenplay Systems sent emails, they just didn't pay. The idea is that the longer they took to pay, the more interest they made from the money still in the bank.

CHAPTER 91

ARCHIVES I

I became involved in Dad's career and history. Dad had passed away in 1988 from a gall bladder malfunction. He had taken over nine hours of 8mm film, had twelve or thirteen books of photos carefully labeled. I saw with dismay that some of the photos had been ripped out of the books. Peggy explained that cousin Gaby had asked for them and she had given them to her. I tried to get Peggy to understand that these were priceless bits of movie history, but to her they were merely photos her husband left with no particular value at all. In any case she did not want to part with the books because they were "all I have left of his memory." Nothing budged her. There they sat, moldering in the closet. As for the photos that cousin Gaby had, she would not even show them to me, much less return them.

I contacted Howard Prouty, the archivist at the Academy of Motion Picture Arts and Sciences. Explained to him what we had, and of course he was interested in collecting them for the Margaret Herrick Library in Los Angeles, where they would be stored in temperature and humidity controlled rooms to prevent deterioration. None of this impressed Peggy, who kept insisting that these were the only memories of Dad she could keep and she would not release them.

CHAPTER 92

SHERIFF'S RESERVE NEWS

Another UPM who lived nearby was a friend, Sheldon Hayutin. He and his wife, Joyce, Sarah and I went to dinner regularly. Shell was a captain in the Los Angeles County Sheriff's Department Reserve. He was a sworn officer who went on patrol from time to time. We discussed it, and I joined the Sheriff's Department as an unpaid volunteer. We were in the Media Unit. Our job originally was to create training videos or various aspects of police work. We also wrote and edited the Reserve News, a bi-monthly publication. My job was copy editor, correcting spelling and grammar errors before we went to press. We had monthly meetings, usually at "Twin Towers," the downtown Los Angeles jail. The cooks were inmates. They routinely did their level best to ruin lamb chops, pork, mashed potatoes, anything they could do to make us uncomfortable. It was awful. Swill. After the first couple of meals there I ate before going, and just took a prepackaged orange juice from the drink machine.

The meetings were interesting, dealing mainly with media matters. There were two or three other sworn officers there, one the Department's senior advisor for media. This gentleman worked closely with Shell on the subjects of the articles, format, and so forth. We had pretty much a free hand in publishing the magazine as the advisor seldom if ever interfered with what we were trying to do. We had special articles about search and rescue teams, mounted patrols, anything unusual of interest.

CHAPTER 93

AERO SQUADRON

One of my clients was the director, André de Toth. A dignified, cantankerous Hungarian nobleman, he had only one eye, but had directed arguably the greatest 3-D movie up to that time, *House of Wax*. During WWII he had a pilot's license. Owned a war surplus T-6 trainer that he flew around Southern California. When war broke out he found that he was not allowed to fly anywhere within 150 miles of the coast, which mean that he couldn't fly. Among his friends was the Sheriff of Los Angeles County, the legendary Eugene Biscailuz. Biscailuz deputized André, gave him the job of patrolling the coast. When André wasn't filming, he went out at 4:00 am and patrolled the coastline, looking for Japanese submarines. That was the time they would be vulnerable, having surfaced to charge their batteries and fill their oxygen tanks over night. This enabled André to have his plane's tail painted with the yellow stripe that made it an official Sheriff's plane. There were a number of people from Hollywood who kept flying the same way: Robert Taylor, John Ford, W.S. Van Dyke, among others, Jerry Fairbanks. They all went out early in the morning, in different shifts, looking for submarines.

André's friend Tom Sommermeier was also in the group. André mentioned several times that he would be interested in seeing Tom again. Shell and I had lunch with André and discussed it. Turned out that the Sheriff's Department had never recognized the service of these early birdmen. Here was a chance for us to do a good deed.

It took a year, but Shell convinced the Department that they should have a memorial lunch for the survivors of the Aero Squadron. Sheriff Lee Baca would present plaques to the survivors, of whom only André and Tom were still alive. The current flyers, both fixed and rotary wing, and anyone in the intervening years, along with the top brass of the Department, would meet for lunch at a hangar at the Long Beach Airport Sheriff's facility. We would cover it for the Reserve News.

But where was Tom Sommermeier? All we had was a faded roster from 1947 with old addresses and phone numbers. We could always try the telephone book. By golly, there was a Thomas Sommermeier in Beverly Hills. We phoned him, and it was the right man. Made an appointment to see him the following week. He gave us his address, on the corner of Rexford Drive and Sunset Boulevard.

We arrived at the appointed hour, went through some very intimidating gates, into a two-acre estate in the heart of Beverly Hills. Tom was waiting at the front door. We parked between the house and the tennis courts. The swimming pool was on the other side. We entered the foyer, which was framed by two ten-foot elephant tusks. These nicely complemented the wildebeest head on the wall. We were ushered into the living room, decorated very tastefully with paintings, photos of Tom's various aircraft. He was rated on rotary-wing (helicopters) as well as fixed wing. There were model planes on the table. He proudly showed us a model of the Jetstream, his private jet he piloted himself. He also had his wings and his old Sheriff's flight suit. He would love to go to lunch with the sheriff, and he would especially love to see André again. Tom's wife, an excellent hostess, appeared with coffee and pastries for us. Tom was excited about getting a plaque, and was very willing to tell us stories about his Sheriff's patrol days.

I couldn't help but notice that the house was truly grand. Doubtful that he earned this by flying for the Sheriff's Department. He answered by telling us that his family owned the Jergens Lotion Company. Oh.

On the day of the event Shell, Joyce, Sarah, and I picked up André and drove the hour and a half to the Long Beach Airport. André kept asking when Tom was going to arrive. He was like a kid in a candy store. He was in a wheelchair, but he was still bursting with energy and good will. We were seated at the table of honor. Presently Sheriff Baca appeared, came and greeted us, very cordially, very warmly. But where was Tom?

Tom arrived, all right. He flew his Jetstream in, parked it right outside the hangar, and walked in with his wife and his copilot. He was eighty-five years old and never flew alone any more but he had piloted it down from its hangar at Van Nuys Airport. Remembering our hour-and-a-half hour drive, I asked him how long the flight was. It was less than ten minutes. The lunch was a big success. Sheriff Baca gave out the plaques as promised. The current aero squadron members all lined up to shake the hands of Tom and André. The current department aircraft were also parked just outside the hangar and all the guests were given a chance to inspect them. Sergei Sikorski, son of the helicopter inventor, gave a speech also. It was a grand affair. André enjoyed himself immensely. We had a great story. I took a page full of photos for the Reserve News.

Actually I had helped André to format his memoirs, later published in Europe as *Fragments*. A great book. Not an autobiography in the normal sense of the word. I showed André how to use Microsoft Word, which enabled him to write and format his own work. We became great friends. Even after his book was published we kept having dinner together.

CHAPTER 94

PEGGY

Peggy was still living in the house she shared with Dad in Leisure Village, and the bachelors were still hanging around her. She was such a sweet person that she couldn't say "No!" to anyone. One, "Bill," was a stalker. He was desperately in love with Peggy and refused to leave her alone. I didn't know how dangerous he was until the day she took him to church with her. At the end of the service, the minister suggested that all the members of the congregation hug the person on their right and left. Peggy turned to the person on her left, not Bill, and hugged him. Bill grabbed her and threw her to the floor. The next day I saw Bill at Peggy's house in the morning. He always came to her house early and made coffee for them. I drove out to meet him. I told him he could not see her any more. I put a note in the guard kiosks at Leisure Village not to let him in. He told me that he loved her very much and he would not do anything I said. I told him that if I found him trying to see her I would call the police and register him as a stalker. He stayed away from her for a while, then took to driving up and down the street in front of her house and yelling at anyone whom he saw with her. Luckily he died of a heart attack a couple of weeks later.

Another case was when Peggy received phone calls from someone claiming to represent the widows and orphans of policemen who died in the line of duty. This is a common scam in Leisure Village among older people, Peggy included. She always wrote out a check for $25 or so. I explained to her that they are crooks, that the money never goes to the charity they claim, they just keep it. Peggy did not stop giving them money. I called her attention to it again, told her these were scam artists. She said that may be true, but if she doesn't donate, who will support all those widows and orphans? Eventually she stopped.

CHAPTER 95

LEISURE VILLAGE

Sarah and I wanted to remain in the Los Angeles area because I was still lecturing at UCLA. We looked around in several neighborhoods, including Northridge, Valencia, Newhall. We looked at condos and houses in Calabasas and Agoura. I phoned Ann, Sarah's sister, who worked with a real estate agency in Westlake Village. She arranged for us to look at properties in the hills around Westlake. At first I didn't want to go much farther because of the drive back into Los Angeles to lecture. All my friends and my sons live in the Los Angeles area. Did we really want to go far out? On the other hand Sarah's mother lived in Ventura, the rest of her family, uncles and aunts, lived in Santa Paula, and Peggy lived in Camarillo.

We were spending more time with Peggy. She was prey to every charlatan in Camarillo, and all the predators were after her. After Bill's death she began seeing Claude Anderson, one of the elderly, handsome gigolo types who hung out at the weekly dances at the Rec Center at Leisure Village. He didn't live in Leisure Village, had an apartment in Ventura at the harbor, but he conned his way into the Village for the dances. He was one of those who preyed on rich widows. He kept going to the dances, looking for victims. He found one in Peggy, the most trusting innocent soul. She started buying him presents, a wide-screen TV, a stereo system. Peggy always loved good music. Dad had it playing in the house day and night, and Peggy did likewise. Peggy was so kindhearted that she could never refuse anyone anything. With Dad she didn't have to worry, but now that there were sponges like Claude around she didn't know when to deny someone. This would require looking after. Perhaps it would suit for us to buy a home in Leisure Village.

Leisure Village is a retirement community at the east end of Camarillo. It consists of 2,136 homes, some free standing, some attached. There is a recreation center with a huge heated swimming pool, an 18 hole golf course, tennis, paddle ball, bocce, wood shop, ceramics. It's like a big summer camp for adults. All sorts of activities. There are regular dances, bingo every Wednesday, square dances, yoga classes. The residents themselves manage all these activities. There are three guarded gates requiring a pass to enter. The guards are all CPR-trained. Just outside the main gate is an ambulance service with EMTs on duty 24/7.

Ann found us a house in the middle of the Village, one of three attached homes.

Perfect for what we wanted. Two bedrooms, two baths, large living room with a dining room built off it. Walking distance to Peggy's house. We closed on the house and moved in March of 2000.

We lived very happily in Leisure Village. Peggy was becoming tired of keeping her house up and decided to rent out her house and move into the Motion Picture Country Home in Calabasas, where movie stars go in their golden years. She had a nice two-room apartment there with all the amenities. She no longer had to worry about doing her own laundry or making her bed. The staff did it all.

By now I was entirely self-sufficient. I was collecting my full DGA pension, and that was enough to pay the mortgage, food, all our expenses, and then some. Anything else would be frosting. And I was still lecturing. I now had the luxury and pleasure of attending to the considerable stock of photos, films, memoirs, and memorabilia of my own career and Dad's. Even better, Peter, my brother, had spent some time with Dad in 1983-84 getting Dad to narrate his autobiography into a tape recorder, so we had hours of his voice explaining and clarifying events in his childhood and his later career in film.

It became difficult for me to remain working with the L.A. County Sheriff's Department. A new Deputy Advisor had just taken over the publishing chores, and he wrote an article for each issue. His articles were so badly written with such terrible spelling and grammar that it took major surgery to repair the damage. He did not like that. He also insisted that he could insert several paragraphs into his articles telling everyone how wonderful his grandchildren were. I told him that had no place in a serious magazine for policemen. He insisted that his work be printed untouched and unedited, and told me that I did not have to edit the magazine any more. I told him that I am a volunteer, and he didn't seem to care about that. I never had anything to do with the LASD after that. Shell Hayutin resigned at the same time. It was a long drive anyway from Camarillo to downtown L.A. for the meetings.

I went to the local Camarillo Police Department, a branch of the Ventura County Sheriff's Department, and asked at the desk if they had a newspaper. They did not but they invited me to discuss it with the Crime Prevention Officer who coordinates the department volunteers. I told Sr. Deputy Jim Aguirre what my background had been with the LASD. He told me that they did not have such a magazine in Ventura, not even for the regular deputies. But they did have the Camarillo Citizen Patrol, a volunteer organization adjunct to the regular sworn officers. They do traffic control when necessary, search and rescue, and community PR activities. Eyes and ears of the VCSD. I applied and six months later I was invited in for an interview. I must have passed the test because I next was fitted with a uniform and entered training. I've been a member now for more than twelve years.

I was still lecturing at UCLA, and still traveling and lecturing in Washington, New York, Canada, and Florida. Sarah and I were doing fine. She began making trips herself to visit her children, Ed in Colorado, and Seth and Margaret in various Army camps around the country. Both were career soldiers. All three of her kids had become personal friends of mine. They accepted me and in a few respects considered me their father, a role I really felt privileged to play. I could never take the place of her late husband Gary of course, but I was myself, and we got along just fine.

In 2002 Sarah's arthritis became acute. She needed a knee replacement. The insurance would pay. We found a highly respected surgeon, Dr. Gumbs, in Northridge, and he operated. Completely successful. Sarah was laid up for a while, and needed therapy to recover, but we worked through it very well and soon she was up and around as if nothing had happened.

Something terrible did happen. In fact it happened a few days before she went in for surgery. While we were driving to the doctor's office my cell phone rang. It was cousin Gaby, telling us that Peggy had been in a very bad auto accident and was in the hospital. Could we come immediately. I said that we were on the way to the doctor and would be there as soon as we returned. I already knew what had happened.

The evening before, Peggy had phoned me. She was staying in Claude's apartment in Ventura over night and wanted to return to her apartment in the Motion Picture Home the next morning. She phoned me and asked me to drive her. Claude was legally blind. I had offered to show the two of them some of Peggy's films on our video but he always said he couldn't see the screen. What was he doing driving? He still had a valid license because the DMV had forgotten to test his eyesight when they renewed his license a couple of years before. He did not want to be denied the privilege of driving, no matter how dangerous he was. Peggy admitted that she was terrified to drive with him because not only could he not see the traffic but also he seemed to feel that every drive was a race between him and the other cars. Not a good combination.

The next morning I could pick Peggy up and drive her into town. I got up, took a shower, had a quick breakfast. Then I noticed the answering machine beeping. I listened to the message. Peggy said that Claude wanted to drive her home and I didn't have to come and get her. Oh-oh. I would have insisted if I had answered the call, but now I was too late. Hopefully the drive would be safe for her.

Claude had collected Peggy as a trophy. He enjoyed showing her off to his friends. He enjoyed spending time with her, driving her around. Taking her home would give him another half hour with her.

Claude, speeding along Highway 101, did not see the cars stopped in front of him in his lane, and rammed the car in front at 70 mph. He had never slowed down. His car careened across the freeway and ended up across the lanes. The car he hit was damaged beyond repair and the occupants had to be hospitalized. The car in front of that also suffered major damage and the occupants had broken bones. It was a terrible accident. Peggy had five broken ribs, a collapsed lung, a broken wrist, a broken leg. If she survived she might never walk again. She might not survive. She was in frightful pain. She could barely speak. She was in the emergency room at St. John's Hospital. The worst part was that her neck was broken.

As soon as Sarah and I returned home we went to the hospital. Peggy was in guarded condition. She looked like she had just been in a terrible accident. She was bandaged; her arm was in a cast; her body was immobilized; her neck was in a brace. She looked out of slits for eyes. She was all doped up with medicine and pain killers. I asked her why she didn't wait for me to drive her, she answered that she had made a mistake. I didn't mention it again.

Peggy lasted for two months of terrible pain and suffering. My brother, Peter, and his wife, Joanne, came down from Oakland to be with her. He would be here off and on for the next two months.

For a time it appeared that Peggy was getting better. She even got up and began to walk very slowly with the help of the therapist. She was speaking more clearly. Beginning to take solid food. She was still in an obscene amount of pain, however. No amount of drugs or morphine was able to take the pain away. Then she decided that she didn't want therapy any more. It was just too painful. We watched as she slowly sank. She lost her speech. We gave her a pad and pencil so she could write to us what she wanted.

Almost two months after the accident Peggy contracted pneumonia. Her organs began to shut down. The doctor told us that she would probably last another two or three days. Peter and I discussed it. We asked Peggy what she wanted, and she wrote, "Go to Bobby." "Bobby" was her nickname for Dad, who had died fourteen years before. With that, we told the doctors to remove all but the pain medicine, and within a day Peggy was gone. A horrid end for such a lovely lady.

The memorial service was held a few days later at Peggy's church in Camarillo. After that Peter, Joanne, Sarah, and I got in the car and drove with Peggy's ashes down to Point Mugu. Peggy had requested to be scattered into the sea. Peter and I sat on the rocks overlooking the ocean for a few minutes, then we slowly poured the urn's contents into the sea. I remembered all the good times we had had with Peggy, and for the life of me I could not remember anything bad about her. She was pure good. Not a bad bone. Not a bad word about anyone ever. Just pleasant thoughts. I was happy that she had no more pain.

CHAPTER 96

ANDRÉ

André de Toth and I had become close friends. We and our wives had dinner many times together. Immediately after Peggy had passed away I had lunch with him. He told me that he wanted me to be the funeral director for his funeral. I had no idea what to do, having never done this before. Furthermore, although he was Catholic, he had seldom been in church. He knew a priest in Burbank who would conduct the ceremony. Besides that, André had specific wishes for his funeral. Having directed many western films he wanted two songs specifically to be played at the ceremony: "Ghost Riders in the Sky" by Vaughn Monroe, and "Back in the Saddle Again" by Gene Autry. He didn't really care what else was played as long as it stayed with the western theme.

Oh yes, and one more thing. André was to be cremated and his ashes buried in Forest Lawn Cemetery in a plot he had chosen overlooking the San Fernando Valley. He wanted his ashes to be buried in a plain brown paper bag. Hmm. I asked Ann, his wife. She said "Oh, not that again." André was adamant. Ann was less than amused. We would see.

I still don't know how he did it. Less than a week later André died of a heart attack in his apartment in Burbank. I hope I go like he did. He dropped, and that was the end.

I went to the office at Forest Lawn Cemetery and spoke with the person in charge of André's funeral. Gave her the CDs of the requested music. I also told her about the paper bag request, but got almost no reaction. That was apparently still in question.

Two or three days later André's friends gathered to pay their respects in the chapel at Forest Lawn. It seemed like hundreds of them. There were several movie directors I knew, some actors who had worked with André, a couple of his children. Some critics. Actually a very distinguished gathering of movie people and friends. There was a ceremony in the chapel, officiated by the priest, then we all repaired to the site of André's grave where his ashes were to be buried. I took the priest aside and told him about the paper bag request. He allowed as how if that was what André wanted, that was what we should do. Ann gave her assent.

The priest made a very heartfelt and touching presentation at the gravesite, and then said "André's friend, Bob Koster, wishes to speak."

I had the paper bag from Von's supermarket folded in my inner coat pocket. I said that André had asked me to perform a few last chores at his grave side. I said that he wanted to be buried in a paper bag. With that I pulled out the paper bag, opened it, and placed the urn inside it, at the side of the grave. The brief moment of silence was broken by a few giggles, then laughter and applause. This was so typical of André, everyone knew that he would have done one last outrageous act, and this was it.

CHAPTER 97

ARCHIVES II

After Peggy passed, Peter and I finally had the 8mm film and still photos of Dad's life. We donated them to the Academy of Motion Picture Arts and Sciences at the Margaret Herrick Library. The Academy promised to restore and preserve them, and to give us high-definition copies of the film on DVDs. Their restorations are so good that people have asked me where Dad got his 35mm movie camera! I also spent four months at the Academy scanning the photo books in very high resolution. Peter and I have copies of all the material, which we have made available to schools, and to producers who are making documentary shows about that era.

Sarah's and my life had picked up considerably. We went to Europe. We traveled in Switzerland, Austria, Germany, the Netherlands, Hungary. I learned that Filmarchiv Austria was making a TV show about the exiles, those German film artists who migrated to Austria after Hitler became chancellor. Dad had the only existing behind-the-scenes movie footage of those artists in action, and the producers, Dr. Armin Loacker and Martin Prucha, and the director, Kurt Mayer, wanted it for the film. No problem.

I went to Vienna and spent a couple of weeks working with Armin and Kurt on the concept. This was to be a joint project under Filmarchiv Austria and ORF, Österreicher Rundfunk, the Austrian state-owned TV network. Luckily, Hans Holt, the star of one of Dad's films, *Katharina die Letzte*, was still alive, and we would interview him also. I would narrate much of the film. The Archive already had many stills from the period, but no movies. That was my contribution.

I had seen *Katharina die Letzte*. A delightful piece of fluff. Hans Holt was an excellent actor, sort of a Clark Gable type, but much lighter. Great humor. He and his wife, Renate, felt a kinship to us because they had met on *Katharina* and had been married ever since, sixty-eight years.

Kurt Mayer, Armin, a small TV crew of four, and I drove out to Baden bei Wien, a small town south of Vienna, to the Altesheim there. It was a kind of Kunsthaus, a retirement home for artists, actors, directors, musicians. We had a regular video camera and a few lights with us. Armin had spoken to Renate before we left. She told us that Hans did not want to speak with us. He was over ninety years old now and did not want to be reminded of the past at all. She would speak with us briefly. We would not be able to see him. I was disappointed because I had a copy of his autobiography with me, *Jeder Tag hat einen Morgen*, "Every day has a morning." I wanted him to autograph it for me.

We arrived at the Altesheim just after lunch. The manager ushered us into a most impressive living room, red velvet hangings, wooden paneled walls, the aroma of Franz Joseph's own cologne buried in the furnishings. Presently a very dignified lady in her late eighties approached us. She spoke very good English. She greeted me warmly, a bit more cursory toward the TV crew. Armin and Kurt spoke with her briefly. Hans was up in their flat and did not wish to come down. We were not allowed up in the rooms. She would speak with us. Kurt had his hand-held handycam and could use that. She did not want to disrupt the tranquility of the place with a crew, so the crew and equipment would remain in the wagon.

I interviewed Renate for about fifteen minutes. What had they been doing since *Katharina die Letzte*? What was it like to work in Austria with Herman Kosterlitz? How did they fare during the war? What was the last film Hans had done? The usual questions. I had to improvise. I had never interviewed an Austrian acting legend before and did not want to step out of bounds. I thought that Kurt or Armin would interview her but they thought it better that I do it.

Renate said that she had to return to their flat to check on Hans and she probably would not be back down. The interview was over. I grabbed my book and handed it to her. I told her that I would be honored if he would kindly autograph it for me. She could do that but she did not know if he wanted to sign anything. She went to the elevator. I followed her, trailed by Kurt and his video camera. I asked her for a personal favor. Could I please, please just go up with her in the elevator and stand outside their apartment. I only wanted to see him if possible, not to intrude. It would mean a great deal to me. She agreed reluctantly.

I rode up in the elevator with her. The elevator door was across the hall from their apartment and I could clearly see their living room. Hans was sitting at the table. Renate took the book to him and told him something I did not hear. He signed the book for me, then looked out the door directly at me and gestured for me to enter. I said, "Ich bin der Sohn von Herman Kosterlitz." "Ah, wilkommen!" He shook hands warmly. He bade me to sit. Kurt, meanwhile, silently came in the door and stood against the wall with his handycam photographing the moment. Hans and I spoke for about five minutes with my broken German and Renate translating when necessary. Then she stood next to him, placed a hand on his shoulder, and said, "Hans is tired. He has enjoyed meeting you but now you must say goodbye." Hans turned and kissed her fingers, resting on his shoulder. I was very touched.

Kurt and I talked on the way back to Vienna. I learned that his brother, Peter Mayer, was the dean at the Universität für Musik und Darstellende Kunst in Vienna, the University for Music and Performing Arts. Would I be interested in lecturing there? Hmmm?? I gave it some serious thought for a second or two and then allowed as how it might be possible. The next day I was in Peter Mayer's office discussing a weekend seminar on scheduling and budgeting. I would return in a few months after he had a chance to properly publicize it. I would lecture on a Saturday and Sunday. I would be paid enough to cover the expense of travel and hotel. I requested one more thing—a dinner at Sacher's, the legendary restaurant in Vienna in the Hotel Sacher, birthplace of the Sachertorte, one of the more sinfully delightful pastries ever devised by man. Seeing the chance to have a good dinner on the house for his wife and himself, he agreed immediately. We exchanged information and I returned to the hotel.

A few months later I returned to Vienna for the seminar. On the same trip I visited Berlin to go to the Deutsche Kinemathek, where some of Dad's papers were held. Gero Gandert, a representative of the Kinemathek, visited Dad and tried to collect as much memorabilia from him as possible. Dad had donated the majority of his collection, 16mm copies of his films, scripts, notes, etc., to the film archives of Brigham Young University. The archivist there, James V. D'Arc, was very persuasive. There were still some items left over. The Deutsche Kinemathek wanted them. I suppose it was a way for the German establishment to recapture something of those who had to flee Germany because of the Holocaust.

Dad had given Gero some letters and papers, nothing very exciting, and the Kinemathek was preserving them. They were kept in a file box in the same room with the papers of the agent, Paul Kohner, donated by his son, Pancho. A reporter was there from the Berlin newspaper, taking photos of Henry Koster's son visiting Berlin for the first time. Dad was a celebrity in Germany. They were anxious to claim him for their own. Gero explained the importance of keeping the papers in a carefully controlled environment so they would not deteriorate. He brought out the box of letter and papers, placed it carefully on the table in the middle of the room. Then he made a sweeping gesture with his had pointing out all the Kohner papers around the walls. With that, the tail of his coat caught the box of Dad's papers and knocked it off the table, scattering the papers across the floor in complete disarray. The reported kept snapping photos, and Gero was saying, "Oh no, no more photos" but the press must have its day. I was laughing.

When I was about three or four years old Dad had made for me a book of his own paintings and hand-lettered pages, in which he showed some famous men of the past: Abraham Lincoln, George Washington, Albert Einstein, William Shakespeare, Ludwig von Beethoven, and a few others. He had painted their pictures in watercolors and hand-lettered one-page biographical overviews. It's a lovely little book. I knew that the Kinemathek was having a grand opening of its new facility, a big glass and steel building on Potsdamerplatz in Berlin. Brought the book for them to show at their opening as a personal memento from Henry Koster, who was born in Berlin. I told them that after the opening they were to send me back the original. They could make a copy if they wished but I wanted the original for the family.

I took the book to the Kinemathek myself and gave it to Gero, who was naturally very excited to have such a unique artifact in his hands. He accepted it, temporarily, on behalf of the Kinemathek.

I also visited the studio at Babelsberg where the great German films were made during the Weimar Republic time, films such as *M, Metropolis, The Last Laugh, The Joyless Street,* and other classics by Lang, Murnau, Dupont. Erich Pommer was the principal producer for UFA then. The studio was relatively untouched by the war. It had been in the East Berlin area so had been under control of the Communists until a couple of years before when the Berlin wall came down. The facilities had been rebuilt. Everything was updated. The studio was actively courting Hollywood productions to come and use the facilities. As a visiting Hollywood person I was given the VIP tour by the studio manager.

The wardrobe department was the best I have ever seen. It ranged from loincloths for primitive peoples to full-dress uniforms for almost every military organization from every time period in history. There were suits for the rich and rags for the poor from the Roman Empire through World War II. I could have spent days there but very little of it fit. The prop department was similarly impressive. Paintings, rifles and pistols, sconces, scrolls, books. Seemingly miles of it. Everything carefully catalogued. The prop master in charge could take you instantly to whatever you needed.

Their pride and joy was the sound department. The re-recording studio had a brand new 60-channel mixing panel. They could record anything from gunshots to Beethoven's Ninth Symphony. Their sound effects library was similarly impressive. Need to hear a gunshot from a chassepot rifle? They had it. A hummingbird's mating call? No problem. They asked if I wanted to meet the head of the sound department. "Hey, Bob! How's it going? Don't you remember me? I was in your class at UCLA four years ago! What a pleasure to see you again!" Neither the first nor the last time that had happened.

The studio boasted a backlot with sets representing both pre- and post-reunification Berlin. Checkpoint Charlie was prominent.

Then we were ushered into the studio manager's office for a little conversation. The studio was recovering from two generations of Communist management. With rare exceptions the union workers had been paid whether they worked or not. So, sometimes they showed up for work and sometimes they did not. Sometimes they were prompt and sometimes late. The financial incentive to work harder for advancement was not there, and they had fallen into an attitude of nonchalance about the work. It was just a job. The studio management was working to repair the damage, and I am sure that by now they have done so. But at that time it was difficult.

Adventures In Hollywood: A Memoir By Bob Koster

Several things happened in Europe that reinforced my belief in the basic goodness of mankind. At least the basic goodness of the Swiss and the Austrians.

I took Sarah to Europe on a trip. We stopped in Berne to see some of the sights. Sarah was walking quite well and I wanted us to take advantage of the European fall. Her birthday fell on a day when we were in Berne. I arranged for us to take a train ride to the Schilthorn, a high peak in the Alps around two hours away, and take the funicular railway to the top where there was a revolving restaurant with an unbelievable view of the Alps, including the Mönch, the Jungfrau, Mont Blanc, and the Eiger. Getting there was an adventure. We took the train to Interlaken, changed trains for Steckelberg, right next to Reichenbach falls where Professor Moriarty killed Sherlock Holmes in the famous books by Sir Arthur Conan Doyle. From Steckelberg the funicular travels up the mountain to the Schilthorn. The restaurant was location for a famous scene in *On Her Majesty's Secret Service*, resulting in their serving the James Bond Salad, the James Bond Hamburger, the James Bond Dessert, etc. Surprisingly there was no James Bond wine.

We enjoyed our meal, walked around at the top of the mountain for a while, then started back to Berne. The funicular ride was spectacular as we descended into the clouds below, then out of the clouds to Steckelberg. Took the train to Interlaken to change trains there for Berne. At Interlaken we walked across the train platform to the train marked "Berne," took seats in the front car, and waited for the train to start. Presently the engineer came on board without so much as a glance at us, started the train, and drove it around 300 meters down the tracks where he stopped. A workman appeared with a large garbage can and began cleaning out the car. Something was wrong here. I also noticed that we were the only passengers in the car. I went to the engineer's glassed-in compartment, knocked, and showed him our ticket. He put his hand to his head. Told us we were on the wrong train. The real train was still in the station. He saw that Sarah had arthritis and couldn't possibly climb down from the car and walk back up the tracks to the station. So he did something I never saw before and will probably never see again. He backed the train into the station so she wouldn't have to walk. I cannot imagine that happening anywhere else in the world. We were incredibly lucky to have chosen that train and that engineer, under those circumstances. We caught the right train and went into Berne. Had a grand dinner that night in the Bellevue Hotel on the banks of the River Aar, pronounced "Aar."

Eventually the Austrians had enough footage of me, home movies, snippets of film from the productions, to make a very respectable TV show called *Unerwünschtes Kino*, "Undesirable Movies." I went back and forth a couple of times to Vienna to help, and to record narration. By now Kurt had left the show and it was produced and directed by Petrus van der Let, a documentarian with a wide-ranging interest in all manner of things, and an even wider smile. He brought a film crew to Hollywood to photograph some of the areas where Dad and the others had lived and worked. He came to our house in Leisure Village, where I recorded more narration. It took a few months but there was a workable print. The Filmarchiv decided to have a grand premiere in Vienna's first-class Metro Kino, the house where most of the cinema revivals were shown.

I flew to Vienna to introduce the show. Staying at the Carlton Suites hotel on Mühlgasse, just a few blocks from the Vienna Opera and two blocks from the famous Naschmarkt, the outdoor food market. Metro Kino was about two miles away, just a tad too long to walk. I had the hotel phone for a cab to take me.

We arrived in plenty of time at the theatre. I paid the cabby around €7 or 8 with another two for tip. Ran into the theatre, saw Armin, and asked when I was supposed to speak. He took me into the auditorium. I then had a random thought. Wanted something to drink. There was a bar in the lobby. I went there and ordered a glass of wine, and then realized that I had left my wallet in the cab. What a sinking feeling that was. The wallet had my passport, credit cards, around 300 Euro and a few dollars. Now what? I went to the theatre office hoping to phone the hotel to call the cab company and ask that the driver return. There was a secretary on the phone with her boyfriend who did not want to give up the phone. Asked me to wait. I went back to the lobby, told Armin what had happened. I looked for a pay phone but everyone in Europe has a cell phone. Stifled, I went out the front of the theatre to get some fresh air in my lungs and plan my next move. As I stood at the curb the taxi drove up and the cab driver handed me my wallet. Not a thing was missing. Nothing. I wanted to tip him but he would not accept a tip. What a lovely gentleman. The rest of the evening went beautifully.

I was also invited to lecture at the Austrian Directors Association but it did not come to pass. I was there on time but only one student showed up, so the lecture was canceled. The association made me an honorary member as a consolation prize.

One good thing was that I found the organization that collects royalties for cinema artists in Europe. I joined the Verwertungsgesellschafft Dachverband Filmschaffenden Genossenschafft mit Beschränkter Haftung. It took less time to join the group than it did to pronounce the name. Dr. Walter Dillenz, the head, has become a friend. A few years later he told me that they had shortened the name to Verwertungsgesellschafft der Filmschaffenden Genossenschafft mit Beschränkter Haftung. What a relief.

Speaking of cell phones, we have just begun to use their capabilities. I saw the following in Berne. A young man walked up to a soft drink machine, punched a few buttons on his cell phone, and a bottle of soda came down the chute for him. He must have paid electronically using the cell phone. I haven't seen that in the USA yet, not as of this writing.

I was still waiting for the Deutsche Kinemathek to return Dad's picture book. About a year after I left them the book of Dad's paintings of famous men I had received a very well made digital copy of the pictures and the handwritten bios, but not the original book. I sent emails to Gero, to the head archivist, Dr. Werner

Sudendorf, and anyone else whose name I knew up there, but nobody responded to my queries. I assumed that the book was gone, never to be returned.

Two years after that Gero came back to Los Angeles to collect more things. He phoned me and asked for a meeting. I went to where he was staying. He asked if he could look at Dad's papers. I explained that my book of paintings had never been returned. I had a copy but not the original. He said that was terrible, how could they have made such a mistake, he would look into it as soon as he returned to Berlin, they never should have done that, and so forth. I met him for lunch at Pancho Kohner's house, and I mentioned the "mistake" they had made in front of Pancho and his wife. Gero was very embarrassed, as he should have been.

After he left there was a flurry of emails, all sent by me to Berlin. The Kinemathek never bothered to answer. Two years after that I finally received the original book back in the mail. The scum at the Kinemathek never apologized, never acknowledged that anything was wrong. They did say that next time I was in Berlin I should stop by and see the new museum.

CHAPTER 98

TEACHING II

Teaching was fine. I started teaching at the local university, California State University at Channel Islands, extension division, specializing in history of media. Because of my research into Dad's history I had expanded my studies to include the birth of radio, TV, and film. This was fascinating to me. I gave classes on the history of musicals, propaganda films, documentaries, horror films. I was still teaching off and on at UCLA Extension but this would not last long. The drive was too long, the parking too difficult. CSUCI was much easier and paid better too.

Europe called. After the original lectures in Vienna I was hired by the University of the Danube at Krems, Austria, to lecture on production. I made that trip three or four times. The students were more than receptive; many stayed in touch with me over the years and asked advice on matters relating to their careers and production problems.

I also began to lecture in Europe on film history. Hans Toonen, a journalist from Holland, wrote the biography of Philip Dorn, a Dutch actor who became well known in Hollywood. He contacted me because Dad had given Dorn his start in Hollywood, and I had numerous pictures and films of Dorn when he first arrived here from Dad's collection. Hans did much research in Hollywood in the studios and archives for his book. After he returned to Wijnandsrade in Holland he sometimes contacted me to get more information from the archives for him. I was glad to help.

When his book was released Hans invited Sarah and me to Holland to lecture at the screenings of the newly restored film *De Kribbebijter*. As the director's son I was privileged to introduce the film and to give lectures on the history behind the film, Dad and Philip's relationship, and other relevant historical data.

The trip was a great treat for us. I lectured in Amsterdam, Scheveningen, the Hague, and Maastricht. We ate at some of the finest restaurants in Holland, and stayed at interesting places.

CHAPTER 99

SAN FRANCISCO

Back in the USA I was contacted by the Directors Guild of America to lecture to the San Francisco branch on film production. Sarah had always enjoyed San Francisco as well, and here was a chance to visit my brother in Oakland. I had a big box of Dad's personal papers, letters, and other memorabilia. Peter and I would go through it and see what he wanted and what I wanted and we would throw the rest out. None of it had any historical significance, so museums wouldn't be interested.

I did the two-day seminar. As usual, the San Francisco UPMs and ADs were more than welcoming and we enjoyed the time together. On the Monday following Peter came up to the hotel room. We opened the box and went though the contents for about an hour and a half. We discussed most of the items, put some back, made another box for Peter's stuff.

CHAPTER 100

EUROPE 2007

In the spring of 2007 we took a major trip to Europe, visiting our friends in Germany, Hungary, and Austria. Sarah and I flew to Berlin first. Stayed in the grand old Hotel Kempinski on the Kurfürstendamm. Dad had stayed there when he was filming in Berlin in the late 1950s. We were tourists most of the time. I paid a visit to the Deutsche Kinemathek to see if they still had Dad's papers or if they had been thrown out yet. They were there. My previous experience having been a bit rocky, I didn't trust the Kinemathek people any more. Gero was a very sophisticated snake oil salesman. He introduced me to Dr. Werner Sudendorf, the head of the archives. This version of the old snake oil salesman welcomed me with open arms, told me how sorry he was about the misunderstanding with the book of paintings. We chatted for a while. Gero appeared and took me on a personalized trip through their rather impressive museum. Dr. Sudendorf asked if there were anything else they might have from Dad's collection. I mentioned the digitized restorations of the home movies, and he started salivating all over his desk. Especially because there were scenes taken in Europe before the war. I told him I would send him copies if he would give me a written agreement that he knew that the family owned the copyright, and that the Kinemathek would never use the footage for anything but research. They could never exhibit the films for money. He told me to return tomorrow and the agreement would be ready. I did, it was, and we both signed it.

When we returned to Los Angeles I sent the DVDs with a request that they let me know when they are received. It is now four years later and I am still waiting. Gero was stupid enough to phone me twice in the meantime when he was in town and I reminded him about the receipt. He had the speech memorized. He said that was terrible, how could they have made such a mistake, he would look into it as soon as he returned to Berlin, they never should have done that, and so forth. So far nothing has happened. I still do not know if they received the copies. Heck of a way to run a business. I put them in the same category of *sheisskopf* as the AFI with Dad's home movies. I'll never have anything to do with them again.

Sarah knew nothing of this. My two visits to the Kinemathek took maybe three hours total. She was with me for the tour of the museum, and she was in the hotel when I went back to sign the release. Other than that we were tourists. We enjoyed the city, one of the most beautiful in the world. Had some excellent dinners at various German restaurants, enjoyed the comfort of one of the world's great hotels.

We traveled to Dusseldorf and stayed with a friend, Anna-Marie Heidenheim. She was the daughter-in-law of Gabriel and Elsbeth Levy. Gabriel had produced *De kribbebijter*. Anna had a packet of over 200 letters of correspondence between Dad and Gabriel, from 1936 to about 1956. Gabriel had remained in Amsterdam, but since his wife was not Jewish they had food and he was not arrested. Also, he knew when to hide under the bed. These letters are a valuable historical document and I hope to have them published some day. Anna-Marie and I remained in contact over the years.

CHAPTER 101

VIENNA

Sarah and I next went to Vienna. Sarah's daughter Margaret joined us there. We had a splendid time together touring the city, and meeting with Armin. Great guy. He showed us around Vienna, took us through the Filmarchiv Austria offices, and generally was very warm and welcoming to us. He even cooked us a home-cooked Austrian meal in his apartment, and we talked until the wee hours. We had a couple of great dinners with Petrus van der Let as well, and his family. His daughter wanted to come to Hollywood and be an actress and I dissuaded her. I hope. Sarah, Margaret, and I went to some of the better museums, did the tour of Schloss Schönbrunn, where the Empress Maria Theresa lived. Toured Rosenhügel Studios where Dad had directed in 1934-35. Showed Sarah and Margaret the very sound stage where Dad had made *Katharina die Letzte* back in 1935. Then we went to the restaurant at Sacher's for their famous Sacher torte. It was a splendid trip.

CHAPTER 102

BUDAPEST

We enjoyed Vienna for about a week, then took the hydrofoil boat down the Danube to Budapest. I had never been there before. I had brought some memorabilia from Kiraly and Solti, my mother's parents. I knew they were well known in their own time, but I had no idea how beloved they were by the Hungarian people even today. We were constantly surprised. Kiraly Ernö lived in a hotel on the Kiraly Utca, one of the major streets of Budapest (Utca = Boulevard). He appeared in the Kiraly Szinhaz (Szinhaz = Theatre). Kurutz Marton, one of the main people at the Magyar Nemzeti Filmarchivum (Magyar=Hungarian, Nemzeti=National, Filmarchivum=Film archive) took us under his wing and showed us around the beautiful city. There were buildings relating to my history. We saw the apartment house where my grandmother and mother lived after Kiraly divorced Solti. We saw the hotel where Kiraly lived, a block away. We went to the school my mother attended when she was a child. There were still marks from the war and from the 1956 revolution that had not been erased yet, bullet holes in the walls, half-demolished buildings here and there, but for the most part the city was in good shape. The people were wonderful.

There was a remarkable difference between the Hungarians and the Germans and Austrians I was used to. In the Germanic countries many of the people spoke English. They were proud to show off their knowledge of the language. In Hungary no such thing. Since it had only recently been freed from the Soviet influence, many of the people spoke Russian, not English. Knowing the Hungarian national pride I doubt that many of them even spoke Russian. Over the centuries Hungary has been conquered by many but assimilated by none. Hungarians have always retained their own national character, language, cuisine, architecture, and manners. It did not matter if the Mongols, Turks, or Communists were in charge. And Hungarians were always an amazing fountain of creative force in every kind of art, and have had a hugely disproportionate number of scientists, novelists, philosophers, and others sprouting from this little country.

Marton was delighted with the materials I had brought and he made copies of everything. For the originals he suggested that perhaps the Budapest Theatre Museum would be more appropriate. Even though Kiraly had performed in several films of which Marton gave me copies, his primary work was on stage and that is how he is remembered in Budapest. Marton took me to the Petofi Irodalmi Múzeum, the Literature Museum of Petőfi. They were having an exhibit showing the history of jazz in Hungary, and since both Kiraly and Solti were jazz singers in their day, there was a prominent display of their clothing, music, musical instruments, Kiraly's cane, his top hat, her fan, the kind of memorabilia one would expect. The curator had the unlikely name of Gergely Thuröczy, nicknamed "Cottage Cheese" for some reason. The museum was closed at the time so I had a private tour of the place. We finished in front of Kiraly and Solti displays. Very thorough and very well presented. Nearby was a stand on the floor with two or three sets of earphones. They told me to put a set on. Music started playing, and I suddenly heard Kiraly and Solti singing a duet of "Alexander's Ragtime Band" in Hungarian, recorded in 1912. I had never heard them before and had not seen them for fifty years, and I began crying. Cottage Cheese smiled indulgently. I didn't expect that. It was a highlight of the trip. When I left they gave me the CD.

Sarah, Margaret, and I had some excellent dinners, some with Marton, some with his assistant Gyöngi. I was learning things. In one of the finest restaurants in Budapest I ordered a salmon dinner. The waiter asked if I wanted anything with that. I chose rice and veggies. And I ordered a little dinner salad. The waiter made it obvious that I had committed sacrilege. I asked what was wrong. "Sir, one NEVER orders salad with salmon." Remember that for the next time you are in Budapest. I wanted above all to have a genuine Dobos torte in Budapest where they were invented. After all, I had a Caesar salad in Caesar's restaurant in Tijuana, Mexico, where they were invented, and a Sacher torte in Sacher's in Vienna. There was no Dobos restaurant because the pastry was named after József C. Dobos, the chef who invented it. The word "Dobos" means drum in Hungarian. The pastry is shaped like a drum and has a thick, hard caramel topping that makes it look even more like a drum. Marton took us to the Café Mozart on Erzsebet Korut. (Erszebet = Elizabeth, Korut = Road) Roughly equivalent to Rodeo Drive or 5th Avenue. As it happened they were almost out of Dobos torte. The one piece they had left we bought and shared among all of us there.

Too soon it was time for us to leave. The three of us flew to Frankfurt where we caught planes to the U.S..

Unfortunately Sarah was not able to enjoy the rest of the year. She passed away suddenly on August 1. Went swimming at Malibu and drowned. I was devastated, lived on autopilot for a few months while the shock became more and more distant in the past. I would not wish that experience on my worst enemy.

But life does go on. A few weeks after that I flew to Vancouver, Canada, to lecture to the Directors Guild of Canada on scheduling and budgeting. The DGC put me up in a fine hotel in mid-town, close to the conference room where I was to lecture. Doug Dean, an AD from Los Angeles, has memberships in both the

DGA and the DGC. He lives full time in Vancouver. He attended the seminar. He also took me under his wing, and we had a couple of really nice dinners together. I stayed an extra day and toured the city with him. Vancouver is one of the more beautiful cities in the world. It took my mind away from the recent past.

CHAPTER 103

A NEW LIFE

I began to return to the Citizen Patrol and go out with a partner again. Camarillo was holding another Citizen Academy a month later. I was the official still photographer, so I attended all the classes. I had been doing this for several years and knew the routine. My job was to stay in the background, take photos of the lecturers and the people attending, put them in a good light. When we visited the Sheriff's Academy at the Camarillo Airport, I photographed as many as possible pointing the laser pistols and trying to use the driving simulators. When we toured the CSI offices I photographed them all peering through the microscopes at the bullet markings. People love to see themselves doing police things. The Citizen Patrol was a pretty harmless way to ease back into a normal routine.

The Camarillo Citizen Academy is held twice each year, in the spring and fall. It consists of twelve meetings, once a week in the evening, three hours each. It gives the average citizen a fairly thorough understanding of police work. One week there will be lectures by a judge, a district attorney, and a public defender. The next week there might be the bomb squad, hostage negotiations, and the K9 unit. Another time we visit the CSI center in Ventura, and dispatch where all radio communications are handled for the entire county. There is a tour of the jail and another of the Academy. The last class is always graduation night. The mayor and the police chief give each person who completes the course a diploma and a graduation photo is taken. Like most of the volunteers I try to stay in the background and take photos when possible without being obtrusive. This is for the citizens, not for us. Graduation night I have to stand out in the room with camera and tripod and look like a portrait photographer. I really enjoy taking photos so this is not work for me.

This graduating class had a number of interesting people in it. One of them was a man who showed up drunk and had to be taken out of the class because he was making untoward advances to another class member. The legal limit for drinking is .08 blood-alcohol level. He took a breathalyzer test and blew a .28, nearly four times the legal limit.

I was still suffering from the aftershocks of Sarah's passing. I had to stop going out on patrol for a few months because I found myself becoming very angry at inappropriate times, and that is not good for someone in uniform in a patrol car. I took a leave of absence from the CCP. I kept teaching, however, giving more classes at CSUCI in movie history. Planning and delivering these classes was great therapy.

CHAPTER 104

TEACHING IN GERMANY

I had a friend in Germany, Dr. Helmut Asper. He lectures at the Universität Bielefeld, in the Fakultät für Linguistik und Literaturwissenschaft, specializing in Wissenschafft (Academics) und Geschichte (History) der Kinemastudieren. At least he was not a member of the Verwertungsgesellschafft Dachverband Filmschaffenden Genossenschafft mit Beschränkter Haftung. Or maybe he is. I never asked. In any case he invited me on behalf of the Universität Bielefeld to come to Bielefeld and lecture on the origins of movies. I asked him why he would go through all the trouble of bringing me to Germany when there were so many expert film historians there, himself included. He answered that I am from Hollywood. Oh.

I was all alone and free as a bird. I rented a car in Düsseldorf and spent a week visiting with Anna-Marie. Had plenty of good, home-cooked German food, walked along the banks of the Rhine. Went shopping on the "Kö", the Königsallee, the King's road, the Rodeo Drive or Fifth Avenue of Düsseldorf. I drove down to Wijnandsrade and spent a few days with Hans Toonen and his wife. Learned that Dutch cooking is exquisite also, and some of the restaurants are truly *uitstaand* (Dutch for ausgezeichnet). Since everything is so close to each other in Europe, we were able to have dinner in Holland and dessert in Belgium. In fact we ate ice cream at a combination of ice cream shop and video store. What a brilliant idea.

The Germans have two or three very good traffic rules. 1) No passing on the right. None. Only on the left. 2) There are few stop signs on street corners. The rule is that the person on the right has the right-of-way. You slow down when you come to a four-way corner, and if there is someone on your right they may pass first. If someone on your left, you go first. 3) There are also roundabouts or traffic circles in many places eliminating the need for stop signs.

The autobahn is fun. I rented a Skoda, the Czech equivalent of the VW. In fact VW owns Skoda. The car was a diesel and gave excellent mileage. Driving it was exactly like driving a gasoline car. Quiet, comfortable, and very economical. They should sell such cars here in the USA. I was only able to get the Skoda up to around 170-175 KPH on the Autobahn. Around 105-110 mph. I stayed in the #2 lane because the Audis, Porsches, and Mercedes were zooming past in the fast lane. Heck, the VWs were too. I saw a few Ferraris, Maseratis, and one Cobra, but only for a few seconds. I cruised at around 130-140 kph since I didn't want to stress the little Czech car too much, and anyway I was enjoying the countryside. Almost every spare part of the beautifully kept fields had some wind turbines, and many homes and businesses had solar panels on the roofs. These people are serious about saving energy. Maybe some day we will mature enough to do the same.

Bielefeld is a large small town near Hannover. It has a few big city ills but not many. Helmut and his girlfriend live on the outskirts of Bielefeld. They were kind to give me a room while I was teaching. This was easy because I taught on Friday and Saturday of one week and Friday and Saturday of the next. Four days; that was all, eight hours a day. They asked me to lecture in English because even though the class was on the origins of film, it was part of the English Department. Go figure. During the week between the two weekend lectures I traveled into what was East Germany just to see what was there. I discovered that my German is passable, the German people are lovely, the countryside no matter where is breathtakingly beautiful. I had a ball. Even in former East Germany all the better hotels have wi-fi so I could stay in touch by email. I could not have had a better working holiday to cleanse all the cobwebs out of my system.

As frosting on the cake, Helmut cooked me a superb pheasant dinner when I was about to leave. Never had it before. What a treat. In fact every meal in Germany was a treat. The institutional food at the university was gourmet quality. I asked about the difference. The food in Germany is pure food. There are no chemicals included for preservation. The food hasn't been genetically altered to make it bigger. In Europe in general they call American food "Frankenfood" for good reason.

CHAPTER 105

HOME TO CAMARILLO

I returned home refreshed. The teaching fee paid for the trip and I had some really good side trips as an added plus. I had time to take stock. I was sixty-eight years old, getting on towards over the hill, at least climbing it. Most likely my social life would pick up but my romantic life was obviously over. I was sure that my friends would try to "fix me up" with eligible ladies. I was a target. In fact in Leisure Village there is the "casserole patrol" that gathers whenever a widower appears. A couple of times I came home to find well-cooked casseroles sitting in front of my door. One lady actually became angry with me when I turned down her offer to cook me a home-cooked meal. I had become pretty good at that myself and I usually cooked for myself at home. I had no problem going out for lunch or dinner alone, although I much preferred the company of friends.

I slowly eased back into the life I had before, teaching, lecturing. I rejoined the Citizen Patrol and began going to meetings again. After a few months I began patrolling in uniform again. It felt good and I enjoy the friendship of the others. In the more than ten years I have been on the Citizen Patrol I have never found one member, not one, whom I disliked. I had instant rapport with the deputies also. One deputy took me on a ride-along whom I found to be quite sour and harsh. Two or three years later he was a member of the K-9 unit and the dog must have changed him. He is now one of the kindest, gentlest men, and an excellent deputy as well.

Over time I began to get back into a routine of sorts. I taught at the local university. I slowly got over my anger, and as it left me I began to go out on patrols again, briefly at first, later for the full eight-hour day. The anger never entirely stayed away, but it went into the background. The sorrow as well.

Now I am at peace with myself.

I teach and lecture.

I write.

I go out on patrol. I have also been elected to the Board of Directors of the Camarillo Citizen Patrol.

I love my sons. The rest of my extended family, too, all of them very much.

Life is good.

INDEX

Numbers in bold indicate photographs

Abrahams, Mort 209, **210**
Abrams, Morrie 64, 71, 189, 191, 287-288, 289, 290, 293
Ackerman, Bettye 260
Ackerman, Harry 296
Addinsell, Richard 9-10
Adler, Luther 209, 212
Agishi, Dr. Akiko 204, 205, 206
Ahern, Fred 265, 266
AlaPoten, Gary see LaPoten, Gary
Alatis, Tony 83, 86, 94, 212, 340
Allen, Corey 265, 266, 267, 268, 298, 299, 300, 320, 334
Allen, Marty 174, 175-176
Allen, Woody 71, 143-144
Amerika 307, 308
Anders, Luana 164-165
Anderson, Claude 346, 348
Anhalt, Edward **210**, 212
Arbus, Allan 160, 161
Arbus, Diane 159, 160
Archer, Anne 296
Arness, Jim 274, 275, 276
Aspis, Eddie 121
Aubrey, James T. 182, 184, 185, 187, 198, 228, 230
Audley, Mike 266
Avildson, John 148, 221

Babcock, Barbara 292
Bach, Steven 242, 243
Baker, Kurt 103, **129**, 182
Balaber, Barney 76
Balaber, Helen Oursler 76-77
Bananas 143-144
Banyai, George 13-14
Barony, The 214-218, **214**, **215**, **216**, **217**, 319
Barrett, Rona 185, 198

Barron, Bob 145
Barrymore, John 21, 275
Bartel, Paul 38, 263
Basil, Toni 165
Bearcats 162-163
Begelman, David 275
Belasco, Bill 182, 184, 185, 187-188, 198-199
Belkin, Alan 289, 293
Bell, Earl 245-246
Benjamin, Joe 180
Bercovici, Eric 274
Berenger, Tom 250-251, 252
Bergholtz, Emmett 236, **236**
Bernstein, Jack B. 248
Between the Darkness and Dawn 295
Bibb, Leon 38, 117
Bing, Maximilian 240, 274, 286
Birnie, Dick 274, 279
Black, Karen 219, 220
Blood and Sand 76-77
Blore, Clara 37, 38
Bob and Ray 70, 251
Bohrer, Jack 207
Boone, Pat 40
Bowman, Chuck 319, 320, 321
Boyle, Peter 148, 221
Bozo Show, The 75, 78
Brando, Marlon 11-12, 175
Brandt, Jerry 332
Brand, Tony 201, 202
Brooks, Mel 97, 240, 333
Brother Theodore 145-146
Brown, Tommy "Mother" 109
Brother Jessup 22-23
Brynner, Yul 204, 214, 215-216, **216**, **217**, 228
Budget Book, The 327, 331, 332
Buerlin, Justin 308, 309
Burke, Paul 108

372

INDEX

Busch, Augie 85
Butch and Sundance, the Early Days 132, 242-243, 250
Butcher, Ted 308-309, 316

Cain, Chris 289, 292
Caldwell, Steve 278, 281
Campus, Michael 304, 305
Can Ellen Be Saved? 197, 198-199, 200
Carfagno, Eddie 259
Carmel, Eddie 159-160
Case of the Hillside Stranglers, The 325, 327
Casper, Ed 103
Cassidy, Joanna 299-300
Chan, George 265
Chapman, Ben 139
Chason, Gary 230
Children of God see *Can Ellen Be Saved?*
Chicago Story 274, 279
Clark, Dick 137, 329
Clark, Fred 8, 9
Clouse, Bob 214, 216-217, **216**
Codename Foxfire 298-302
Coleman, Harry 80-82, 83
Collins, Robert J. 259, 299, 300
Columbu, Franco 263
Condominium 256-257
Conrad, William 265, 266
Cook, Alice 75-76
Cooper, Jackie 320
Cooperman, Jack 282
Corea, Nick 278-279, 281, 282
Corman, Gene 207
Corman, Roger 207, 223
Coster, Nicolas 255-256
Costikyan, Andy 144
Crenna, Richard 287, 325, 326
Crichton, Michael 228, 289
Crowe, Tonya 271, 272-273
Culp, Robert 194, 195, 197
Curtis, Dan 219, 220, 308, 309, 310, 311, 314, 315
Cutts, John 279

D'Amico, Salvatore 76
Dangerous Moonlight 9-10
Daniels, Bill 108
Darby, Kim 139, 140
Dark Night of the Scarecrow 271-273, **272**, **273**, 287

Darktown Strutters 207-208
Davis in Vegas 174, 175, 176
Davis, Jr., Sammy 174-175, 176, 177
Day, Francisco "Chico" 107, 108
DeBakey, Dr. Michael 228, 229
De Govia, Jack 245, 246, 247
De kribbebijter 17, 359, 362
DeMille, Cecil B. 61, 104, 252
Dennis, Sandy 98
De Souza, Steven 319, 320, 321, 322
De Toth, André 343, 344, 350-351
De Young, Cliff 178, 179
DiCenzo, George 238, 275
Diegh, Khigh 200-201
DiGangi, Jimmy 209
Diller, Barry 252
Domberger, Minoru Terada 204, 205
Donfeld see Feld, Don
Donnelly, Darby 34-35
Dorn, Philip 17, 359
Downey, Sr., Robert 156, 157, 158, 159, 160, 161, 164, 165, 166, 178, 179
Drake, Larry 271-272, 273
Duel, Peter 139, 140
Duke, Patty 108
Dunn, Eli 107
Durbin, Deanna 5-6, **6**, 11
Dwinnell, Bill 86, 88, 91, 94
Dye, Capt. Dale 319

Edens, Roger 128, 131
Edwards, Vince 237-238
Elgar, Peter 109-110
Estevez, Emilio 289, 292
Evans, Mark 286
Everson, Les **210**, 212
Exodus 69, 73, 211
Eye on New York 83-86, 111

Fabian 61
Fairchild, Morgan 323
Fantasy Island 160, 269
Farina, Dennis 325
Farrell, Mike 191
Feld, Don 58
Felsen, Milt 73-74, 93, 143
Ferrara, Abel 303
Ferrer, José 258, 260
Ferrigno, Lou 286

Fier, Jack 58, 238
Fiorello, Tommy 98
Flesh and Blood 132, 250-252
Flower Drum Song 10, 65, 255
Fonda, Henry 258, 259-260
Food of the Gods 223-227
Ford, John 62, 343
For Love of Ivy 117-120, 304
Forman, David 165
Foster, Phil 119
Franklin, Pamela 223, 225, 226
Freddie the grip 60
Freeman, Morgan 291
Fried, Lucy 86, 87, 90, 91, 92, 94, 95, 99, 102, 105, 112, 120, 121, 153, 156, 163, 164, 167, 168, 170, 173, 174, 180, 186, 189, 190, 191, 192, 201, 226, 227, 233, 234, 244
Friedman, Seymour 58, 238, 253, 269, 284, 285, 286
Fries, Ava Ostern 326
Fries, Chuck 319, 320, 321, 322, 323, 324, 325, 326, 327
Fries, Diane 327, 328
Fries, Tom 323, 324, 326
Funt, Allen 151-152
Fury, Ron 194, 195
Futch, Sarah-Jane 22, 26, 32, 42-43, 44, 61, 64, 65, 321, 326, 334, 336, 337, 338, 339, 342, 344, 346, 347, 348-349, 352, 356, 359, 360, 361, 363, 365, 367-368
Futureworld 103, 228-232

Gabor, Eva 269
Galfas, Timothy 113-114
Gallagher, Tim 251
Gallant, Michael 308-309, 310, 315
Gallett, Booth 244, 245, 248, 249
Gandert, Gero 354, 355, 357, 358, 361
Garrett, Jerry 33, 35
Gavilan 278-283
Gavin, Jr., Tommy 84, 103
Generation 139-141
Gerber, Daisy 271, 287
Gerber, David 237-238
Gethers, Stephen 325
Gideon, Clarence Earl 258, 259
Gideon's Trumpet 258-261, 264
Gilman, Sam 11-12
Gladiator, The 303

Gless, Sharon 296
Glickman, Joel 117-120
Glouner, Dick 114
Gluck, Steve 105
Godfrey, Mike 33, 35
Godowski Jr, Leopold 154
Goldberg, Leonard 279, 282, 283
Golden, Dave 182
Goldfarb, Phil 115-116
Gordon, Bert I. 223, 224, 225, 226, 227
Gordon, Flora 224, 225, 226, 227, 228
Gortner, Marjoe 223, 224, 225-226
Gould, Elliott 130
Gray, Hugh 38
Greaser's Palace 126, 156-167, 200, 269, 270
Greenberg, Dave 182
Greenfield, Steve 317, 321, 336
Greenwald, Ken 38, 39, 68-69, 94
Griffith, D.W. 51, 65, 84
Grossberg, Jack 143, 144
Grow, Ron 283
Gunsmoke 274, 276

Haas, Dolly 85
Hallmark Hall of Fame 122, 258
Hancock, Mike 276
Hanks, Tom 195, 220
Hansen, Chuck 260-261
Hantz, Bob 182
Hardesty House 306-307
Harmon, Larry 78
Harrison, Jeanne 86, 87
Hartke, Senator Vance 122
Harvey 8, 65
Haworth, Ted 240-241
Hayutin, Sheldon 342, 343, 344, 347
Heffron, Richard T. 194, 196, 228, 230, 231
Heiblim, Marco 163
Hello Dolly! 128-132, **128, 129,** 133, 197
Henderson, Albert 165
Herman, Matt 265, 266
Hickox, S. Bryan 320, 322, 325
Hiller, Arthur 209, **210**, 212
Hirschfeld, Al 85-86
Hitchcock, Alfred 12
Holt, Hans 352
Holt, Renate 352, 353
Honath, Norm 261, 306, 307, 314, 315
Horan, Don 135

INDEX

Hornstein, Marty 103, 192, 214, **214**, 216-217, 228, 230
Hough, Bill 58
Houseman, John 258, 259
House of Westmore 40-42
Hughes, Howard 58, 127
Huntley, Chris 317, 321, 336
Hustler of Muscle Beach 262-264

Inch, Jimmy 222
Incredible Hulk, The 278, 286
Incredible Melting Man, The 221-222
Ives, Burl 37-38

Jablonsky, Yabo 153, 154
Jaeckel, Richard 319
Jaffe, Sam 259, 260
Jagger, Dean 259, 260
Jaglom, Henry 145-146
Janssen, David 140-141
Jeffords, Bob 299
Jellinek, Herb 192, 306
Joe 148, 221
Jones, Claude Earl 272
Jordi 153, 174-175, 177
Joyce, Michael 306, 307
Judge Dee and the Monastery Murders 126, 200-203
Judgment at Nuremberg 211-212
Jump 148-150
Jumps, Charlie 201-202, 214, **217**
Justman, Robert H. 258, 259, 260, 274
J. Walter Thompson Advertising (JWT) 86, 87-92, 94-95

Kagan, Jeremy Paul 200, 201
Kahan, Saul 33, 38, 333
Kalser, Konstantin 68, 71
Kamiel, Fred 154
Kaplan, Jonathan 262
Katharina die Letzte 4, 95, 352, 353, 363
Katzka, Gabe 242
Katz, Marty 192, 194, 197, 198, 219, 306
Kaufman, Jerry 103-104
Kazan, Elia 71, 109
Kelly, Gene 128, 130
Kelton, Richard 218
Kennedy, John F. 85, 147
Kennedy, Robert 131

Kilmer, Val 304-305
Kiraly, Erno (grandfather) 2, **3**, 3, 29, 39, 68, 364, 365
Kiraly, Katalin "Kato" (mother) 2-3, 4, **4**, 5, **6**, 7, 8, 9, 12, 13, 14, 15-16, 17, 18, 19, 20, 24, 26, 27, 28, 30, 31, 32, 36, 38, 40, 44, 47, 49, 50, 51, 66, 89, 92, 94, 295, 337, 364
Kiraly, Miklos 13, 18, 68
K-9000 322
Kohn, Joe 89
Kohner, Paul 169, 354
Koppleman, Norman 109
Koster, Christopher 99, 102, 105, 120, 142, 173, 190, 192, 240, 270
Koster, Henry (father) 1-12, **4**, 15, 17, 30, 31, 32, 35, 36, 37, 38, 44, 49, 57, 58, 59, 60, 61, 65, 66, 68, 69, 85, 89, 92, 95, 167, 168, 169, 190, 191, 243, 255, 262, 268, 274, 326-327, 341, 345, 346, 347, 349, 352, 354, 356, 357, 358, 359, 360, 361, 362, 363
Koster, Kevin 120, 142, 169, 170, 173, 190, 192, 240, 270, 334
Koster, Nick 7, 8, 9, 10, 11, 170, 255
Koster, Peter 7, 8, 11, 94, 170, 198, 347, 349, 352, 360
Kosterlitz, Herman see Koster, Henry
Kotis, Arnold Farquhar Trelawney 104
Kovacs, Laszlo 38, 242
Kratina, Dick 145, 187
Kronenberg, Bob 91

Ladd Jr., Alan 240-241
Laemmle, Carl 4-5
Lamas, Fernando 278
LaPoten, Gary 319
Law and Order 107, 325
Law of Burning Sands 52-54
Lawrence, Claude 303
Lawrence, D. H. 284
Learman, Richard 235, **235**
Leavitt, Sam 211, 212
LeBlanc, Deirdre 275
Lester, Richard 42, 242-244, 246, 248
Leuker, Art 58, 60
Levinson, David 281
Levy, Elsbeth 17-18, 362
Levy, Gabriel 17-18, 362
Lewis, Harry 20-21
Lewis, Marilyn 20-21

Lincoln, Abby 117, 118
Lindberg, Gary 291, 292
Lindsey, John 96
Loacker, Dr. Armin 352, 353, 357, 363
Love Me and I'll Be Your Best Friend see *More Than Friends*
Lowe, Dick 114
Lusby, Kool 271
Lustig, Branko 308, 309, 315
Luter, Frank 52-53

MacArthur Stretch 255-256, 259
Maffeo, Neil 262, 263, 264
Magnum P.I. 311
Magnus, Anita 10-11
Manduke, Joe 148, 149, 150
Man in the Glass Booth, The 126, 195, 209-213, **210**
Mann, Danny 117, 118, 119, 304
Man Who Broke 1000 Chains, The 304-305
Marshall, J. Howard 35-36
Marshall, E. Pierce 35-36, 136
Marshall, Penny 253
Marton, Kurutz 364-365
Marvin, George 89
Marvin, Ronn 24, 28, 31, 32, 44, 50, 94, 337
Mason, Marlyn 194, 196
Mathias, Harry 323
Matthau, Walter 128, 129, 130
Mayer, Kurt 352, 353, 356
McCann, Chuck 77
McClain's Law 274-276, 278, 279, 316
McEvily, Bob 75, 79
Meeker, Ralph 223, 224
Menzies, Heather 278, 281
Merman, Lewis B. "Doc" 57-58, 59, 61, 65, 107
Merman, Nat 58, 59, 60
Midkiff, Dale 329-330
Miner, Jan 135
Mitchum, Robert 308, 310
Montalban, Ricardo 269, 278
Moon Is Down, The 76
Moran, James 72
Moran, Peggy (stepmother) 7, 10, 168, 169, 259, 320, 338, 341, 345, 346-347, 348-350, 352
More Than Friends 253
Moses, Robert 85
Mosier, Wilbur 248
Mostel, Zero 84

Mr. Hobbs Takes a Vacation 57-64, **62**, **63**, 117, 194
Murphy, John 117
Murray, Forrest 164

Narizzano, Silvio 125
Naughton, James 286, 295
Naylor, Cal 265, 266, 267, 307
Naylor, Tiny 265, 266
Nettleton, Lois 209, 212
Newman, Paul 115-116, **116**
Nicholson, Al 325
Nicholson, James 223, 255, 259
No Highway in the Sky 9, 267-268
Norris, Chuck 197

O'Brien, Liam 235, 259
O'Connor, Donald 8, 259
Ogle, Chuck 185, 188
O'Hara, Maureen 58, 59, 60
O'Herlihy, Michael 236, 320
Olivier, Sir Laurence 125, 195
Olsen, Carl 236, 274
On the Waterfront 11, 65, 107, 175
Outrage. 194-197, 228, 329-330

Pacelli, Eugenio Maria Giuseppe Giovanni see Pope Pius XII
Pahle, Teddy 95
Palance, Holly 284
Palance, Jack 284, 285
Papp, Frank 95
Parker, Don 191, 192
Parks, Gordon 182, 184, 186, 187, 188
Parsons, Jr., Lin 182, 188
Passions 287-288
Pasternak, Joe 2, 3, 4, 5-6, 9
Patterson, Captain Dale 309, 320
Patton 148
Pendulum 122-124
Peppard, George 122
Peters, H.G. 137-138
Peters, Lauri 61-62
Peyton, Father Patrick 334
Phantom of the Mall 323-325
Phillips, Bill 286
Phillips, Frank 260
Phillips, Michele 256
Pilcher, Jimmy 259

INDEX

Pleshette, Suzanne 250, 251
Poitier, Sidney 117, 118, 119
Police Story 204, 233, 235-239, **235**, **236**, **239**, 240, 274
Polito, Gene 228-229, 230
Pope Pius XII 12, 15-16
Porte, Jack 109
Powell, Peter 165-166, 178
Preminger, Otto 73
Pressman, Larry 209, **210**
Prouty, Howard 341
Putney Swope 156

Quincy, M.E. 254

Rachel, Rachel 115-116, **116**
Rafner, Lee 211, 326-327
Ransohoff, Martin 103
Reeves, George 258-259
Reiner, Rob 253
Return of Frank Cannon, The 265-268
Reynolds, Debbie 169, 262
Rich, David Lowell 296
Rickards, Joe 57, 58, 60
Rintels, David W. 258
Ripley's Believe It or Not 284-285
Robertson, Bern 72
Robson, Mark 107
Rockefeller, Nelson 146-147
Rogers, Charles 5, 243
Rogers, John W. 242, 295, 303
Rohauer, Raymond 77
Rolsky, Bob 233, 234
Roosevelt, Franklin D. 32, 136, 308, 309-310
Roselius, John 251
Rosenfelt, Scott 290
Roses Roses 240
Rossman, Al 38, 174, 176, 177, 332
Rossi, Steve 174, 175-176
Rothstein, Roger 97, 103
Rubin, Cyma 156, 161, 166
Rydell, Mark 240, 241

Sachs, Bill 221-222
Saeta, Eddie 275-276
Safe Place, A 145-147
Safier, Emil 317, 318, 321, 327-328, 331, 332
Sales, Soupy 78
Salven, Dave 108, 122, 123, 124

Samet, Jerry 146
Sargent, Joseph 255
Savarese, Ralph L. 153-155, 174-177
Saxon, John 62, **63**, 198
Schell, Maximilian 195, 209, **210**, 213
Schaefer, George 122, 139
Scherick, Ed 117, 118
Schick, Elliott 224, 226, 227, 230
Schiller, Joel 211
Schirmer, Bill 282
Schneider, Bert 145, 146
Schneider, Bob 97, 103, 296, 304
Schneider, Harold 146, 147
Schwartzenegger, Arnold 263-264
Seberg, Jean 122, 124
Seiden, Hal 84, 86, 87
Sellstrom, Brent 231
Selverstone, Hank 88, 89, 91, 94
Semcken, John 309
Shaw, Robert 209, 212
Shear, Barry 237
Sheffer, Craig 292
Shigeta, James 255
Shore, Pauly 323
Singing Nun, The 169, 262
Singleton, Ralph 331
Sky's No Limit, The 296-297
Smith, Anna Nicole 35-36
Smith, Bill 217-218
Smith, Bud 157-158, 178
Smith, Lane 258, 271
Solti, Hermine (grandmother) 2, **3**, 3, 38, 89, 364, 365
Sommermeier, Tom 343-344
Space Force 240-241
Staabs, Gaby 168, 341, 348
Starr, Harrison 115
Star Trek 103, 240, 258, 260
Star Wars 243, 319
Stern, Sandy 287
Stewart, Jimmy 8, 58, 59, 60, 61, 62, **62**, 65
St. Johns, Richard 276
Sticks and Bones 178-179
Stone Boy 289
Strangis, Gary 299
Streisand, Barbra 128, 129, 130
Stuart, Mel 284
Sudendorf, Dr. Werner 358-359, 361
Supercarrier 319-322

377

Adventures In Hollywood: A Memoir By Bob Koster

Supercops, The 103, 107, 165, 182-188, 189, 198, 199, 200
Superman 75, 258-259
Swartz, Charles 321
Swope, Mel 235, 238
Sword and the Switchblade, The 174, 175

Tatelman, Harry 255
Tate, Sharon 107-108
Taylor, Elizabeth 34, 65
Tenneson, Bill 87, 94
That Was Then, This Is Now 289-293
Toonen, Hans 359, 369
Top Hat 55-56
Towne Payne, Julie 278
Trauma Center 286
Trilogy of Terror 219-220, 308
Troop Beverly Hills 326

Under the Law: The Tracy Thurman Story 329-330
Upp and Addam 175-176
Up the Down Staircase 98-100, 108
Urich, Robert 278, 279, 281
Urich, Tom 278

Valentine, Joe 12, 15, 16
Valley of the Dolls 107-108
Van der Let, Petrus 356, 363
Van Dongen, Frits see Dorn, Philip
Verebes, Ernst 7, 8-9
Vidor, Zoltan 89
Vietch, John 122, 124
Villechaize, Hervé 160-161, 269-270
Viola, Joe 207, 208
Von Bülow, Erich 219
Von Sydow, Max 214, 215, **215**, 216, **216**

Wagner, Lindsay 287
Wahl, Ken 303
Wald, Jerry 58-59
Wallace, Dee 296
Waller, Ron 38, **41**, 332
Walt, Norm 83, 84
War and Remembrance 308-316
War Games 282
Washington, Denzel 250, 252
Wasserman, Lew 298-299
Waxman, Franz 7, 9

WCBS 83, 84, 111
Weisbart, David 107
Weld, Tuesday 145
Welles, Orson 145, 146
Werris, Snag 175-176
Westmore, Frank 61
Westmore, George 40
Westmore, Perc 40-41, 61
Westmore, Wally 61
Westworld 215, 228
When the Whistle Blows 256-257
Wilck, Laura 20, 40
Wilson, George 320-321
Winds of War, The 308, 310
Winston, Stan 201, 209, 211
Wizan, Joe 271, 273, 287
Wizard of Oz, The 110, 196
Woodward, Joanne 115, **116**, 287
WPIX 75-79, 84, 111
Wrye, Donald 307
Wyrtzen, Jack 75-76

Youngerman, Joe 64, 71, 189, 191-192

Zachary, Ted 97, 103
Zane, Billy 325-326